LEGALISING THE DRUG WARS

Where did the regulatory underpinnings for the global drug wars come from? This book is the first fully-focused history of the 1961 UN Single Convention on Narcotic Drugs, the bedrock of the modern multilateral drug control system and the focal point of global drug regulations and prohibitions. Although far from the propagator of the drug wars, the UN enabled the creation of a uniform global legal framework to effectively legalise, or regulate, their pursuit. This book thereby answers the question of where the international legal framework for drug control came from, which state interests informed its development and how complex diplomatic negotiations resulted in the current regulatory system, binding states into a degree of global policy uniformity.

John Collins is Director of Academic Engagement, the Global Initiative against Transnational Organized Crime, Vienna. He is also a Fellow at the Centre for Criminology, University of Hong Kong, and Editor-in-Chief for the Journal of Illicit Economies and Development, LSE Press. John's contemporary policy interests focus on the political economy of international drug control and the evolving dynamics on national and international policy reforms.

LEGALISING THE DRUG WARS

A Regulatory History of UN Drug Control

JOHN COLLINS
Global Initiative against Transnational Organized Crime, Vienna

CAMBRIDGE
UNIVERSITY PRESS

CAMBRIDGE
UNIVERSITY PRESS

University Printing House, Cambridge CB2 8BS, United Kingdom

One Liberty Plaza, 20th Floor, New York, NY 10006, USA

477 Williamstown Road, Port Melbourne, VIC 3207, Australia

314–321, 3rd Floor, Plot 3, Splendor Forum, Jasola District Centre, New Delhi – 110025, India

103 Penang Road, #05–06/07, Visioncrest Commercial, Singapore 238467

Cambridge University Press is part of the University of Cambridge.

It furthers the University's mission by disseminating knowledge in the pursuit of education, learning, and research at the highest international levels of excellence.

www.cambridge.org
Information on this title: www.cambridge.org/9781316512326
DOI: 10.1017/9781009058278

First published 2022

A catalogue record for this publication is available from the British Library.

Library of Congress Cataloging-in-Publication Data
Names: Collins, John, 1986– author.
Title: Legalising the drug wars : a regulatory history of UN drug control / John Collins, Global Initiative against Transnational Organized Crime, Vienna.
Other titles: Legalizing the drug wars
Description: Cambridge, United Kingdom ; New York, NY : Cambridge University Press, 2021. | Includes bibliographical references and index.
Identifiers: LCCN 2021020820 (print) | LCCN 2021020821 (ebook) | ISBN 9781316512326 (hardback) | ISBN 9781009061032 (paperback) | ISBN 9781009058278 (epub)
Subjects: LCSH: Drugs of abuse–Law and legislation–Criminal provisions–History–20th century. | Narcotic laws–History–20th century. | Drug control–International cooperation–History–20th century. | Single Convention on Narcotic Drugs (1961 March 30) | United Nations. Commission on Narcotic Drugs–History–20th century.
Classification: LCC K5282 . C65 2021 (print) | LCC K5282 (ebook) | DDC 345/.0277–dc23
LC record available at https://lccn.loc.gov/2021020820
LC ebook record available at https://lccn.loc.gov/2021020821

ISBN 978-1-316-51232-6 Hardback

Dedicated to my wife, Adrianna; my parents, Brian and Miriam Collins; and family, Andrzej and Ewa.

CONTENTS

ACKNOWLEDGEMENTS

I would first and foremost like to thank my PhD supervisor, Professor Nigel Ashton, for having faith in this research undertaking and providing absolutely invaluable guidance and insight. Further thanks to my advisor, Professor Piers Ludlow, for his guidance and support throughout.

I would like to thank Professor Virginia Berridge and Professor James Mills for agreeing to serve as examiners for my dissertation. I have learned tremendously from their work. I am immensely grateful to Finola O'Sullivan for her belief in this book project and her patient and tireless work in bringing it to fruition. Thanks also to Marianne Nield for all her diligent support and work on this project.

Further thanks and gratitude go to the many outstanding people I had the chance to work with and learn from at the London School of Economics (LSE). These included Professor Arne Westad, Professor Michael Cox, Dr Nicholas Kitchen, Dr Luc André Brunet, Dr Michael Shiner, Professor Peter Trubowitz, Professor Simon Hix, David Coombe, Dr Paul Keenan, Dr Anthony Best, Dr Svetozar Rajak, Professor Steven Casey and Dr Tanya Harmer.

I am grateful to Professor Danny Quah and all the members of the LSE Expert Group on the Economics of Drug Policy, as well as the contributors to the Governing the Global Drug Wars Special Report. I have learned immeasurably from their work.

Thank you to Dr Kasia Malinowska-Sempruch, Matthew Wilson, Diego García-Devis, Mame Bougouma Diene, Denise Tomasini Joshi, Daniel Wolfe, Marc Krupanski and the incredible people I have had the pleasure to work and interact with at Open Society Foundations; to Dr Ethan Nadelmann and to the entire Drug Policy Alliance; to Daniel Brombacher, Julia Jesson and the team at the Global Partnership on Drug Policies and Development programme, implemented by the Deutsche Gesellschaft für Internationale Zusammenarbeit.

Thank you to the many dedicated and incredible friends and colleagues in global drug policy who have had a substantial impact on my own work; in particular, Dr Joanne Csete, Dr William McAllister, Professor David Courtwright, Professor Joseph Spillane, Dr Katherine Irene Pettus, Professor Peter Reuter, Professor Alex Stevens, Professor Caitlin Hughes, Dr Damon Barrett, Dr Rick Lines, Dr Gabriel Feltran, Luiz Guilherme Mendes de Paiva, Catalina Mahecha Cruz, Emile Dirks, Dr Emily Crick, Blaine Stothard, Tony Duffin, Jack Harrington, Niamh Eastwood, Baroness Molly Meacher and many others too numerous to mention.

To the remarkable leadership, staff and network at the Global Initiative against Transnational Organized Crime, particularly Director Dr Mark Shaw and Deputy Director Tuesday Reitano.

ABBREVIATIONS

BO	Burma Office
CAB	British Cabinet Papers
CND	Commission on Narcotic Drugs, UN (1946–present)
CO	Colonial Office
DND	Division on Narcotic Drugs, UN (1946–present)
DSB	Drug Supervisory Body (1933–67)
ECOSOC	Economic and Social Council, UN (1946–present)
FBN	Federal Bureau of Narcotics, US (1930–68)
FO	Foreign Office
HO	Home Office
INCB	International Narcotics Control Board
IO	India Office
LON	League of Nations
OAC	Opium Advisory Committee (League of Nations)
PCOB	Permanent Central Opium Board (1928–67)
PRC	People's Republic of China
UK	United Kingdom
UN	United Nations
UNGASS	United Nations General Assembly Special Session
UNO	United Nations Organisation
US	United States of America
WHO	World Health Organization

HISTORICAL OVERVIEW: THE INTERNATIONAL DRUG CONTROL SYSTEM

- 1907: Ten Year Agreement
  - Britain, China and India agree trilateral framework for ending Indian opium exports to China within ten years.
- 1909: Shanghai Opium Commission
  - Initiated under US leadership as the first truly international drug control meeting.
  - The Great Powers examine ways to suppress international opium traffic – particularly traffic bound for China.
  - Largely ends in discord but leads to 1912 Opium Convention.
- 1912: Hague Opium Convention
  - Formal beginning of international drug control system.
  - States encouraged to end drug 'abuse' but remains vague on the mechanisms to achieve this.
  - Signatories must prevent shipment of opium to states which bar its entry.
  - Enters into force in 1919 and co-opted into the new League of Nations.
  - US leadership undermined by its ambiguous relationship with the League-administered system.
- 1925: Geneva Opium Conventions
  - Establishes first mechanisms to enforce a supply control framework.
  - Creates the Permanent Central Opium Board (PCOB) to monitor international imports and exports of narcotics.
  - US fails to secure an end to all 'non-medical and non-scientific' drug use. Walks out of proceedings and never signs.
  - Treaty gains widespread adherence over time.
- 1931: Conventions
  - US cooperates with the UK, Germany and other industrialised states to fashion a workable control scheme.
  - First introduction of 'schedules' into international treaties.

  - Creation of system of estimates to be administered by the new Drug Supervisory Body (DSB).
  - Formalises international distinction between licit and illicit drug trades.
  - Both PCOB and DSB function as quasi-judicial bodies independent of the League of Nations.
- 1936: Convention
  - Aimed at suppressing growing illicit traffic.
  - United States again fails to successfully advocate for end to all 'non-medical and non-scientific' drug use. Its delegates withdraw active cooperation for remainder of treaty negotiations.
  - Achieves limited ratification.
- 1939–40:
  - States consider negotiating international production control agreement. Interrupted by World War II.
- 1939–45: World War II
  - Certain PCOB, DSB and League functions transfer from Geneva to Washington.
  - Continue to function (minimally) throughout war.
  - United States extracts commitments from Britain and the Netherlands to end opium monopolies in the Far East.
  - Exceptions remain. France follows suit in 1945.
- 1945–6:
  - United Nations becomes new custodian for administration of existing treaties.
  - Continuity with pre-war system maintained.
- 1948: Synthetics Protocol
  - Brings synthetic narcotics under international control for the first time.
- 1953: Opium Protocol
  - Prescribes more severe limitation of agricultural production of opiates.
  - Forced through by the US, France and other allies.
  - Rejected by agricultural producing countries, consumer countries and moderate states.
  - Never becomes operational.
- 1961: Single Convention
  - Unifies previous Conventions (except 1936) into one document.

  - United States works to thwart its ratification, and instead bring 1953 Protocol into force.
  - 1964: Single Convention enters into force. US initially refuses to ratify.
  - PCOB and DSB are merged into one International Narcotics Control Board (INCB).
  - INCB retains a 'quasi-judicial' role.
- 1967: US ratifies Single Convention.
- 1971: Convention on Psychotropics
  - Brings Psychotropic (psychoactive) substances under international control, but in a less stringent form than applied to opioids, coca and cannabis.
- 1972: Protocol Amending the Single Convention
  - Product of US efforts to strengthen the Single Convention and INCB.
  - Six decades after first Opium Convention, international system remains overwhelmingly focused on supply control issues.
- 1972: UN Fund for Drug Abuse Control (UNFDAC) created.
  - Nominally independent but reliant on US patronage.
  - Heavily supply control focused.
- 1988: Illicit Trafficking Convention
  - Primarily aimed at tackling organised crime and trafficking.
  - Introduces extensive precursor controls.
  - Addresses demand issues by recommending criminalisation of personal consumption.
- 1998: United Nations General Assembly Special Session (UNGASS)
  - States commit to massive reductions in drug use and supply within ten years.
  - Slogan: 'A drug free world. We can do it!'
- 2016: UNGASS
  - Marks solidification of a period of increased fragmentation, flexibilities and overt breaks with traditional war on drugs conception.

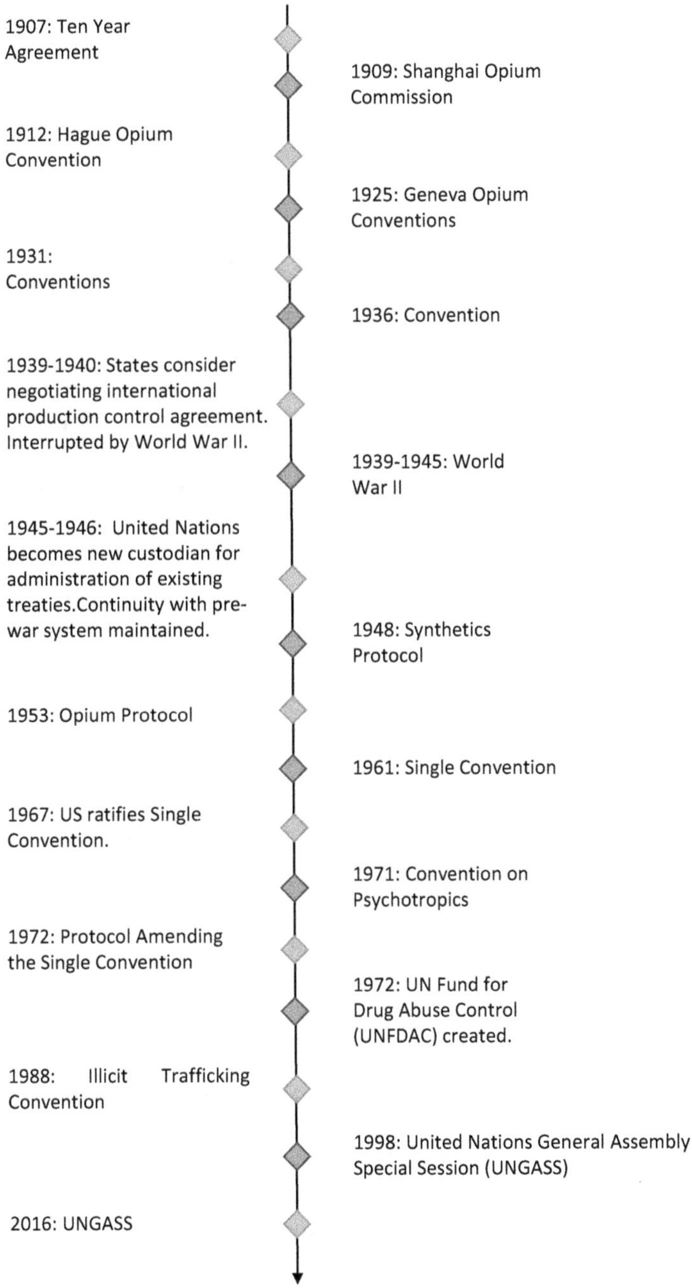

Figure 1 Historical Overview: The International Drug Control System

Introduction

Where did the regulatory underpinnings for the global drug wars come from? This book looks to answer this question. Most popular conceptions point to Richard Nixon declaring a 'war on drugs' to the Whitehouse Press Corps in June 1971. Thus began, for most contemporary analyses, a now five-decade, counterproductive and institutionally racist drug war at home and abroad. The modern drug wars, for there are many across the world, did not in fact begin with Richard Nixon. Instead, one must first look to the legal-institutional foundations laid in the United Nations (UN) and its predecessor international treaties. This book serves as the first fully focused history of the *UN 1961 Single Convention on Narcotic Drugs*, the bedrock of the modern multilateral drug control system and the focal point of global drug regulations and prohibitions. Although far from the propagator of the drug wars, the UN at least enabled the creation of a uniform global legal framework to effectively legalise, or regulate, their pursuit. This book thereby answers the question of where the international legal framework for drug control came from, what state interests informed its development and how complex diplomatic negotiations resulted in the current regulatory system, binding states into some degree of global policy uniformity.

Based on five years of archival research, my numerous publications on the topic and a decade of policy engagement with the contemporary UN drug control system, this book will shed much-needed new light on the debates and discords surrounding the creation of UN drug control. It is the first work which seeks to link in-depth historiographical analysis with contemporary policy debates. It is also the first historical work to provide an extensive, in-depth and systematic regulatory history of the creation of the UN Commission on Narcotic Drugs (CND) in 1946 through to the signing of the 1961 Single Convention and ending with the latter's eventual modification and solidification in 1972. It then links these historical discussions with a contemporary and novel evaluation of the

Single Convention's legal legacy and its positioning within international relations analyses more broadly.

Multilateral drug control originated at the turn of the twentieth century with the aim of managing the spillovers associated with the production, manufacture, trade and consumption of certain substances globally. Initially focused on opium, as the century progressed, the range of substances, bureaucratic oversight of trade and the scope of control expanded. So too did enforcement efforts, culminating in the onset of the 'war on drugs era'. This book examines the full story of the system's transition following the partial collapse of the League of Nations drug control system at the outset of World War II, through its eventual recreation under the UN. It looks to the diplomatic positions of the old colonial powers in Europe against the idealised policies of prohibition vigorously promoted by the US and its key diplomatic ally, China. It highlights the early role of countries such as Iran, India, Afghanistan and Turkey in efforts to limit global opium production as well as their jockeying for position as producer states within a globally regulated 'licit' market. Finally, it will examine the role of transatlantic relations, specifically the vital British–US divide over regulations and prohibitions and the shifting leadership roles assumed by Britain and the US. This ultimately resulted in the defeat of the US with the failure of the 1953 Opium Protocol and the coming into force of the consensus-oriented 1961 Single Convention.

The book will conclude by examining the intersection between regulatory-legal history and contemporary multilateral drug policy debates. It will situate the historical narrative within ongoing debates about the limits and flexibilities of the current global drug control system. In particular, it will focus on the divide between regime 'integrationists' and system 'pluralists'. Integrationists adhere to a strict doctrine of systemic coherence, arguing that the legal contours of the system are absolute and certain, binding member states within a straitjacket of global prohibitions. Reformist integrationists, in particular, conclude that the system is ultimately a US-led prohibition regime and one irreconcilable with national-level policy reforms, such as cannabis legalisation.

Pluralists, on the other hand, have argued from a position of historical regulatory complexity. Further, they argue the pragmatic utility of a less integrated system in the near term as policies evolve and adapt at local levels and thereby expand the global evidence base. This book, following in the pluralist lineage of its author, highlights the fundamental historical inaccuracy of the US-led prohibition regime narrative. It instead points to the regulatory complexity of the system, built on an intersection of member state interests and agendas, of which the US is only one part. It points to past decades of disagreement and dissensus under which the system, far from fracturing and collapsing as many integrationists predict, merely evolved and adapted into an ever more complex body. The book thereby concludes by drawing on the experiences of climate change and intellectual property governance and the application of 'regime complex' theories to these fields. By drawing together the historical lessons of the UN drug control system, this work suggests that the analytic lens of a regime complex serves as the best tool with which to understand the present challenges, flexibilities and functional utilities of the current international drug regulatory system.

An Overview of Interests and the 1961 Single Convention

The period 1939–67 was perhaps the most important in the creation of the modern international drug control system. It began with the collapse of the League of Nations drug control system and culminated in the coming into force of the 1961 Single Convention on Narcotic Drugs in 1964, followed by eventual ratification by the US in 1967. The League system had its origins in the 1909 Shanghai Opium Commission and collapsed with the outbreak of World War II in Europe. Its normative and technocratic underpinnings, however, were to survive the war in the hearts and minds of the 'Gentlemen's Club' of narcotics control advocates.[1] This was a small community of individuals committed to a vision of a tightly regulated international trade underpinned by prohibitions around non-medical and non-scientific usage. For many, the ultimate vision was, as Harry Anslinger wrote for the US in 1965, 'to abolish legal opium production entirely'.[2] For others, such as the UK, it was about creating a well-regulated 'ethical' trade in a problematic international commodity.[3]

The technocratic elements of the system escaped to Washington, DC, in 1940 and remained there until peacetime. World War II, meanwhile, reshaped international narcotics control in many key respects. It achieved what previous conferences could not: a tangible commitment by colonial powers to prohibit most non-medical and non-scientific consumption of opium in their colonies and end the monopolies that supplied them. These had been a key stumbling block to control in the 1930s and, with their removal, states could look towards the all-encompassing international regulation of drugs from production through to consumption. The framework of manufacturing regulation, created under the 1931 convention, remained the most consensual aspect of the system. Reverse integrating production controls would be a far more complex aspect, while issues around consumption and managing drug 'addiction' remained unresolved into the 1960s and beyond.

The 1961 Single Convention came into force in 1964 despite US efforts to kill it and secure the 1953 Opium Protocol in its stead. Behind this story lies complex and overlapping interests, processes, diplomatic struggles, Cold War politics and national idiosyncrasies. This book argues that international drug control efforts between the collapse of the League of Nations system and the coming into force of the 1961 Single Convention are best understood as a triangulation of three blocs: control advocate states, led by the US; producing states and their non-interventionist allies, led by Turkey and the Soviet Union; and moderate manufacturing and consuming countries, led by the UK. In this triangulation process, the US and UK remained the core actors in international drug diplomacy and the two main policy strands within the system: prohibition and regulation, respectively.

The British–US, regulatory–prohibitionist drug relationship saw overlap and division in policy interests resulting in both cooperation and competition. The overlap was around the pursuit of a global regulatory framework for managing the flows of licit 'dangerous drugs' internationally. Their division centred on the peripheral or frontier aspects of this: namely, where to draw the line between licit and illicit consumption; how tightly to restrict, regulate and prohibit global supplies; how much interference in national affairs to allow international organisations; and how to deal with existing drug-consuming populations.

Where their policies overlapped and when Britain and the US worked together, international political progress was possible. Where the two diverged, around strict adherence to prohibitionist principles, overly restricting the manufacturing sector's ability to procure cheap raw materials and imposing repressive 'closed institutional' models for dealing with 'addiction', political momentum stalled. This book argues that the 1961 Single Convention developed as a hybrid regulatory system, underpinned, as all regulatory systems are, with prohibitionist aspects. However, the book also argues that the 1961 Single Convention ultimately represented a victory for the UK-led regulatory strand over the US-led prohibitionist strand.

The UK and other European powers such as the Netherlands represented the deep regulatory strand. This sought to manage global narcotics issues and the expectations of prohibitionist states by establishing a moderate international framework overseeing commodity flows and gently encouraging states towards suppression and better domestic management. Their means to achieve this were consensus and multilateral decision-making, with the goal of utilising this issue to advance other areas of international cooperation.

The US represented the strong prohibitionist, control advocate, strand within the system. It utilised diplomatic pressure, bullying, sticks-and-carrots. Since the early 1900s, US policy maintained an almost fanatical belief in prohibitionism as the sole means to resolve the global drug issue. This stemmed from a supply-centric vision that the cause of drug 'abuse' was excess and unregulated supplies of 'addictive' drugs. By removing the supply, instituting harsh and mandatory penalties for transgressing laws and ensuring compulsory 'treatment' for 'addicts', the US believed the issue to be fundamentally soluble. Within this prohibitionist mentality, the core drug diplomat and key protagonist of this story, Harry J. Anslinger, looms large. He was, at base, a bureaucratic opportunist and key functionary in a broader US vision based on the desire to pursue the 'evil' to all corners of the globe. Underpinning this approach was a self-interested belief that prohibition, underpinned by police enforcement and political will overseas, was the best defence against increasing use in the US.

Anslinger essentially channelled the US approach to narcotics. The same impulses would likely have been present in his absence but perhaps with less national and international traction. He spent four decades at the helm of US drug control, commanding a formidable personality, a strong domestic constituency ('Anslinger's Army') and intense bureaucratic and political savvy.[4] His 'army' was a mixture of domestic interests and lobby groups which supported stringent national and international controls. Part of the grassroots stemmed from traditional prohibitionist organisations such as the Women's Christian Temperance Union. Others represented the domestic drug manufacturing sector, which looked to Anslinger to protect their interests in international negotiations. Others emerged as sympathetic members in US press institutions, most importantly the Hearst Press. Others still represented elite Washington, DC, policy insiders, most prominently the small but powerful group of the Foreign Policy Association (FPA) which had taken an early interest in drug control during the 1920s and 1930s, likely, in part, as a means to further US cooperation with the League of Nations. Meanwhile, the UK had a far less important drug control lobby with no clear indication that domestic opinion had a major policy impact. Instead, Britain's policies, like other European powers, were driven by technocratic impulses, intra-bureaucratic battles, national pharmaceutical and medical interests which disliked invasive international regulations, concerns over international prestige and an overarching desire for international cooperation.

During this period, the two diverged over the relentless US drive to shrink the global market, with little concern for manufacturer or consumer concerns, or the early British desire to accommodate opiate consumption in their colonies via 'quasi-medical' maintenance. Further, European powers favoured a less invasive, free and open market with relatively minimal international oversight. Part of this derived from domestic economic concerns. For example, for the UK, any increase in drug costs would be borne by the new National Health Service (NHS), created in 1946 and implemented in 1948, and could weaken the competitiveness of their pharmaceutical exports relative to new synthetic narcotics and those derived from new manufacturing processes on the continent of Europe.

For the US, the economic downside to stricter regulation was lower and could be borne by its established pharmaceutical sector. The goal was therefore to drastically raise regulatory standards and export a strong prohibitionist framework. Throughout this story the US remained at the vanguard of control advocacy, occasionally falling out entirely with the system when moderate states refused to go along with its designs. At the opposing end was a heterogeneous mix of recalcitrant states, centred largely around drug-producing countries which sought to avoid troublesome and invasive international regulations. Britain traditionally served as a middle-ground manufacturing state. During the interwar years, however, Britain's control of a number of key producing states (Burma and India for example) meant it frequently served as a recalcitrant to the US vision. After World War II, however, an ostensible end to the opium monopolies and decolonisation processes meant that Britain worked to carve out its middle-ground role as the head of a moderate coalition of producers, manufacturers and consumer states. These had various economic interests in the system and a desire to see some international framework but were reticent to follow the US vision.

The US and UK visions would continue to differ over whether the goal was to manage and contain the size of the global market (the British–European vision) or to try and shrink the size of the market (the US vision). Supplementing this core regulated market were prohibitionist aspects, aimed at suppressing non-medical and non-scientific consumption.

However, the implementation of these prohibitionist aspects was left purposely vague and ill-defined, seeking, on the one hand, to incorporate the US normative framework of repressive prohibitionism, while preventing the imposition of concrete obligations on states which had no desire to accept them, on the other.

Academic Contribution

What role did the treaty system have in the origins of the modern drug wars? Orthodox policy narratives, adopting a limited historical perspective, often portray the UN treaty system, specifically the UN Single Convention, as *sui generis*. It was, under this understanding, part of the process towards a US-led global 'war on drugs' and, by inference, a product of US drug diplomacy which drove states into a rigid international framework that would generate unforeseen hardship and toil. Under this reading, UN drug control is inextricable from the US-led drug wars. This book provides a revisionist and more complex account, one highlighting the fundamental continuities between the UN system and the League of Nations system which proceeded it. It further challenges the idea of the system as a US construct, imposed on other states. It instead points to the wide body of primary documents highlighting the Single Convention as a consensus framework as well as a US diplomatic failure. Ultimately, the US sought to sabotage the Single Convention in favour of the 1953 Opium Protocol, as will be discussed. For much of this period the US watched from the sidelines, a key actor in many ways, but not the predominant one. For example, as producer nations sought to divide up the global 'licit market' for opium production, the US was purposely excluded from meetings. As such, breaking out of the orthodox teleological and dichotomous policy narratives which predominate contemporary drug policy debates, this book highlights the fundamental legal, diplomatic and geopolitical complexities underpinning the regulation of drugs at the global level.

While a small number of other works have broadly sought to cover this topic, none yet go into the depth required to reconstruct this key period. William McAllister comes closest with his broad and formidable 2000 work, *Drug Diplomacy in the Twentieth Century*.[5] His book is ultimately constrained by a broad time period and parsimony, providing historical snapshots of key issues and debates but missing a sequenced reconstruction of some major events and processes, such as this book will provide. Further, McAllister's work serves more usefully as an institutional history and gives limited elaboration on the detailed regulatory debates underpinning the system. For example, the key producer state negotiations in the early 1950s are dealt with only in passing. Lastly, given that no major historical work on the UN drug control system has been written since his work two decades ago, this area is ripe for a re-evaluation.

This book is the first comprehensive diplomatic-legal-institutional history on the UN genesis period and certainly the first published manuscript on the topic since William McAllister's groundbreaking 2000 work.[6] It embarks on this endeavour with the hindsight of a new wave of nationally oriented historical research on drug control in the Americas, South Asia and East Asia. It further can incorporate the lessons and debates of more recent scholarship on the continued changes within the system, for example David Bewley-Taylor's reiteration of the 'Prohibition Regime' theoretical analyses[7] as well as my later 'flexibilities' analysis[8] and 'regime complex' framework.[9] These only serve to supplement more recent human rights analyses of the global control system from the analytical perspective of a 'Suppression Regime'.[10] Further, this book approaches the subject with the insights of an active policy analyst and participant in the UN General Assembly Special Session on Drugs (UNGASS) in 2016 and the subsequent High Level Ministerial Segment in 2019. While debates continue on the future evolution of the control system, this book provides an important historical account into the vacuum of primary source–based research, one that can help inform contemporary legal-political theoretical debates.

Historiography and Theories of Drug Diplomacy

For a field that has influenced such a wide range of socio-economic and political outcomes globally, there remains a remarkable dearth of in-depth international historical analysis. There are three main historical works addressing the creation of the UN Drug Control system. Arnold Taylor's (1969) study of international drug control as a 'humanitarian' endeavour inaugurated the study of drug diplomatic history. It concludes its story in 1939, thereby providing a basis for understanding the UN era, but leaving it otherwise untouched.[11] Brunn et al.'s 1975 work, *The Gentlemen's Club*, provides a vital link in the historiography, albeit one fundamentally limited by a lack of access to any notable archival sources and thereby a reliance on publicly available documents and interviews with policymakers.[12] As William O. Walker III suggests, it is 'less satisfactory as a broad, comprehensive study but of considerable value as an interpretive administrative history'.[13]

McAllister's *Drug Diplomacy in the Twentieth Century* changed the field when published in 2000.[14] Matched only in breadth by its comprehensive use of archival sources, McAllister painted a compelling account of the creation of UN drug control and the role of key actors within the system. However, specific regulatory issues and debates, which this book covers in depth, are in McAllister's work necessarily relegated to a broad institutional historical narrative. For example, receiving a brief mention in McAllister's manuscript, it was a further eighteen years before an analysis of the British–Dutch prohibitions of opium smoking during World War II, a vital moment in global drug history, was published.[15] Further, there has, as yet, been no in-depth coverage of the emergence of the globally regulated market in opiates over the period 1946–61, something McAllister covers in passing but that remains in significant need of fuller elaboration and analysis. This book seeks to heavily correct and fill these vital gaps in the field and provide much-needed historical development and insight.

Virginia Berridge stated two decades ago that 'large areas of policy history, at both the national and international levels, remain untouched.'[16] Since that time, some areas of drug historiography have emerged as vibrant fields of study, but precious few new works have augmented multilateral historiography. Instead, we have seen a number of national-regional histories. For example Paul Gootenberg and Isaac Campos have led the way on reappropriating drug policy histories within Latin American contexts.[17] James Mills leads on a reappraisal of Britain's role within the earliest drug treaties[18] as well as a systematic rethink of cannabis's role within the international system.[19] Similarly, new research on the history of South East Asia has shed important light, for example James Windle's 'How the East Influenced Prohibition'[20] as well as my own works 'Breaking the Monopoly System',[21] 'War, Decolonisation and the Birth of the Illicit Opium Trade in Burma',[22] and 'Imperial Drug Economies, Development, and the Search for Alternatives in Asia, from Colonialism to Decolonisation'.[23] These latter works seek to augment earlier imperial histories such as Carl Trocki's political economy classic *Opium, Empire and the Global Political Economy*[24] or William O. Walker's regional histories.[25] The Middle East has been slower to birth a new generation of historical research but is slowly catching up. For example, Bradley Hansen's look at Iranian drug history[26] and Maziyar's Ghiabi's look at Iranian drug politics.[27] More recently, James

Bradford's important study on Afghanistan provides another national drug policy history.[28] Again, all pursue a country-level approach with limited scope for explaining global institutional and policy developments. In furtherance of these works, this book breaks substantial new ground on Asia and the Middle East, particularly Afghanistan, Egypt and Iran, from an international perspective. This book should thereby serve as a timely link between these national-level historiographical developments and a new regulatory history of UN drug control and its relation to national-regional policies.

David Bewley-Taylor's work inaugurated a more international relations–focused analysis of drug control. Ultimately it did so from a relatively limited basis of historical investigation. It therefore added considerably to theoretical discussions on drug policy but provided minimal primary-based research. Bewley-Taylor is the main proponent of the orthodox 'global prohibition regime' school. This approach has its origins in Ethan Nadelmann's groundbreaking article on 'Global Prohibition Regimes'.[29] Bewley-Taylor developed this school in his first book, *the United States and International Drug Control, 1909–1997*, through a hybrid of international relations theory and international history.[30] The core historical narrative draws heavily on Bruun et al.'s book *The Gentlemen's Club*.[31] Bewley-Taylor extends this narrative through a central thesis that the US created a 'global prohibition regime' via 'hegemonic stability' and other forces.[32] Criticised for lacking archival depth and some historical inaccuracies,[33] his earlier work serves more as a conceptual approach rather than an in-depth historical account.

Bewley-Taylor developed this US-created 'global prohibition regime' thesis in his later work, *International Drug Control: Consensus Fractured*, drawing on new secondary diplomatic historical material to argue that the consensus around the 'core prohibitive norm' of the control 'regime' is 'cracked' and may break apart.[34] He uses contemporary international relations theories around 'regime defection' to elaborate his claims.[35] Earlier examples of 'regime defection' theories being applied to the field of drugs can be found in H. Richard Friman's *NarcoDiplomacy: Exporting the U.S. War on Drugs*.[36] Ultimately this book differs from Bewley-Taylor's and other analyses that the core 'norm' of the system is prohibition. Instead, I highlight that it is a system of commodity regulations underwritten (as all regulatory frameworks are) by prohibitionist aspects. Further, it contests the notion that the US was the key driver of the system's outcomes, but instead argues for a more nuanced picture of interstate cooperation. Further, it points to recent systemic resilience in the face of fragmentation as undermining the empirical validity of Bewley-Taylor's thesis.

The concluding chapter of this book will address these theoretical debates by suggesting a move beyond the prohibition regime approach and instead looking to a 'regime complex' analysis. Raustiala and Victor define a regime complex as 'an array of partially overlapping and non-hierarchical institutions governing a particular issue area'.[37] Scholars have utilised the term to explain the complex multidimensional web of governance arrangements in climate change and intellectual property rights.[38] The Conclusion will highlight that ideas of fragmentation of 'governance architectures' have yet to be applied rigorously to the field of drug control. Similarly, long-standing debates have seen international legal scholarship escape from dichotomous ideals of uniformity and coherence. What becomes clear when one de-exceptionalises drug diplomacy, this book argues, is that the tensions within international drug policy mirror those found in other areas of global governance. For example, the broad battle between those advocating policy pluralisms and those imploring integrated governance architectures.[39]

The Conclusion will provide a short overview of the 2012–2020 period of drug control and argue that a deeply resonant story can be found. Namely, drug policy reformers divided among those arguing for greater 'flexibility' and those arguing for a radically new integrated alignment in favour of human rights. Just as global governance and legal scholarship has been forced to come to terms with a more contingent and complex operating environment, so too will conceptions of the global drug control system. This book will argue that, absent the fundamental characteristics of coherence and concentration that characterise a 'robust regime', the concept of the regime complex better conceptualises the current long-term changes underway. This book will be the first manuscript to apply it to the field of drug control. Thus, it concludes by linking history to the present.

Conclusion

This book draws overwhelmingly on primary source archival research to reconstruct the historical processes, goals and ideas that shaped the UN drug control system. It does so by drawing out more extensively issues discussed in passing or at times overlooked by McAllister and others, for example the British decision-making process surrounding the ending of the opium monopolies in 1943; the role of the Judd Resolution in US post-war policy formulation; or the struggles to create a unified national narcotics control in Germany and, to a lesser extent, Japan. All of these receive only passing examination in existing historical accounts. Further, the thesis draws out, far more extensively, the political economy of the 1953 Opium Protocol and the 1961 Single Convention. It does this via a more thorough examination of the reasons given by states for their support or rejection of certain provisions. It thus brings discussions, in many cases, down from broad historical brushstrokes to detailed appraisals of state actions at specific moments and highlights the ad-hoc evolution of policy via sequential decision processes.

By beginning its story proper at the outbreak of World War II, it brings a new historical perspective on the role of the War in reshaping the trajectories of international control efforts. McAllister's work is the only one at the time of writing to cover this era in depth and tells the story as one of strong continuity between the League of Nations and the United Nations. The analysis that emerges here highlights continuities with the pre-war system but also the existence of multiple competing conceptions and possible counterfactuals during 1944–6. First, however, we must look to the eighteenth century and the emergence of the drug issue as a focus of interstate relations.

1

Drug Diplomacy from the Opium Wars through the League of Nations, 1839–1939

1.1 Introduction

This chapter begins by outlining the geopolitical and socio-economic contours underpinning the Opium Wars. As a great power conflict between Britain and China, the wars laid many of the foundational elements for the coming global drug control system. These included straining bilateral relations between great powers as well as the emergence of nationalist and moralist coalitions of diplomats and missionaries driving 'reformist' agendas globally. Coinciding with its rising global role and its expansion into formal empire in the Philippines in the early 1900s, the US became not only an ideological proponent of global prohibitionist policies but a key implementer in its effective colony. Britain, meanwhile, eventually cut a deal with the Chinese state to end India's involvement in their lucrative export market. Britain continued, however, to differ from the US on the best approach to managing opium smoking within colonies. Where the US pushed immediate and uncompromising prohibitions, Britain, the Netherlands, France and other European powers pursued an incrementalistic regulatory-oriented approach. Thus, when the great powers met in Shanghai in 1909 for the first truly multilateral gathering, the battle lines for the coming century were largely already drawn.

Tempestuous and discordant, the Shanghai meeting grudgingly mapped a path towards an international plenipotentiary conference. This meeting at The Hague produced the 1912 International Opium Convention. The aim of this first, and indeed all subsequent drug treaties, was to create reciprocal state responsibilities for limiting the flow of mind-altering drugs. After World War I, the new multilateral drug control system was quickly absorbed by the League of Nations with the creation of the Opium Advisory Committee (OAC). However, the US's simultaneous interest in the issue and unwillingness to join the League of Nations proved complicating. Nevertheless, throughout the 1920s and

1930s a whole series of treaties and institutional changes gave the system regulatory shape. The most important of these were the 1925 International Opium Convention and the 1931 Convention for Limiting the Manufacture and Regulating the Distribution of Narcotic Drugs. Together, they enabled a closed monitoring system, thereby formalising the international distinction between licit and illicit drug trades which continues to the present day.

Ultimately, the course of drug diplomacy mapped the decline of the interwar multilateral system. The League OAC, precursor to the United Nations Commission on Narcotic Drugs (CND), ultimately sank. The enforcement and monitoring bodies, however, survived and, with the support of US Federal agencies, fled Geneva for the safety of Washington, DC. The chapter concludes with a brief introduction to the main diplomats who would drive international controls through the wartime era into the new UN. Unquestionably the most relevant, controversial and diplomatically luminescent protagonist was the commissioner of the US Federal Bureau of Narcotics (FBN) Harry J. Anslinger, a career drug official whose involvement would run from the 1920s virtually uninterrupted until the end of the 1960s.

1.2 The Origins of the Modern Drug Issue

The modern drug trade was in many ways a product of globalisation and technological development. Local drug trades grounded in social rituals and norms interacted with processes of globalisation to become increasingly global phenomena. As technology exponentially increased the gross tonnage of production and transportation processes, traditional mechanisms of social control appeared to break down.[1] The transition of drug economies from relative scarcity to ubiquity drove increased efforts to control their use and exchange. So too did state interests in monopolising the economic outcomes of the trades. Thus began a displacement problem where societies had an incentive to maximise the supply of opium and eventually other drugs to external markets whilst simultaneously trying to limit and control their internal markets. As McAllister and Spillane write, 'The central question' at the turn of the twentieth century 'was not whether the state would ultimately restrict some aspects of distribution and sale, but whose authority would be privileged in the process of creating and implementing those regulations.'[2]

The seeds of modern multilateral drug control can be traced to the Sino-Indian opium trade of the nineteenth century. This trade had solidified under Portuguese, British and Dutch traders who transformed a fragmented and localised trade into integrated imperial structures, culminating with the monopoly of the British East India Trading Company (EIC). The EIC quickly rendered India as the dominant global actor in the drug trade and one of major geopolitical significance. This process, fuelled by mercantilist trade concerns, collided with regional geopolitics as the crumbling Chinese imperial state sought to redefine its relationship with opium.[3]

The growth of opium consumption within China fuelled rising existential fears which then merged with isolationist impulses. Opium became associated with foreign influence and smuggling and thereby something to be repressed. The prohibitions of 1729 were a manifestation of this concern, magnified by a sense of imperial emasculation as the government perceived a loss of control of its southeast coast.[4] Soon, the incorporation of Western practices of consumption, namely mixing opium with tobacco to form smokable opium, or 'madak', solidified its perception as both a foreign cultural influence and one which posed escalating health and economic costs.[5] Soon, the extent of these economic costs became visible as silver flowed out of China into India in exchange for opium, thereby helping correct British trade imbalances around tea, porcelain and silk. This, so general historical analysis holds, helped propel British power in the region, with scholars such as Trocki suggesting a direct correlation between British imperial growth and opium revenues.[6] Attempts to counter this process saw China and Britain meet headlong in a series of great imperial conflicts known as the Opium Wars.

China's defeat in the Opium Wars saw its enforced opening to Western trade and the legalisation of opium. Formalised under the 1860 Convention of Peking, part of the legalisation impetus arose from the unquestionable need to raise Qing government revenue. Moreover, the Qing state proved unable to control opium production within its own territory, evidenced by the emergence of a massive alternative economy within Yunnan, one which, as Bello describes, 'thrived' on the state's weakness and provided a powerful source of income and political power to 'indigenous peoples, Han peasants, and merchants, as well as local dynastic officials'.[7] Moreover, while the regions highlighted the increasingly tenuous grasp of the political centre, the central government also found itself increasingly reliant on the opium revenues it sought to limit. As such, faced with a choice between a local industry or an external one, the Chinese state ultimately grew reliant on south-west opium, a process which eventually supplanted imported Indian opium.[8]

Opium spread outwards from China, its path mapping onto transnational labour flows as China became the first large-scale source of 'free wage labour' for the South-East Asian region. Workers moved in large numbers to Malaya, southern Siam, Tonkin, Borneo and Sumatra to toil in the tin and gold mines or plantations of rubber, sugar, tobacco and pepper. With them flowed outwards traditions of opium growing and consumption.[9] As European powers encountered these opium consumption patterns, they sought regulatory solutions to limit their impact, derive state revenues and minimise their imperial cost base. One widespread model was revenue farming, in which empires 'farmed out' revenue collection to local elites through an auctioning of taxation or monopoly rights for goods such as opium, alcohol, sex work, gambling and others. Opium proved particularly profitable, generating large cash flows and thereby an ease of accumulating capital stocks. Trocki goes so far as to argue that the opium farming systems in parts of India, China and virtually all of South-East Asian territories 'were important adjuncts of capitalist development within the region'.[10] He continues,

> The farms also financed commodity production and helped to generate the infrastructure for consumer economies. These institutions helped to create the finance and state structures that protected businessmen and their profits [. . .] In fact, all Asian governments depended upon opium farms for major portions of their revenue.[11]

Nevertheless, much of the history of colonial opium economies was determined by changing opium regulations, operating in a dialectic with imperial politics imposed from the core and local governance exigencies. The EIC initially operated via a contract system for opium. Accusations of corruption, abusive labour practices as well as quality concerns saw a transition to the 'Agency System' in 1797. Private cultivation was outlawed, while agents would provide capital advances to producers that would operate for the company, with farmers growing in specified areas and delivering to agents. This opium would largely transit through Calcutta auctions and into the hands of privateers, who would complete the supply chain into China. For almost a century, the EIC wielded formidable monopoly power and profits remained substantial, as did predatory market practices aimed at limiting potential competition. By 1860, when the British Crown assumed direct administration of India, ending the EIC, opium accounted for 17 per cent of the government of India's revenues.[12]

This Indian revenue story was hardly unique. In the final decades of the nineteenth century, the Netherlands Indies' opium farms generated 18 per cent of total colonial revenue, with similar figures found in French Cochin-China and Siam.[13] In 1907 the government of Siam ended the farming system, establishing a direct government monopoly on the opium trade. Burmese policy, meanwhile, had proven a mix. Responding to rising consumption, nineteenth-century rulers prohibited opium's use among ethnic Burmans but allowed it to continue for Chinese, Shan and Kachin populations. British conquest led to an attempted standardisation with Indian policies. Local production was prohibited with the Indian opium monopoly extended into Burma. As Britain conquered Upper Burma in 1885, they soon adopted a similar policy to the previous Burmese rulers, instituting prohibitions for Burmans while enabling the continued supply to Chinese and other non-Burman populations through licensed opium shops. For British administrators, this experiment in social control proved too taxing, and soon restrictions on opium shops in Lower Burma were relaxed, allowing their expansion. Opium continued to be supplied by India as well as through seizures of illicit Chinese and Shan State opium.[14]

The socio-economic and political impacts of the opium trade on South, East and South East Asia were immense. As I argued in 2020, there is simply no way to understand the processes of economic development in these regions without an understanding of the licit–illicit opium trade.[15] As Trocki writes,

> Before the nineteenth century, it is no exaggeration to say that capitalism did not really exist in Southeast Asia [. . .] Even those who did produce for the global market rarely sold their goods into the market and they consumed even less from it. Many exchanges were ritualised and took place within relations of dependence. Despite centuries of commerce, there was no real middle class in any Southeast Asian society, nor was there any "free" wage labour. There was no properly commercial forms of production, finance or banking and there were no systems of law that would have protected or regulated such enterprises. Rulers were arbitrary and absolute; wealth in itself could not effectively exist without the protection of the power elites. (Trocki, 2002, 299)

The European empires brought capitalist superstructures which drew these regions into the global economic system. Opium was a key enabler of this, alongside other revenue-farming models. However, it was not solely European influence. Again, as Trocki highlights, it was Chinese communities that created the local capitalist institutions that were capable of interfacing with the global economy. Chinese entrepreneurs tapped these revenue streams developing a preponderance of local wealth and political power, through minimal day-to-day activities. Through these positions they developed roles as key socio-economic intermediaries, coalescing investments and managing large-scale capital investments. As such, the farms became 'the first and perhaps most effective means of accumulation in nineteenth-century Southeast Asia'.[16]

In India, the 1878 Opium Act superseded all provincial regulations, giving the government of India a full monopoly over the regulation of opium from production through distribution and possession.[17] Although the act sought to shrink the areas under cultivation, by the 1880s, opium remained one of the most valuable traded global commodities, with 5,400 metric tons exported from Calcutta and Bombay each year, earning the government 93.5 million rupees.[18] Reformist pressure continued to grow within Britain, with some domestic constituencies calling for outright prohibition of the trade, despite the economic impact this would likely have on the local economies and imperial coffers. A formal Royal Commission on Opium directly challenged reformists, arguing that the trade had a minimal social impact, the limiting of which would be drastically outweighed by the economic dislocation caused by prohibition. Moreover, they highlighted, Chinese opium simply stood ready to step into any void.[19] The report of the commission proved controversial, with many claiming a 'whitewashing'. This division set the basis for intragovernmental debates as Britain entered the twentieth century and a rapidly evolving context with regard to opium.

1.3 Enter Multilateralism

The turn of the twentieth century saw a rapid escalation of drug control as a multilateral issue. Domestic Chinese cultivation had already heavily supplanted Indian opium, while Britain had already made unilateral concession to China on the opium trade, for example relinquishing the treaty right of intervention in China to protect the Indian opium trade. Nevertheless, opium remained a key cash crop for Indian farmers, a large source of Indian government and Chinese customs revenue. Far from the crass economic self-interest widely portrayed within Britain's opium policies at this time, what one instead finds is a complex situation of limited policy options, weak governance, economic needs of small-scale farmers and a reluctance to engage with broad social experiments such as outright prohibition. The post–Opium War Sino-Indian trade formally came to an end, however, with the Anglo-Chinese Opium Agreements of 1907–14.[20]

The US paradigm for international drug control solidified around the turn of the twentieth century. It encapsulated both domestic concerns and economic interests. Domestic concerns had two main strands. First, it was fuelled by a changing perception of drug user ethnicity and demographics by the white protestant population.[21] This was magnified by a nativist fear of immigrants, alien substances and cultural practices.[22] Second, it was built on a latent progressivism that sought to use the state to remove social evils, particularly those seen as bred by intoxicants. This progressivism was to develop a strong internationalist footing under the administration of Theodore Roosevelt.[23]

In the economic sphere, the US sought to build relations with a Chinese population and state apparatus that saw opium as embodying all they detested about the European colonial powers. China remained the epicentre of the world opium problem, and the drug had come to represent a potent symbol of national disgrace inflicted during and after the Opium Wars.[24] The US sought to utilise these sentiments to ameliorate their own, largely immigration-related, tensions with the Chinese business community and help open the market to American commercial interests.[25]

The interaction between these idiosyncratic strands of American foreign and domestic relations drove US efforts to export drug control.[26] The first tangible manifestation occurred in the Philippines after the Spanish-American War. Washington ended the opium monopoly, begun by the Spanish administrators half a century earlier, and instituted a policy of strict prohibition, except for medical purposes.[27] This was to serve as the American test case for prohibition, and eventually the model it forcefully advocated for the European colonial powers.

The first US efforts to internationalise this prohibitionist model began with its co-convening of the Shanghai Opium Commission in 1909. Delegates had no plenipotentiary powers, yet immediately clashed. The US and China pushed a strong prohibitionist agenda and the colonial powers dismissed it, defending 'quasi-medical' opium eating and smoking in their colonies. Meanwhile, drug-producing states argued that manufacturing states were being hypocritical by seeking to restrict opium production while leaving their own pharmaceuticals unhindered. These divisions represented the core battles over international drug control for much of the coming century. The Shanghai Commission produced weak recommendations that were largely ignored. Britain, in the midst of the Ten Year Agreement for phasing out opium exports from India to China, broadly wanted to avoid additional international obligations around the trade and its colonies.[28]

Undeterred, the US threw its weight behind a plenipotentiary convention.[29] The resultant Hague Convention of 1912 was a relatively weak document that required universal ratification. Article 6 of the Hague Opium Convention of 1912 committed states parties to the gradual 'suppression of the manufacture, the internal traffic in and the use of prepared opium in so far as the difference conditions peculiar to each nation shall allow'.[30] The outbreak of World War I placed this treaty on hold until 1919 when its ratification was included in the Paris peace treaties at the behest of both Britain and the US. The accession of Sir Malcolm Delevingne as undersecretary for the drug issue at the Home Office in 1913 proved pivotal in bringing British policies closer into line with US policies. Taking a strong supply control stance, he helped overcome Foreign Office reluctance to engage with the issue.[31] This forced Germany and Turkey to accede, and the treaty eventually came into force.[32]

The 1912 Convention was a compromise document, with broad aspirations and no implementation mechanisms. It became the normative foundation for the international system and control efforts over the coming century. Its preamble stated that the international community was 'determined to bring about the gradual suppression of the abuse of opium, morphine and cocaine' and their derivatives.[33] What remained was to agree the means to achieve this goal. This was rendered more difficult by the fact that the US was ostensibly ignoring the effective home of the system – the League of Nations. Further, anti-drug zealots in the US would sooner see negotiations fail than the US weaken its stance of complete prohibition save for 'medical and scientific needs'.[34] Eventually, however, the ground was set for two new plenipotentiary conferences to be held in 1924–5.

British policy represented an evolving mix of normative desires and practical concerns. In the end, practicalities usually carried the day. Opium smoking was permitted within a number of British Far Eastern territories, and its sale through government monopolies continued to provide substantial revenues. The result was a situation whereby Britain's colonies continued a practice that London officially condemned.[35]

Efforts by Malcolm Delevingne to win the abolition of 'quasi-medical' opium use in anticipation of the 1924 Conferences led to a tense bureaucratic fight. This eventually pitted the Home Office and Foreign Office on the one side versus the Colonial Office and India Office on the other.[36] Delevingne argued London 'was being continually pressed by public opinion in the United States, which has the support of the American Government'. He was supported by the Foreign Office, which was uncomfortable with maintaining an apparent hypocrisy on the international stage.[37]

The Colonial Office was concerned with practicalities of prohibition. China would likely serve as a hub for a reinvigorated illicit trade, one that would be politically destabilising for British colonies. Further, there would be fiscal ramifications. Between 1858 and 1947 about one seventh of the revenue of British authorities in India came from taxes levied on the production and export of opium, although this remained in steady decline since 1906.[38] Finally, they worried about opium consumers being pushed towards heroin, cocaine and other substitutes.[39] Eventually the Cabinet sided with the Colonial Office, with the prime minister deciding, 'Although we wish to see an end to the [opium] traffic, we cannot ignore practical difficulties which Americans, in particular, must be made to understand.'[40]

They chose a policy of gradual suppression over a fifteen-year period (on course to coincide with the outbreak of the next world war). A wide loophole, however, made full prohibition contingent on effective suppression in China.[41] The policy challenged America's uncompromising stance. Meanwhile, the two 1924 Opium Conferences met. The first, to which the US was not invited, focused on Asia and almost immediately became deadlocked. The second began in November 1924 and saw the US launch a hardline offensive, throwing proceedings into near disarray. Beneath the tempest, the subcommittees successfully pulled together a number of bureaucratic proposals. Most notable was a system for states to estimate their drug requirements, and a means for reporting these statistics to a new semi-autonomous administrative body – the Permanent Central Opium Board (PCOB).[42]

The first conference concluded in early February 1925, producing the *1925 Agreement concerning the Suppression of the Manufacture of, Internal Trade in, and Use of, Prepared Opium*. Ultimately this achieved little forward progress, owing to the instability in China. One week later, the second conference wrapped up. The US delegation, unwilling to make concessions, had walked out of proceedings and refused to sign. The resulting 1925 Convention instituted the first significant bureaucratic mechanisms to implement the normative goals outlined in the 1912

Convention. It also brought into the control framework other drugs like coca and cannabis, or 'Indian Hemp'. It did not, however, restrict supply, and states were free to continue producing and consuming whatever quantities they desired, provided they reported statistics to the PCOB.[43] Meanwhile, the US had been completely alienated from the drug apparatus and would remain so for the next half-decade until a new drug official steered the federal government back towards the drug control system.

Harry Anslinger was appointed as head of the newly created Federal Bureau of Narcotics (FBN, a branch of the Treasury Department) in 1930. He served as Commissioner of the FBN from September 1930 until his retirement in 1962, and then remaining as a US international drug representative until 1970. Anslinger was a committed alcohol prohibitionist and was determined not to repeat the failures of the Volstead Act in the field of drugs. One of these failures, he believed, was an unwillingness to institute harsh penalties for individual consumption. As late as 1928 he submitted a plan to a national competition offering his 'better ideas' on how to administer alcohol prohibition more effectively. Anslinger's feelings for Britain were, at best, ambivalent. He had cut his diplomatic teeth with the State Department, negotiating the 'Anslinger Accord' with British officials administering the Bahamas in the 1920s. It established a certificate system for shipping, to counteract the overt alcohol bootlegging into the United States from the port of Nassau. This success led to his being poached by the Treasury Department.[44]

Anslinger would dominate American, and for prolonged periods international, drug control efforts for the next four decades. A young and extremely capable bureaucrat, he had a shrewd political instinct, a willingness to massage and fabricate data, and an ability to cultivate the media and loyal domestic constituencies ('Anslinger's Army') and leverage them to forward his control agenda.[45] More pragmatic than his legion domestic detractors gave him credit for his overarching priority remained to build and maintain the FBN as the US's lead drug agency. His single-mindedness on the drug issue betrayed a certain moral zealotry, but this was usually outweighed by a desire to protect the FBN and his suzerainty over it. He was in this sense more of a bureaucratic entrepreneur than a moral entrepreneur.[46]

1.4 Prelude to War

By 1930 conditions in the US had sufficiently changed to allow a re-engagement with the nascent drug control system. An internationalist constituency argued for engagement with the League on this issue as a means towards broader cooperation; the drug manufacturing industry feared an agreement imposing unfair conditions; and the State Department wished to cleanse the spectre of the 1925 Conference from its relations with the League.[47] Moreover, the recently appointed Anslinger, together with his State Department ally Stuart Fuller (the two would remain a close and formidable team until Fuller's retirement in 1941), quickly showed themselves determined to re-internationalise US drug control efforts.[48]

Within the League, a sense of collective responsibility to vindicate international cooperation, particularly regarding arms control, led delegates to surmount the large obstacles to agreement.[49] The resultant 1931 *Convention for limiting the Manufacture and regulating the Distribution of Narcotic Drugs* was a compromise treaty, but one that imbued the drug control system with a new coherence, and created a tangible distinction between the global licit and illicit traffic in manufactured drugs. It also added some oversight teeth to the work of the PCOB through the creation of the Drug Supervisory Body (DSB).[50] Meanwhile it served to further enshrine a supply-centric approach to drug control as the underlying principle of the international control framework, with little consideration given to demand issues.[51]

The cooperation proved short-lived. Soon afterwards, Malcolm Delevingne retired from the Home Office – albeit remaining active within the international control apparatus until 1948.[52] London quietly continued to work to square its colonial interests with its international commitments.[53] Meanwhile, the US quickly wearied of compromise. Taking up the diplomatic leadership reins from Britain, Anslinger and Fuller forged ahead with a US vision for immediate prohibition of non-medical and non-scientific consumption in an uncompromising and divisive manner.[54]

In 1931 the US had warned that:

> There is but one real method by which to suppress the evil of opium smoking in the Far East [... it] is complete statutory prohibition of the importation, manufacture, sale, possession or use of prepared opium, coupled with active enforcement of such prohibition.[55]

Britain and other European colonial powers continued to profess agreement in principle but refused to prematurely commit. Meanwhile, a growing illicit market accompanied the implementation of the 1931 Convention.[56] States doubled down and looked to cross border anti-smuggling cooperation as a remedy, while broader security issues in Europe and Asia threatened to engulf the League. The last major act on the control front was the 1936 Illicit Trafficking Conference. During this, Anslinger and Fuller attempted, but failed to win, criminalisation of all non-medical production and distribution. Unwilling to compromise, they sought to walk out but were prevented by a State Department anxious to avoid a repeat of 1925. Remaining on at the talks, the pair mocked the proceedings and eventually refused to sign the *Convention for the Suppression of the Illicit Traffic in Dangerous Drugs*. The treaty would eventually come into force in October 1939, by which stage war had intervened.[57]

1.5 Conclusion

At the outbreak of war in 1939, the drug control system stood as a mixture of contradictions and uncertainty. On the one side were the strict control advocates, led by the United States. Having exploited League insecurities to further their hardline conception of control, they struggled to encourage compliance with, and widespread acceptance of, their approach. On the other side were producing states, agrarian countries whose economic, cultural and political systems were entwined with – and often in some ways dependent upon – the very drugs the system sought to limit.[58] Success for control advocates was often a function of how much leverage could be brought to bear on these producer states. In the middle were the old colonial powers, of which Britain was perhaps the most prominent example. European powers recognised the role that addiction and the opium economy played within many of their colonies. Britain, in particular, thereby sought to balance its desire for international cooperation (which required US interest in this issue to be encouraged) with the realities of imperial governance and commercial interests.

As the decade drew to a close, the League OAC became consumed with the goal of designing a production limitation treaty. A conference was tentatively scheduled for 1940, by which time war had already indefinitely postponed it. In the meantime, Britain had ignored US efforts to impose a specific timeline for eliminating both its opium monopolies and the practice of opium smoking in its colonies.[59] Seeing this as a major domino in ending the colonial trade, Anslinger would look to the confusion of wartime as a means to secure his desired end. This issue, so symbolic of the divide between the prohibitionist United States and the old colonial regulatory system, was soon to come to a head.

2

International Drug Control in Wartime, 1939–1945

2.1 Introduction

The outbreak of war would fundamentally reshape international drug control and set the basis for the system that was to be enshrined in the 1961 Single Convention and which endures to this day. For the first and only time in its history the evolution of the system would be determined by specifically bilateral efforts rather than multilateral ones. Moreover, it was US-led bilateral efforts, driven by its wartime leverage, while other states were confined to rearguard defensive actions. The US was to emerge after the war as the dominant world power and a lead nation in international drug control efforts. Instead of recreating the previous ambiguous association with the League drug apparatus, the US would take centre stage in the new UN control system. None of this was predetermined. The reshaping of control efforts during wartime was in many ways the result of aggressive wartime diplomatic manoeuvring on the part of the US FBN Chief Harry Anslinger and key members of the Washington drug control lobby.

In many ways this Washington group fundamentally altered key interests underpinning the system and changed the arithmetic for post-war control. The most radical departure occurred in 1943 when Britain and Holland promised to adopt a policy of total prohibition of opium smoking and monopolies in their Far Eastern Territories upon repossession. This shift was the outcome of an aggressive and risky strategy of bluff by Anslinger and his allies. Neither country believed their colonial interests were best served by immediate prohibition. Nevertheless, owing directly to US pressure, both Britain and the Netherlands eventually caved. Their acquiescence helped ensure the post-war control system would not revert to the immediate deadlock of the interwar years. Instead, it offered a path to a reinvigorated focus on production control. In the interim it also ensured that the US could bring new pressure to bear on the traditional system recalcitrant states such as Iran and Afghanistan and thereby further set the stage for a post-war production limitation treaty.

However, as peacetime loomed in 1944 Britain, the exiled European powers and the US held very different policy focuses. The US drug lobby's immediate goal was to push Iran to ratify existing conventions. From this position they hoped to use their post-war leverage to push for a new international poppy limitation convention that would finally restrict opium production to medical and scientific purposes. Under this agreement India and other producer states could finally be forced to further curtail opium production and use. Without the acquiescence of traditionally recalcitrant states like Iran and Afghanistan, however, the illegitimate international trade would render efforts to limit 'legitimate' production worthless.

Britain's prime concern in 1944, meanwhile, was Burma. Coupled with the intense military drive underway, London needed to decide civilian government policies along with the precedents these would set for other liberated territories. Enforcing immediate prohibition on smoking and opium eating was viewed as a practical impossibility, particularly in frontier regions. It would result in smuggling, undermine government power and potentially spark social unrest. Britain sought a way to square their practical concerns with their awareness of US anti-opium sentiments, particularly since American forces would be operating in Burma. The result was a drawn-out policy process that revealed a strong British belief that US opium policy was naïve and impractical. Countering this was a continued fear that the Washington anti-opium lobby were a politically dangerous and unscrupulous collection of people who could readily damage British interests.

As 1944 progressed, a consensus hardened within the US government to use their wartime leverage to force the issue when needed. It was not until late in 1945 that the extent of their disagreement over Burma became apparent to both the US and Britain. By this time, the US interpreted the British policy as reneging on its November 1943 commitments. This then combined with Britain offering only qualified support for a new production limitation convention and resulted in a large diplomatic blow-up. All was occurring in a context where control system politics were once again coming to the fore and various actors began jockeying for leverage within the emerging UN framework. Underneath it all, existing policy differences continued to smoulder and complicate drug diplomacy. While the war had enabled forward momentum on some issues, it also laid bare the fundamental flaws, contradictions and interests underpinning a multilateral approach to drug control.

2.2 The Early War: September 1939–1943

By 1939 the international control framework was underpinned by a number of multilateral treaties, implemented via national legislation. The League OAC was established by a General Assembly resolution and acted as the policy organ of the control system. The PCOB and DSB had independent treaty bases – although depended on the League Secretariat for administrative functions. The PCOB was charged by the 1925 and 1931 Conventions with supervising and reporting upon the movement of opium, coca leaves and other narcotic drugs throughout the world, and to 'sound the alarm' when excesses accumulated in any territory. The DSB was the product of the 1931 Convention and oversaw the 'system of estimates' for governments' 'medical and scientific needs', and thereby could determine what quantities each country could manufacture, import and export.

The 1931 Convention had almost universal adherence by 1933 and applied to 177 territories. Most complied, and the PCOB retained the power to request that states parties impose an embargo on further exports to those that did not. In practice, this option was avoided, with quiet diplomatic pressure instead preferred. For those states that did not, or could not, supply statistics (including those that had not ratified the 1931 Convention), the DSB was empowered to establish estimates on their behalf, which were legally binding on states parties.

The US maintained official relations with the PCOB and DSB but not the League OAC. The US and its control advocate allies, such as Canada and China, believed the encroachment of national economic interests into the OAC and the League drug secretariat had fatally weakened the interwar system. The PCOB and DSB were perceived as having remained above the politicisation of the OAC. When war broke out, the League drug apparatus hoped to remain aloof. The PCOB requested all governments to continue sending statistics, and the vast majority complied. Britain remained strongly supportive of maintaining the entire League system.[1] The US focused on saving the DSB and PCOB. In October 1939 the State Department publicly affirmed that,

> It is upon the operation of these two boards ... supplementing and coordinating the efforts of independent nations, that the entire fabric of international drug control ultimately rests and the American Government regards it of the highest importance ... to the entire world, that they should be enabled to function adequately, effectively and without interruption and should enjoy the cooperation of all nations.[2]

By the close of the OAC meeting in Geneva in May 1940, the Netherlands had surrendered to Germany and soon France would sign an armistice. Thereafter the pretence of normalcy ended, and attention shifted to a salvage operation.[3] As Anslinger described it, staff suddenly began 'jumping around in Geneva like chickens before a hurricane'.[4] Evacuation of the PCOB and DSB to the US soon appeared to offer the best hope for the system's survival.

In 1940, President Roosevelt had approved the transfer of 'non-political' League services to the Institute of International Study at Princeton. The goal was to preserve the League's technical apparatus and gain intelligence about Germany's economic situation.[5] The PCOB and DSB were not invited because the distinction between their work and the League Secretariat was not grasped within the State Department.[6] Nevertheless, Anslinger and other advocates like Helen Howell Moorhead and Herbert May for the Foreign Policy Association (FPA), conducted a quiet campaign to overcome State Department opposition – the most determined coming from Assistant Secretary of State Breckinridge Long.[7]

Britain, meanwhile, evolved a general wartime policy of 'keeping alive the organs of the League which are able to do useful work'. In 1940 they were already 'strongly in favour of the transfer of as many officials as possible concerned with narcotics to the US'.[8] At the same time, wartime conditions fostered the emergence of a new London-based relationship between top League drug personnel stationed in Britain, the Foreign Office and the Home Office. The Chairman of the PCOB (and India Office official) Sir Atul Chatterjee had, in July 1940, opened a four-way correspondence with Roger Makins, Deputy Head of the Foreign Office Central Europe Department, Sydney Harris, Undersecretary of State at the Home Office and DSB Chairman Sir Malcolm Delevingne. Hereafter the group is referred to as 'the London Four'. Chatterjee's initial motive was to gauge State Department opposition to the transfer.[9]

The four-way correspondence quickly blossomed into a relationship of strong mutual utility. The PCOB and DSB officials provided timely expertise to the British government who were bewildered by the issue's wartime potency and struggling to prevent it poisoning other areas of Anglo–American relations. In return, the British government provided these officials with valuable access to the Washington-based League apparatus. Both functions became increasingly important as US influence and internal machinations became more apparent. By 1943, the DSB Chairman Sir Malcolm Delevingne was acting as the main Foreign Office advisor on the opium issue.

In 1940 the State Department appeared likely to refuse the PCOB and DSB move to Washington. They suggested League officials look to Portugal, Cuba or South America as alternatives. Chatterjee, trying to mollify State Department concerns, promised a minimalist role, 'reception, collection and publication of statistics'. His sense of urgency increased as his correspondence with League headquarters in Switzerland was cut off. A quiet Washington lobbying campaign continued under the leadership of Herbert May and the FPA.

May was vice president of the PCOB; acting chairman of the DSB; and board member of the FPA. He came to represent a core member of Harry Anslinger's wartime 'inner circle' but also a true system old hand, commanding broad international respect and admiration. May had served on the PCOB since its founding in 1928. Since the early League days, the FPA had served as a surrogate for the US government on the opium issue. It undertook public relations work, lobbied US elites and became an incubator for policy ideas. It was a central plank of Anslinger's wartime inner circle. The 'inner circle', a term originated by William McAllister, was a group centred around Harry Anslinger and Washington DC-based control advocates and lobbyists during the war. It played an instrumental wartime role.[10] It had three main actors, one of whom was Herbert May. Helen Howell Moorhead chaired the FPA Opium Research Committee and was perhaps the most important non-state actor in the formation of international drug control. As William McAllister describes, for over a quarter of a century 'she provided social lubrication, acted as a go-between among governmental representatives, floated policy options, and served as a back-channel communications conduit.'[11] Joseph P. Chamberlain served as president of the FPA and law professor at Columbia University. He took a less activist role in the day-to-day workings but served as an extremely effective figurehead particularly using his high-profile international contacts. All three frequently acted in a personal capacity, as the FPA Charter prohibited policy advocacy.[12]

The inner circle also included a number of Anslinger's chief international allies. Most important was Col. Clem Sharman of Canada (see below). At times it included Dr Victor Hoo, China's Vice Minister of Foreign Affairs from 1942 to 1945. Hoo had served as China's lead representative to the League from 1931 until 1942 when the opium issue was a chief foreign policy concern. He would continue to work closely with the US, as we shall see.[13]

George Morlock from the Division of Far Eastern Affairs was Anslinger's chief ally and counterpart at the US State Department. Morlock and

Anslinger worked together closely, although Morlock was more deferential to broader State Department concerns than his predecessor Stuart Fuller, with whom Anslinger had formed an extremely tight bureaucratic alliance during the 1930s until Fuller's death in 1941.[14] The inner circle also came to include Arthur Elliott Felkin, the diligent and earnest PCOB secretary and former British bureaucrat. While in Washington, Felkin, already disillusioned with old League Secretariat members, came heavily under Anslinger's influence. It further included Leon Steinig, an exiled Jewish Austrian who had escaped Nazi occupation to the US with Anslinger's help, eventually becoming a US citizen. He had served a key role in drafting the international drug treaties during the 1930s and was the main secretariat figure in the DSB.[15]

Eventually Herbert May secured State Department consent for the PCOB and DSB move.[16] Opposition folded when it became apparent that Secretary of State Cordell Hull held a 'strong interest' in the drug issue. Logistical barriers remained, however. For example, the Spanish government initially refused a travel visa for Arthur Elliott Felkin. Anslinger eventually extorted one by threatening to withhold future narcotic supplies from Spain.[17] It was an early example of the powerful leverage his opium stockpile afforded him.

Political and logistical constraints ensured minimalist functioning of the PCOB and DSB in Washington. Reports were reduced to bare bones statistics, removing all commentary not mandated by the conventions. They were officially 'branch offices' of Geneva headquarters. With increased US patronage came increased US influence. The PCOB and DSB were dependent on the goodwill of their hosts and the assistance of Anslinger. As Herbert May described it when Anslinger helped solve a complicated office lease issue, 'Good old Harry, always to the rescue!' Reciprocating, members of the apparatus provided statistics and political intelligence to Anslinger and became a core part of the inner circle.[18]

Anslinger also used the situation to inculcate the American approach to addiction 'treatment' to the officials stationed in the US. This involved arranging extensive tours of prisons, federal narcotics farms (detoxification hospitals) and various regional FBN bureaus.[19] As Felkin described one visit to a New York penitentiary to Anslinger, '[a]s you know, I am a child in these matters, but I want to tell you how strong a general impression of keenness and efficiency I got.'[20]

By 1943 Anslinger commented that it was 'gratifying to know that the structure we have helped to erect over the past years has not toppled'.[21] Herbert May later recollected the PCOB and DSB were 'among the very few international institutions which continued to operate fully all through the war ... nearly all League activities had stopped too and the Opium Advisory Committee ... was not able to operate.'[22] Although May overstated their functioning, it was a good example of continuity between the League and the UN. In 1941, 88 per cent of the 177 states and territories covered by the 1931 Convention submitted statistics.[23] Further, officials, expertise and technical frameworks would be available for reinstitutionalisation after the war. Other organisations collapsed or became tainted by their presence in occupied territories. The League of Nations Health Organisation, perceived as coming under 'German and Vichy influence', needed a complete remoulding after the war.[24]

With the technical apparatus saved, but the OAC and the League drug secretariat placed into limbo, the system's political momentum ground to a halt. Anslinger and his allies continued to work behind the scenes to circumvent and make redundant these latter aspects of the League system they so hated. Political evolution had shifted to bilateral interactions, largely independent of the multilateral framework. US drug control advocates would take the lead on these efforts, thoroughly exploiting its wartime position, whilst the old colonial powers fought a stumbling rearguard action. The war would help reshape the international control system, but traditional stumbling blocks continued, particularly between the UK and US. It is towards some of these issues that we now turn.

2.3 Britain, the US and Wartime Narcotics Concerns

Wartime conditions caused widespread disruption to the licit and illicit markets. Conflict increased the demand for painkillers and other medicines. This fuelled expanded production – eventually leaving new excesses that could leak into the illicit market, particularly when the war ended.[25] Narcotics were also vital to each nation's war efforts. A tenet of economic warfare became preventing enemy access to drugs or precursor raw materials. For example, states engaged in 'preclusive buying' while trying to destroy opponents' drug-manufacturing capacities.[26]

Opium itself was seen as a direct weapon of war, particularly in the US. After Pearl Harbor, Anslinger seized on the opportunity to further link the drug issue with national security concerns. Japan was already believed to be conducting a 'narcotisation' campaign against China's population – a charge eventually levelled at many Japanese officials during the Tokyo War Crimes Trials.[27] Meyer and Parssinen argue that the narcotisation charge was part of a broader 'myth of conspiracy' surrounding drugs and 'what looked like genocide and conspiracy at the highest levels . . . in fact was political compromise in pursuit of larger goals.'[28] Nevertheless, soon after war broke out Treasury Secretary Morgenthau publicly claimed that 'Japan's war on Western civilisation started ten years ago, an offensive in which the weapons were narcotic drugs.' Anslinger opportunistically claimed that America 'experienced Pearl Harbors many times in the past in the nature of dangerous drugs from Japan which were meant to poison the blood of the American people'.[29]

Another pervasive fear was that wartime conditions bred addiction among soldiers. They could then bring their consumption back home to the general population. It was a recurring US fear stretching back to the Civil War, when morphine addiction earned the name the 'army disease'.[30] In Britain, World War I press hysteria contributed to the passage of the Dangerous Drugs Act of 1920, which limited cocaine, morphine and heroin prescriptions to medical professionals. The historiography of wartime addiction epidemics suggests that they were often more imagined than real but proved an enduring public perception of the dangers of war.[31] Anslinger carefully monitored all reports of addiction among US soldiers and their interactions with local drug trades. He received a stream of reports from commanders on the ground and his own sources within the Office of Strategic Services (OSS). Many were forwarded to the War Department for remedial action.[32] Britain was acutely aware of US fears for their troops during joint operations in Asia, as we shall see.[33]

Anslinger also grasped opium's potential as a weapon of economic warfare. He had spent the late 1930s building up America's reserves and by 1940 was sitting on roughly six hundred thousand pounds of opium – a four-year supply. This afforded him tremendous strategic leverage and apotheosized him to a 'de facto global drug czar'.[34] For example, in August 1940 the Netherlands East Indies sought emergency supplies of manufactured drugs equivalent to one ton of opium. Anslinger insisted that they provide one ton of raw opium they were holding ready to be processed into smoking opium.[35] Only Britain, meanwhile, with its large pharmaceutical industry, remained in a position to challenge US drug hegemony.[36]

For Britain, war raised immediate practical concerns. Unlike the US, it had no stockpile and had to battle to ensure adequate supplies for its factories, colonies and pre-existing export markets, of which Canada was one of the largest. This was all before additional wartime demands. Britain had a delicate balancing act: meeting wartime needs; protecting pre-existing export markets; preventing currency outflows; and making inroads into the traditionally German and American dominated pharmaceutical export markets of Latin America.[37]

Britain's concerns for its colonies also centred on ensuring supplies for their monopolies. Absent these, administrators faced growing black markets; collapses in government revenues and consuming populations suddenly deprived of legitimate supplies, all at a time when they could least afford civil unrest. By 1940 London was sufficiently worried about its international bargaining position vis-à-vis producer countries such as Iran that it considered joining forces with France, and possibly the Netherlands. Tehran's Monopoly appeared to be reneging on part of a 1939 contract for one thousand chests of opium, each weighing roughly 72 kilograms.[38] Fears about their reliability only increased as the Monopoly talked of price hikes and began demanding payment in dollars, something the Treasury flatly refused.[39]

The Colonial Office soon became alarmed over the Straits Settlements' dwindling stockpiles. Meanwhile the Hong Kong monopoly pushed for permission to source alternative supplies through a disreputable private firm operating under the family name Nemazi. The firm had been blacklisted after causing a minor opium scandal for British shipping interests in Hong Kong in 1927.[40] The Colonial Office was told to sit tight while an arrangement was sought for a purchase that would cover both colonies.

After some further false starts with negotiations, the situation in Malaya and Hong Kong grew urgent and the Colonial Office began looking to Turkey and Afghanistan as potential substitutes.[41] The Foreign Office offered no objections, and instead noted that Kabul was anxious to sell for fiscal reasons and that Indian was anxious to help them sell. Some in the Foreign Office suggested purchases from Turkey would help the Turkish pay for tin and rubber and so recycle money back to UK colonies.[42]

As 1940 drew to a close, both Afghanistan and Turkey were prepared to offer supplies of opium in exchange for sterling, and on relatively favourable terms.[43] Meanwhile the Iran contract affair had reached all the way to the desk of British Foreign Secretary Anthony Eden, who was marked to receive a full report in early 1941.[44] This early wartime experience as a hostage consumer nation left an indelible mark on Britain. As we shall see in later chapters, London would vigorously oppose US attempts to restrict the global supply prerogative to a 'closed list' group of nations, instead demanding market competition and consumer choice.

2.4 Anglo–American Tensions and the US–Canadian Special Narcotic Relationship

Canada was one of Britain's largest pre-war export markets for manufactured drugs. Canada was also the United States' closest drug diplomatic ally. Canada's top drug official, Colonel Clem Sharman began representing Canada at the League OAC in 1934. From then until his final retirement from the control system in 1958, he and Anslinger were virtual alter egos on the international stage. The two engaged in a prolific correspondence and shared a belief in controlling supply at the source as well as the pursuit of strict criminal penalties. Britain would later characterise Sharman as 'obsessed with the purely police aspect of the [narcotics] problem'.[45] Both also shared a latent disdain for the colonial opium policies of Britain, the Netherlands, France and other European powers.[46]

Sharman's wartime position was reinforced by the fact that the prime minister had previously served on the Canadian Delegation to the first international opium conference and retained a strong interest in the issue.[47] Overall Canada's hard-line position derived from Sharman's strong issue suzerainty and his skill at manipulating international forums without risking Canadian prestige. As we shall see, the Canadian position would moderate sharply on his retirement in 1954.

Anslinger and Sharman's personal relationship resulted in a de facto regional framework and strategy. For example, the two occasionally cooperated to secure cross-border market access for their best behaving drug-manufacturing firms. This simultaneously strengthening their domestic positions as industry gatekeepers, providing them with non-statutory powers to dole out benefits and punishments to firms.[48] Sharman's relationship with London, meanwhile, was largely fraught, and interactions centred on safeguarding Canada's supply.

Canada had taken quick action to curtail domestic consumption with the 1939 War Measures Act, which banned all non-prescribed opiate use. With the fall of Holland and Belgium in mid-1940, Canada lost half its supply of its main opiate, codeine, and a significant portion of its supplies of morphine and heroin. They were now completely dependent on Britain at a time when the Atlantic was an increasingly perilous supply line and Britain's own survival was in doubt. Although Canada's supply situation was a source of concern, it never became acute, as Ottawa had, with Anslinger's assistance, secured a US promise to act as its supplier of last resort.[49]

Aside from economic competition Anslinger quickly became critical of perceived British inaction over wartime smuggling. He had begun the war on reasonable terms with his British counterparts. He and the Chief Inspector of the Home Office Drug Branch, Major William H. Coles, enjoyed a mutual respect at the League OAC. When war broke out, Coles was reassigned, and his role fell to Deputy Chief Inspector Francis Thornton. Anslinger's overt response was concern while he expressed hope that Coles had not severed his connection with the issue.[50] This initial response set the tone for the relationship until Coles's return in 1945, during which time Thornton would inspire a lack of faith in Anslinger (and Sharman) that would eventually become disdain.

In 1940, Anslinger praised signs that the UK was toughening its police response to domestic drug use. He was particularly glad to see high-profile press stories about drug-addicted members of the medical profession being prosecuted. However, in early 1941, Liverpool caught press attention as a trans-shipment port for the illicit traffic into North America and by 1942 was even being raised within the State Department. Anslinger's initial response was to quietly reach out to Thornton and the Home Office 'to work out something'.[51] Increasingly furious at Thornton's seeming inaction, Anslinger remained relatively muted until after 1943, when he returned aggressively to the issue. A further simmering source of Anglo–American wartime tension was Britain's interactions with Latin America, as we shall see. These Anglo–American drug disagreements strengthened Anslinger's resolve to use wartime confusions to secure an end to the British opium monopolies in the Far East.

2.5 Ending the Opium Monopolies Issue

Article 6 of the Hague Opium Convention of 1912 committed states parties to the gradual 'suppression of the manufacture, the internal traffic in and the use of prepared opium in so far as the difference conditions peculiar to each nation shall allow'. The United States continued to push for immediate suppression, while European colonial powers sought gradual measures to suppress prepared opium use. Many argued that consumption was diminishing as a direct result of the monopoly system. Further, they claimed it was an effective mechanism to prevent the illicit traffic 'which stimulates consumption'.[52]

At the outbreak of war, opium smoking was legal, under proscribed conditions, in the Netherlands Indies, British Malaya, the Unfederated

Malay States, Brunei, Sarawak, Burma, India, Ceylon, British North Borneo, Hong Kong, French Indochina and Thailand. European governments maintained that monopolies adhered to the 1912 Convention and were preferable to total prohibition. The US and China had demanded throughout the 1930s that large and mandatory annual reductions in supplies to these monopolies be included in any production limitation agreement. Conversely, the British and the Dutch had maintained that a production limitation agreement was first needed to reduce the leakages into the illicit market from China and Persia and then abolition of opium smoking and eating might be possible, 'provided that a reasonable transitional period is allowed'.[53] For the US, China and to a lesser degree Canada, the monopoly system sustained the illicit market, addiction and non-medical use while serving as a barrier to a production limitation convention.[54]

By the beginning of the 1930s, China remained the epicentre of the global trade and the key to control in the region. Meanwhile, a League Commission of Enquiry reported in 1930: 'Contact with Chinese Immigrants has in other Far-Eastern territories usually been the cause of the indigenous population acquiring the opium-smoking habit.'[55] During the 1920s and 1930s, China had disintegrated into warlordism, civil war and then war with Japan. The political economies of these wars fuelled a process whereby local politics and the black market grew in symbiosis, as all sides used the illicit trade to finance military operations.[56]

In 1935, the Chinese nationalists began the most vigorous domestic anti-opium campaign they would ever undertake. This Six-Year Opium Prohibition Plan aimed for total suppression by 1940 but proved largely unsuccessful.[57] The government nevertheless began declaring victory in areas it controlled, while claiming areas under Japanese control were getting worse and that China's successes were being undermined by neighbouring 'places where opium is openly sold by the local governments'.[58] These narratives were echoed publicly and uncritically by Anslinger, congressmen and other US officials. Many in Washington recognised that facts on the ground were more complex and that generals and local politicians loyal to Chiang Kai-shek were likely complicit in the trade. They nevertheless remained effusive in their public support for Chiang, finding a useful tool to bludgeon Japan's aggression and build goodwill with the Chinese government.[59] Other powers, such as Britain, found little cause to parrot Chiang's claims, while China's criticism of the opium monopolies was recognised as a significant public relations problem, particularly in the US. Soon, China and the US would join forces against Britain and the Netherlands at a point of intense vulnerability for the latter.

By 1942 the inner circle, led by Helen Moorhead and Herbert May, were examining principles for post-war control and the ending of colonial opium monopolies. On the other side were, what Sharman described as, the '"wait and see" army' led by Malcolm Delevingne and Bertil Renborg of the League Secretariat. The latter, adopting a conservative position, suggested examining the idea of consolidating the existing conventions into 'a single instrument', or single convention, while also planning for re-establishing international controls for when hostilities ceased.

Both Sharman and Anslinger despised Renborg, viewing him as emblematic of the old League drug apparatus they wanted to kill off. They had no intention of engaging with his machinations, while George Morlock, Anslinger's counterpart in the State Department, agreed suggested they should wait until US broader post-war multilateral policies were clear.[60] Anslinger viewed 'Sir Malcolm's ideas' as 'typical of British Imperial policy' and suggested the US and Canadian governments 'march along together on a concrete plan involving the abolition of smoking opium after the war and limitation of production'. He went on, 'if we do not get agreement with the British Government before the war is over, we might as well give up the idea of progress as they will fall back to the pre-war tempo.' Sharman agreed but argued that mid-1942 was 'the worst possible time to take the initiative' as 'the dice would be loaded more heavily' against them. He suggested bringing Russia on board as he and Anslinger charted a path forward.[61] Anslinger let the matter stall, but in September 1942 he spotted his opportunity. As he wrote to Sharman:

> I have been asked to instruct naval officers who are being trained to take over administration in occupied territories in the South Pacific, on narcotic administration. The thought occurred to me that it would be a good thing to indoctrinate them well with the idea of abolishing the monopolies immediately after they take over. Victor Hoo called the same day with the same idea, stating that the Chinese intended to take similar action and that if we also took this action and the monopolies were out during the armistice period, one, two, or three years, the British could hardly re-establish these institutions if, as, and when they regain possession.[62]

Sharman quickly agreed 'whole-heartedly'. However, Anslinger's strategy involved a great deal of bluff. The US would have the right to establish any form of government in areas of which they had unilateral control.

In areas of joint control, the US could not act unilaterally. Morlock met resistance to the idea within the State Department but privately suggested that Anslinger pursue it with the War and Navy Departments by suggesting that closing opium dens was a US legal obligation.[63]

In the meantime, Bertil Renborg had drafted two memos outlining post-war planning options. These arose from meetings of the PCOB and DSB in London during 1942, which the inner circle had largely boycotted. Renborg sought to circumvent the inner circle by gaining the support of the Acting Secretary General of the League, Sean Lester. The latter had expressed an interest but intended to reserve his decision until he received the final plans. Renborg set to work consolidating them and finally forwarded them on to Anslinger and Sharman on 28 December, two full months after the London meeting. By this stage, Anslinger and the inner circle had separate plans in motion and had little intention of supporting Renborg.[64]

Renborg's vision focused on consolidating the treaties, continuity of function of the system of estimates and the wholesale transfer of the League apparatus. Regarding the monopolies and quasi-medical consumption, he dismissed radical action, suggesting 'prohibition could not be expected by itself to bring about the desired result' and suggesting further study.[65] Upon receipt of the documents Anslinger wrote back angrily:

> the two most important subjects in a post-war world, namely, limitation of opium production and abolition of smoking opium monopolies, were given the same treatment which they have had in the past – the old political run around. It is my opinion that if any progress is to be made … the approach will have to be entirely different from that set forth in the vague program.[66]

Sharman responded with similar criticisms. Renborg moved quickly to assuage doubts claiming that the informal 'consensus' was that opium smoking would be abolished and that effective measures would be included in any peace settlement. Sharman and Anslinger remained unimpressed.[67]

Over three meetings, between December 1942 and March 1943 the 'inner circle' pressed ahead. The meetings were unofficial, convened under the independent and unthreatening banner of the FPA, but were choreographed to suggest US government backing – for example being held in Anslinger's office, ostensibly because FPA conditions were too cramped. The US government had no consensus policies on post-war planning, let alone the drug issue. In December 1942, Anslinger (FBN), Helen Moorhead (FPA); Professor Chamberlain (FPA); Herbert May (PCOB; DSB; FPA); Dr Victor Hoo (China); Dr Liu Chieh, Minister Counsellor of the Chinese Embassy; and George Morlock (US State Department) met to strategise.[68]

Burma became the focus of the discussions given the expected allied military drive. Dr Hoo suggested that prohibition, despite Britain claiming it was a civilian health issue, was arguably 'a military necessity for the safety and welfare of troops'. This became the core argument for the US and China as the group looked to reconvene in early January 1943.[69] At the second meeting, the inner circle moved to develop a Pacific consensus to isolate the British and the Dutch by including the 'obviously unaware' representatives of Australia and New Zealand. Sharman, given the political sensitivities, sat this meeting out. Anslinger and Morlock sounded out the two governments and suggested the US government was merely deciding how to approach relevant governments. With little substantive progress the inner circle made their move. They convened another meeting on 17 March, including representatives from Britain, the Netherlands, China, Canada, Australia and New Zealand.[70]

The Dutch quickly agreed to send an 'observer' from their Washington Embassy.[71] The UK Foreign Office sought the Home Office's views.[72] The London four relationship, between Harris (HO), Chatterjee (PCOB), Delevingne (DSB) and now a Mr M. Williams (FO), emerged as a strong counterweight to the inner circle. Delevingne, by now the Foreign Office's main opium advisor, immediately rang alarm bells. He read it as a bureaucratic flanking manoeuvre around League structures and warned it was 'certain' that opium smoking would be raised. He pointed out that the government of Burma was already looking at the question, while Malaya and Hong Kong would have to examine it closely before Britain could formulate a coherent position, let alone have a lay Washington Embassy official discuss it.[73]

Consequently, London refused to be represented but allowed the Ambassador discretion to send 'an observer'. The Foreign Office were curious as to the official attitude of the US government. They began what was to prove a long and vigorous interdepartmental discussion by soliciting the Colonial Office's views.[74] The latter called the question 'premature' given wartime uncertainties and their expectation that Japan was 'fostering' opium smoking. They suggested a regional solution, based on a convention with surrounding territories.[75]

Lord Halifax, anxious to oblige and unaware of the diplomatic minefield, opted to send an observer. It was a decision he quickly came to regret as his representative was blindsided at a meeting designed specifically backfoot Britain and force the colonial issue.[76] Choosing his words carefully, Anslinger said that 'one cannot have the Four Freedoms and still sell opium.' He then attacked past British colonial opium policies, while Herbert May suggested Britain had the worst international opium reputation. Moreover, they warned that the US press was snooping around the issue, viewing it as linked with other international problems.[77]

Anslinger pointed to China's supposed success and claimed that in the event of an occupation of Burma, China would enact strict prohibition on its sale. Sharman and Chamberlain closed ranks, also praising China's domestic control efforts. Sharman, however, was careful to make explicit that the views expressed were his own and that a formal Canadian policy had not yet even been discussed. Anslinger then argued that China's policy could lead to a clash with the British given his expectation that US forces would follow a similar policy of immediate suppression in the areas that they occupied.[78]

Anslinger was bluffing. The State, Treasury, War and Navy Departments had not yet expressed a specific policy, let alone suggested that they would override their uniform occupation policies already agreed by the Combined Chiefs of Staff. Unilateral US measures were explicitly not envisaged.[79] Further, a precedent had already been set in North Africa where the French had reopened their hashish monopoly, while the US could merely forbid its occupation forces from using the shops.[80] In a broader sense, the Roosevelt administration, and Secretary Hull in particular, were careful to avoid airing alliance politics publicly at this time.[81] George Morlock sat in silence at the meeting as Anslinger set the US up for a potentially embarrassing climb down should the colonial powers refuse to fold. His silence, however, helped create a perception that Anslinger spoke for a unified US government.[82]

London privately labelled Anslinger's portrayal of China as the work of 'foreign and Chinese propagandists'. They maintained the main obstacle to total prohibition in colonies adjacent to China remained 'smuggling by and on behalf of the Chinese communities resident therein'. London saw itself as at least being honest in refusing to enact a policy it could not enforce. One Foreign Office official naïvely argued that 'Americans with their experience of prohibition should be the first to appreciate the importance of avoiding a situation where the law itself is brought into contempt.' China, on the other hand, was seen as publicly enacting broad laws of suppression while privately allowing profitable monopolies to function under the name of an 'Opium Suppression Bureau', marketing the drug as 'anti-opium medicine'.[83]

The Dutch Observer was conciliatory during the meeting but quickly requested the minutes be changed to express his defence for the monopoly system as the best means to prevent smuggling. Further, he sent on an article by the former Dutch OAC member, DeKat Angelino, which justified the Dutch position. It claimed the results of prohibition in the Philippines were not 'encouraging' and suggested advocates for immediate prohibition were misguided. It argued that the current Dutch policy prevented the growth of the illicit traffic, corruption and opium consumers from turning to cocaine and heroin.[84] Anslinger simply dismissed it as 'the old opium bloc argument'.[85] By June 1943 the inner circle had no indication of whether their strategy had succeeded in shifting the British or Dutch positions, with their immediate reaction suggesting 'a repetition of their former position'. Anticipating little progress, they began to examine 'further avenues'.[86]

In London, foreign policy goals quickly outweighed practical administrative concerns for the Foreign Office. Anthony Eden accepted the difficulties but hoped to avoid 'unfriendly criticism'. The Foreign Office recognised the political capital China would draw from British intransigence and 'disproportionate importance' placed on the issue in the US.[87] Discussions between the Foreign, Home, Colonial, Dominions, Burma and India Offices soon concluded that more concrete action was necessary.[88]

2.6 Changing Colonial Policies

A core determinant for the shift in British policy was a change in costs and benefits. Following the 1925 conventions, the colonial governments in Borneo and Malaya imposed a system of registration and rationing for smokers. Gradually rations were reduced alongside ostensible efforts to improve social conditions. Registration for the Malayan monopoly was effectively closed in 1934 with the expectation that existing addiction would be confined to an aging cohort and thereby not spread to a new generation.[89]

Hong Kong was unable to adopt a similar course due to its proximity to Mainland China.[90] During the 1920s civil disorder in China caused an influx of black market opium. Rather than suppression, the goal of government policy was merely to coerce consumers into buying monopoly opium. Further, fiscal benefits of the monopoly militated against efforts to change the system.[91] However, with these fiscal benefits and the concerns about administrative practicalities muted by Japanese occupation, the desire to appease American demands in 1943 outweighed these former obstacles. This wartime logic applied across the various British territories occupied by Japan.

The Dutch unilaterally decided to acquiesce in August 1943 but postponed to allow a simultaneous British announcement.[92] The secretary of state for India and Burma said later that the Dutch decision made it 'difficult to resist American proposals'.[93] Britain risked becoming a regional pariah. In September 1943 the Interdepartmental Opium Committee convened at the Home Office and agreed a broad policy of suppression along with a draft public statement (after subsequent tweaking) that the UK:

> has decided to adopt the policy of total prohibition of opium smoking in the British and British protected territories in the Far East which are now in enemy occupation and, in accordance with this policy, the prepared opium monopolies formerly in operation . . . will not be re-established on their reoccupation [emphasis added].[94]

London no longer felt in a position to say 'no'. Acutely aware of the US public sentiments, they feared a public relations disaster should the monopolies be blamed for 'infecting' US soldiers with addiction.[95] Further, they expected a US public relations windfall from the announcement, which could help alleviate broader colonial policy tensions. Moreover, the administrative costs of prohibition were viewed as significantly less than decades prior, particularly as the Japanese occupation removed the administrative benefits. Finally, sacrificing the monopolies in British territories occupied by Japan would help appease American demands before they could be extended to cover the more problematic case of India.[96]

The policy shift would not apply to India, where the traditional method of opium consumption was by eating not smoking. Mainland India was also not 'in enemy occupation'.[97] Burma proved the most complicated case and would drag on through the war and into the post-war era as we shall see. Consequently, reiterating previous reservations, the 1943 Statement explicitly warned that success would 'depend on the steps taken to limit and control the production of opium in other countries' (i.e. China).[98]

Anslinger, unaware of his victory, moved to initiate a public relations offensive in the US, stoking fears of a resurgent heroin trade driven by the monopoly system if allowed to infect US troops. Congressman Carroll Reece gave a widely publicised speech in the US House of Representatives mimicking Anslinger's talking points. Anslinger also worked with his international allies, particularly Dr Hoo to forge a Sino–US response to expected Anglo–Dutch intransigence. Simultaneously, Anslinger's domestic allies exerted political pressure in both the US and UK. The FPA reached out to the British Council of Churches, fishing for intelligence on Whitehall interdepartmental discussions. Even if successful, Helen Moorhead wanted a change in policy to seem 'the result of British opinion, not American pressure', to help 'save their face'.[99] Ultimately, this overture seemed to go nowhere, and there is no indication that British public opinion and domestic lobby groups played a significant role in determining government policy around opium.

The US federal government eventually reached a consensus to do everything possible to effect suppression, but that it could not technically be forced upon the colonial powers.[100] Anslinger and his domestic allies focused only on the first part of the consensus statement and declared victory, seeing it as 'steady forward movement'.[101] The State Department issued a polite aide-memoire to London, the Netherlands, China and Portugal restating US pre-war views and suggesting they limit opium use to strictly medical and scientific purposes. They also asked the British government to consider 'a common policy' for forces under allied command, while reserving the right to take any independent measures 'deemed necessary for the protection of the health' of US forces.[102]

This document sparked confusion in London and mild panic in the Washington Embassy. The Embassy, unaware of the policy shift already agreed in London read it as a 'threat ... which the Americans might easily put into effect, with the full support of their public opinion'. Furthermore, they feared it would 'compromise the position which is being slowly built up, of leaving control of civil affairs in British territory to British authorities'. The Embassy asked that it be 'considered urgently' warning that 'the people interested here are fairly unscrupulous in their methods' and 'if there is what seems to them undue delay they may start some kind of propaganda campaign which might be damaging to us.'[103]

Back in London, the reference to strict 'medical and scientific' usage was initially misread as an escalation of US demands. Departments worked to ensure that the public relations offensive would address the concerns highlighted, but on points of substance, it was eventually just ignored.[104]

Some historians have suggested that the Embassy's concerns drove British policy. William McAllister argues that Britain and the Netherlands feared that the US 'might delay or terminate plans for returning civil administration to the previous colonial masters'.[105] This may be true in a broader sense, but at no time was it made explicit as a reason for the policy shift on opium. The Embassy's fears were the most alarmist, and the policy shift had already been decided and remained unchanged despite the misinterpretation of the aide-memoire. At no point did there appear an imminent fear that opium would be the trigger for America to thwart British repossession of its colonies. William O. Walker, meanwhile, plausibly suggests that a fear of being pushed out of Asia weighed on the British policymakers regarding this matter. He does, however, incorrectly suggest that the policy shift was not decided upon until after the aide-memoire was received.[106]

Overall, it was a decision largely based on a cost–benefit analysis. The British government had not been a long way from enacting some form of suppression prior to the 1924 conferences when the balance ultimately had tipped in favour of colonial concerns over transatlantic ones. By 1943, the equation had reversed. Negative publicity and the alienation of powerful figures in the US government could adversely affect broader foreign policy goals at a time when none of the monopolies' administrative benefits were being felt. Anslinger had timed his *coup de grâce* perfectly and navigated a complex grey zone of US government and Anglo–US policy to great effect. Had Anslinger not bluffed and forced this issue, it seems unlikely that Britain would have embarked on such a broad and coherent policy shift upon retaking its possessions. The situation on the ground would more than likely have called for a recreation of the monopoly system and the pre-war status quo, in the short term at least.

London began choreographing its statement to obtain 'the fullest possible publicity value, especially in the US'.[107] By 16 September, both Anslinger and Sharman were celebrating. As Sharman described it:

> This is the most happy solution to what might well have proved ... a major conflict of policy between the United States and Great Britain at or before the Peace Conference ... I am abundantly satisfied that your personal influence, as also your action in having the unofficial show down meeting in Washington last March, was by far the most influential factor.[108]

Anslinger labelled it 'the first concrete post-war agreement for which Treasury is responsible.'[109]

On 10 November 1943, in response to a prepared question in the House of Commons, the secretary of state for the colonies recited a prepared two-paragraph statement. It was accompanied, on the same day, by the Netherlands' announcement. The acting secretary of state noted the announcements 'with satisfaction' and gushed that: 'the problem of smoking opium should now be susceptible of solution.'[110] Drug control advocates went to work drawing press attention in the US.[111] Sir Malcolm Delevingne wrote in *The Times* of London claiming that it would 'make a not unimportant contribution to the cause of Anglo-American cooperation particularly in the Far East'. Congressman Carroll Reece, in a speech on the House floor, described how Anslinger, through his informal negotiations, was 'largely responsible for this diplomatic triumph'.[112]

Chiang's government publicly welcomed the announcements, claiming China was among the 'principal advocates' for total prohibition.[113] Britain was infuriated at being placed 'on the defensive' and the Foreign Office privately cursed the Chinese as 'hypocrites' who 'cleverly ... conceal their hypocrisy!'

Some voices of dissent surfaced in Britain. For example, Mr Clifford Bellairs wrote in a letter to *The Times* of London:

> I have had some 30 years' experience of the opium trade and this I can prophesy with certainty: if the Government merely prohibits the import and sale of smoking opium in the Far East the illicit traders, smugglers and dope peddlars will return en masse to make enormous profits to spread the vice, and it will not end the comparatively innocuous smoking of opium ... but will open up further fields for the illicit consumption of morphine and cocaine, each a hundred times more deadly.[114]

Another regional domino would fall in 1945 when the French announced a policy of prohibition in their colonies.[115] The paradigm for the post-war world was being shaped and old stumbling blocks removed. It seemed that much of the deadlock of the interwar years could be headed for extinction. Having won this wartime coup, Anslinger had earned significant leverage both at home and abroad. He quickly turned his sights towards the Middle East and Iran in particular.

2.7 Taming the Iranian Market

Iran was one of the world's major opium producers. Its support for international controls had traditionally been weak, drawing scorn from control circles, particularly the US. It had signed the original 1912 Convention with a major reservation, rejecting one of its central principles, article 3(a): that an exporting country was responsible for preventing the shipment of opium to countries that prohibited its entry.[116] Iran's motives appeared purely economic, in that it would close the lucrative Chinese market. Iran further refused to adopt an international import/export certificate system as per the 1925 Convention.[117] Shifting Iran's international policies became a central plank of Anslinger's wartime drug diplomacy. Britain, on the other hand, proved unwilling to undermine relations with Iran in pursuit of drug control.

By 1917, opium was Iran's second most valuable export and had a substantial domestic consumption market. The regime of Reza Shah, running from 1921 to 1941, pursued a course of modernisation and westernisation that required new sources of government revenue. Opium seemed an obvious source and one encouraged by US advisors, specifically Dr Arthur Millspaugh who had the official role of Administrator General of the Finances, 1922–7.[118] During the interwar years, India had ceased opium exports to China. Iran quickly took up the slack. Its crop peaked in 1936 at 40 per cent of the world's morphine supply, and 15 per cent of Iran's foreign exchange earnings.[119] By the outbreak of war, it was also viewed as a main source for the global illicit market, particularly for Japanese forces in China.[120]

The Anglo–Soviet invasion of Iran in 1941 disrupted the Iranian-Japanese–Chinese opium trade. Britain ceased issuing navicerts allowing neutral ships to pass through wartime blockades, cutting off shipments to Japanese firms. The US Consul in Tehran noted that through 'the British contraband control, Iran [was] cut off from its former profitable Far Eastern Market'. Around this time, the new regime of Mohamed Reza Pahlavi expressed a desire to curtail opium production and consumption. Washington's drug establishment remained sceptical, particularly after an Iranian Treasury Official stated in December 1941 that their Monopoly would treat opium sales as a purely commercial transaction, regardless of the consequences for the countries it was selling to.[121] In this, the Americans heard a clear restatement of the original Iranian reservation to article 3(a) of the 1912 Convention.

In 1942 Anslinger was nevertheless forced by the State Department to temporarily lift the ban on Iranian opium imports to improve relations.[122] A drawn-out US–Iranian wartime opium engagement ensued. The latter periodically promised adherence to the drug conventions, the former promised access to its domestic market after the war. Anslinger then tentatively welcomed an olive branch from the Chief of the New York–based Iranian Trade and Economic Commission, Allah Yar Saleh to try to regularise the US–Iranian opium trade. For Iran it was part of a broader trade rapprochement with the US in 1942–3. For Anslinger it was an opportunity to press Iran to improve domestic controls.[123]

In 1942 the State Department began free trade negotiations with Yar Saleh covering sixty commodities, possibly including opium. Both Anslinger and Morlock opposed opium's inclusion, preferring deference to the drug conventions and warning that the US could not legally buy Iranian opium after the war unless Tehran adhered to drug conventions. Further, they suggested it would be a perverse reward given Iran's record, and would ignore the good behaviour of convention adherents like Yugoslavia and Turkey.[124]

Elizabeth Washburn Wright suggested tying the trade agreement to American drug control demands, thereby adding new pressure on the Iranian government to adhere to the drug conventions. It is not clear how Anslinger viewed her proposal, but George Morlock was unequivocal that 'the trade agreement was too important to be tied up with the small matter' of opium and the suggestion should be 'thrown out'. He preferred instead a 'voluntary' exchange of notes between the two countries on the opium issue.[125]

Bertil Renborg, meanwhile, the increasingly sidelined League drug secretariat old hand spied an opportunity to show the League Secretariat's continued relevance. He asked the British Home Office to use 'its influence' in Tehran to obtain some progress on drug control. The Foreign Office argued that it was not a 'specifically British interest' and that they already had 'enough more important matters' on their hands. Further 'a pipe of opium is one of the few consolations a Persian can enjoy in these days and any attempt by us to interfere would only add to our unpopularity.'[126] Their flat refusal highlighted the place of opium within the hierarchy of Britain's foreign policy concerns at the time.

Just as Renborg's efforts were falling flat, the US and Iran concluded their 1943 Free Trade deal. It was the twenty-seventh deal America had signed under the Reciprocal Trade Agreement Act of 1934, the sixth since the outbreak of war, yet only the second with a country in the 'Near East' (Turkey was the first). Iran received concessions on 95 per cent of products exported to the US as of 1939. Opium would still be strictly controlled by the FBN and the change in the tariff rate was not expected to strongly impact the volume traded. It did, however, lessen Iran's comparative disadvantage, given the relatively low morphine content of its opium vis-à-vis other suppliers such as Afghanistan. In order to activate the trade concessions in opium, Iran first needed to enact a system of import/export certification as per the 1925 Convention, and ensure domestic laws were sufficient to confine opium to legitimate channels.[127]

By the end of the year, it was apparent that Iran was making no progress towards stricter controls.[128] Anslinger was undeterred. Flush with success after the Anglo–Dutch announcement of November 1943, he entered 1944 ready to refight his battle with Iran. His position was considerably strengthened by a change in Afghan drug policy during 1943.

2.8 Afghanistan Coming in from the Cold?

The US had previously refused to supply Afghanistan with manufactured opiates due to its non-ratification of the 1912 Convention (although it had ratified the 1931 Convention). By 1941, Kabul appealed to the State Department to reconsider. Initially they refused, claiming the commissioner could not legally authorise supplies to non-adherents of the 1912 Convention. Afghanistan promised to take 'any steps' necessary 'to comply with American laws' while the State Department privately acknowledged that in 1912 Afghanistan's foreign affairs were conducted by Britain. The Treasury Department agreed to issue export authorisations on a temporary basis. In October 1943, the US received word that Kabul had ratified the 1912 Convention. Although this did not solve the Afghan drug problem, it did represent another feather in Anslinger's wartime cap. It also augmented his credibility when pressing other recalcitrant states, not least Iran. The US, meanwhile, continued to press Kabul to tighten domestic controls throughout 1944 by politely threatening to cut off its market access when the war ended.[129]

2.9 Egypt as a Regional Leader

Sir Thomas Russell Pasha was a colourful British bureaucrat who had served the British police apparatus in Egypt since 1902. Perhaps best described as the Anslinger of the Middle East, he was the closest thing the region had to a drug czar. He served as the commandant of the Cairo City Police and chief of the Central Narcotics Intelligence Bureau (CNIB) for the duration of the war.[130] Like Anslinger, Russell Pasha was a remarkable bureaucrat, a shrewd media operator and occasionally an informal regional drug diplomat. Like Anslinger he was a strong advocate for control of narcotics at the source, and he ably stirred up local and international press coverage to further these strategic ends. In these pursuits, any loyalty to the British government often appeared secondary to his self-described 'drug habit' and bureaucratic suzerainty.[131] This latter attribute was perhaps his greatest similarity with Anslinger. For both men, their bureaucratic survival was synonymous with the survival of drug control efforts.

The Anglo–Egyptian Treaty of 1936 further drove Russell Pasha towards his US allies. With the fulfilment of its European Police Clause, he expected that the drug issue would be handed over to an incapable, Egyptian-run apparatus and his decades of work would be undone. He increasingly sought US patronage and cultivated a strong personal relationship with a number of the US drug control lobby particularly Mrs Corinna Lindon Smith – an advisor on narcotics to the American General Federation of Women's Clubs. Anslinger described her as one of Russell Pasha's 'very sincere friends and a great admirer'.[132]

With the outbreak of war, the flow of 'white drugs' (namely heroin) into Egypt dried up while 'black drugs' (namely hashish) poured in from the surrounding Levant states. In 1941, the *Egyptian Mail* attributed the drought to 'war conditions and the strict supervision exercised on shipping in the Mediterranean by the British Fleet'. Russell Pasha described the war as 'a golden opportunity which must not be missed' before the 'British police disappear[ed]' and CNIB became subsumed into the Ministry of Interior. He advocated a post-war Arab front against the illicit drug trade, one based on sustained Western support. In September 1941, he began a new diplomatic campaign against hashish cultivation in the Levant states. He wrote that anti-hashish efforts required 'a certain ruthlessness for the feelings and pockets of the big landlords, notables and Ministers of Syria', as well as 'efficient organisation of police, Gendarmerie, Law courts, etc.'. He argued that by getting the Syrian administration to kill cultivation for a few years, it was far 'harder for an independent Syria . . . to start . . . again'.[133]

To Russell Pasha's frustration, Britain was unwilling to intervene militarily in the drug trade in the Levant in 1941. He believed this encouraged a French 'attitude of laisser-faire' and gave 'the impression that the British authorities were not interested in the matter'.[134] As with the case of Iran in 1943, it was a correct impression to draw. British military forces were far more absorbed with other matters in 1941 and had no desire to complicate relations with regional groups and generate new military entanglements in pursuit of long-term hashish control.

This lack of British interest drove Russell Pasha further towards the US. In a bizarre moment of candour, he wrote to Anslinger in March 1942 that 'our American Colony here is growing greater daily!' It was a statement that both Anslinger and Assistant Secretary of the Treasury Gaston privately described as 'interesting'. In the meantime, Egypt announced its intention to ratify the 1912 Hague Convention. This promise, coupled with a request by George Morlock that Egypt be given 'sympathetic consideration', led the Treasury to approve shipments of US-manufactured opiates to Egypt. Their speedy ratification – by June 1942 – was then happily touted by the US later that year when Iran questioned the feasibility of wartime ratifications.[135]

Despite their convention ratification, Russell Pasha quickly became impatient with the Egyptian government. He complained to Anslinger that his 'masters ... have had a wonderful opportunity of inserting non-growing of hashish into the treaties they have been discussing with Independent Syria and Lebanon, but they've done nothing'. He also expressed dismay at the lack of a suitable Egyptian candidate to replace him as head of the CNIB, lamenting that 'no Egyptian has ever taken up the anti-drug traffic as a hobby.'[136]

He warned that Egypt would 'go down like a pack of cards before the narcotic attack that is coming'. Demand remained high, and once international communications reopened, 'white drugs' would pour in from the Balkans and Far East. He wanted to stay on in the role but feared that advocacy by the British Embassy for him doing so would be misinterpreted. He suggested a multi-state effort involving Britain, the US, Canada and League of Nations.[137] The UK Foreign Office and Home Office thought his fears 'fully justified' but preferred it be taken up 'on an international basis' so Britain was not 'saddled with the job'.[138] As 1943 drew to a close, the future of Egyptian control remained uncertain. With Egypt's ratification of the 1912 Convention, Anslinger refocused his limited regional attention on Iran and Afghanistan.

Meanwhile, Russell Pasha continued to reach out to a number of actors regarding his post-war role in Egypt. Anslinger was non-responsive, either because the letter was misplaced or because he was focused on other issues. Russell Pasha continued a broad press offensive and undertook a diplomatic mission to Lebanon and Syria in March 1944, where he found conditions disheartening. Neither was free from French control nor could avoid a difficult suppression campaign by claiming a lack of autonomy. Notables were 'a law unto themselves in their own district', ignoring the central government and frequently stipulating that fellahin tenants cultivate cannabis. High prices were further driving cultivation into North Syria, where government control was even weaker than in Lebanon. Russell Pasha secured the support of General Holmes, British Commander of the IXth Army, who provided material assistance for suppression efforts. Holmes, a convert to the opium cause, assured him that tackling the traffic was, in his view, part of the war effort and a high priority.[139]

Russell Pasha argued that Turkey remained the main threat for heroin. He had received an angry rebuke from the Turkish officials for suggesting Turkish opium was being smuggled into Egypt via Syria but maintained that seizures in Aleppo suggested Anatolia was the origin. He attributed the angry Turkish response to the poor relationship between the French authorities in Syria and the Turkish authorities. Overall, he claimed the Lebanese and Syrian 'problem' could only be completely solved 'after the war when something similar to the League of Nations takes shape'. States could then be pressured through the international system to ensure they met obligations.[140]

Anslinger finally responded to Russell Pasha in March 1944 (five months after his initial contact). Offering platitudes, Anslinger remained non-committal. He said that 'no greater calamity could befall … narcotic control in the Middle East', than Russell Pasha leaving and predicted 'a very speedy recrudescence of the "white" drug traffic'. He promised that he was pushing the State Department 'to make some move' but warned that 'the time is not far distant when the curtain will fall on the stage for you, Sharman, and myself.' He also intimated that he was focusing on 'the limitation of production project and our chief attack is on Iran'.[141]

The cases of Iran and Egypt, and to a lesser extent Afghanistan, highlighted a sharp divide in Anglo-American policy. British attention to the issue throughout the war only became live when direct interests were at stake. In the Far East, the opium issue touched on important questions of colonial governance. In the Middle East, it was a battle fought over abstract international obligations. When faced with a choice of expending even minor political capital in pursuit of control efforts, every time Britain chose to ignore the issue. The US, although subsuming the issue when broader interests were at stake, for example trade agreements, nevertheless proved willing, time and again, to expend some diplomatic leverage on it.

2.10 Transatlantic Tensions

Towards the end of 1943, opium smuggling via Liverpool to North America re-emerged as a 'common interest' for Canada and the US. Throughout 1944, the two continued to report seizures of Indian Monopoly opium. Anslinger and Sharman sent angry letters to Thornton at the Home Office calling Liverpool 'neck and neck' with Basra as a centre of illicit traffic. They claimed that opium, was 'freely available', the prices 'extremely low' and penalties 'negligible'. Both men attributed the problem to a lack of will or capacity on the part of Britain.[142]

Requests from the UK and other branches of the US and Canadian governments to Anslinger and Sharman to turn a blind eye to the trade and leave offending crew members aboard ships in furtherance of the war effort only fuelled their anger. Thornton's responses did not alleviate the tension. Anslinger had dispatched Arthur Elliott Felkin, PCOB secretary and Washington 'inner circle' confidant, to London to 'vigorously' press the issue. Thornton claimed ignorance and vowed to look into any reports forwarded. Hearing this, Anslinger wrote to Sharman: 'it isn't any wonder that the traffic thrives. It doesn't need to be organized.'[143] The commissioner was quietly compiling these complaints, particularly those against the Indian opium monopoly, into a dossier that could be used at a post-war production limitation conference. Nevertheless, with the monopolies issue now out of the way, Anslinger decided the time was opportune to make his feelings known to Thornton.

In August 1944 Anslinger wrote 'we understand each other well enough to use plain language'. He claimed that he had initially mistaken the statistics regarding British penalties for smuggling for those handed out by Japanese courts before the war. The US Treasury had in 1942 publicly characterised the Japanese penalties as 'an open scandal'. He went on to say that these 'pointless and ineffective fines' were not a deterrent 'but actually encourage the traffickers'.[144] Unmoved, Thornton simply dismissed Anslinger's complaints for the remainder of his tenure and as he did so Anglo–US drug relations grew ever more frosty.

Canada and Latin America, meanwhile, had become a further sore spot for the transatlantic alliance. Between 1943 and 1944 Britain squeezed opiate supplies to Canada while quietly increasing exports to Latin America to increase market share and improve dollar earnings. By December 1943, they were providing only 50 per cent of the minimum

Canadian requirements. Britain blamed a 1943 supply disruption from Turkey causing 'severe shortages' of opium. In early 1944 supplies tightened further, and the High Commissioner in London needed to make 'strong' representations on Canada's behalf. This time, he was permitted to include incriminating intelligence that Anslinger had privately supplied to Sharman showing that manufacturing firms in Britain had been exporting narcotics to Chile while an Indian supply mission had recently offered US firms one hundred thousand pounds of raw opium cake.[145]

By supplying Chile, Britain was undermining Anslinger's regional strategy. Anslinger offered to supply Chile's narcotic needs in return for an end to their domestic production and manufacturing. Further, he believed Chile was self-sufficient and simply re-exporting all narcotics imports to other countries – including Argentina and Brazil. Argentina had not ratified the 1912 Convention, and the US had refused to supply it with narcotics. Both Anslinger and Sharman believed Thornton was knowingly permitting excess supplies to be sent to Chile as they believed he had done for Cuba and Mexico in 1941–2, at a time when Anslinger was pressuring both to reduce consumption, production and smuggling.[146]

Anslinger continued to feed Sharman intelligence, and in July 1944 forwarded a Brazilian government acknowledgement that Britain had replaced Germany as its main supplier. Meanwhile, in another regional victory for Anslinger, Brazil promised to prohibit post-war cultivation 'in compliance with [his] wishes'.[147] For Sharman, these cases highlighted that Britain was lying. When the evidence was presented to London it suddenly claimed a 'marked improvement in supply'. It then began to argue that 'manufacturing capacity' was now the main obstacle to supply. Neither Sharman nor Anslinger believed it. The Home Office would later offer the unconvincing explanation privately to the State Department that the supply shortages arose from the accumulation of stocks for use in liberated areas. The 'sufficiently improved' situation facilitated increased exports to Canada. Although welcome, it did not fulfil Canada's yearly requirements, nor compensate for their drained stocks.[148]

In the meantime, the PCOB provided Sharman with further ammunition releasing an analysis of 'Trends in Trade' in narcotics for 1938–42. This claimed that 'the markets lost by Continental Europe [were] now largely supplied by the United Kingdom' which 'undoubtedly . . . had become the principal exporter in the world'. Germany's loss had been

Britain's gain. The vast majority of this shift was in Latin America, where Britain's market share grew from 1 per cent in 1938 to 77 per cent in 1942.[149]

The Dominions Office offered a complicated and unconvincing series of explanations. Wishing to leave the affair behind them, and undoubtedly regretting a July 1943 suggestion that Canada seek some of her supplies from the US, London reiterated their commitment to meet Canada's needs. Sharman described this as 'an attempt to justify a situation that cannot be justified'. Nevertheless, careful not to overplay his hand, he acknowledged the situation had 'largely been ameliorated' thanks to the 'force with which the facts were communicated'.

The severe shortages Canada had faced in 1944, where some hospitals reported being unable to obtain codeine, were not repeated in 1945, and a more sustainable Anglo–Canadian arrangement gradually emerged.[150] Further, by the close of 1944, the US and Britain had reached an arrangement regarding Latin American whereby both would be limited to exporting half of any country's annual estimates. This meant countries could not double up on purchases. Thornton's subsequent efforts to spin this agreement as evidence of British shortages emerged were unsurprisingly met with scepticism by his North American counterparts.[151]

In October 1945, Major Coles informed Anslinger he had resumed control of the Home Office Drugs Branch and looked 'forward to a renewal of ... collaboration'. He immediately picked up on a pending correspondence with Thornton, welcoming Anslinger's suggestion for an arrangement with India to station a US representative to flag up illicit shipments headed for the US and UK. Anslinger's wrote to Coles that 'it is with a great deal of pleasure that I read your note.'[152] The two had not always seen eye to eye during the League days but had a sufficiently amicable working relationship, and Anslinger hoped they could move beyond the stonewalling of the Thornton era.

2.11 The Burma Dilemma

Britain's Burma dilemma centred on placating American wishes while accommodating local logistical barriers. Despite US paranoia, Britain remained sceptical of the risks of troops becoming addicted to opium, claiming there were no recorded cases for British troops operating in the region.[153] London had warned in a memo to the US government in Washington that their 10 November announcement would 'not immediately be so sweeping' regarding Burma. Nevertheless, since Burma was an area where US troops would be operating, the federal government read the announcement to include Burma.[154]

The practice of smoking prepared opium was not widespread compared to 'quasi-medical' opium eating, which was supplied through a system of government run shops. London maintained that complete suppression was unattainable until cultivation in the neighbouring Yunnan Province, China, was halted and highlighted that prohibition's success depended on 'other countries' in the 10 November Statement.[155] Highlighting a divide between British and US visions, London believed that they had restricted drugs, via 'stringent regulations, to medicinal and scientific purposes'.[156] The challenge was to convince or secure US acquiescence in this vision.

London sought to reframe the Burma opium question as a long-term reconstruction and development problem. The government of Burma convened an Expert Committee in late November 1943. It quickly adopted a conservative approach, building on the existing policy legacy rather than advocating any radical changes. They re-examined the high-profile 1931 'League of Nations Commission of Enquiry Report' that had triggered the 1932 commitment to total suppression of eating and smoking. Towards this eventual end the government had taken steps to minimise opium's availability, mostly by tweaking state-controlled supply channels and regulations. The Committee praised the government for being 'most scrupulous in observing its commitments' and argued the 1931 Report had been overlooked by 'recent discussions in America'. They suggested that long-term policy should amplify existing trends based on the twin pillars of increasing control of opium consumption and accelerating suppression. Conscious of international opinion, they recommended avoiding any actions that appeared driven by monetary concerns. Government policy had to appear to be driven by public health and safety concerns, not economic exploitation.[157]

Turning to the short term. the Committee simply noted, in what became known as 'Paragraph 28', that policy fell to the chief civil affairs officer in Burma. He had drawn up policies, with the governor's approval, and had already enacted them in areas under British control. These short-term policies aimed to balance strictness with flexibility. It committed the military administration not to reopen opium shops unless forced by local circumstances. If reopened, their goal was to ensure opium was obtained through licit channels, with stiff penalties to discourage the illicit market. British forces could also use opium as currency to procure goods and labour from locals if necessary. Perhaps most controversially, it allowed the extension of cultivation to areas where it was hitherto prohibited until normal civil government could be restored and regular supply channels reopened.[158]

In January 1944, despite this self-assured report, the Burma Office questioned if the US would accept the short-term policy. They were adamant that US demands for immediate prohibition were 'out of the question' and fraught with 'positive dangers'. Further, they wanted to use the issue to draw a red line between civil and military command and make clear that 'actual administration will be in the hands of the British Civil Affairs officers.'[159] Nevertheless, they reopened discussions on 'Paragraph 28'.

At the same time, dissent within the Expert Committee surfaced. Emerging as a strong contrarian voice was Lt Col K. Lindsay, a medical officer with first-hand experience. His views had been suppressed, as they would have been inflammatory to US opinion, so he bypassed the Committee. He criticised the 'pre-arranged policy of the League of Nations' and the 'well meaning but misinformed bodies in Europe and America trying to force their ideas on oriental people'. He referred to the former as 'an international ring of statistics-bound opiophobes' and 'anti-opium propagandists'. He wrote that he originally viewed opium as a pure vice, but had come to appreciate its benefit, particularly for the coolie class whose work 'is about the hardest in the world'. Offering his 'medical and social view', he said that total prohibition 'would be foolish as well as wrong'.[160]

The Foreign Office remained on the sidelines as the Burma and Colonial Offices thrashed out these questions. However, their private comments proved sympathetic to Col. Lindsay's assertions. One official remarked that 'no doubt there is truth in what he says but it won't affect our policy'. Another wrote:

> I cannot say how whole heartedly I endorse Col. Lindsay's views. Most unfortunately it will not affect HMG's policy. One only wishes the voice of moderation and common sense could sometimes be heard![161]

By February 1944, the State Department were enquiring about the implementation of the November 1943 Statement and the Foreign Office prodded their colleagues for a preliminary response.[162]

After their 'defeat' of the colonial powers, US drug policy splintered. Anslinger's immediate efforts focused on Iran. Meanwhile, League old-hand, Elizabeth Washburn Wright, both invigorated by and jealous of Anslinger's achievement over Britain and the Netherlands, clumsily orchestrated her own campaign.[163] Out of the friction between these various manoeuvres, a US drug diplomatic doctrine was given a new legislative basis. This legislation merged the traditional US drug policy ideological goals with wartime outcomes, creating a clear strategic reference point for US officials going forward into peacetime.[164]

Congressman Walter Judd was a stalwart supporter of China and had spent many years in the country as a medical missionary in the 1920s and 1930s.[165] In February 1944 he began championing legislation, seemingly at the behest of Elizabeth Washburn Wright and independent of Anslinger's manoeuvres, which would eventually come to be known as 'the Judd Resolution' with a speech in the House of Representatives.[166]

In words that would become the exact language of the 'Judd Resolution', he argued that the war risked an explosion in the illicit opium traffic but also an 'unprecedented opportunity' for eliminating it. The British and Dutch November 1943 announcements meant the US had 'for the first time the support of certain western empires without whose support our efforts have been doomed to failure'. Success, he argued, would now depend on opium-growing countries. Iran, as the world's 'greatest producer', could reignite the supply line to US opium 'addicts'. However, lend-lease money and materials was making countries like Iran newly 'dependent' on the US, which could use this 'special influence' to encourage production limitation to the world's estimated legitimate needs of 400 tons a year. China, he claimed, had largely suppressed cultivation; Japan was 'going to be smashed'; the Russians had 'controlled opium very rigidly in their own land'. The US now had the opportunity to 'eliminate it from the world as we eliminated it from the Philippines'. He claimed, 'the Asiatic peoples trust us on this' and that 'such a unique opportunity may not come again in years.' Like the Civil War, he suggested, 'it would seem that it is taking another war to bring about the abolition of another form of slavery even more destructive of the dignity of and well-being of man.'[167] It was a speech that pulled together decades of US policy and moulded it to the changed geopolitical and drug control circumstances.

Meanwhile, the Burma Office and War Office were awaiting the final decision from Admiral Lord Louis Mountbatten, the Supreme Allied Commander South East Asia.[168] He had been briefed to keep in mind a number of complicating factors, including the potential hardship to native growers; political difficulties in districts where the habit was endemic; negative side effects of increased smuggling; and the impact of Yunnan Chinese supplies nullifying prohibition.[169] The Foreign Office and the Washington Embassy were told to sit tight.[170]

This sparked an agitated response from Ambassador Halifax. He was 'not very happy about the attitude of the Civil Affairs Authorities in Burma' and warned their 'insistence on ... compromising with local customs and conditions, is likely to meet with strong opposition from the Americans, whose penchant for drastic measures is illustrated in the ... State Department's Aide Memoire.' He warned of ramifications for broader Anglo-American relations: 'if the people interested in this opium question get excited and go out to attack our policy they will mobilise pretty substantial public support.'[171]

The Foreign Office asked that the War Office give 'full weight' to his warning, but the latter bucked against interference.[172] They considered the short-term policy decided, and Halifax's concerns relating to 'a far wider issue'. They also reiterated that allowing 'uninformed American public sentiment to interfere' would 'open the door to similar interference in any other sphere of imperial domestic policy'. They initially tried to avoid forwarding the ambassador's letter to Mountbatten but succumbed to Foreign Office insistence.[173]

Around this time, a frank meeting took place between the Home Office and the State Department about opium. The former pointed out that the government was still considering the Burma question. George Morlock angrily concluded they were 'hesitant to permit the military to close the monopolies and suppress opium' and were trying to delay. He suggested to Anslinger that the US consider unilateral action.[174] The stage was set for a potential diplomatic blow-up.

2.12 The US Drug Doctrine: HR 241 – the Judd Resolution[175]

The US House of Representatives and Senate passed HR 241, the Judd Resolution, unanimously in June 1944. It stated, 'this World War ought to be not an occasion for permitting expansion and spreading of illicit traffic in opium, but rather an opportunity for completely eliminating it.' The president was 'to approach the Governments of all opium-producing countries' urging 'they take immediate steps to limit and control the growth of the opium poppy and the production of opium and its derivatives to the amount actually required for strictly medicinal and scientific purposes'.[176]

The State Department served international notice they would be pursuing it as official US policy.[177] This had major implications for

Britain, where a central tenet of its opium strategy was to deflect attention from India.[178] The Judd Resolution brought new US attention to India, along with Iran and Afghanistan. Acting Treasury Secretary Gaston wrote an open letter to the House Committee on Foreign Affairs highlighting the centrality of India to the post-war system. He claimed that five thousand shops in the Indian States sold opium which was showing up in US seizures. He argued that India was growing 200–300 tons annually for domestic non-medical purposes which served as a 'reservoir' for the illicit traffic.[179] Secretary of War Stimson wrote a public letter painting production control efforts 'both as a war measure and as a part of the permanent program for peace'.[180]

The Resolution also represented a strong shift in locus away from the FBN towards the State Department. Anslinger had filled a power vacuum created by exceptional wartime conditions. The State Department was always likely to reassert control once these conditions ended. The Judd Resolution accelerated and formalised this bureaucratic realignment. Anslinger would retain a potent international role, often through private channels, but the State Department once again became the lead on US drug diplomacy.

The US had moved from having no unified strategy to a unanimous Congressional Resolution urging the president to pursue Anslinger's framework on a bilateral and multilateral basis. It largely represented a reiteration of traditional US goals but married these broad ideological aspirations with the changed geopolitical circumstances and Anslinger's strategic vision. The Judd Resolution served as a vital focal point over an era of increasingly fractured and uncertain policies and tangible rallying point for US diplomats. In so doing, it set the stage for a new diplomatic offensive, a significant portion of which would be directed towards Iran but also Afghanistan and India.

2.13 China Prepares for Post-War

Britain remained sceptical of China's claims of progress and worried that a return to civil war would render opium control impossible, particularly with the wave of addiction expected in the wake of Japanese occupation. Under these circumstances the trade would simply be 'continued by Chinese enterprise'.[181] The practical implications for British colonial opium policy were enormous. For the US, meanwhile, China remained its key drug control ally.

1944 saw opium politics re-emerged as a conflict point within nationalist–communist politics. The Kuomintang had worked to weaken communist support during 1943 by accusing them of planting poppies. The US Embassy at Chungking expressed disbelief and saw the claims as part of a 'propaganda campaign' to discredit the communists and lay the public relations groundwork for a military campaign in the northwest. Further, the Embassy had numerous reports of Chiang loyalists' complicity, particularly transporting opium from occupied areas into the unoccupied ones.[182] Anslinger, aware of these issues but also cognisant of the pro-Chiang Washington climate, remained silent.

Chiang continued to burnish his anti-opium credentials. His annual Opium Suppression Day message in June 1944 claimed huge successes while outlining new eradication and anti-smuggling efforts. The narrative, however, came under increasing press scrutiny. A *New York Times* reporter, embedded with the communists, found no evidence of cultivation. The article led Assistant Treasury Secretary Gaston to describe Kuomintang accusations as 'another pretty little Chungking invention'.[183]

In March 1945, London shared an internal memo with their US counterparts. Although Chiang's resolve was 'undoubted', the nationalists were outmatched. Illicit profits were 'fantastic' and the main sources of supply were areas under warlord control and/or inhabited by non-Chinese tribes people with local potentates strong enough to ignore central government fiats. Further, the British argued there was no evidence to support the 'frequent rumours, believed to have been put out by Chungking propaganda sources', that the communists were growing opium.[184]

By the close of war, the problem remained undeniably acute in both occupied and unoccupied areas. Moreover, opium loomed so large in the Chinese public consciousness that all sides fought for the moral high ground. Chiang had little real control over the trade but sought the anti-opium mantle to counteract the communists' wartime public relations gains. Furthermore, anti-opium efforts, synonymous with anti-imperialism in China, would mitigate against his appearing too close to his Western allies. However, by trying to paint the communists as the perpetrators of a trade his own generals were complicit in, Chiang undermined his credibility with US government agencies. US support nevertheless remained unwavering, particularly since Chiang's image as an anti-opium crusader had assisted with broader US regional drug control strategy. The US was now focused on imposing its vision on core producing states. Meanwhile, China would continue as the lynchpin for the implementation of European colonial prohibitions.

2.14 Pressuring Britain, India, Iran and Afghanistan

The State Department produced a framework for implementing the Judd Resolution. States were asked to: (1) strictly limit production to medical and scientific purposes; (2) adhere to a system of estimates equivalent to the 1925 Convention; (3) commit to take part in a post-war production limitation conference. These were then directly transmitted via a series of memoranda. The British Foreign Office received two memoranda in September 1944. The first urged Britain to consider taking steps to limit production in Burma and India.[185] The second was a copy of the memorandum sent to the Iranian Government. The US asked that Britain help by making representations to the Iranians and said a similar request was being made to the Soviet government.[186]

These memoranda called for restricting cultivation to a closed list of countries; establishing a control body with 'absolute and complete independence' to enforce compliance; mechanisms to ensure fair pricing, product standardisation and a fair system of distributing the costs of administration; and limitation to annual world medical requirements as they stood in 1944 – around 400 tons. The US estimate for actual world production in 1944 was 2,400 tons, leaving an excess production of around 2,000 tons.[187]

India had traditionally bucked against all US pressure. Opium eating was far more prevalent than smoking, and in 1939 they had pre-emptively rejected new production limitation obligations. They warned the League in 1939: 'No such obligation could be taken until the organisation of medical services throughout the country has been greatly advanced.'[188] The Indian position was unchanged in 1944, but the US State Department pushed on two indirect pressure points. The first related to export legacies. India had largely stopped exporting opium after 1935. However, it continued to export for medical purposes to the UK and minor amounts of raw opium to French and Portuguese settlements in India, Nepal, Zanzibar and Pemba. All were technically legitimate under international law as they were exported at the request of the recipient state. Nevertheless, the US argued that the British 10 November Statement militated against export of raw opium for use in the manufacture of smoking opium.[189]

The second pressure point was the Indian states, for which the government of India was not in a position to enter into binding obligations. The government claimed it had maintained their cooperation through persuasion not injunction. The State Department now wished to impose concrete obligations on these 570 states, which contained over one-fifth of the population of India. The US claimed they produced 185 tons of opium (almost half of world medical requirements) sold through thousands of shops. As such, the US wanted these states either 'directly' or 'indirectly' represented at future conferences.[190] Past experience suggested long odds of success. Nevertheless, by late 1944 the US believed their best option was to focus on negative publicity and hope that they 'could work the same game on the India Office Policy that we did on the Colonial Office on Smoking opium'.[191]

Meanwhile, Anslinger's 1943–4 diplomatic 'attack' on Iran had failed. They had introduced no new legislation, reneged on a promise to establish an import/export certificate system, and cultivation and consumption patterns appeared unchanged. Many in the US concluded government control was too limited and Anslinger was receiving OSS reports that government stores were flouting basic domestic controls and reselling opium stocks to US merchant mariners and Indian troops.[192] With his efforts stalled and following the passage of the Judd Resolution, Anslinger appeared content to step aside and watch the State Department lead the charge.

However, internal pressure for reform was stirring. In June 1944, a vocal anti-opium movement emerged, led by the Iranian Anti-Opium and Alcohol Society. It began publishing statistics, often contradicting official ones, and reached out to the US government for help. Simultaneously, the Iranian Majlis (Parliament) witnessed visceral speeches, which US officials acknowledged were 'grossly exaggerated' and had 'little basis in fact'. Domestic conspiracies that 'other foreign powers with more imperialistic designs than the United States might be interested in preventing' the abolition of opium took root. Partly in response to these stirrings, the Iranian foreign minister began to sound out US willingness to provide crop substitution assistance.[193]

The US eventually offered an economic package to incentivise control. Iran would receive a 125-ton share of the post-war licit market – perhaps 'guaranteed' through a tripartite successor to the Turkish–Yugoslav agreement. This would mean drastic reductions from their estimated average annual production of 750 tons. To mitigate these reductions, the US promised extensive technical assistance; to continue US purchases of Iranian opium; to refrain from growing poppies in the US; and to discourage opium production in the American hemisphere.[194] The efforts, once again, came to nought. Practical cooperation actually deteriorated when the new director of the Opium Monopoly ceased his predecessor's 'habit of furnishing the consulate informally with information', leaving the US dependent on unreliable Anti-Opium and Alcohol society statistics. Further, there remained no movement on the Iranian legislative front.[195] The failures in Iran were made all the more visible in comparison with Afghanistan.

Early in 1944, the US pursued a delicate balancing act of trying to prod Afghanistan towards suppression, without alienating them. As discussed, the US had temporarily suspended their practice of not purchasing opium from countries without an import–export certificate system. In January 1944, the US ambassador warned the Afghan foreign minister, 'in a friendly spirit' that unless such a system was established, the US would have to cease importing Afghan opium after the war. He also offered a slice of the licit post-war market and pointed out the competitive advantage of Afghan opium with its relatively high morphine content. He also highlighted there would be no legitimate market for smoking opium in the Far East after the war.[196] With no particular sticks available to wield, the State Department left the Afghan government to examine their options.

In November 1944, the Afghan government shocked observers by announcing the complete prohibition of *all* opium cultivation after March 1945. This went far beyond US requests and was quickly touted by Representative Judd as the first successful outcome of the Judd Resolution. The State Department praised the decision as driven by 'humanitarian sentiments' in the face of 'financial sacrifices' and expressed the hope that other producers would follow suit. The reasons for the far-reaching decision were not clear. The Council of Ministers claimed that despite its profitability they lacked the necessary controlling organisations to regulate the trade. As a result, the social costs (both moral and material) of continued cultivation were claimed to outweigh the benefits.[197]

Representative Judd sought to use the decision to pressure Iran. He gave a press interview claiming Iranian lend-lease ports had become a 'seat of opium infection threatening the United States directly'.[198] Iran remained unmoved, and the State Department avoided applying tangible pressure. With the lack of traction over Iran, the overall US strategy once again appeared to stall. Soon the Burma issue would also re-emerge and undermine the very successes the US had touted regarding the old Colonial powers.

2.15 Britain, the Monopolies and the Judd Resolution

In August 1944, the War Office maintained that, despite 'American anxiety', complete prohibition in Burma was impractical and the goal was to minimise the illicit market: 'in one word, the Military Administration aims at control.' Lord Mountbatten reframed the problem as one of socio-economic development and suggested a twofold response: 'gradual restriction of availability of opium with a gradual improvement in standards of living and education'. The War Office went further and reinterpreted the Judd Resolution as referring only to the 'spread of illicit traffic'.[199]

Other Far East commands had been 'holding back', waiting to see if Burma's directive would resemble that expected for Malaya. It was now apparent that Burma would not be able to give a 'clear-cut directive', leading the Colonial Office to change tack. Britain could issue substantially similar directives for Malaya, Borneo and Hong Kong and so decided to move ahead with them independent of any Burma directive.[200] The question remained, then, whether and how to coordinate a Burma directive with the US.

By this stage the decision on whether to consult the Americans was informed by three main factors. First, the State Department aide-memoire had reserved the right to take unilateral action to protect their troops. Second, Britain had promised to consult with the Americans over the implementation of their policy. Third, and conversely, the recent Charter of the Colonial Civil Affairs Committee now explicitly gave Britain the right to unilaterally prescribe civil affairs policies on liberated territories. This technically removed the obligation to consult. However, Lord Halifax's fears, coupled with the threat of American unilateral action, drove a decision to consult the US first via an explanatory statement of policy.[201]

Lord Mountbatten, meanwhile, began to second-guess his own government's policies – possibly due to private contact from Ambassador Halifax in Washington. He feared the long-term policy had not been made explicit enough to the US. Further, he warned he could not 'deplore too strongly a solicitude for the native growers of opium which I detect' in the arguments assigning blame to Siam and China and that opium profits should be 'the very last consideration we should allow ourselves to be influenced by'. He feared Britain would be accused of protecting opium producers in Burma from foreign competition. and these would become harder to dislodge. He further suggested that 'if we do not intend to come into line with the rigid American point-of-view we should say so as soon as possible.'[202]

The Burma Office sought to quell Mountbatten's misgivings. They argued that the long-term policy of 'ultimate suppression' had long been clear, and the UK was being 'quite frank' with the US over short-term accommodations. Further, they sought to alleviate Mountbatten's concerns surrounding the extension of cultivation:

> The tribesmen of the various Kachin Hill tracts use opium in their tribal religious ceremonies and also attach considerable importance to its medicinal properties. Prior to the Japanese Invasion cultivation was prohibited in most areas and Government provided a limited supply for these purposes. When Government officers retired from the hills the tribesmen were informed that the prohibition against cultivation was withdrawn; as Government could not meet the tribesmen's requirements it was only reasonable to allow them to grow what they needed. This will be the situation on our return and an immediate renewal of the prohibition orders would cause unrest. Opium production in these areas is very small and the quality is so bad that no-one outside the hill tracts would use it.[203]

The Burma Office admitted US criticism seemed 'unavoidable'.[204] Mountbatten nevertheless feared the 'policy may be misrepresented by ill-disposed critics' and his military administration was being used for 'economic and sociological experiments' with 'little regard for either the truth or for my good name!'[205] In January 1945, the secretary of state promised that the note for the US government would be re-examined in light of Mountbatten's observations.[206]

In February 1945, the Burma Office completed a revised note regarding control measures. The Foreign Office agreed to frame it as a series of 'positive' proposals so the US would have to find reasons to object.[207] Ambassador Halifax was to transmit it, along with an explanation that, 'although it does not follow verbatim' the State Department September 1943 memo's suggestions, it covered 'precisely the same ground'. Privately, the Foreign Office expected the US would 'welcome it'. When, towards the end of March 1945, the State Department had not replied, the Foreign Office became 'disturbed' and urged the Embassy to make enquiries.[208] In the meantime, the US State and Treasury departments expressed full satisfaction with the separate policy directive for Borneo, Malaya and Hong Kong.[209] Also, some potentially useful information came to light. Two young officers serving with the Burma rifles reported to the Burma Office that:

> The American forces operating in Burma have caused rather an awkward situation, since the British Forces were prohibited from supplying opium

> to the populace as payment for goods and services, except in very exceptional circumstances, but the American Forces made payment with opium freely and in large quantities, and consequently, secured labour, etc. which the British Forces were unable to secure.

One Burma Office official wrote: 'This fact, if true, would be a useful card to have up our sleeve if the Americans should try to take any high moral line about our proposed policy in regard to opium.'[210] London adopted a wait-and-see approach, with the added confidence that they had the potential counter to 'United States idealism in unofficial negotiations'.[211]

After receipt of the two US Judd Resolution memoranda in September 1944, an administrative blunder saw the Foreign Office misplace them until December. In a quick flurry of activity, they sought advice from Britain's embassy in Iran and other departments.[212] In August 1945, Britain finally responded. They promised 'sympathetic consideration' to furthering US goals and promised both the UK government and the government of India would participate in a post-war production limitation conference. However, Britain preferred to leave specific provisions to the conference, when producing states would be present and a consensus could be built. It was exactly the kind of consensus-oriented approach that Anslinger was trying to get ahead of. As for the suggestion that Burma and India prohibit production and export for other than medical and scientific purposes, London simply refused, restating old arguments. Further, regarding the request to lobby Iran on production limitation, Britain reiterated that it was best left to the production limitation conference, but that Britain would advocate that Iran participate.[213]

One week later, on 8 August 1945, the State Department responded to British opium policy in Burma. They acknowledged the difficulties but argued the short-term policy was 'not consistent with established United States policy' and therefore they could not agree. In particular, they took exception to shops potentially being reopened, given the presence of US troops. They also pre-empted and neutralised the British trump card regarding US troops trading opium. The Note claimed that Narcotics authorities in the US had only recently learned about the practice and that the War Office, having been notified that it was a violation of US policy, immediately instructed theatre commanders to prohibit further use.

The State Department memo tore into British policy. They presumed that the reopened shops would dispense opium for smoking as well as eating. This, they pointed out, was not 'at all in consonance' with

Britain's November 1943 Declaration and claimed that the experience in Hong Kong showed that government-licensed shops had failed to undermine the inflow of illicit opium from the Chinese mainland during the 1930s. They argued that the only effective policy was prohibition, together with enforcement, and Britain's policy would worsen the regional and global situation. They urged Britain 'to reconsider'.[214] The response threw London into a tailspin, and they quickly convened a meeting of the interdepartmental opium committee.[215] The question of opium in Burma, it seemed, was destined to drag into the post-war era and potentially represent a significant sticking point in Anglo–American drug diplomacy for the foreseeable future.

2.16 Conclusion

At the outbreak of war, the core control question dividing states was how to deal with the existence of colonial opium monopolies and opium smoking.[216] Key questions around production control and the expansion of the system stumbled on the fundamental divergences on this issue which saw states divide into three camps. On the one side were the US and its allies who advocated strict adherence to medical and scientific usage. On the other were producing states, many of whom were economically dependent on the very opiates these control advocates sought to eradicate. In the middle were the old colonial powers, torn between their desire to fulfil the normative goal of eradicating opium abuse and the recognition of the practical difficulties of immediate prohibitions. It was this old colonial buffer which had blunted production control efforts in the interwar years. With the resolution of this issue, the stage was set for a renewed focus on production limitation in the post-war era.

The wartime years 1939–45 had witnessed significant shifts in the international drug control system. With London's blessing, the technical arm of the League drug apparatus had fled to Washington and came under increased US influence. Simultaneously, a set of relationships had developed in London that would serve as an information exchange and counterweight to this new US influence. The rapid realignment in the British–US international power balance, coupled with changes in British strategy, had enabled the US to heavily influence British drug policy. The colonial opium issue was the clearest example. Anslinger successfully bluffed a high level of US resolve, and Britain came to view its options in rather stark terms. The first option was to fight to sustain colonial monopolies it did not currently hold and whose benefits it did not currently feel, while swimming against the international regulatory tide. The potential consequences were stoking US public opinion and angering a key ally, upon on whose future cooperation they were growing ever more dependent.

The second option was to agree to US demands as far as possible, ignore the administrative problems until the colonies were firmly back under their control, and reap whatever public relations victories it would bring. Faced with this choice, it is perhaps unsurprising that Britain conceded. Nevertheless, had Anslinger not ably used his wartime leverage and pushed the issue, the outcome was unlikely. By the close of 1943, the commissioner could justifiably feel that he had had gambled and won. He then quickly pivoted to using his strategic opium reserve to try to force recalcitrant producing states into joining the control system.

Although a number of derivatives of the colonial issue remained, Britain had reduced its economic interests in opium and gained a new stake in a supply-centric system. Controlling opium use in its colonies would require illicit supplies to be suppressed in other territories. The potential for a drug détente between the US and Britain appeared altogether possible after 1943, particularly as both were drug-manufacturing states. Despite this convergence of interests, however, their approaches to international control remained quite different. For Britain, pragmatism, self-interest and consensus remained the default setting. For the US, it maintained a single-minded commitment to strict controls in all parts of the globe. These differing approaches, the US favouring immediate and strict prohibition and the UK favouring incrementalism and various forms of regulation, would determine not just their own relationship, but also the shape of the international drug control system going forward.

The Anglo–US division over Burma highlighted the policy divide. Britain, while paying lip service to US prohibitionist impulses, sought to reframe the issue as one of regulation and socio-economic development. Being successful in these latter points could lead to ultimate success in the former but necessitated a deference to incrementalism and gradualism. Britain's approach to opium control in Burma and the Far East remained driven by regulatory impulses, not a commitment to immediate prohibition. The quiet move towards a new form of opium maintenance, in the more sanitised form of opium pills, would highlight this point strongly, as we shall see.

In these final wartime years, the UK focused most closely on Asia while the US focused on the Middle East. The UK maintained no ostensible interest in the latter region despite efforts by the US and others, such as Bertil Renborg and Russell Pasha, to encourage a more active role. This bilateral wartime slowly ground to a close and the drug control world tilted back towards multilateralism. Britain merely had to stall issues of contention, such as Burma, India and production limitation, claiming they were best left for multilateral responses. The broader British–US divide would be co-opted into the post-war institutional processes, representing deep fissures within the system.

Meanwhile, these final wartime years witnessed major domestic changes, particularly in the US. The Judd Resolution paradoxically shifted drug diplomacy back to the State Department, thereby ending Anslinger's wartime cowboy diplomacy. He had made highly effective use of the American strategic opium reserve, the hiatus of the PCOB and DSB in Washington and the general wartime confusion to instigate diplomatic initiatives. Now, the construction of the post-war system would become the explicit remit of the State Department, and one which they would be extremely reluctant to relinquish back to Anslinger's hands. The State Department generally proved more measured in approach and tone and sought to balance the issue with other US interests. Nevertheless, their strategy, enshrined in the Judd Resolution, was that largely developed by Anslinger and his allies throughout the war.

3

Creating the UN Commission on Narcotic Drugs, 1945–1946

3.1 Introduction

As we have seen, the technical remnants of the League system had been hiding in Washington. Anslinger and his Washington-based 'inner circle' allies used the wartime confusion to push an aggressive bilateral agenda. Now, the transition to the post-war era offered a tantalising opportunity to reshape the international system. However, many states, including Britain, initially aimed for conservatism and continuity with the League. Britain's broader policy focused on maintaining its great power status by building the great power alliance into the post-war international order.[1] Against broader geopolitical issues, narcotics control appeared extremely low on this list of concerns and remained a largely functional issue. Britain was willing to engage with and support the issue, provided there was no direct impact on other UK interests and priorities.

How far the US would cooperate with the League to transfer the drug apparatus to a new international organisation, how aggressively the State Department would pursue drug diplomacy, and whether the US could work with its wartime allies to construct a post-war system remained open questions. The transition period represented a time of significant opportunity but also risk. Should the inner circle lose the political initiative, an impotent or even retrograde system could emerge. Neither of these prospects was particularly worrisome to the Britain which favoured consensus and continuity while building an 'honest broker' role for itself.

The Judd Resolution had enabled the State Department re-exert control over US drug diplomacy, thereby officially ending Anslinger's wartime freewheeling machinations. Now, as the Allies edged closer to a new United Nations Organisation (UNO) alliance politics and a widening gulf between the West and the Soviet Union saw Anslinger almost entirely pushed out of the decision-making process. Despite this he continued to utilise every means to try reimposing himself. Britain also witnessed a change in domestic leadership as Major Coles took up the reins at the Home Office drugs branch and proved keen to re-exert Home Office suzerainty and wrest influence away from the Foreign Office.

Washington's relationship with Britain on this issue, lacking the animosity of the past, turned increasingly on questions of personnel and administrative matters. The broad strategic questions dividing the two nations had narrowed considerably and a new era of relative harmony seemed to prevail. Britain viewed itself as close to the vanguard of the new post-war drug control order. Pragmatism and self-interest remained the core of their policy, but they felt increasingly comfortable evangelising the merits of the control system while quietly directing it in ways congruent to their broader economic and political goals. The key question, therefore, was whether the allies could agree a framework to reconstitute the League system within the new UNO and how far they were willing to go in promoting this outcome.

3.2 The Remnants of the League System

The Opium Advisory Committee (OAC) was the pre-war system's 'principal organ' and policymaking arm, comprising government representatives. It was a creation of the League General Assembly as a committee of the League Council. The Council selected the countries represented, which had traditionally been open to all that had expressed an interest. It began with eight members but by 1939 had grown to twenty-four. Germany, Italy and Japan had withdrawn cooperation and the Soviet Union had never been a member. The OAC had ceased operation during the war and how to reconstitute it remained the most highly contested question.[2]

The Drug Supervisory Body (DSB) was a creation of the 1931 Convention. It oversaw the creation of a set of estimates for international manufactured drug requirements, including those countries that could not or would not provide their own. It would then issue estimates of world requirements for manufactured narcotics. In this way, supply could be matched to demand and thereby, in theory, eventually eliminate excess global supplies and starve the illicit market. The Permanent Central Opium Board (PCOB) was a creation of the 1925 Convention. It provided a general supervision of the international trade, trying to ensure that excess quantities were not building up in certain jurisdictions. It compared national estimates provided to the DSB with the eventual national statistical returns, allowing it to ensure governments remained within their estimates.[3]

Within the League Secretariat, a specialised staff dealt with drug issues led by its own chief, Bertil Renborg. Given the divided opinions on Renborg and the operation of the League secretariat, the question of where to situate the drug secretariat within the broader UNO secretariat became a hotly contested question during negotiations as we shall see.[4]

3.3 Towards a Production Limitation Convention?

As Bertil Renborg wrote, the 1931 Convention had created:

> a planned economy on a world-wide scale. It regulates a whole industry throughout the world, from the point at which the raw materials enter the factory to the point at which they finally reach the legitimate consumer. The only missing link was at the time the limitation of the production of the raw materials. [5]

Controlling production became the defining post-war issue. Prior to 1939, twelve countries actively produced raw opium. Of these, only India, Yugoslavia, the USSR and Japan manufactured morphine and other opiate medicines. Iran, India, Turkey, Yugoslavia, the USSR, Korea, Afghanistan and Bulgaria produced raw opium for export. China and Indo-China produced for domestic consumption alone and not for licit export. According to rough PCOB estimates, between 1934 and 1937 world production stood at 18,504. Of that, roughly 65 per cent was in China; 17 per cent in Iran; 6 per cent in Turkey; 2 per cent in the USSR; 1.5 per cent in Yugoslavia and roughly 1.5 per cent in Afghanistan, Korea, Japan, Indo-China and Bulgaria combined. Chile meanwhile accounted for an insignificant 45 kg over the four years.

Of the estimated 18,504 tons, 83 per cent was unaccounted for. Further, only 1,350 tons (7 per cent) was used to for legitimate medical morphine. Eight hundred tons was exported to opium-smoking territories (Thailand, British Malaya, Indo-China, Formosa, Kwantung, the Netherlands Indies, Macao and Manchukuo) and 1,100 tons was used for domestic consumption by 'addicted' populations. Neither of these uses was considered legitimate by the US and its control advocate allies. Although lacking official statistics from China, estimates suggested that all 12,000 tons produced was consumed domestically.[6]

Around the time the 1925 Convention had come into operation, Hungary had discovered a new method for extracting morphine from the whole dried poppy plant, known as 'poppy straw'. This eliminated the intermediate 'opium' stage and thereby lessened the risk of leakage into the illicit market. The process was soon adopted by Australia, Czechoslovakia, Denmark, Germany, Hungary, the Netherlands and Poland. Traditional producer states saw the method as an economic threat, and many called for an outright ban as a precondition for even discussing a production limitation convention.

Since production was not covered by any conventions, statistics covering production, trade or stocks were unavailable. The question of how to control this industry remained open. Further, the emergence of synthetic drugs such as dolantine offered the tantalising prospect of a world without the need for opium poppy. Control advocates welcomed these developments and the leverage they provided. Producer states, meanwhile, recognised the threat to their valuable export commodity.[7]

Turkey worked throughout the 1930s to corner the global licit market and cultivate its image as the tightly regulated global good citizen producer. It favoured levelling up the playing field through a production limitation convention and thereby reducing competition. Yugoslavia represented the broader concerns of the producer bloc. It was 'in principle' supportive but set 'essential' prerequisites that poppy straw production should be forbidden; a clear distinction be drawn between opium for smoking and opium for manufacture of drugs; alternative development provisions be included to assist producing countries and share the costs of global regulation; minimum prices for producers be assured as well as the destruction of confiscated drugs rather than their repurposing into licit channels. Yugoslavia had successfully worked in the 1938 OAC meeting to establish these as the bedrock principles of the producer bloc and won the support of a number of consuming nations. It was widely expected that these principles would become the basis for any post-war production limitation discussions.[8]

Canada had articulated the sceptics' position, based on its interests as a key consuming nation, worried about the effect of supply restrictions on the price of and access to opium. 'Sympathetic' towards the goal, it questioned whether there was a sufficient foundation of facts and cooperation and argued that statistical data was weak. For example, statistics were almost completely lacking from Afghanistan, China, Manchuria and Jehol. In cases like Iran, they were approximate; in others vital information was lacking, such as for the prepared opium monopoly in Peru. Meanwhile, India would be obliged to make formal treaty reservations for the Indian states. The latters' stocks, Canada pointed out, exceeded legitimate medical and scientific needs of the entire world.[9]

Other states downplayed these obstacles. British India claimed to control the only routes through which opium could leave India and that leakage into the illicit traffic had been minimal. France, Poland and Belgium saw the obstacles as surmountable, highlighting that the 1931 Convention had been concluded with similarly insufficient data yet produced 'excellent results'. Switzerland was similarly supportive but wanted to ensure the agreed mechanism guaranteed access to manufacturing supplies.[10]

An essential question therefore centred on how to design a production limitation system. The two alternatives proposed were a quota system or a free order system. Producing-exporting countries (Bulgaria, Greece, Turkey and Yugoslavia) largely preferred a quota system, arguing that supply and price stability and guaranteed market allocations would compensate for increased regulatory costs. Iran favoured a free order system, presumably to minimise regulatory constraints and recognising it would need to shrink production under a quota system.[11]

Consuming states also advocated a free order system to maintain market competition and lower prices. A 1939 compromise suggested a quota system allowing for a preference in orders to provide some consumer choice. A suggested way to administer it was to establish an international selling office based on the centralised model of the Turko–Yugoslav Opium Combine of the 1930s. This had formed an effective monopoly for the two countries and was something the US sought to recreate and expand after the war. Success, however, still depended on reaching agreement between the various producer countries on allocating quotas. Most states agreed that an internal monopoly was the best way to regulate production, although some objected. Bulgaria claimed that a monopoly would place too heavy a regulatory burden on small producers and advocated merely a 'special organisation'.[12]

Following passage of the Judd Resolution in 1944, the State Department began requesting producing countries to prohibit non-medical or scientific production and export and to suppress illicit activity. The responses were mixed and highlighted the remaining political and economic barriers to multilateral agreement. Afghanistan declared in November 1944 that it would prohibit all cultivation from March 1945. Mexico and China reiterated their commitments to suppressing illicit cultivation. The USSR said that it was studying the issue. The Turkish government promised to engage with any production limitation conference that would ensure 'equal conditions for all producers'. The UK and India expressed interest in a production limitation conference but refused to commit to strict medical and scientific use in all jurisdictions immediately. Iran and Yugoslavia gave no response. A number, including Bulgaria, Indo-China and Siam, were unable to engage given wartime conditions.[13] Production limitation, however, represented just one strand of a process to create a new international drug control system. The most immediate and pressing problem was how to recreate a functioning multilateral framework.

3.4 From the League to the UNO

Unlike the OAC, the PCOB and DSB had their own treaty basis and would not dissolve with the League. They had maintained some continuity for the 'system of estimates' throughout the war from their branch office in Washington, but they ultimately depended on a facilitating international organisation.[14] States agreed that continuity was essential, while far from being bystanders in the UNO creation process, members of the PCOB and DSB assumed a prominent global role, often speaking on behalf of the system and even advocating policies for specific countries such as Germany.[15] The PCOB in particular pursued a greater political role, facilitated by the inner circle which viewed it as an effective tool in pushing a control agenda on reluctant countries.

As early as 1941 Sharman and Anslinger had contemplated the shape of international control in the event of a Peace Conference being called. In May 1941, Anslinger had even reached out to his German counterparts, Werner Thomas, head of the Rauschgiftzentrale of the German Kriminalpolizeiant in Berlin, to hedge his bets in case of a British loss, or a peace agreement. He wrote that he hoped 'that your Government will return you to this work in due course, and that after the war we shall be able to see each other again and to collaborate as we did in the past'.[16] By November 1941 both Anslinger and Sharman were tilting towards having 'an all-inclusive treaty' ready to table at a peace conference. They were also aiming to do it 'outside the orbit' of the League Secretariat and its Swedish head Bertil Renborg.[17] The two men were already contemplating the radical opportunities a new post-war order would provide to remould the system. This impulse only grew stronger over time. First, however, Anslinger and Sharman would need to circumvent 'the Big Swede'.[18]

The inner circle had been highly reticent to see Renborg come to Washington during the War. Helen Moorhead described him as 'stupid', while even the British Foreign Office viewed him as a 'clumsy ass'.[19] He had faced no danger in Geneva and was seen as having good relations with the German government. Further, his role as head of the drug section of the League Secretariat would raise complications for the PCOB and DSB 'branch offices'. Ignoring these political difficulties, he descended on Washington and almost immediately created new problems. As Moorhead wrote: 'he wanted everything to carry on in the most correct foreign office style . . . he could not realize that it was better not to raise certain questions . . . to have certain letters go unanswered.'[20]

An angry correspondence between Renborg and the Canadian government in 1942 convinced the inner circle to push him out of Washington, especially as it became apparent there was a divergence between their post-war visions. Renborg favoured a conservative approach of 'strict codification of existing engagements'.[21] The inner circle wanted an activist agenda pushing for a new production limitation convention and a radically redesigned OAC.

Matters worsened when Renborg blocked the Chinese inner circle ally, Dr Victor Hoo, from appointment to the PCOB in 1942. Anslinger and Sharman assumed this was because 'he realized that Hoo would go along with both the United States and Canada in all policies.' Renborg secured the nomination of another Chinese national, Dr Woo. The action, orchestrated from London, led Anslinger to conclude that it had 'all the earmarks of the Renborg-Delevingne combine'. Robbed of this opportunity to strengthen their grip on the PCOB, Anslinger accelerated efforts to marginalise the London-based remnants of the League. The first step was pushing Renborg back out of Washington to London or Geneva, where he could cause fewer problems. The FPA took the lead in advocating his removal.[22]

As early as February 1942, Renborg moved to control the post-war planning process. He pushed for a meeting of the OAC to discuss various matters including post-war control. Anslinger and his State Department ally George Morlock successfully worked to 'drop something on it from a great height', and his plan died.[23] Undeterred, in March 1944 Renborg drafted a plan for the post-war international organisation. Once again it received no US support.[24] He reworked it in September 1944 and this time pursued international support. He noted that his views were 'entirely unofficial' but declared himself 'in favour of the status quo' since it 'worked reasonably well' and hoped to see the League system moved and adapted to the UN.[25]

Renborg favored a distinct secretariat section because drugs represented 'a very special problem' with 'no or few similarities to other questions'. He feared that lumping drugs in with social or health questions could result in irrelevant aspects becoming 'overemphasized' and non-experts addressing highly technical questions.[26] He argued that simplification was 'an urgent necessity' but rejected amalgamating the PCOB and DSB with the OAC. The former was 'expert bodies with specific functions and powers of criticism and sanctions'. The latter was a policymaking body. He also argued that amalgamating the PCOB and DSB would be difficult. The resulting body would 'be the judge in its own case'; that is, estimating requirements and then judging government compliance.

Renborg also pushed to clarify the precise competence of the expert organs. He wrote: 'they should not intervene with Governments with regard to their administrative systems or to their drug policy.' If they had concerns, they should report them to the OAC's replacement, which could then make investigations and recommendations. He argued for a continuation of the past arrangement in which all countries who desired membership were allowed to join. By 1944 there were nineteen countries producing raw materials and as many as twenty-five countries manufacturing drugs. This was all in total opposition to the 'inner circle' conception which favoured a small, handpicked OAC replacement and a more politically potent PCOB. While Renborg's efforts represented the League old guard's continuity efforts.

3.5 The Inner Circle Post-War Plan

By 1943, the FPA was taking the lead, crafting the inner circle post-war settlement framework. Acting as a public face, they left Anslinger freer to operate below the radar. Their goal was to salvage the DSB and PCOB and destroy the remnants of the OAC. This, they hoped, would result in a new, leaner and more activist committee. Producing a clear 'independent' organisational blueprint ready for adoption became central to their strategy.[27]

By 1944 it was clear that the US State Department and the Canadian Department of External Affairs would handle all international organisational questions 'from top to bottom', including opium control. This meant Anslinger and Sharman had to inject themselves through backchannels while appearing to remain distant. For example, US officials in charge of post-war international organisation planning were barred from consulting outside the State Department. However, George Morlock was able to informally consult Anslinger and relay his views to his State Department colleagues.[28]

During a frosty April 1944 London meeting between George Morlock and British drug officials, US–League divisions began to emerge. Sydney Harris for the Home Office made clear his preference for continuity with the League system. He argued that any new production limitation agreement should be left to a reconstituted OAC. The inner circle believed he and 'the Home Office pundits' hoped to deflect 'criticism or publicity' by returning to the toothless OAC consensus framework. Morlock refused to commit and suggested ten to twelve experts meet and discuss the situation. The US, he warned, was interested in 'practical steps to combat the illicit traffic but ... not interested in meetings dominated by obstructionists'.[29]

Sharman was asked by Hume Wrong at the Canadian Department of External Affairs to give his opinion. Sharman strongly echoed the US vision of a much smaller OAC consisting of eight to twelve members, not the previous twenty-four, and a 'technical' committee consisting of country experts not political appointees who at OAC had 'nothing to contribute except defence of their own countries' interests'.[30]

A 'technical' committee comprising national drug administrators was attractive for several reasons. First, it framed the inner circle conception as technocratic as opposed to political. Second, it would foster supply-focused and police enforcement–oriented national control agencies and expertise. Sharman and Anslinger hated health professionals attending OAC, as they were unfamiliar with policing issues, the illicit traffic and tended to 'complicate matters, as so much of what they say ... sounds like "expert material", which it very definitely is not'. Third, it would ensure that Anslinger drove US drug diplomacy rather than the State Department. This would simultaneously strengthen his position in Washington, including against potential federal reorganisation.[31]

Anslinger's more radical hope was that government representatives would appear before experts to argue against resolutions they did not approve of. Thereby the burden of proof would lie with political representatives, and the experts could decide whether to accept, modify or reject the case. Herbert May anticipated 'considerable opposition from some "Foreign Offices"'. Further there was a grudging recognition that some level of politicisation was inevitable. Ensuring government buy-in 'without letting technical questions be affected by ... political considerations' seemed the key.[32]

The inner circle aimed for an OAC of eight 'technical experts' with the option to expand as countries developed expertise. Sharman argued to the Canadian Department of External Affairs that the 'most efficient and result-producing body' had functioned for ten years prior to the war. This was an unofficial gathering of six to eight national administrators in a hotel room in Geneva and continuing correspondence throughout the year. They would exchange intelligence and coordinate cross-border police efforts. Even when Germany had ceased cooperation with the League, the German narcotics chief, 'an exceedingly efficient man' continued to attend, although using a fictitious name and national affiliation. Sharman argued that this cooperation continued to bear fruit even after the Anschluss when, for example, Germany imprisoned an Austrian trafficker.[33]

Similar to Renborg, the inner circle wanted to see the drug secretariat remain independent of other UNO secretariat functions. This would prevent the medicalisation or 'social welfarisation' of the issue, with the potential that the opium secretariat could come under the leadership of health experts.[34] Converting these aspirations into political reality was the next step.

3.6 Towards the Commission on Narcotic Drugs

Movement one way or another was initially stalled by uncertainty about the post-war organisation. By October 1944, proposals for the new UNO began to emerge and the inner circle quickly moved to action. The State Department soon concluded that opium would be subsumed into the Economic and Social Council (ECOSOC). Remaining non-committal, they welcomed FPA proposals and permitted George Morlock to begin building a coalition of overseas supporters by disseminating proposals through US diplomatic missions. Both the US State Department and the Canadian Department of External Affairs were sceptical of achieving an apolitical successor to the OAC. Nevertheless, Anslinger and Sharman viewed matters as 'starting off on the right foot' and pressed ahead. Representative Judd's vocal support helped solidify the US position, while Sharman ensured the Judd Resolution received favourable attention within the Canadian government.[35]

Before the OAC officially dissolved with the League, Renborg aimed to hold a final wartime meeting to draft an agenda and proposals for the new organisation thereby ensuring a fait accompli of continuity. In Washington, Helen Moorhead wrote that she 'would very much regret the calling of a meeting of the old O.A.C. that is now pretty completely dead. It would be too bad to revive it . . . and then shortly afterward wipe it out altogether by the new set-up.'[36]

Renborg received the support of the London Four (HO, FO, PCOB and DSB) and was awaiting approval from the acting secretary general of the League. The American position was to formally abstain, given that it was not a member of the League, but to attend as an observer. Anslinger, Morlock and Sharman meanwhile once again set about circumventing Renborg's efforts.[37] As Sharman wrote:

> we should let the dead past bury itself, if they can be convinced that death has actually taken place and that mortification is due to set in, and . . . we should not aid in any attempt at resurgence.[38]

They should aim instead for:

> a new born child in the narcotic world which will grow up and develop into something which will be well worthwhile, unfettered by the ideas and activities of grandparents or great grandparents of a bygone age.[39]

Sensing a policy vacuum, Morlock took the initiative and began to advocate for a 'Narcotics Advisory Committee' (NAC) to replace the OAC, composed of all parties to one or more of the conventions. The real work would be done by a Standing Committee of the NAC composed of representatives designated by ECOSOC chosen from the US, UK, USSR, China, France, the Netherlands, India, Canada, Egypt, Turkey, Yugoslavia and Mexico. Representatives would be heads of their domestic narcotics administrations. Voting would be on a majority basis, and the UN secretary general would establish a Narcotic Drugs Section (NDS), separate to any other division of the UN Secretariat. The inner circle quickly solidified around Morlock's criteria and also looked forward to the prospect of unifying the conventions into a single 'all inclusive' convention and central committee with unified executive, administrative and judicial functions. They recognised these ambitious goals could take years.[40]

After the Dumbarton Oaks agreement, it became clear that the League would voluntarily dissolve. The State Department then began to formulate a coherent strategy for the new UNO and asked Helen Moorhead to draft 'the very best plan' for drug control she could envisage, and they would 'give it every consideration'. Moorhead urged that it be considered an independent subject under ECOSOC. She strongly argued against considering it a social issue and sought to reframe it as an economic problem:

> the international control apparatus . . . [is] directed to keeping a commodity, the production of which is restricted, in legitimate channels. And

> while it has social as well as public health implications, the control, with its special enforcement and prevention machinery lose its effectiveness . . . if associated with a social welfare or public health agency . . . The opium problem is at present, and will continue to be for a foreseeable period, largely a restrictive economic and policing problem.[41]

Soon Moorhead's FPA memo became the de facto, albeit unofficial, US framework. Meanwhile, formal League dissolution and the drafting of the UN charter would be decided at the upcoming San Francisco Conference, where all eyes now turned.

Britain's post-war foreign policy strategy was based on Anthony Eden's 'three pillars'. First was the creation of a 'World Organisation embracing the bulk of the nations and eventually, perhaps, all nations'.[42] London saw narcotics control as a consensus 'technical' issue, above politics and a means to strengthening multilateral representation and involvement and thereby a beacon to other areas of international cooperation. The details of drug cooperation were, from the start, secondary to the goals of consensus and relative harmony.

The San Francisco Conference proved highly unsatisfactory to the inner circle. Drug control received comparatively little attention, and Anslinger was almost completely shut out by the State Department. This was unsurprising given broader tensions within the 'big three' alliance between Britain, the US and Russia and the genuine risk the entire endeavour could collapse in discord. Further, as Hoopes and Brinkley point out, smaller states were increasingly wary of the power concentrated in these three states. With these fundamental issues and deep divisions over major foreign policy concerns, such as Poland, the structure of the United Nations and its General Assembly, the US took a strong activist role in guiding the conference through to conclusion.[43] This inevitably meant deprecation of avoidable issues, such as drugs, lest they cause unforeseen hiccups.

The US delegation made a 'declaration of principles' on drugs but took no tangible leadership. These principles advocated that:

> the [UNO] will be entrusted with supervision over . . . international agreements . . . and that there shall be established an advisory body to advise directly [ECOSOC] and that the existing agencies be regarded as autonomous agencies to be brought into relationships with [ECOSOC].[44]

Soon 'newcomers' in the State Department began advocating a complete merging of the PCOB, DSB and OAC successor into one body composed of non-governmental experts. Anslinger was horrified, privately pointing out that he could not think of one potential 'expert' whose advice he would wish to follow.[45] Further, he expected it would 'meet with hearty British disapproval'.[46] Sharman described this 'complete divorce, without alimony, between narcotic control in the domestic governmental and international fields respectively' either 'amusing or pathetic, depending on the point of view'. DSB President Malcolm Delevingne agreed 'it would be a great mistake' and expected a cold reception from the UK, who would likely push back against excluding government representation.[47] Elliott Felkin, secretary of the PCOB, was similarly vocal in his opposition.[48]

Overall, San Francisco was viewed as a defeat by the inner circle, which quickly launched another lobbying offensive to ensure drug policy was not lost in the post-war agenda. They focused on UN Preparatory Commission negotiations set to take place in London. Anslinger began by orchestrating a national press campaign. In October 1945 the Women's Christian Temperance Union claimed that the San Francisco Charter left 'the world open to traffic ... of the scourging drug' opium and that opium control was 'left out of the Charter in deference to the profit motive of "certain nations"'. Hearst Newspapers supported this view with a string of editorials.[49]

Meanwhile, Bertil Renborg emerged as the favourite to head any new drug secretariat. Anslinger and Sharman worked feverishly to prevent it and ensure Leon Steinig, 'in whom everyone has confidence', assumed the role.[50] In August 1945, Anslinger wrote to the US UNO Preparatory Commission delegation decrying Renborg's 'absence of impartiality, inability for straightforward action, excessive ambition and lack of judgement'. This, he claimed, surely disqualified Renborg from the role given the competence requirement outlined in Article 101 of the UNO Charter.[51]

Renborg's machinations further provoked their ire. In November 1945, he circulated a memo suggesting that narcotics control could be viewed as a 'means of preventing international aggression'. Sharman described the suggestion as 'tripe' and 'extraordinary that mental excrescences of this kind should emanate ... from the holder of a position which would normally imply the necessity for brains and judgement'.[52] He and Anslinger worked to portray Renborg as incompetent and therefore unsuitable. When this didn't succeed, they suggested Renborg was a Nazi sympathiser.[53]

Canada was strongly opposed to Renborg but did not wish to appear to block his nomination because he was not a national of the UN, nor did they wish to be on the opposing side to the British. Major Coles of the Home Office Drugs Branch remained a staunch advocate for Renborg. He correctly surmised that the Canadian opposition stemmed from a personal quarrel between Sharman and Renborg and maintained that Renborg was the best person for the position. Regarding alleged Nazi sympathies, Coles claimed to have no knowledge other than rumours that Renborg had visited Finland during the Russo-Finnish War and become involved in 'undesirable activities'. London decided to try clear up the allegations. The US threw their weight strongly behind Leon Steinig, but Britain felt he was not 'big enough for the job', labelling him, in crudely anti-Semitic terms, an 'intellectual' who 'does not make a formidable impression'. Although finding no evidence of Nazi sympathies, the British recognised that Renborg had lost the confidence of the US, Canada and a number of others. In the end they accepted Steinig.[54]

When Major Coles had returned to the Drugs Branch, he was determined to reassert Home Office suzerainty based on two strategic tenets, continuity and conservatism. As Sharman had remarked in mid-1944, 'I note with interest the British attitude, which I have long prophesied, that they want the limitation problem to continue to be handled through the [OAC].'[55] Further, Britain sought a cosmetic change in their international opium reputation and consistently sought to portray themselves at the vanguard of control whenever possible.

London's main disagreement with the inner circle was over how much to leave undecided for the new UNO. On more general points, the Home Office agreed that the OAC successor should be made up of government representatives, not merely a body of experts. They were open to a smaller committee with 'more carefully selected members', since some OAC members had only been there 'for reasons of prestige'. The PCOB and DSB could not be allowed to lapse and should maintain their 'special position' as 'impartial non-political organs'. London was willing to consider amalgamation of the PCOB and DSB, but only after the UNO became fully operational and after broad consultations.[56] Overall, Britain was aiming for minimal activism before the UN met, merely a stable transfer of League functions. Once reconvened, difficult questions could then be addressed.

Somewhat unexpectedly, Philip Noel-Baker, the British minister of state for foreign affairs, who had a long engagement with the drug issue, began to advocate more radical proposals. He suggested all questions be left to the General Assembly. This was completely contrary to inner circle goals to have Preparatory Commission recommendations ready for the first General Assembly. Further, he wanted all the existing machinery, including the PCOB and DSB to be 'integrated' into the UNO. Lastly, he wanted to see the creation of two or three international factories supplying all global medical requirements of drugs. The Home Office flatly refused this latter point.[57]

He quickly alienated the India, Colonial and Burma Offices by failing to consult them, and the Home Office soon moved to quell his enthusiasm. They called a meeting of the Inter-departmental Opium Committee to clarify British policy. At the meeting, the consensus position was to support the UN Preparatory Commission, retain members of the PCOB and DSB temporarily in their positions, and have the General Assembly request ECOSOC to appoint a committee to advise on system adaptation. ECOSOC would then seek international agreement to appoint new members of the PCOB and DSB, pending revision of the conventions, and the secretariat question would be left to the Secretary General. The British delegation was ready to introduce this resolution in the Preparatory Commission meeting but eventually deferred to the Chinese delegation's resolution.[58]

Noel-Baker refused to give up, and in January 1946 sought the support of the Secretary of State for India Lord Pethick-Lawrence in pushing more radical proposals. The Home Office responded angrily and resolved to clearly reassert suzerainty. The Interdepartmental Committee was reconvened, and the various departments closed ranks with the Home Office. The Foreign Office was left awkwardly defending Noel-Baker's behaviour as mere bureaucratic crossed wires. The Home Office claimed that Noel-Baker 'underestimated' the success of the interwar system and that the present issue was taking up from where the League had left off, rather than rebuilding the system from scratch.[59] Despite a difficult few months, by January 1946 Britain had finally outlined its post-war drug vision. Part of this represented the reassertion of control by the Home Office over the Foreign Office. Soon, the complexity of the UN process saw other agencies happily divest responsibility. The Colonial Office was glad to see the Home Office take the lead and admitted their interest only became 'live' over 'methods of control'.[60] Nevertheless, Noel-Baker was not finished and would take his efforts to the Preparatory Commission.

For the inner circle, Helen Moorhead left for the Preparatory Commission in London to try and unofficially influence events. The Commission would prepare the Agenda for the first UN Assembly. As she departed, Moorhead wrote to Anslinger that she would 'try to think each time what you would have done'. She worked her way into important meetings, to many of which even the former Acting Secretary General of the League was not invited. Some access was gained 'irregularly and must be kept quiet' and she was careful to direct communications privately to Anslinger, avoiding regular Treasury Department channels. As she watched events proceed, she was soon lamenting to Anslinger that it reminded her of San Francisco, with the inner circle being cut out by the State Department.[61]

The State Department had promised Anslinger to support proposals for an independent commission reporting directly to ECOSOC. Soon it became apparent that no such instructions had been sent, and the US delegation was avoiding leadership. Morlock wrote bewildered to Anslinger on 5 November that 'All our efforts have been in vain.' Anslinger thought it 'discouraging' and felt his since San Francisco was 'nullified'. The Chinese delegation, expecting the US to propose a new independent commission, soon stepped in to take the lead with their own resolution. The US delegation remained silent on this and Anslinger privately fumed that they appeared to have 'laryngitis'.[62]

Anslinger had written to the Chinese official Victor Hoo in October, saying that his 'splendid' views were entirely in line with the US.[63] Now he asked Hoo to be his eyes in London. Events, he said, needed 'very close watching'. He feared that 'we have been thrown together with and subordinated to "social welfare"' and wondered 'how often must the same error be repeated within one generation?'[64] Anslinger soon learned the US delegation had instructions to leave the matter to the General Assembly, as it would raise difficult questions for other matters, such as the Fiscal Commission. The State Department did not want to come out in favour of a special commission for opium with direct contact to ECOSOC (i.e., a decentralised opium commission) and thereby tie the US to this course more broadly. Morlock learned from within the State Department that the US delegation were hoping another country would take the lead and were generally sceptical of the issue's relative importance.[65]

In London, Adlai Stevenson, the head of the US delegation, took little interest and his staff warned Helen Moorhead to keep a 'sense of proportion'. She lamented to Anslinger that if only they could get instructions sent to the delegation, the Chinese resolution would pass. She wrote, 'Other countries are waiting [for] our lead.' Anslinger worked to prod from Washington. He arranged a General Federation of Womens' Clubs resolution calling on the State Department 'to take prompt action to bring about the creation of an [OAC] not related to health, welfare or other section but to report directly' to ECOSOC. In the meantime, Anslinger demanded a 'show down' with the State Department.[66]

Victor Hoo and the Chinese delegation pressed ahead with their Resolution recommending the creation of a new OAC reporting directly to ECOSOC and sought Moorhead's advice in drafting it. On 30 November Anslinger's efforts bore fruit. The State Department telegrammed their London delegation to support the Chinese resolution, although the precise terms were to be left for ECOSOC determination. The State Department were also aware that Britain had a similar resolution ready to be tabled. They asked their delegation to ascertain British intentions and the content of their resolution and potentially outsource the diplomatic heavy lifting. Victor Hoo, meanwhile, secured the support of a number of delegations, including the USSR.[67]

On the same day, Anslinger and the State Department met for their 'showdown'. The State Department blamed a clerical error for the instructions not being sent. Anslinger claimed that the US was not taking the lead and asked whether they would push for a separate narcotics section within the UN Secretariat, independent of health or social welfare. The State Department refused to be drawn, preferring (like the British) to defer secretariat issues to the secretary general. Anslinger lamented that the recent US record 'did not look well' but the State Department retorted that it was 'a question of timing, not of substance'.[68]

The Chinese resolution passed unanimously on 6 December. It recommended that a Commission on Narcotic Drugs (CND) be established at the first session of ECOSOC. It was the only one of its kind, with every other suggestion by the Preparatory Commission labelled 'possible' or 'for consideration'. Back in the US, Anslinger went to work promoting the achievement through the Hearst press, and made sure to credit Victor Hoo as the man who 'formulated it and steered it to unanimous adoption'. He privately thanked Hoo for his 'magnificent work'.[69]

Moorhead concluded that the 'inner circle' had been pushed out of the negotiations as 'the result of not having a top ranking official in the State Dept. to support Anslinger'. She met with Adlai Stevenson before departing London and warned the US 'had won a battle, but not the war'. She told him that the US delegation at ECOSOC should have a drugs expert and that Anslinger was the most competent. Stevenson remained non-committal. Moorhead also reported a changed British dynamic. Delevingne was unwell and had been pushed out by Major Coles. Noel-Baker remained unpredictable. Delevingne said the Home

Office would try to control him in the Assembly, but there was a risk he would 'go off on his own and make a "rousing speech"'. For Moorhead this was just another reason for Anslinger to attend. She had witnessed their 'new born child' coming into being. It now required a 'guardian' within the US delegation, not an 'outsider' like herself.[70]

Overall, the 'inner circle' had mixed results from the first round of political battles. They had not radically reshaped international control. The State Department deprecated the issue and minimised US involvement. Through a mixture of bureaucratic 'oversight' and machinations Anslinger had been excluded from the official process. Meanwhile, Delevingne was pushed back out of the British policy process and the Home Office had fully re-exerted control under Major Coles. However, part of the inner circle agenda, of securing a solid institutional basis for the new CND, had been salvaged by the work of Victor Hoo and the Chinese delegation. A significant question now was whether Anslinger and Sharman could inject themselves into the UN process.

3.7 The UN First Session

During the plenary of the General Assembly in January 1946 the UK delegate, Arthur Henderson, made a statement in support for the Chinese proposal and lauded the international control system as 'an object lesson in international cooperation'.[71] His speech set the tone for the meeting. The British and Chinese delegations proceeded to take a clear lead while the State Department quietly advocated long-standing US goals. They instructed the US delegation to support a ten- to fifteen-member commission. Further, thanks to lobbying by Anslinger and Moorhead, the US delegation pushed for Leon Steinig to head the drugs Secretariat and advocate its independence from any health or social unit.[72]

Anslinger had suggested ten to start, the US, UK, China, France, India, Canada, Egypt, Turkey, Mexico, the USSR, plus the presidents of the PCOB and DSB as voting members. Each had a central narcotic administration, implying that the head of each would be the country representative. For the US it would be Harry Anslinger and for Canada it would be Col. Sharman. Further, it promised a reliable bloc of inner circle (US, Canada and China) and allied states (Egypt and potentially Turkey, Mexico and the USSR) who could outvote more conservative states like the UK, France and India. The Netherlands and Switzerland were left off the list likely for this reason, but ostensibly because they did not have narcotic 'problems of sufficient importance'.[73]

The UK favoured fifteen members, plus the two presidents. China favoured fifteen maximum. Anslinger and Morlock eventually yielded on giving voting rights for the presidents of the PCOB and DSB in the face of determined opposition yet maintained the CND should be composed of no more than thirteen members.[74] In the end they agreed on fifteen state members. The PCOB and DSB presidents could act in a consultative capacity but would not be members, nor have voting rights. On US recommendation it was explicitly stipulated that representatives should be directors of narcotics administrations or similarly qualified persons. China, the UK, USA, USSR, France, India, Netherlands, Canada, Mexico, Turkey, Egypt, Iran, Yugoslavia, Peru and Poland would be represented. The question of amalgamating the PCOB and DSB was postponed until the first session.[75]

Anslinger described progress as 'almost too good to be true'. Moorhead described herself as 'very satisfied'. Thanking her old friend Arthur Henderson for his opening speech, she called for CND to become '[a] group of law-enforcement officers, getting together to bring more effective pressures on the illicit world'.[76] On 18 April 1946, the Assembly of the League asked Member States and League officials to facilitate the UN's assumption of the League's roles on the issue. By August, the UN secretary general had established an independent Division on Narcotic Drugs (DND) within the Department of Social Affairs of the Secretariat of the UN. Further, the UN Secretariat assumed provisional responsibility for administrative and financial support for the PCOB and DSB and their secretariats. Leon Steinig was named director of DND.[77] Arthur Elliott Felkin became secretary of a new combined PCOB/DSB Secretariat. With these actions the UN had assumed political and secretarial functions of the drug control system. The League era had officially ended, and the UN era had begun. The First Session of the CND was fixed for 27 November 1946.

3.8 Conclusion

As Sharman wrote later, 'the Narcotic Commission was one of the first bodies, if not the first body, created by the Assembly.'[78] The inner circle and the League officials had successfully salvaged the system's key apparatus during the war, overseen its transfer to the new UNO and ensured it was highlighted as a priority for post-war international cooperation. Far from a clear inner circle success, however, the battles around the creation of the UNO represented a mixed outcome. The inner circle had spent most of their time fighting a rearguard action. What emerged was a moderate coalition centred on China, the UK and the US State Department. The inner circle had done much of the heavy lifting on designing the institutional framework. However, none of the delegations proved willing to push the envelope, and the result was a consensus-oriented system that would await the return to multilateralism before making any major forward momentum on the great questions of controls and goals.

Meanwhile, the episode highlighted the innate possibilities for closer Anglo-American relations. Part of this stemmed from the changed colonial arithmetic. Despite Anslinger's role in pushing Britain towards the policy shift, with Anslinger and the hardliners marginalised from the process, the State Department sought a path of least diplomatic resistance – at times even trying to outsource efforts to the UK. The UK on the other hand was anxious to demonstrate its commitment to drug control efforts, while avoiding any major forward momentum or radical changes before the CND properly emerged. They relished the opportunity to cooperate with the moderate US delegation which would only serve to strengthen broader Anglo–US relations at this critical juncture. It was for these reasons, and the low political costs of the issues at stake for the UK, that a functionalist US–UK relationship emerged over the creation of CND and supported or at times driven by consensual Chinese and Canadian attitudes.

In one sense, the outcome represented a failure by the inner circle to utilise a moment of tremendous uncertainty to remake the system. Nevertheless, this underplays the changed dynamic. The large bilateral shifts in policy, particularly surrounding the opium monopolies, and the occupation of a number of important states, had begun a new trajectory towards control and had changed the governing arithmetic within the system. True, they had not resolved the key questions of control prior to the UN meeting as they had hoped. However, their work during the war and in preparation for the UN General Assembly helped set the trajectory of policy towards realisation of many of their goals. It would simply take time, patience, normative and interpretive shaping, precedence and perseverance. As time progressed, it became clear that some issues which had deadlocked the interwar years had been left behind. However, it also became clear that key policy, political and economic divisions remained.

4

Reconstructing Drug Control in Europe, Asia and the Middle East

4.1 Introduction

This chapter examines the post-war national and regional efforts to secure drug markets, re-regulate industries and provide precedents which could ultimately drive international regulations. As peace arrived, and the creation of a UN drug control system looked certain, questions of national and regional controls loomed large. First was the question of re-establishing regulatory frameworks in post-war Europe. Germany was key given its historical centrality to licit manufacturing as well as its geopolitical lynchpin status. If national controls could be re-established in Germany, then the existing international regulatory framework would likely be preserved and potentially strengthened. The Allies had minimal ideological differences about how to implement administrative controls in Europe. Further, the regulatory tenets were largely mapped out under existing treaty law and German domestic legislation. The key question was whether the Allies could bridge widening geopolitical fault lines. For Britain, reeling from a post-war economic crisis, protecting their successful drug export industry from a resurgent European market was vital. US drug officials focused on ensuring the continuation of European narcotics control and thereby viewed success in Germany as a vital concern. In the case of Japan, the US had a potential prohibitionist and regulatory beacon for the rest of Asia. Harry Anslinger, supported by local agents, expended huge lobbying efforts and political capital. With the strong support of the General Douglas MacArthur Administration, US goals would be far easier to achieve in Japan than in Germany.

The next major issue was re-resettling the political frontiers of international drug policy reform. Momentum towards a production limitation convention had stalled prior to the war. The actual shape and dynamic of potential production limitation remained chimerical as potential producers proliferated, while the scale of the regulated market only shrunk as more and more types of opium consumption and trade were deemed illicit. The future role of China, the world's largest opium producer, remained a key technocratic problem, but one rendered insoluble by geopolitical crosscurrents. Avoiding the China issue, the US initially focused on creating a tripartite Turkish–Yugoslav–Iranian producer agreement. This would, they hoped, prevent the proliferation of small opium producers in Latin America and the Balkans. The feasibility of this grand design was challenged by Iranian and Afghan opium, as well as aggressive market expansion by British and US pharmaceuticals in the traditionally German markets of Latin America and beyond. Further, the question of 'quasi-medical' opium use in British and other European colonies remained a transatlantic dividing line. If Britain could continue a non-smoking form of opiate consumption in Malaya, Hong Kong, Borneo and Burma, it would provide an alternative to the US model of outright prohibition. On the other hand, if the US could demonstrate in Japan that the strict implementation of its prohibitionist framework worked, then it would claim vindication.

4.2 Re-establishing the System of Estimates

Prior to the war, ten territories had ceased cooperation with the drug control system. Germany, which remained a special case; Austria and Luxemburg, which had quickly re-established post-war cooperation; Danzig, Estonia, Latvia and Lithuania, which were no longer independent entities; the USSR, Bulgaria, Hungary, Romania, Yugoslavia and Siam, none of which had, as of 1946, resumed full cooperation. As a result, there remained extensive areas in East and South East Europe, including important producing countries, which were not sending statistical returns. To rectify this, the PCOB focused unprecedented political efforts on Europe.

In its May 1946 Memorandum, the PCOB pushed to establish its headquarters in Europe to allow 'close contact' and 'technical advice' to governments rebuilding narcotics control. In the Americas, Argentina, Brazil, Colombia, Uruguay and others had continued to provide 'excellent' returns. None were received from Bolivia, Ecuador, Nicaragua or Paraguay, which made estimating the size of the global cocaine market difficult, but immediate progress on this seemed unlikely. In Asia, missing returns all centred on former Japanese possessions, but the PCOB were confident the US would drive a speedy return to reporting. Many quickly began sending statistical returns in 1946.[1]

As national controls were re-established, the PCOB further tried to fill a political vacuum left by the collapse of the OAC. By November 1945, Elliott Felkin was cajoling and encouraging governments to re-establish national controls. He was often assisted by Anslinger and his agents who, for example, helped ensure Italy was 'on the way back' by November 1945. Holland and Norway were weakened as records had been destroyed, but both proved 'anxious' to re-establish cooperation. Greece was slow, while Bulgaria and Romania proved 'very difficult'. Yugoslavia seemed 'easier' and likely to restart cooperation quickly.[2] Anslinger wrote in December 1945, 'the Board is taking a very particular interest in the narcotic controls set up in the four zones' of Germany.[3] This political interference soon backfired, as we shall see, and a chastened PCOB was soon ready to cede politics to the UN and return to number crunching.[4]

The DSB maintained a strictly statistical role but struggled to build an accurate picture of the post-war market. It had to provide 'estimates of requirements' for states which did not provide any. In 1945, fifty-one countries and eighty territories provided estimates, while the DSB provided them for twenty countries and twenty-six territories. In its 1945 estimates it warned that for some countries it had not received estimates for years and was forced to establish estimates based on normal peacetime requirements. It highlighted that as governments were restored, they should try to ascertain actual requirements as soon as possible. Further it had to base its estimates on the territorial situation in 1939 and would need to readjust for any post-war settlement.[5]

4.3 Europe: The Case of Germany

Allied, and particularly US, goals for European narcotics control were twofold. First, ensure the supply of narcotics in legitimate trade. Second, keep the illicit traffic and addiction to a minimum. The division of Germany into zones rendered it the most complicated case. Despite an Allied rhetorical emphasis on developing a national framework, zone-based systems quickly emerged. Under these, enforcement varied, and the distribution of drugs was highly unequal, with shortages in some areas and surpluses in others.[6] In Germany, unlike in Asia, Anglo–American policy interests sufficiently overlapped to allow unified action. Britain welcomed narcotics regulation in Germany, especially if it could help manage a resurgence of the German drug industry. Further, by highlighting their commitment to narcotics control in Europe, Britain could deflect attention from its policies in Asia.

Reich drug policy implementation was generally seen as strong. Anslinger wrote in November 1945 that 'German laws are stricter and have a better constitutional basis than our own.'[7] Making these laws operational again and re-establishing international cooperation would be the key challenge. With its withdrawal from the League of Nations in 1933, Germany had relinquished its membership of the OAC, and the German member of the PCOB resigned. Nevertheless, it continued close unofficial cooperation and submitted statistics as per the 1925 and 1931 Conventions. In September 1939, the German government recommitted to the conventions regarding tackling illicit trafficking and statistical collecting but began withholding information until the cessation of hostilities.[8] A key Allied goal was be to obtain these outstanding statistics.

The immediate concern for the US was to secure existing stockpiles, re-establish a control apparatus and ensure adequate medical supplies. The threat of a resurgent illicit traffic loomed large, as one US narcotics official wrote:

> The opportunities are not lacking. Milling thousands are without sufficiently gainful occupations; the highways are thronged with homeless seeking shelter and means of profit and support; the general chaos of German economic life; a surplus of currency in the hands of Allied soldiers which they cannot send home and are anxious to spend; adequate chemical knowledge to produce the drugs; thousands of acres of poppies to furnish the raw materials; all these are invitations to the narcotics trafficker.[9]

The collapse of Germany had scattered statistical information, and there was no clear authority to meet international obligations. Lt General Lucius Clay, General Eisenhower's Deputy on the Control Council, promised to uncover all available information and forward it on to Anslinger. It soon became evident that these records and personnel were located in the Soviet Zone. The US decided to use the PCOB, with whom the Soviet Union had previously maintained relations, to request access to these records for a PCOB report on Germany.[10] Time would show the approach misjudged, as we shall see.

US officials viewed zonal controls as 'extremely unsatisfactory and ineffective' and decided to bring a narcotic control officer from the US to their zone. Initially offered to Anslinger, he turned it down citing his focus on the UN and appointed FBN agent Samuel Breidenbach instead. Short-term fixes sought to bring order to the licit market, while press stories stoked fears of a burgeoning black market. Imports and exports were blocked, and military government officials sought to control the trade, from manufacturing through to physician prescriptions as well as trying to ascertain the situation in the other zones.[11]

The US and PCOB began pushing a unification of German narcotics control. Elliott Felkin met US officials Captain William Weatherwax and FBN agent Breidenbach in Paris to plan strategy and an eventual official visit to Germany. They decided to work towards a unified Western Zone policy, and eventually approach the Soviet authorities. In September 1945, they met the French Minister of Foreign Affairs Gaston Bourgois and the Director of the French Bureau of Narcotics Mr Razet. The minutes of the meeting were then forwarded to the British government and eventually found their way to the Home Office.[12]

Anslinger was encouraged.[13] He expected Soviet stonewalling since ‘they must submit everything to higher levels’, but he also expected ‘that traffickers will have poor pickings in the Russian zone’. He believed the prospect for coordination with the British and French zones was strong. By September, however, progress had ground to a halt. Weatherwax was trying to get ‘out of the mess’ and back to the US, while Breidenbach tried to ‘break’ the deadlock but claimed the Army was simply ‘passing the buck’. He feared an acceptance of a zone set-up but warned that nothing ‘short of a centralized national administration’ would prevent a resurgent illicit traffic, which would eventually threaten the US.[14]

Anslinger agreed but worried it ran afoul of State Department policy of avoiding centralised government in Germany. He worked to secure their support and counselled patience:

> Even some control in the American, British, and French zones with proper uniformity and coordinated effort would be acceptable in lieu of the centralized idea. You should be prepared to accept as much. However, keep hammering away . . . we can retreat to still relatively safe ground.[15]

The US Group of the Allied Control Council immediately cleared Breidenbach’s control proposals for the US zone and sought to pass it through the broader Allied Control Council. However, on 1 October, the French delegate objected to any central administration before French demands for the internationalisation of the Ruhr had been met. The Soviet delegate, meanwhile, argued that the central administration outlined in the Potsdam agreement should be set up before any others. General Clay temporarily withdrew the proposal rather than have it rejected. The French position soon hardened when De Gaulle publicly rejected any discussion of a central administration before the internationalisation of the Ruhr and Rhineland.[16] Meanwhile, the minutes of the September meeting with Elliott Felkin in Paris circulated in Whitehall. London initially advocated 'examination' but 'not implementation'. They deprecated US concerns about troops and viewed the risk as being confined to Germans and therefore German responsibility.[17] Initially, the US appeared a lone voice for coordinated control.

However, upon receipt of the September Paris meeting minutes, the Home Office began forcefully advocating 'concerting action' and echoing US concerns.[18] Sydney Harris, Under Secretary of State at the Home Office, warned the War Office that there was 'a real risk that . . . control may break down' and that it was 'important that the British military authorities should keep in step not only with the French but also with the Americans who . . . attach the greatest importance to this particular subject'.[19] Without this Home Office advocacy, the issue could easily have been overlooked. The Military Attaché's Office had initially described the PCOB enquiry as 'a secondary matter' and passed it off to colleagues to mollify Felkin and the PCOB.[20] After Harris's intervention, UK military officials quickly concluded that 'effective control can only be taken through central agreement.'[21] Thus began an Anglo–American convergence on a unified narcotics control policy in Germany.

Breidenbach, meanwhile, pushed ahead in US zone, re-establishing the German Opium Law of 1929 with some minor changes creating opium offices in each of the Zone's three Lander. Administration was in the hands of the German officials, with supervision by the US narcotics official. The eventual goal was to channel all information through the headquarters in Berlin, which would also eventually absorb the three offices. The manufacture and sale of heroin was abolished, as were imports of narcotics into the zone from outside Germany. Exports had to be approved by the chief of the Public Health Branch.[22]

The US directives did not live up to Breidenbach's hopes, but he viewed them as 'a basis' for improvement. Meanwhile, the PCOB enquired as to the situation in Germany, but the Soviet authorities requested extra time to clarify the relationship between the PCOB and the League. Breidenbach wrote in frustration, 'the Russians hang back for one reason – the French for another.'[23] Progress was discernible, but painfully slow.

After numerous delays, in January 1946 the Allied Public Health Committee updated Felkin and the PCOB that they were studying the question.[24] The Soviet delegate refused a formal response, however, as they now associated the PCOB with the League and thereby defunct.[25]

Shortly thereafter, a greatly disheartened Breidenbach returned to the US. He believed he had left a 'legacy of possibilities', but was not optimistic for real results.[26] His replacement, Arthur Giuliani, arrived in Berlin on 8 April 1946. He wrote to Anslinger that he was immediately informed by General Stayer, of the Public Health and Welfare Section, that:

> protocols of the League, or the PCOB are not to be mentioned at all, particularly in quadripartite circles ... he stated that Mr. Breidenbach ignored his wishes in that regard, a matter which caused him some embarrassment vis-à-vis the Russians.[27]

Both Giuliani and Anslinger saw the matter as 'a tempest in a teapot'. Nevertheless, until the PCOB could be explicitly brought within the UNO, the Soviet Union would veto any German cooperation. Giuliani found a general appetite for the UN to take the lead in facilitating the centralised control. In the meantime, he adopted a minimalist role, sticking to the letter of his mandate and working 'to establish good will throughout the organization'.[28] By May 1946 the position of the PCOB began to be clarified and the Soviet delegates stopped viewing it as 'League of Nations Business'. Anslinger further expected that CND would make clear recommendations that Germany carry out its obligations under the various conventions when it finally met in 1946.[29]

Giuliani described the situation in the US Zone in May 1946 as 'bad, but not so bad as any other Zones, where no attention whatever has been given to' the issue. The black market had created 'a mentality of law breaking similar to that which existed in the U.S. following [alcohol] prohibition' but it could be tackled through 'more efficient policing'. He focused on organising a system of reporting and control which the other zones could emulate and thereby pave the way for unified control.[30]

Giuliani believed that the British had 'considerably more' control than the French. He spent a tremendous effort trying to 'pierce the Iron curtain', but many US officials believed their secrecy stemmed from 'fear of embarrassing their own people, many of whom are involved in the black market'. Reports suggested there was no active control and no production, with shortages being filled from Russia. The situation in Berlin, meanwhile, was 'ludicrous'.[31] In August 1946, the US made its first shipment from the US zone to Berlin to relieve an acute shortage there.[32]

In July 1946 Giuliani advocated a Working Party to achieve some uniformity, even if centralisation remained political 'dynamite'. The 1929 German Opium Law was the law of the land in each zone, but implementation and enforcement varied. His goal was to make some minor adjustments to the law and then draft a directive through the working party that would apply to all zones. Further, since he was the only person trying to begin compiling statistics, he could try to use the working party to ensure some uniformity of statistical collection across all zones.[33]

In June 1946, the British Zone's military government issued instruction 95, 'Regulations governing the control of narcotic drugs'. This recognised the German Opium Law of 1929 and later amending decrees. It differed in some ways from the US Zone, for example there was no restriction placed on the manufacture of Heroin and no restrictions on imports. British officials believed they had made 'a good beginning'. Violations seemed minimal, narcotic supplies were controlled, and there was little evidence of illicit imports. Effective policing was credited with lower lawlessness than the other zones. Giuliani even concluded British Zone law enforcement was superior to the US Zone. His overarching fear, nevertheless, remained accepting divergence between zonal regulations preventing eventual unification of control.[34]

Giuliani entered August 1946 with renewed British and French support and found the prospects for a working party 'more encouraging now than ever'. The Soviet delegate, while agreeing in principle, remained obstructive. Giuliani described how the British delegate 'argued at least as vehemently as we did . . . showing extreme annoyance at the illogical way in which we were being stymied' on easily manageable technicalities with the Soviet delegate claiming 'that the Americans were using "secrecy" in their "personal project"'.[35] The matter was postponed until September when the Soviet delegate unexpectedly withdrew his objections and the measure passed. Giuliani found the shift 'inexplicable'. One hypothesis derived from his discussions with a member of the Allied Control Committee,

> This business of fighting up to the last minute is typical, and is followed by capitulation as complete as this . . . It may be that the delegates cannot make decisions, but must get them from upstairs.[36]

Regardless, Giuliani wrote to Anslinger, 'we did the most we could do and . . . [w]e are now on the table.'[37] Publicly, Anslinger maintained pressure, stating at CND that 'the division of the country into zones and Berlin into sectors, all contribute to making impossible the fulfilment of the international drug conventions.'[38] Offering solace to the PCOB, Giuliani wrote to Anslinger,

> Mr. Felkin should not feel too bad about rebuffs he may have received, for his efforts . . . have been the starting point of this whole business. This, of course, excepting your own efforts, which people seem to take for granted.[39]

Giuliani promised to make US Zone returns to the PCOB and to try to get German officials back in the 'habit'.[40] In the meantime, the DSB would produce estimates for Germany as a whole.[41]

The working party first met in Berlin in September 1946. They agreed that Giuliani would draft proposals for amending the 1929 law and the group met again in November to discuss this draft. The British and French delegates approved with minor changes. The Soviet delegate immediately took issue with technicalities and Giuliani concluded they had 'every intention of blocking the general proposal'. He held individual meetings with his French and British counterparts. He found expertise and interest extremely lacking in the French Zone, and they 'show interest only when the productive capacity of the area is threatened'.[42]

In contrast, he found himself 'in complete accord' with his British counterpart, with only two exceptions: forbidding the manufacture of medical heroin and that no trade application be denied on the basis of need. Giuliani recognised that heroin was unlikely to be banned, given that its manufacture and sale was permitted everywhere else in Europe. The latter point, however, highlighted a deeper Anglo-US ideological division. Giuliani was pushing for a decentralised provision mechanism based on the approval of order forms and import certificates, and the establishment of a quota system, if necessary. The British delegate pushed for a command economy based on a centralised system of control. Giuliani 'pointed out that this was quasi-socialization of medicine, a system which is generally regarded with disfavour at the moment in the [US]'. The two failed to reach agreement and left the matter to the working group.[43]

By December, Giuliani concluded that accord was impossible and 'from the very first, the Russians sabotaged my whole proposal.' The French delegate suggested moving ahead with a tripartite agreement. Giuliani wanted to continue 'until all hope of reaching agreement is gone', particularly if the UN could manage to 'force the issue in the meantime'.[44] In December 1946, Anslinger and the US Delegation introduced a CND resolution, unanimously adopted, urging the Allied Government to 'establish ... effective narcotic control for all Germany'.[45]

Giuliani called it 'gratifying', but shortly thereafter, the Soviets attacked the working party for failing to achieve anything. Finally, at their fifth meeting in January 1946, the Soviet delegate stated that no revision of the 1929 Opium Law was needed, making it impossible for the working party to continue.[46] Efforts to effect a unified control in Germany appeared dead, a victim of emerging Cold War politics. The US, Britain and France would continue to work together while the Soviets would pursue their own course. Giuliani wrote in January 1947 that the 'PCOB is a long way from getting the statistics!'[47] He refocused his efforts on building narcotic squads in the US Zone and ensuring the issue remained on the agenda of the Allied Health Committee, even if no forward progress was possible.

The US had spent significant energy and political capital trying to establish centralised narcotics control in Germany. The British, in consonance with broader economic and foreign policy goals, as well as recognising it would place them alongside the US, readily offered support. France, seeing the likely futility of the effort and the negligible political cost, similarly offered support. Further, the issue fit within a broader trend of Western zonal cooperation. The PCOB, despite being burned for its political overreach, had also played a key role in facilitating this Western coalescence. Still, the PCOB and DSB would remain wary of running afoul of emerging Cold War politics going forward and consciously avoided any potential claims of regulatory overreach.

4.4 The Divided Asian Paradigm

The divergence between transatlantic policies came into relief in Asia. Whereas Britain, France and the US worked together over Germany, an essentially conservative and technocratic endeavour, they diverged once again when it came to the frontiers of narcotics control, the implementation of complete prohibitions in Asia. Britain maintained an essentially pragmatic attitude underpinned by a willingness to compromise with local needs. The US saw Japan as the perfect opportunity to implement its strict prohibitionist model. Further, the US prosecuted Japan's violations of the narcotics conventions as war crimes. US control advocates, meanwhile, found an important ally in Japan with General Douglas MacArthur.

Unlike Germany, the US had unified control of Japan and its territories. The American commanders had little notion of what to expect when they took control. The received wisdom was that Japanese forces pushed opium onto their Chinese, but that Japan had minimal domestic opiate use. Japan was a signatory of the 1912, 1925 and 1931 Conventions and had passed a series of domestic regulations beginning with the 1898 Opium Law. All raw opium and coca leaves produced were subject to licences mandating that they be sold to the Government. Only government opium could then go to market. Permits and authorisations for use and possession were granted to physicians, dentists, veterinarians, pharmacists and drug manufacturers, while all wholesaling operations were kept under strict government and police supervision.[48] Imports and exports were also subject to a system of certification.

Drugs could be purchased with a medical prescription and drug addiction was a matter to be reported to the police by physicians. By the end of 1938 there were 3,600 registered 'addicts', the majority of whom were supposedly Korean. Treatment and 'cure' were provided by charity organisations, which claimed high success rates. For example, in 1938, 310 out of the 316 'addicts' in treatment were reported as being 'fully cured'. Opium smoking was strictly forbidden, with severe penalties. There also existed an Advisory Opium Commission, created by an Imperial Ordinance in 1931, tasked with examining control in all Japanese territories. The Tokyo Metropolitan Police Bureau was responsible for the illicit traffic and maintaining contact with control authorities in other countries. By 1939, 27 tons of raw opium was produced in Japan proper, while 26 tons was produced in Korea.[49]

In August 1945, Anslinger announced that hundreds of civil affairs officers would follow US troops into liberated territories in East Asia, expressly trained to suppress the illicit narcotics traffic. He told reporters how the 'officers and their aides will start back on the road to health the peoples who fell victim to drug addiction through Japanese connivance to rule them by weakening their wills with narcotics.' Suggesting the British, Dutch, French and Chinese policies were in lockstep, he claimed, 'it should take only three to four months to get most of those addicts back to normal once the process starts . . . but it will be a matter of putting them on cold turkey to get them back.'[50]

China wanted the US to ensure the total de-narcotisation of Japanese policy with complete prohibitions on production and manufacture written into any peace treaty. George Morlock was non-committal and suggested that the Chinese CND representative Dr Sze, take up the matter at the proposed production limitation conference.[51] General MacArthur, meanwhile, pressed ahead with domestic controls. It is possible that he was influenced by his personal lineage with the

Philippines and had internalised the US prohibitionist policy implemented there around the turn of the century.[52] He moved quickly to establish a five-point program of control, with reports to be made to him within thirty days. Within fifteen days the administration had compiled an itemised statement of all stocks of narcotics, including location and owner.[53]

By October 1945, Anslinger was part of an effort within the US to use the violation of international drug conventions as grounds to indict members of the Japanese government for war crimes. An FBN Agent was appointed to uncover information to be furnished to the War Crimes Office.[54] The inner circle viewed this as a potentially important precedent with Sharman writing in 1946,

> It is, I think, good policy to establish in practice the principle that a deliberate Government policy involving the use of narcotics in direct defiance of international conventions previously subscribed to is an international offence.[55]

In October 1945, General MacArthur issued a directive to the imperial government that all new cultivation was prohibited, and existing crops were to be destroyed. All stocks were frozen, imports required his approval as supreme commander, while exports were completely prohibited. His actions rode a wave of positive press in the US, with some claiming it would knock out 90 per cent of the world's illicit supply. Others contrasted US policy with British imperial policy. The latter, they claimed, had used the trade to finance its empire, while the US took every opportunity to extinguish it. In General MacArthur's statement, he justified the policy in light of 'well-documented evidence of Japanese use of opiates in attaining their quest for an empire and as a means of subjugating conquered peoples'.[56]

Days later MacArthur issued similar instructions to forces in Korea. Within two weeks, press reports pointed to an illicit cache valued at US$50 million seized by US forces. Anslinger also worked with Elliott Felkin to ensure that the government of Japan properly filled out PCOB forms.[57] General MacArthur, meanwhile, continued to take a strong personal interest. A former FBN agent, Lt W. L. Speer related a story about a meeting between himself, FBN agent Oyler and General MacArthur to Anslinger:

> Mr. Oyler had walked out to the elevators ahead of me, and when I came out he was talking to General MacArthur. All I heard of that part of the conversation was the 'Bureau of Narcotics', after Ralph introduced me to

> the General as 'the narcotic control officer, a former agent in the Bureau of Narcotics', the General asked, 'How am I doing with narcotics', Ralph replied, 'pretty good, General'. The conversation lasted about three minutes much to the astonishment of everyone as I have never seen the General stop to talk to anyone before.[58]

Speer reported 'good cooperation' from Japanese officials who were 'eager for suggestions'. He argued that the main problems stemmed from insecure stocks and poor record-keeping.[59] By December 1945, US officials were assisting the imperial government in drafting a new directive. It was largely modelled after US domestic legislation, the 1914 Harrison Act, at the suggestion of Oyler, although he was careful that the FBN not be seen to be playing an overt role. Anslinger wrote that 'the results speak for themselves' and that he was 'greatly pleased with the intelligent approach' taken by Speer and Oyler.[60]

Efforts continued apace, and by late 1946 Japan was held up as an international exemplar in post-war control. The October 1946 PCOB report both condemned Japanese actions during the war and praised the US military occupiers for their efforts. Anslinger suggested bringing the report to the attention of General MacArthur, whom he was 'sure' would 'be as pleased as we are'.[61] International control advocates believed they had effected a de-narcotisation of Japan's foreign policy.

How much the reinstitution of controls in Japan would impact on the global illicit market remained to be seen. As with the Philippines four decades previously, the US brought an ideologically prefabricated policy to an area it occupied. Yet Japan represented a radically different policy environment, with a wide chasm between its policies on the Chinese mainland and Korean peninsulas and its regulations at home. Like the Philippines, the US press was quick to highlight all indications of success and attribute them global significance. Success implementing the US vision was conflated with success in outcomes. Japan, like the Philippines before it, became a poster child for US anti-opium efforts and a counter to the supposed half-measures of the old colonial powers, particularly Britain.

4.5 Britain in Asia: Malaya, Hong Kong and Borneo

Malaya, Hong Kong and Borneo highlighted the difficulties faced by Britain as it sought to implement opium-smoking bans. The ban had been decided under US pressure in 1943 when the political arithmetic favoured placating the US and ignoring post-war policy costs. In 1945, these administrative costs had to be paid. The opium dilemma remained unchanged. On the one side were the local realities of existing 'addicted' populations, for whom there was no 'cure', and even if there was, no medical infrastructure to implement it. On the other was the political necessity of deferring to the US concerns, even if they were viewed as irrational and unworkable.

The Colonial Office hosted a meeting in April 1945 to discuss Malaya given its relatively high level of 'addiction'. Administrative difficulties quickly came into relief. There was little success in obtaining staff for the Civil Affairs Administration, with only three doctors filling eighty places. This, the Colonial Office decided, necessitated maintenance of consumers on a prepared form of opium until a longer-term solution could be found. They would issue 'prepared opium on medical certificates', but this raised a question of supply. One option was to re-establish their factory in Singapore 'in a modified form', but they feared accusations of reintroducing the opium monopoly in a disguised form.[62]

They decided that 'opium tablets' would be supplied to 'satisfy the genuine needs of confirmed addicts' and avoid the necessity for re-establishing the Singapore factory. Certificates would be issued by medical officers or authorised practitioners. To pre-empt US criticisms, it would be made explicit that 'addicts' would 'as soon as practicable' be provided treatment in government institutions. Further, to demonstrate resolve, enforcement of the ban on opium smoking would be made the responsibility of the police, with ex-Malayan customs officers drafted in to assist.[63]

Because the question 'was solely one of medical treatment' the Colonial Office decided that tablets would not be denied even if consumers were not already registered to receive smoking opium. As a 'political gesture' to the US and to mitigate against the perception that they were switching one form of opiate addiction for another, vague instructions on 'the desirability' of diminishing provision would be issued. Medical officers bucked at the idea of being 'restricted' in treating their patients and overall, the Colonial Office agreed that the officers 'could be relied upon to exercise discretion'.[64]

Malcolm Delevingne argued that no revenue should be seen to derive from sale, given past US 'suspicions'. The Colonial Office rejected this on the basis that medicine was normally charged for in government hospitals, and issuing free opium could encourage increased consumption. The US State Department had requested that all seized stocks be destroyed, but this was also rejected due to supply shortages and transport difficulties.[65]

The Colonial Office also paid lip service to treatment options, such as examining the methods used by Chinese doctors, and social antidotes to drug consumption such as the provision of 'recreational facilities as a counter attraction to opium smoking'.[66] Forty five million tablets were provided for the post-military phase, at a cost of £45,000, to be met by 'Malayan funds'.[67] Some provision was also made for supplying tablets to Borneo and Hong Kong; however, neither was viewed as being as 'greatly troubled with the opium problem' as Malaya.[68]

Overall, British policy aimed for as much continuity as possible, while trying to defer to US wishes. Opium smoking was to be abolished, although the success of implementation remained to be seen. The US perception was that the problem was one of political will. Governments needed to resolve to eradicate non-medical supplies and force 'addicted' populations into treatment. The British viewed this approach as impractical for many colonies. Medical infrastructure, assuming effective treatment even existed, was largely absent in many colonies. The medicalisation of maintenance was a middle ground between outright prohibition and the continuation of quasi-medical usage. The former was seen as practically unworkable while the latter was seen as politically unsustainable. Burma and India, however, which had not committed to immediate eradication of non-medical and non-scientific consumption, remained a different story. They served only to further highlight that the response in Malaya, Hong Kong and Borneo was driven largely out of a desire to satisfy American wishes.

4.6 Unfinished Business in Burma and India

In February 1946, the State Department, under renewed pressure from Congressman Judd, pushed for a response to their note on opium policy in Burma. Judd intended to publish both the note and the British reply.[69] By June the British Foreign Office continued to 'stall', as the Burma Office had not responded. The Foreign Office believed that 'the State Dept. clearly do not wish us to have our tails twisted over this opium question, but it may be difficult to avoid unless we state our position over it clearly soon.'[70]

By August 1946, the Foreign Office was still awaiting a reply.[71] The political costs of inaction on Burma seemed to have decreased drastically and with the first CND approaching, the soft State Department attitude suggested the issue had fallen right down the US agenda. Anslinger also figured little in discussions. In September, the Burma Office finally provided a reply to the Judd memo. Although 'not perhaps quite as full as we may have wished' it was agreeable to the relevant Foreign Office officials and Major Coles as UK representative to the CND.[72]

Stalling by the Burma Office had allowed the situation on the ground to change. US forces had withdrawn and there were no reported cases of US troops acquiring the opium habit in Burma. The practice of opium smoking, meanwhile, would be made illegal, and they would abolish the system of licenced shops supplying registered consumers with opium for eating.[73] Opium eating for 'religious and ceremonial purposes and for "quasimedicinal" and scientific uses' would be exempted and an, as yet undetermined, form of opium maintenance would be provided.[74] They warned the US government that the ban would take time to become effective.[75] The State Department proved willing to declare victory and move on and the secretary of state politely noted 'with satisfaction the decision' to prohibit smoking and abolish the system of licensed shops. Other details were glossed over.[76]

Prior to the war, opium limitation within the nominally sovereign Shan states in the border regions of Burma and the Wa states, located to the northeast of the Shan states, was largely omitted from formal international discussions. Further discussion of these areas was left out of the formal reply to the US. Most of the trans-Salween Shan and the Wa states only came under some form of administration following agreement with China as to the frontier in 1941. These areas produced surplus quantities of low-grade opium which tended to enter the illicit market either via 'Ministerial' Burma, China or Siam. Just prior to the war, the government of Burma began to admit to its position as a producing country. This fact was now solidified by the inclusion of the Shan and Wa states, even though administration in those areas was extremely light. With the CND first meeting looming and discussions turning to a production limitation agreement, the Burma Office expected the issue to draw attention.[77]

London decided the government would highlight their commitment to a long-term strategy, that first aimed at controlling production in the area, then limiting production and consumption in the Shan states and eventually a total prohibition on production. London believed, with this long-term strategy in place, it would be defensible for the government to purchase surplus opium stocks in these areas and use them partly to meet local demand for opium eating.[78] Prior to the first meeting of the CND, extensive details remained 'to be filled in', but the Foreign Office warned that a production limitation convention may necessitate 'the ultimate elimination of opium production in the trans-Salween areas as soon as may be practicable'.[79]

Major Coles at the Home Office seemed less concerned and defended the Burma Office proposals as 'a very satisfactory scheme for dealing with a very troublesome subject.' Thus began a strong UK exceptionalism around Burma. Further, Major Coles suggested there may actually be an international market for surplus Burmese opium and suggested determinations be made whether it could be 'workable commercially'.[80]

India remained steadfast in its response to the Judd Resolution in protecting 'quasi-medical' opium eating until medical facilities could be expanded.[81] They supported the proposed production limitation convention in principle but refused to 'undertake any fresh obligations'.[82] Although US circles had sporadic bursts of interest in pressuring India, few thought serious diplomatic leverage was an option or that Indian intransigence would be overcome. A production limitation convention appeared the best hope.

4.7 Iran: The Key Recalcitrant

Member state representation on CND began to loom large in 1945–6. In 1945, the Iranian Desk at the State Department inquired whether Iran could be represented, arguing it would be preferable to have them 'in' than 'out' and that it could be a diplomatic 'lever' to to increase controls. Anslinger responded angrily. Repeatedly frustrated by Iranian promises, he lacked any faith in their ability to change and pointed out that during the League OAC meetings it had been represented by the 'head sales manager for the Iranian Opium Monopoly, and who not only tried to sell opium to the representatives of the other countries but opposed everything of a constructive nature.' Anslinger originally only wanted one representative from opium-producing countries: Turkey.[83]

Iran had delayed responding to the US State Department official note of September 1944. A bill introduced into the Majlis for the ratification of the 1925 Geneva Convention was still pending. No bill had yet been introduced ratifying the 1912 Hague Convention without the much-maligned reservation to Article 3(a). In a final Judd Resolution push, the US Embassy was asked to try to 'persuade' the government to limit production, suppress the illicit traffic and consider joining a reconstituted Turkish–Yugoslav opium agreement. The Embassy made little effort and warned that 'patent instability' was of such a 'critical' nature that little progress could be expected.[84]

Within Iran, however, a new domestic movement for prohibition had emerged. The Anti-Opium and Alcohol Association published a brochure written by Mahmoud Fateh, a former minister of qgriculture. It argued for complete prohibition of cultivation and for poppy to be replaced by cereals.[85] Despite these stirrings, little tangible changes appeared to be likely.

The US Embassy pointed out that the government was preoccupied with the situation in Azerbaijan but promised to 'keep pressing ... pointing out [the] particular desirability at this time of publicity favorable to Iran'. In March 1946, the prime minister created a commission to study how 'to stop production of opium and smoking of this deadly poison'. On 10 April, he issued instructions to the governors of all provinces that all cultivation should cease within the year. The Ministries of Agriculture and Finance were told to draw up the necessary enforcement measures. Further, the sale of opium in shops as well as its eating and smoking was prohibited. The State Department doubted that the decree would be implemented, while their Embassy wrote that the '[d]egree of compliance will depend in part on the development of the present government towards totalitarianism' and warned it 'will be extremely difficult to enforce the Prime Minister's orders'.[86]

US press and political circles nevertheless responded jubilantly. Representative Judd, speaking on the floor of the House of Representatives, claimed it as the second success of the Judd Resolution, after Afghanistan. Others within the US noted the action was 'In consonance with his General Program to do away with elements of [the] economic and social structure ... that make Iran open to foreign criticism that it is reactionary or backward.'[87]

Initial indications suggested the effort was in fact genuine. In June, Prime Minister Ahmad Qavam announced that all government officials had fifteen days 'for total cure' and stated that the order would have 'secret agents' carrying it out. In July, the Council of Ministers made clear that the Opium Monopoly had to be disbanded with complete prohibition of cultivation and use. Government efforts at suppressing the 1946–7 crop appeared to cause an increase in illicit activity, as well as prices. Anslinger and the Treasury Department believed there to be 'every indication' Iran was sincere and pushed again for ratification of the drug conventions without reservations.[88]

The State Department remained sceptical. Analysts at the US Embassy questioned whether the goals were achievable and warned that no crop substitution had been outlined to mitigate economic hardship to growers. They suggested the Iranian government seek US government assistance, and the Iranian Ministry of Finance made clear that they would. Reports emerged that the Anti-Opium Commission had placed an order for 100 million 'anti-opium tablets' with the USSR, while black market prices continued to rise. The US Embassy expected that less accessible parts of the country would disregard the decree and that years of more intensive government activity would be needed to eliminate the cultivation.[89]

Elizabeth Washburn Wright imposed herself onto discussion, arguing that complete prohibition was premature and would result in continued cultivation in 'inaccessible regions'. Further, she claimed that Iran was needed to balance against the Turkish–Yugoslav duopoly. She questioned, 'where would America and the manufacturers of medicinal opium in other countries turn?' US efforts had been to develop a tripartite licit supply system, which aimed to prevent smaller countries becoming exporters. This, she claimed, would be undone, with a proliferation of smaller exporters in the Balkans, Europe and South America and 'the world would be flooded with the uncontrolled drug.'[90]

Wright lobbied in Washington to build support for this view. Anslinger was non-committal, warning that 'until we know what the real situation is in Iran, we should proceed very cautiously.' The State Department also sought to quell her interest, requesting that she leave the matter to Anslinger and the upcoming CND.[91] As the CND met, the Iranian question remained unresolved. The difficulty the US experienced in articulating a clear strategy for Iran highlighted its complicated and central role in enabling a global production control system.

Iran presented an example of US policy being driven by pragmatism over orthodoxy. The State Department pushed back against overzealous Iranian moves towards total prohibition, without effective economic alleviation. Unlike Japan, there were real obstacles to diminishing opium consumption and production. Like Malaya, Burma and other British possessions, Iran had limited medical or enforcement infrastructure and in areas outside government control, little capacity to enforce anti-opium decrees. Over Iran, the US acted more like the old colonial powers – willing to subsume a strict anti-opium policy orthodoxy to pragmatic geopolitical and local concerns.

4.8 Rebuilding the Global Licit Market

The Turkish–Yugoslav Opium Agreement dated to December 1934. It gave the Central Opium Bureau at Istanbul the exclusive right to sell opium grown in either Turkey or Yugoslavia. The agreement divided markets, with Yugoslav opium supplied to the US and Turkish opium supplied to Europe and others. By 1938, 'perpetual difficulties' had undermined it. Iranian opium, which had traditionally found a home in Asia, increasingly competed for European market. Prices became depressed relative to the US – which prohibited Iranian opium imports. Yugoslavia offered compensation, but Turkey demanded a repartition of markets and a levelling of prices.[92] By 1939, the agreement became increasingly difficult to sustain, as the two sides sought to carve up the international market against a backdrop of deteriorating European politics.

In 1940, the monopoly raised its prices when it learned US manufacturers would not be permitted to buy Iranian opium under any circumstances. Anslinger warned Ankara that the US would re-evaluate its policy if US importers continued to be 'subject [to] unfair price disadvantage'. After some discussion he promised to support the monopoly for 'the time being', but would explore his options.[93] Eventually, as we have seen, broader geopolitical concerns drove the US to temporarily lift bans on the import of Iranian and Afghan opium. Both were warned, however, that this was a temporary wartime measure and that after the war Turkish–Yugoslav opium would again become preferred.

In July 1945, the US approached Turkey and Yugoslavia to suggest a revival of the agreement, possibly now including Iran. Yugoslavia suggested it was premature and Turkey declared that political stability needed to return to Yugoslavia and Iran first.[94] Eventually, with the political deterioration in Yugoslavia, the declarations by Iran and Afghanistan that they would prohibit all cultivation, and the relatively low morphine content of Indian opium, Turkey quickly emerged as the key to the post-war licit market.

During the war, the Allies purchased Turkish opium to supply their war efforts, but also to deny the crop to the enemy. This latter act was known as 'preclusive buying'.[95] By the close of 1943, Britain and the US had come to different conclusions about its efficacy. Bertil Renborg claimed it was ineffective, demonstrated by the apparently large stocks in Belgium, Norway and other German occupied countries. The State Department agreed and wanted to cease efforts. The British Home Office rejected Renborg's analysis and insisted it be continued.[96] Eventually Britain prevailed, and the practice continued.[97]

The Allied wartime opium relationship with Turkey thereby developed along exceptional lines and would eventually need to be recalibrated for peacetime. For Britain, the key was ensuring availability without suffering price gouging, something they felt they had so far achieved through good relations with Turkey.[98] Perceptions of Turkey in US control circles remained overwhelmingly positive and were helped when Turkey expressed full agreement with the Judd Resolution in July 1945.[99]

As the war drew to a close, Britain and the US were increasingly in competition for Turkish opium. The British Directorate of Medical Supplies labelled the situation 'undesirable' and called for a clear 'apportionment' and pricing so that Britain could resume sales to their traditional markets.[100] The two initially agreed to divide the 1945 crop equally.[101] However, Britain came to believe the US had bought up a significant portion of the 1944 crop, while having major reserve stocks on hand. Britain now felt entitled to a larger portion of the 1945 crop. Thus, US and British 'competitive buying' of Turkish opium crops emerged.[102]

By May 1945, Britain had secured 30 of the 50 tons deemed 'urgently required' and requested the US allow them to purchase the additional 20 tons.[103] Eventually Anslinger agreed Britain could purchase 75 per cent of the 1945 crop.[104] Despite this, Turkish supplies quickly deteriorated, and prices doubled. The monopoly claimed large quantities were being diverted to illicit markets and smuggled through Syria, reducing the 1945 crop by roughly half, to 100 tons. Further, with the French, Swiss and Belgian governments all now seeking Turkish opium, they could assure Britain only 35 tons for the coming year.[105] Britain had foreseen this issue and had advocated that one single source should buy all opium on behalf of the Allies to prevent Turkish price gouging. London had already purchased opium on behalf of the Dutch government in 1945 and was examining the possibility for the Belgian government.[106]

Britain's core goal was to keep downward pressure on prices long enough for a more predictable post-war market. For this to happen, conditions in Yugoslavia, Iran and Afghanistan needed to become clearer, as would the general trajectory towards a production limitation convention. For the US, sitting on large opium stockpiles, these issues were less pressing than goals of global supply reduction. Overall, great uncertainties hung over the licit market. British–American cooperation or competition would no longer act as the predominant determinant of global demand, supply and prices. The emergence of post-war competition in an imperfect and partly regulated global licit market presaged difficult negotiations ahead for the new UNO, as we shall see.

4.9 Conclusion

The German and Asian narcotics cases strongly correlated to broader geopolitical trends. They also highlighted the alignment of interests in the international drug control system. When discussions centred on questions of European-style regulation of a narcotics industry, as the German situation did, transatlantic cooperation was possible. Where questions centred on difficult issues of total prohibition, as the Asian colonial questions did, agreement was not possible. How large an issue the US wished to make out of divergences depended on internal US politics and external geopolitical calculus. As the world moved to a post-war framework, narcotics loomed relatively small for broader State Department regional policies and, in most cases, Anslinger failed to place it on the agenda. The State Department had no desire to hold British feet to the fire on this issue in Asia in the face of serious governing concerns, while Anslinger had lost his wartime leverage.

A battle for the narcotics peace had quietly raged in Asia along the traditional European–US divide. On the one side were the British, trying to find national regulatory frameworks that satisfied US demands as far as possible, while working to accommodate local obstacles rather than run roughshod over them. On the other side was the US, advocating the absolutist vision for prohibition but increasingly unwilling to exert political leverage on its allies to achieve that vision. How far Britain could make its incremental regulatory approach work would have a major impact on Anglo–American drug relations and international control efforts more broadly. Similarly, how well the US could adhere to its own absolutist vision as it encountered new governing and geopolitical exigencies in Asia and the Middle East would determine the direction of international efforts.

As the immediate crises around the occupation of Germany and Japan settled down and the two powers faced a plethora of post-war issues, neither had any appetite to refight old Anglo–American battles over narcotics. The crux of British–US narcotics relations, and thereby the emerging global approach, increasingly centred on the division of a global licit market and negotiating a production limitation convention. Britain and the US would have to work together to unite the various social, economic and political interests around the world behind a new convention process and throw all their efforts into producing consensus. This would involve deploying a mixture of sticks and carrots, which only a joint Anglo–American effort could effectively wield. Both appeared to recognise their role in this process, saw the desirability of a production limitation convention and implicitly acknowledged their reliance on one another to enable it. These factors became only more apparent against a backdrop of a deteriorating geopolitical environment. By 1947, with the battle for the narcotics peace largely secured, and a UN framework in place, a new era of narcotics multilateralism was underway, now based at the United Nations. It is towards these multilateral processes that we now turn.

5

Old Battles Anew at the UN Commission on Narcotic Drugs, 1946–1948

5.1 Introduction

Emerging from the tense post-war negotiations, the key uncertainties for CND were how it would operate in practice, how it would fit into broader geopolitics and whether it would function as a talking shop or a tool to enforce a specific framework. The most coherent vision came from Anslinger and Sharman. They sought an enforcement body advocating prohibitionist and repressive responses. The first three meetings of CND in 1946–8 would be pivotal. The first two meetings served to sound out the political context and how the structures would function in practice. Following this, a major political push would occur around the Third Session towards a new Protocol; advancing discussions on a new production limitation convention; and even advocating a new 'single convention' unifying all previous agreements.

Most immediately, however, states sought to ensure a sound legal basis for the system. Britain took the lead, offering legal expertise and driving a consensual process around ensuring the continued functioning of DSB, PCOB and the existing conventions. Once this was secured, states began to look towards enforcing the existing conventions and extending the prohibitions on opium smoking to all territories. Once they had enshrined this as a universal legal norm, control advocates planned to redirect global efforts towards enforcing the prohibitionist framework. On this, the US ostensibly took the lead – although its ability to act as bilateral enforcer, utilising the UN as a bully pulpit, became increasingly dependent on State Department willingness to risk broader diplomatic ripples. As time passed between 1946 and 1948, the State Department became increasingly risk averse, to the point where lead US Delegate Harry Anslinger was muzzled in the 1948 CND discussions and even forced to make a positive statement regarding Mexican efforts, which was diametrically opposed to his actual views. Overall, the two approaches indicated the emerging British–US roles as two key pillars of the post-war system. Britain led the consensual-codification approach, and the US led the political activist, enforcement-oriented, prohibitionist approach.

The immediate forward political direction was around extending the control of manufacture to synthetic drugs not previously covered by the 1931 Convention. The international community was able to speedily conclude negotiations, highlighting the relative consensus around regulating the manufacturing point on the commodity chain. Part of this stemmed from the fact that the burden of control fell on wealthier manufacturing states with greater regulatory capacity, who simultaneously had a desire to carve up the market among existing firms and create new barriers to entry through regulatory hurdles.

Next was the question of production limitation. Control advocates hoped a single oversight/enforcement body would enable more aggressive control efforts at the international level. Around opium, it was unclear what the means to achieve this were. Should states aim for an interim agreement, as the Chinese delegation would suggest, or a long-term agreement, encapsulated within a new single convention as the US suggested? In the middle remained states like the UK, which privately professed scepticism as to the political feasibility or practicality of a production limitation convention. Their chief focus remained to protect their own economic interests, including cheap sources of opium. Meanwhile, the question of whether new controls over the coca leaf and cannabis were practical or even required remained an open discussion. Sceptical states, such as the UK, saw no reason to oppose further study on these issues. Control advocates, such as the US, pushed these studies as a means towards setting the trajectory towards stricter control.

Beneath the initial consensus discussions lay a deeper struggle over whether CND would become an enforcement body, or a cooperative environment aimed at facilitating control. The 1946–8 period would be pivotal in answering this question. On the one side remained the control advocates, led by the US and supported by Canada and, to a lessening practical degree, China. On the other side would remain the producer states. A key question was whether a clearly cohesive producer bloc would emerge. Occupying the middle ground once again were European powers, represented most strongly by Britain. Britain settled comfortably into this role and was happy to watch the shape of debates take form before engaging its political capital to resolve potential choke points and conflicts. Britain self-consciously adopted the role as pragmatist-in-chief, whereas the US under Anslinger continued its role as aggressive prohibitionist, while being increasingly muzzled by the State Department.

5.2 Old Issues Converge at CND

A Drafting Committee met in September 1946 to consider the Secretariat's draft Protocol and resolutions giving life to CND. It consisted of representatives of China, Yugoslavia, France, Peru, the UK, the US and USSR. The UK delegation found the draft legally 'inadequate', and the Committee quicky agreed that the UK's observations should form the basis of an alternative draft Protocol.[1] By late September 1946, a unanimous draft Protocol, together with two draft resolutions, were submitted to ECOSOC. This was almost entirely the work of the UK delegation.[2]

One major disagreement arose when the Soviet Union, China and Czechoslovakia strongly opposed inviting Franco's government in Spain to become a party to the Protocol. Others, particularly Britain, disagreed, and the matter was left to ECOSOC. At ECOSOC, the Soviet delegate argued that cooperation on drugs would represent an 'opening wedge to more extensive relations'. The US State Department took the view that purchasing Spanish cooperation on drugs was too costly if bought at the price of losing the 'Eastern group' of states.[3] Philip Noel-Baker, representing the UK, reiterated that they deplored General Franco's government. He argued that the Soviet delegation wanted 'to exclude General Franco from the Convention', while Britain wanted 'to exclude him from the illicit traffic'. With the UK the sole dissenter, and the US abstaining, a Soviet Amendment to exclude the Franco government from the Protocol passed and the issue was temporarily resolved.[4] The UK's approach fit its broader policy, first outlined by Anthony Eden after the Dumbarton Oaks Conference, of ensuring the UN embraced 'the bulk of the nations and eventually, perhaps, all nations'.[5]

CND officially met on 28 November 1946 in New York. Opening discussions centred on procedure. Anslinger tried to set the initial tone of the session by giving a speech on drug addiction in the US. He claimed they had witnessed a large decrease in addiction during 1917–38 due to effective international controls matched by strict domestic enforcement.[6] He then took every opportunity to impress the US approach on the visiting delegates. As a colleague wrote to Anslinger:

> you are doing a marvelous job as far as educating the boys from the other side as to how to handle narcotics. The two members from Holland ... were amazed ... and Mr. Delgorge, in particularly, hoped that they might some day control things as they are done in this country.[7]

Meanwhile, Iran appeared to be moving towards outright prohibition. Whether its laws were being implemented remained to be seen. A law prohibiting all use and cultivation was introduced into the Majlis in 1945 but stalled. The prime minister and Council of Ministers had issued some initial decrees, and on 9 September, the Council of Ministers decreed opium possession and transactions illegal. A date of 22 November was set for when prohibition would come into effect – exempting medical use and government exports.[8]

At CND, the Iranian delegation sought to roll back on its commitment to prohibition, claiming the decree only applied to 1946. Anslinger sent frantic cables back to the State Department urging he be sent copies of their initial decree so he could pressure the Iranian delegation.[9] By mid-1947, the Majlis had still not met, preventing it making the programme legally permanent. Officially, the US maintained 'every indication points to its being a permanent policy' and that 'competent observers' believed that the crop had been drastically curtailed, with quantities in 1947 expected to be at 15 per cent of the previous year.[10]

By early 1948, Anslinger was receiving new intelligence. Political changes had pushed out the chief of the opium monopoly, Mr Nikpay. He began providing US agents with extensive information and claimed that the 1948 opium harvest could be the greatest in history because of a favourable illicit market. He further claimed the government decrees were the direct result of a political revolt in Azerbaijan Province in 1946, where the Soviet-inspired rebel government decided to issue a prohibition decree, despite the fact that no opium was grown in the region. He argued it was explicitly meant as a propaganda ploy to embarrass the central government, which countered by issuing its own national decree. Nikpay claimed the decree was completely ineffective given the scale of agricultural and economic reforms needed to implement it and that the monopoly continued as before, although renamed as the Department of Prohibition. Further Nikpay assured that the parliament would not ratify the decree.[11]

Anslinger privately wrote early in 1948 that:

> Iran has been behaving very badly during 1947. She sold 9 tons of opium to Iraq, which that government did not receive; 18 tons to Syria, which is not reported as having been authorized there; 22 tons to Siam where there is still opium smoking; and one item which gives us great concern, 56 tons to Indochina to be used for 'disintoxification' of smokers.[12]

He went on:

> We have now prohibited all imports of opium from Iran for medicinal purposes because of her actions in supplying the illicit traffic in 1947.

> Accordingly, Iran is not to be trusted in any sense and should be completely outlawed. I have no sympathy whatever for Iran since her reentry into the illicit traffic after the war.[13]

Once again, the US felt burned by Iranian claims. This would present enormous complications for a production limitation convention. Nevertheless, political considerations prevented Anslinger from publicly castigating Iran, as we shall see.

Meanwhile, by the end of 1947, the outlines of Japan's peace treaty provisions emerged. Japan would be prohibited from cultivating or exporting narcotics and would be limited to importing only for strictly medical and scientific purposes. The question was how to oversee this legitimate import trade. The US initially favoured PCOB oversight but realised this would require treaty amendments. It was then suggested that CND appoint a 'supervisor'. Col Sharman thought this 'an excellent opportunity' for CND to adopt an enforcer role, especially if the recommendations were binding. He and Anslinger sought to carve out the most severe negotiating position to allow a retreat to a more minimal position of insisting that, if manufacturing was to be allowed in Japan, it mimic US controls. Both men worried that Foreign Office officials in the US and Canada would be 'anxious to adopt the least penal line'.[14]

Economic experts in the State Department objected to the prohibition of manufacture and export. Maxwell Hamilton, in charge of the Japanese Treaty at the US State Department, worried that singling Japan out for 'punitive treatment' might breed national resentment towards the drug treaty system. Anslinger (an old friend of Hamilton) argued that Japan's historical record necessitated harsh restrictions.[15] States struggled to find a compromise at ECOSOC level. China advocated direct UN control of supplies and a prohibition of Japanese exports. The USSR objected to 'special provision' for Japan. The US State Department suggested a separate oversight body be designated by ECOSOC but baulked at the idea of a UN-style corporation overseeing the trade, particularly given all the expense and logistics that would entail.[16]

Eventually, ECOSOC reached a compromise hammered out by New Zealand, with input from the US and UK. Governments negotiating peace treaties would make the 'most stringent' national controls, while UN bodies would 'be available to give such information and advice as may be requested'. This ensured a clear distinction between international and national controls. China's goal to internationalise control of the Japanese drug market via the UN went unrealised, out of deference to state sovereignty. A core question of post-war narcotics control had been answered: the UN would in no case supersede state control. Overcoming Soviet objections, the UK amendment was adopted, allowing for information and advice to be supplied by UN experts when requested. This meant that, grudgingly, the UN would have an advisory role, but only on the request of member states.[17]

Around this time, control advocates, found a new and welcome ally in the Peruvian delegate Dr Jorge A. Lazarte. After the First Session, Sharman wrote to Anslinger to remind him of:

> The desirability of conveying privately to the Peruvian authorities the fact that their delegate not only made a most excellent impression and put his country right on the map in so far as the Narcotic Commission in concerned but that his attendance as an expert in the field of psychiatry did much to round out the all-round competence of the Commission from practically every angle.[18]

The US sought Peru's support in utilising the UN to suppress indigenous coca consumption:

> It is clear that Indians of South America consume huge quantities of coca leaves and that the effects are distinctly harmful to the Indians and to the economy of the countries that coca-chewing is widely prevalent. The Individual countries will need strong support from the United Nations to enable them to put into effect repressive legislation, as the Indians will make great resistance.[19]

At the Second Session of CND Peru requested that the UN help create visiting expert commissions to investigate coca chewing in Latin America and determine whether it was harmful. Other countries, the UK among them as we will see, were sceptical of these supposed harmful effects or that control was even feasible.[20]

Meanwhile, at its First Session, CND unanimously adopted a US Resolution recommending that ECOSOC urge all remaining countries to prohibit opium smoking. By 1947 the only country where it was not prohibited was Siam and a number of Indian states.[21] Siam claimed it had instituted a ban among its Chinese population and considered rigorous measures to enforce it, including publicly threatening deportation to China where their offences would be tried under Chinese law. Anslinger raised the issue at the Second Session of CND, highlighting that the Siam government derived almost 15 per cent of its revenue from the opium monopoly. The US would continue to use the UN bully pulpit to pressure them to follow the British, Dutch and French lead.[22]

However, although Britain, France and the Netherlands professed adherence, they were clearly struggling in a number of cases with implementation. Major Coles spoke vaguely of mixed outcomes in British territories, but overall portrayed an optimistic trend. In Malaya, he claimed there had been hundreds of admissions to hospital for opium addiction, but none had experienced serious symptoms from deprivation and only minor smuggling from Siam. North Borneo reported no cases of smoking or patients suffering withdrawal symptoms. In Sarawak there remained a large illicit traffic, believed to stem from supplies left by the Japanese, and smuggling from the Dutch territory, while few consumers had received treatment. In Hong Kong the quantity of opium smoked had decreased, although the number of consumers remained the same. There had been a slight increase in smuggling from Yunnan, China into Hong Kong, but this remained well below pre-war levels. Singapore reported 14,000 'addicts'. Government stocks there had been looted before the Japanese invasion, and there remained a fear that these stocks were still hidden somewhere.[23]

In French territories the monopolies had officially ceased selling non-medical smoking opium. Public smoking was prohibited, and only medical needs could be supplied. 'Dis-intoxication centres' were established, and opium for 'progressive dis-intoxication' could be obtained through prescription. Due to enforcement and anti-smuggling efforts, the price of opium was claimed to have risen five-fold in the space of two years. In 1947, they expected the sale of opium to be 15 tons compared to 50 tons in 1939 and 120 tons in 1920. Anslinger was privately critical of these 'dis-intoxication centres' and highlighted that in 1947 Iran had supplied 56 tons to Indochina for these. By 1948, he privately insisted the French government close the centres and cease purchasing opium for them overseas or he would 'expose this situation'.[24] Despite his threats and frustrations, Anslinger would ultimately be forced to mute his concerns out of deference to broader US regional policy.

The Dutch delegate reiterated his government's support for prohibition. He claimed that some hardship had been caused through a lack of provision of dis-intoxication centres. Further, illicit opium was still available and police control was weak. In areas where the Netherlands exercised little authority, opium was sold openly, and Chinese inhabitants continued to request the re-establishment of the monopoly. India had, in November 1946, decreed the total prohibition of opium smoking. They professed similar problems to the Netherlands but despite these great administrative difficulties, claimed to be seeing overall success. Anslinger requested that the question of 'legal opium smoking' remain on the agenda until it had been completely suppressed across the globe. Then the question could shift to the abolition of all opium smoking.[25]

The US maintained that in India and Burma opium eating was prevalent, 'deleterious to health and should be suppressed in the same manner that the smoking of opium' was. The government of India had traditionally opposed suppression, arguing that without medical facilities it was 'not humane'. By the 1930s, the Indian National Congress Party was shifting towards a more prohibitionist orientation, particularly as domestic consumption appeared to decline.[26] World War II disrupted this momentum, but by the Second Session of CND, their delegation announced, 'in view of the world opinion, the Government had changed its attitude' and aimed to discourage eating.[27] This marked a broader shift in India's attitude towards the control system and presaged its emergence as a moderate producer state.

Meanwhile, at its first meeting CND had unanimously approved a questionnaire to further preparatory work on a production limitation convention. The US strongly supported the questionnaire as 'urgent and important':

During the last six years Afghanistan, Iran, Japan and Korea have prohibited the production of opium; Argentina, Denmark, Austria, France, Czechoslovakia and the Netherlands have begun to cultivate the opium poppy for the direct extraction of morphine; Germany, Hungary and Poland have increased their production of poppy straw; and a new synthetic drug, Demerol, is rapidly replacing morphine.[28]

Before controls could be instituted, they first needed to quantify the problem. The League Secretariat had estimated total legitimate world raw opium requirements at 350–400 tons, not including prepared opium. By 1947, the figure for prepared opium had decreased, while the medical needs for derivatives of raw opium had increased, for example the use of codeine had doubled in some countries. The US even openly worried if it would be able to precure enough raw opium for medical purposes in 1947. The Secretariat needed to develop a new figure for world medical needs which could then determine the need for raw opium, and thereby also illuminate the actual influence of poppy straw and new synthetic drugs on the global market.[29]

By the second CND, the US developed a strategy based on dividing the issue, first looking at opium poppies, then coca leaves, then 'Indian hemp', and thereby develop each subject separately. Ultimately, they aimed for a unified production limitation convention covering all three, but absent this, an opium convention was seen as the most urgent.[30] The

Third Session would be pivotal in trying to generate political momentum towards a production limitation convention and the broader goal of a single convention.

The second CND also solidified the normative trajectory for dealing with domestic drug consumption. A questionnaire circulated by ECOSOC in March 1947 was designed to suggest repressive and strict measures as the natural response, such as asking whether provision had been made to isolate drug 'addicts' from the rest of the population.[31] States began vying to outdo each other at CND in highlighting the severity of control and punishment. Soon the arrest of 'addicts', doctors, illicit traffickers and other narcotics laws violators were viewed as metrics of success. Turkey pointed out they had apprehended 142 'addicts' in 1946, with two addicted to morphine, fifteen to hashish, nine to opium and the rest to heroin. They further highlighted that convicted 'addicts' were placed in 'mental institutions' for at least six months or until 'cured'. Harsh prison terms and fines were prescribed for those violating narcotics laws, including increased sentences when actions were deemed to have increased addiction.[32]

Iran pointed out that police had been authorised to enter private houses and confiscate any narcotics found, while the Ministry of Health was taking measures to cure addicts with what it claimed were 'favourable results'. Further, a Bill pending before Parliament contained a provision for the death penalty for anyone found smoking opium in the future. In response to this statement, the US requested and received approval that the CND report noted with satisfaction the measures taken by Iran to suppress the opium traffic.[33]

In this area, Britain and North America diverged. Canada and the US decried UK penalties as inadequate to deter smuggling. Sharman advocated for minimum prison sentences. Major Coles shot back that there was no legislative basis in the UK and that they would be construed as interference with the judicial process. Anslinger pointed out the US judiciary were not so 'sacrosanct' and that his corrective method was to highlight the damage of the illicit traffic to ensure severe sentences. If his advice was not followed, 'the press was notified, and things took a turn for the better.' Colonel Sharman highlighted a Canadian case of a man receiving a five-year prison sentence for possessing fewer than three grams of opium, because he had a criminal record.[34] The divergence between British and North American approaches in this area remained a consistent theme over the coming decades.

CND, with the overt goal of trying to standardise national laws, had the Secretariat undertake major, multi-year studies examining the various national responses. Further, as other UN agencies sought to engage with this issue, CND fought to maintain its issue monopoly. In January 1947, the Social Commission produced a document perceived by Anslinger and colleagues as portraying 'drug addicts being sick persons'. This conception, at variance with the criminal conception held by control advocates within CND, was deleted once discovered and led to an apology by Leon Steinig and the drug Secretariat.[35] Anslinger and Sharman were furious. Sharman wrote that:

> I am beginning to gather the impression that the germ of the old Genevese complaint has been firmly implanted and is flourishing in the administrative body politic of the U.N. Secretariat.[36]

Anslinger agreed, writing that 'we have to be just as much on the alert with the UN as we were with the League crowd.' Sharman and Anslinger were particularly aghast at statements that 'the prevailing opinion is that effective methods are those of re-education rather than repression', that 'drug addicts should be cured rather than punished' and that addiction should be viewed in the context of eliminating other 'vices' and 'social scourges' through 're-education and re-adaptation'.[37] Further, he and Sharman rejected the notion that 'the drug addict who is not re-educated when the drug is taken from him will instinctively seek to find relief . . . in other vices.' As Sharman wrote, 'one would almost think that the Narcotic Commission had not discussed this very subject in public two months previously.' He argued that the CND,

> With our well established machinery . . . would be well advised to keep thoroughly clear of everything except possibly the most tenuous connection with these impractical social uplifters, and that the most we should agree to would be for them to come and listen in at our meetings.[38]

They held their fire and left it to Steinig to undo in the short term, but they intended to raise it at the next session and determine which section of the UN Secretariat prepared the document so that they could 'give them "the works".'[39]

The Peruvian delegate closely parroted US and Canadian conceptions. He spoke of 'criminal addicts' who sought to 'induce others', often giving away drugs for the purpose. He argued that 'such individuals should be confined to institutions' and kept in isolation. Colonel Sharman, exercising the chair's prerogative, agreed with the Peruvian delegate and claimed that 'such addicts derived real pleasure from inducing others to follow the same vice: in this way they increased the number of their potential sources of supply.'[40] The implications were clear: dissenting views from the prohibitionist and repressive approach to reducing consumption would receive critical and dogmatic pushback from control advocates. The latter group would use the UN as a forum to expand, standardise and advocate repressive responses not only to trafficking but also consumption and addiction.

Whether CND would evolve as an enforcement body in line with the original inner circle conception would in many ways be determined by the early test case of Mexico. Anslinger chose to single out Mexico, given political considerations affecting other potential targets, the direct US interest given proximity, and the strong bilateral leverage potential the US held. Britain, conversely, viewed the Mexico question as 'one which almost exclusively affects the U.S.A. and in a secondary way Canada'.[41]

At the second CND, Anslinger claimed that Mexico had nearly 10,000 poppy fields and hosted at least a dozen clandestine laboratories, altogether producing 30–40 tons of opium for the illicit traffic in 1947. He proposed a resolution highlighting these reports and asking ECOSOC to recommend Mexico take measures to fulfil its international obligations. The Mexican delegate protested that the army and air force had been working to eradicate poppy fields and suppress the illicit traffic, but Anslinger and Sharman countered that this had only applied to a small number of fields. After some discussion, the Resolution passed CND.[42]

Regrouping in early 1948, the Representative of Mexico to the UN Dr Padilla Nervo protested to the US ambassador, while their ECOSOC representative warned of 'political repercussions' of passage of the resolution. Further, they highlighted the problems of control: small farmers received 'easy cash' for poppy crops, eradication was 'regarded as the acts of a totalitarian government', and, alluding to US citizens' involvement, the illicit traffic involved people that were 'very hard to touch'. Despite these difficulties, Mexico claimed to be working vigorously against the illicit traffic. Dr Padilla claimed that an ECOSOC resolution would be utilised by domestic opponents and warned that there was a 'hysterical attitude' within the Mexican government towards it.[43]

The State Department quickly stepped in to defuse the issue. Dr Padilla was warned that the US attitude would be determined by Mexican rhetoric and actions. Should the Mexican delegation seek to displace the blame to US citizens the US delegate would have 'no recourse but to set the record straight at some length, with names, dates, and places'. On the other hand, the US government claimed to be sympathetic towards Mexican difficulties and was 'disposed to be cooperative'.[44]

Relieved, Dr Padilla promised that he would use ECOSOC to highlight the 'numerous steps' Mexico was taking stamp out illicit production and that he had no intention of referring to the US or US citizens in any way. In response, the US promised to withdraw support for the resolution and send the issue back to CND to keep 'under review'. Dr Padilla agreed, on condition that Mexico not be treated as 'a country on parole' at CND level. The State Department nevertheless reserved the right for their representative on CND to be 'completely free to be insistent in the examination of the progress that Mexico was making in stamping out this trade'.[45]

The US proved unwilling to expend broader political leverage on this issue and pulled back quickly from any brinksmanship with Mexico over drug policy. They would allow CND to serve as a bully pulpit from which states could be pressured and criticised over the technicalities of their control efforts. Meanwhile ECOSOC would provide a cooling venue to allow political resolutions. CND could hold states' feet to the fire by sending resolutions to ECOSOC. If matters continued at ECOSOC level, the State Department and other Foreign Offices could work to cool issues and return them to CND. Most importantly, this provided the State Department a veto over all Anslinger's initiatives. Mexico, for the moment, remained a key agenda item for the Third Session of CND, and it was the only country singled out for specific attention.[46]

In March, however, leading Mexican newspapers published excerpts of a statement made by Anslinger to the Appropriations Committee of the US House of Representatives in which he parroted his claims made at CND. This provoked a furious response from the Ministry of Foreign Relations. They demanded evidence for the assertions and argued that a 'spirit of cooperation' should define Mexico–US relations, not criticism. The State Department responded that Anslinger's statement was made at CND, a forum where 'any country may be called upon publicly to account for' its control efforts.[47]

Anslinger remained determined to use the Third Session of CND to reiterate his complaints, but Mexican fury saw him overruled by the State Department. They cut a number of paragraphs from his draft statement and added a paragraph highlighting Mexico's successes in the face of great difficulty. As the State Department pointed out to Anslinger,

> There are just at this time other negotiations being carried on between the United States and Mexican Governments in several matters of considerable importance, one of which is of great importance to us from the

> viewpoint of hemisphere defense. It is therefore the hope of this Division and of our Embassy in Mexico City that the statement will be made in such a manner as not to arouse lasting resentment.[48]

In the end, Anslinger's statement praised Mexico prompting CND to express satisfaction with Mexican suppression efforts.[49] By the end of the Third Session, the Mexico outcome had significantly weakened Anslinger's ability to use the UN as a bully pulpit. He had overplayed his hand and had witnessed the narcotics issue being overtly subsumed to broader State Department goals.

Afghanistan, meanwhile, continued as a seemingly insoluble problem. It had announced the total prohibition of cultivation in 1945, but its opium continued to show up on the global market in 1947. The US remained convinced of Afghan sincerity. However, the Afghan Foreign Office informed the British Foreign Office in 1947 that their government had never intended to stop cultivation completely, merely restrict it to medical and scientific requirements, and that cultivation would continue much as before. Major Coles wrote to Anslinger, '[t]his is not unexpected, but it is not often so frankly admitted.' Anslinger felt deceived, responding that 'I could not help but think that this is the same story put up by the Iranian Representative.' Seeking UK support, Anslinger warned Coles that the US and UK should be prepared to 'confront' the Afghan delegate at a production limitation conference with evidence of their broken promises.[50] As with so many issues in the nascent CND, it was quickly becoming apparent that control advocates lacked the diplomatic or political leverage to prevent backsliding.

5.3 The Protocol on Synthetics

Synthetic drugs loomed large at the initial CND Sessions, representing one area of relatively clear consensus. As the UK delegation wrote, 'modern chemistry has produced synthetic drugs, capable of producing and maintaining addiction, but not susceptible to the control imposed by the earlier Conventions, as they are not products of opium or coca leaf.' Anslinger wrote to Malcolm Delevingne in November 1947 that 'we are virtually undergoing a drug revolution':

> Little did we think in 1931, in drafting the Limitation Convention, that we would be confronted with a whole raft of synthetic drugs, which are coming to the front with such lightning speed that we are almost unable to keep track of them.[51]

Drugs similar to opium alkaloids were increasingly being derived synthetically from coal tar. The two most visible were demerol and amidone.[52] However, a synthetic alternative had not replaced codeine, and for countries like Britain it was the main opium product, meaning a large demand for opium as a raw material. Britain acknowledged, however, 'if a synthetic coal-tar substitute for codeine is invented, opium as a raw material for the legitimate alkaloid trade might virtually disappear.'[53] The US echoed that '[t]he use of synthetics is growing so rapidly that there is a strong possibility of their replacing completely the derivatives of opium.'[54] This became a consistent theme over the coming decades. Producer states viewed synthetics as a direct economic threat, while control advocates used their spectre to simultaneously demand stricter production controls and lower prices.

In the interim, states chose not to amend existing conventions, given the complexity and their expectation for a new single convention incorporating the issue. Instead, they opted for a new Protocol covering all synthetic drugs not included in the 1931 Convention. At the 1947 CND, Anslinger proposed language, was seconded by Major Coles of the UK, and received unanimous adoption.[55] Their aim was then to expedite passage at the 1948 CND.

Anslinger optimistically predicted that the proposed Protocol would 'serve the purposes for all time'.[56] It would supplement, rather than replace, the 1931 Convention and apply that convention's system of control to synthetics. The US pushed for 'a temporary but general limitation' of any new drug pending a definitive decision by WHO on its efficacy and addiction potential. This became a core negotiating point heading into the 1948 CND, with Anslinger claiming to have the support of the WHO, PCOB and DSB for preemptive controls. The US was eventually forced to retreat, lacking support from the UK, USSR and the Netherlands who feared stifling of innovation. Under the draft Protocol, CND could simply recommend to governments, pending a WHO decision, that they apply controls provisionally.[57]

The success of the draft Protocol derived from various factors. These included the strong normative uniformity underpinning the system at the time. The new Protocol simply extended the existing normative and regulatory framework rather than innovating upon it. Further, facing no coherent producer or 'organic' state opposition, it proved relatively uncontentious to recarve up the market among existing players, while raising regulatory standards. More broadly, the Protocol offered a beacon of success to which they could point other areas of international cooperation then foundering on the rocks of the early Cold War.

5.4 The Third CND Session, 1948

The Third Session proved pivotal in setting the direction of international drug policy for the coming decades. The mixed results in the first two CND sessions paved the way for a major political push. In March 1948, the US escalated planning for a new single convention that would, it hoped, follow directly on the heels of a production limitation agreement. Major Coles of the UK, meanwhile, retired just prior to the Third Session, marking the passing of one of the system's old hands.[58]

Prior to the session, in 1948 FBN Agent Tollinger reported from French Indochina about the growing sale of opium. Anslinger intended to highlight the issue at CND, but was again overruled by the State Department. In his extensive draft, Anslinger pointed out that although their Federal Ordinance of June 1946 outlawed the sale of opium for smoking, US intelligence suggested that,

> the French Government did not close the opium monopoly dens when it announced the adoption of its policy of prohibition, but transformed them into 'clinics' where addicts could smoke without molestation. The present policy of the French Government is strictly that of taking all possible measures to supply the demand for opium in order to obtain as much revenue as possible at the expense of the addicts.[59]

Many in the State Department supported the statement 'in principle'. As one wrote privately,

> The report of the Treasury agent ... reveals a picture of colonial exploitation which reads like Radio Moscow at its worst. Approximately one-third ... of the ... Indochinese budget for 1947 was raised through the government opium monopoly.[60]

They nevertheless decided that 'the political situation in that part of the world and in France' prevented the US raising the issue and instead suggested that Anslinger take 'non-public corrective action'.[61] Once again, Anslinger had been rolled back on his efforts to use the UN as a bully pulpit.

Meanwhile, in the lead-up to the session, Leon Steinig sought to strengthen the UN Secretariat's role in monitoring the global illicit traffic. He privately sought Anslinger's advice, pointing out that only ten governments sent reports in accordance with the 1931 Convention.

Anslinger suggested they produce a simple table highlighting compliance alongside a CND resolution reminding governments to furnish reports and to make recommendations about improving seizure reporting. Anslinger also warned of the 'great and expensive burden' and that the Secretariat should aim for a 'simple report in narrative form'. The Secretariat prepared a memorandum on states' compliance with Article 23 of the 1931 Convention, concluding that these reports often contained little 'of value to other governments, and most of the reports contain significant omissions'.[62]

The UN drugs secretariat, the Division on Narcotic Drugs (DND) aimed to expand its mandate and become the centre of activity for illicit market reduction in a future convention.[63] Partly, this was driven by a desire to forestall the UN drug machinery splintering into other regional and bilateral frameworks and institutions. The genesis of the modern, UN-centred, illicit market monitoring system had begun. Nevertheless, with the US forced to tailor its criticisms to geopolitical concerns, enforcing a global framework against the illicit traffic appeared uncertain.

The third CND represented a relatively unique moment of consensus. One of the few points of contention from the UK perspective was how to incorporate a 'colonial clause' accounting for metropolitan ratification of agreements on behalf of their colonies, with particular pushback coming from the Soviet delegation. Another issue arose around renewing CND membership, specifically whether Iran would be re-elected. As UK Delegate Thornton wrote:

> There are two considerations here. The first that hardened lying on the part of a Government contributes nothing and ought to be visited with some consequences, e.g. exclusion from the Commission – yet the same could be said in a minor way concerning France (Indo China). The other that it is well to have an offending country on the Commission where its delegate can … be put 'in the dock'. I should incline to keep Iran. The U.S.A. delegate is in doubt but I think there are reasons why the U.S. Government is inclined to treat Iran tenderly and that may determine the matter.[64]

On opium smoking, certain general criticisms were aired, but not in an overly aggressive manner. The Dutch East Indies were criticised for, although seemingly diminishing smoking, having 'not yet gone the whole hog'. Egypt in particular was critical of allowing any continuation of licenced opium smoking. Similarly, Indochina and Macao were criticised for continuing to allow smoking. Thornton privately acknowledged that, for Macao, 'the opium traffic remains a large part of the raison d'etre of the colony.'[65]

Overall, the US delegation, under a State Department muzzle, held its fire on recalcitrant states. Thornton found Anslinger 'friendly' and 'always helpful' but 'very quiet this meeting'. Privately, he thought Anslinger and Sharman represented 'the two countries which par excellence look to international co-operation to mitigate drug consumption in their own countries'. Under this amicable climate, momentum towards a new production control agreement and new single convention accelerated. Despite US enthusiasm, however, Britain remained cautious about rushing headlong into either. As Thornton wrote:

> But for the white drug problem in the U.S.A., and the fact that white drugs were exclusively produced from eastern opium ... suppression of the production of raw materials and their indigenous consumption in a relatively harmless form would have been carried as far as it has. So far as indigenous consumption is concerned there is a fait accompli; but there is a room for caution as regards the chewing of the coca leaf, the essential viciousness of which has yet to be conclusively established.[66]

The UK also first wanted to see the 1948 Protocol prove itself effective:

> It will be interesting to see what the U.S.A. can do to suppress the illicit manufacture of new synthetics. They failed totally to check illicit liquor stills during Prohibition, although, of course, public opinion was with the distillers. If they fail here, there might even be a reversal of the past, with the East as Accuser and the U.S.A., as the producer of the illicit supplies, in the dock.[67]

He went on, highlighting that,

> The whole situation serves to re-emphasise the importance of the United Kingdom. It occupies an intermediate position. It has more sympathy with the position of the raw material producing countries than the U.S.A. has; and it has virtually no domestic consumption to worry about.[68]

Thornton cautioned against 'being drawn too closely into the orbit of the U.S.A., however friendly our relations are'. Instead, he suggested the UK 'redevelop the flow of secret information which we used to enjoy instead of leaving it a virtual monopoly of the U.S.A'. Viewing himself as a newcomer, he took 'a relatively small part in proceedings except in the discussion and drafting of the new protocol'.[69] Thornton's views set the general tone for UK drug diplomacy in the coming years, as the moderating force within CND and the coalition-builder mediating between producer states and strict control advocates such as the US.

Anslinger had not been muzzled on Siam at the 1948 CND. He publicly highlighted their opium traffic as being in 'full swing' and claimed the northern hill tribes produced 80–110 tons of raw opium annually.

Only 30 per cent was distributed legally, and the remainder was smuggled into Bangkok, Burma and China. The Chinese consul general at Bangkok claimed in 1947 that there were 200 smoking dens and 30,000 smokers in Bangkok alone. Government estimates meanwhile placed opium sales in 1947 at 14 per cent of total government revenue. Anslinger was also furious when, in early 1948, the deputy minister of finance announced that the Siamese government would make its future opium purchases from Iran.[70]

The UK were similarly distrustful of Iran's opium dealings and quick to paint the opium issue as another example of Iran's duplicitous methods in pursuit of economic gains. Not far beneath the UK's anger lay their ongoing difficulties over the Anglo-Iranian Oil Company and the renewal of Anglo–Iranian oil concessions.[71] Thornton wrote that Iran's representative to the 1948 Session, Mr Ardalan:

> Lies abroad for the good of his country and with astonishing effrontery. Ready to multiply or divide Iran statistics by ten to meet criticisms and equally ready to restore original figures for the same reason; referred cheerfully to new Iran laws and their present and prospective effect as if all believed him, although he knew no one did.[72]

Nevertheless, in the interest of consensus and stability for the nascent CND, criticism was generally reserved. The focus of this session remained the Synthetics Protocol and building forward momentum towards production limitation and a single convention. Existing international commitments were reaffirmed, but Anslinger had been limited to only mild criticisms of Mexico, Indochina and Iran. He had used his leeway on Siam to fire a warning shot to other states, but he and other delegations could see his freedom for manoeuvre was limited.

Control advocates back in the US viewed the CND as failing in its enforcement roles. As Helen Howell Moorhead wrote:

> There has been much accomplished by the technique of the Protocol in bringing the old Treaties up to date, but grave weakness has been displayed in handling the illicit traffic cases ... We need a "Prosecutor for the defense of public interest", some one free to urge forward the main object of the Commission-to control the movement of the legal traffic, and to attack un-remittingly the illicit traffic.[73]

Whether CND could be moulded into this kind of enforcement environment remained to be seen, but the early experience of Anslinger resoundingly suggested it could not.

The 1948 Session produced three different resolutions on production limitation. A US resolution called for a new single convention, which would include a production limitation provision. A Chinese resolution, viewing a single convention as a longer-term goal, pushed for an 'interim commodity agreement' until a single convention could be agreed. Finally, the Soviet delegation proposed to control the global production of hashish.[74]

Thornton viewed opium limitation as extremely complex, particularly with the proliferation of synthetic narcotics. Regarding coca leaf, he privately highlighted the uncertainties over its danger and the enormity of socio-economic obstacles to control in Latin America. He pointed out that 'Columbia found this when after a year of attempted prohibition of cultivation, they had to rescind their decrees.' More formidable, he argued, would be efforts to control 'Indian Hemp', which grew wild over vast areas of India, Africa and elsewhere. He argued that 'an onslaught on the growth of this plant would be an undertaking of the first magnitude' and would prove 'nearly impracticable'.[75]

The UK remained sceptical of the US proposal. Consolidating past treaties was seen as 'a minor affair' compared to production limitation, which might never be attained and at a minimum would require years of work. Further, until this was overcome, a single convention would prove premature and unnecessary. The UK sought to postpone discussions through recommending extensive studies. Thornton also doubted the utility of the Chinese proposal and abstained – not wanting to be seen to oppose it. Again, he supported further study to have 'something specific to discuss' at the next session.[76] The Russian proposal was 'meaningless', but since 'it only involved studies . . . which will disclose its absurdity, no harm was done by its adoption'.[77]

The Secretariat would undertake a study of coca chewing in Peru. Initially, no other Latin American country sought involvement, and Bolivia remained actively hostile to controlling the coca leaf. The UK remained deeply sceptical but again figured little harm would result from further study.[78] Also, Thornton wished to support the 'brilliant young psychiatrist' representing Peru with whom he had 'established excellent personal relations, which have already proved useful'. Further, London concluded that:

> The Peruvian Government is, overtly at least, "showing willing", whereas the Government of Bolivia, where the habit is equally prevalent, is indifferent to the point of intransigence. It would be unfortunate if Peru's forthcomingness were met by a niggardly response.[79]

Overall, the Third Session proved amicable, and Thornton wrote that it was 'up to best standards for business and atmosphere'. As a venue it was 'almost clear of ideologies; and as such an enduring example of what can be done internationally if goodwill can be achieved'.[80] The session also witnessed the solidification of the post-war coalitions and alignments. India, concerned with international legitimacy and highlighting the 'new era' domestically, played a far more constructive role. France sought a quietly assertive role while deflecting attention from opium smoking in Indochina. Egypt remained the standard-bearer for anti-trafficking efforts in the Middle East, despite the personal weaknesses, and reputation for inebriety, of its delegate, Mr Zaky. China stayed closely aligning with strict control advocates, despite the weakness and lack of knowledge of its delegate Mr Hsia and the worsening domestic situation. Turkey focused on defending its interests and avoided broader system politics. Russia proved erratic, unpredictable and yet relatively quiescent. Their delegate Mr Zakusov was a drug professional with little understanding of international affairs and a lack of interest in the rival international drug control visions. This, coupled with his 'pleasant and courteous' nature, proved a tremendous boost to the session and fuelled the narrative of CND being a UN forum where broader geopolitical issues were checked at the door.[81]

CND recommended that ECOSOC authorise the Secretariat to begin drafting a new Single Convention encapsulating all previous agreements and any new production limitation agreement. In the meantime the Secretariat would study an interim production limitation agreement and establish a Commission of Inquiry on Coca. Further, in a coup for the old inner circle, Sharman was elected as a new member of the DSB, following his nomination by Anslinger. Lastly, the session saw the creation of a UN periodical eventually to be called the *Bulletin on Narcotics*.[82] ECOSOC quickly passed all measures suggested by CND, and an official signing ceremony for the 1948 Synthetics Protocol took place on the 19 November 1948 at the Palais de Chailliot.[83] In July 1948, it was announced that the PCOB and DSB would be moving to the UN Office in Geneva.

5.5 Conclusion

The 1946–8 period was highly consensual when viewed against the backdrop of the previous four decades. It nevertheless produced mixed outcomes. The League system had been fully salvaged and given a stronger institutional footing within the UN. Once again, it was manufacturing states which took the political lead and accounted for the success of the 1948 Synthetics Protocol. However, the UN had not emerged along the lines the inner circle had hoped for. It remained largely toothless, and members like the USSR pushed back against any encroachment on national controls. Attempts by the US and its allies to utilise the system as an enforcement mechanism fell flat in the face of practical difficulties in recalcitrant states, and the necessity of deferring to broader geopolitical goals.

The US continued to place its hope in an ever-strengthened PCOB as an enforcement body and looked towards the Single Convention as a means to toughen controls. As US global influence grew, so too did its need to find accommodations with insoluble local problems such as opium. Washington's willingness to push an uncompromising drug control agenda thereby lessened. Similar to European government in decades previous, the expansion of US power meant that it had to compromise its anti-opium principles in pursuit of broader political and foreign policy objectives.

The UK remained self-consciously pragmatic, steering towards the middle ground. The colonial question appeared largely resolved, and London only expended political capital on core interests, for example, protecting Britain's drug manufacturing industries. The UN framework had been established and member states began to settle into coherent interest-related voting blocs. What was yet to emerge was a coherent producer nation voting bloc, although this was soon to develop under aggressive Turkish leadership.

Meanwhile, the importance of individual diplomats continued to manifest. The extent to which core representatives worked towards achieving their agendas remained a key determinant of outcomes. This would be particularly apparent as Anslinger was muzzled by the State Department, resulting in more consensual negotiations. Meanwhile, the change in leadership for the UK away from the old hand Coles to the new leadership of Thornton would have significant implication for their drug diplomacy. Lastly, the relatively diplomatic Soviet Delegate facilitated consensual negotiations and contributed to the narrative of CND as above international politics.

The shape of the post-war system alignments were coming into relief. On the one side remained the US, with a commitment to prohibitionist policies. On the other side remained producer states, which bucked against excessive interference, a diminished market and new burdensome regulations. For the UK, in the middle, regulation and respect for middle ground policies remained predominant. The relative success of the US in driving through its prohibitionist and strict enforcement vision, or the success of the UK in moderating US demands and coalescing states around a moderate regulatory vision, would determine the direction of international controls over the coming decades.

6

Dividing Up the Global Licit Market, 1948–1953

6.1 Introduction

By 1948, the trajectory of drug control was by no means clear. Iran and Afghanistan rolled back their commitments; colonial administrations struggled to implement prohibitions; and the general international security situation deteriorated. Meanwhile, multilateral efforts became almost entirely sidetracked by efforts to create an interim production limitation agreement that would serve until the Single Convention could supersede it. On this latter front the US remained far more optimistic than states like the UK, who saw only roadblocks.

The 'serene atmosphere' of the 1947 and 1948 CND Sessions quickly slipped into the rear-view mirror.[1] As the 1940s came to a close the UK had assumed a conservative and defensive posture. Its delegation actively avoided controversial issues and was deeply reticent to expand powers of CND, WHO, PCOB or other bodies. The UK maintained a strong vigilance against anything which could damage its vital narcotics trade and further worsen its precarious economic situation. Similarly, anything potentially complicating colonial matters was strenuously avoided.

UK policy was to run CND silent and deep as broader geopolitical conflagrations pushed drug policy down the international agenda. In certain areas, functional relationships were carved out – for example as had been the case of British–US cooperation over Germany. In other areas, unspoken accords emerged, such as the US going lightly on British colonial possessions and overlooking opium-smoking policies or smuggling cases. Overall, London politely dug in its heels and sought to slow the US-generated momentum towards new accords, while maintaining amicable relations with the US delegation.

Anslinger successfully avoided a domestic reorganisation attempt, and soon aimed for an international accord that would reaffirm the independent position of his agency under treaty law. In so doing he worked to lessen the State Department's grip of the strategic tiller and reassert his international influence. He eventually saw the 1953 Opium Protocol as a means to bring forward momentum on production control and thereby dig multilateral processes out of the mud. With this interim agreement on production control, he could redirect attention back to his pet project, the Single Convention.

The UK, on the other hand, seeing the Home Office policy reins change hands a number of times, maintained a pragmatic but essentially conservative approach. The issues around medicinal heroin use and outside criticism of UK prison sentences heightened London's awareness that the UN drug framework, despite initially circumscribed goals, held a tendency towards 'mission creep' and regulatory capture by states advocating the most repressive and control-oriented approaches. Eventually, as states like the US and France pushed ahead with accords in the face of disagreements, irrationalities and hard economic logic, the UK approach became characterised by stern opposition. This resulted in the UK pushing back against drafts of the 1953 Opium Protocol in an occasionally incoherent but resolute manner.

The UK initially sat quietly on the sidelines, not appearing to obstruct negotiations but confidently expecting production limitation to collapse under the weight of its own contradictions. This approach became untenable when France, under the determined leadership and vision of its CND delegate Charles Vaille, assumed the lead negotiator role and became a key Anslinger ally. 1950 marked the beginning of a new Franco–US drug diplomacy, with the strident and abrasive Vaille aligning closely with Anslinger.[2] Both Anslinger and Vaille worked to hammer through a negotiated outcome even if it alienated many states and was unlikely to achieve consensus and adoption. This Franco–US drug alliance became all the more important as the US–Canadian relationship lost its core strength when Col Sharman was sidelined and his successors moderated their approach sharply, aligning with Britain and viewing the British regulatory approach as more conducive to their economic interests as a consumer state.

The period 1948 to 1953 was underpinned by a general lack of bilateral enforcement efforts. Certain states received the occasional dressing down by the US, but these were generally reserved. By 1952, however, Anslinger had found the issue that he believed would help him retake the initiative on US drug diplomacy. Just as he had done a decade previously with Japan, he launched a full-frontal assault on the People's Republic of China (PRC), painting them as the source of an enormous conspiracy to flood the West with illicit opium to earn foreign exchange and sap US will to fight wars.

As the international security situation worsened, the drug control framework began to strain at the seams. States moved towards quiet bilateral cooperation on issues of overlap, such as Western Germany. Meanwhile, on complex issues crossing deep geopolitical fissures, states were careful to avoid publicly stressing drug policy issues for fear of a rupture pulling the system apart. This became harder as the supply framework of the system began to break down in the face of a spike in wartime demand and pre-emptive stockpiling. The regulated market, which control advocates had been working to shrink, suddenly became a sellers' market, with consumer countries vying for stocks of opium. Claims that synthetics were doing away with the need for opium became harder to sustain and producer states sought to cash in on their position. As CND continued to push towards a production limitation agreement, states like Turkey and Iran became more confident and vocal in defending their interests.

Against this background, CND's Secretariat, the Division on Narcotic Drugs (DND), became bogged down in efforts by its head, Leon Steinig, to push through an international opium monopoly against all diplomatic and economic barriers, to the detriment of all other work, such as the Coca Leaf Commission and the draft Single Convention. Eventually, DND overreach alienated key member states and created a breakdown in relations between CND and its Secretariat. Messy discussions around the Opium Monopoly became an embarrassment to the entire UN and all were keen to salvage some agreement.

6.2 Anslinger's Domestic Threat: Reorganisation

In 1949, the Hoover Commission on Organization of the Executive Branch of the Government began advocating that the FBN be transferred from the Treasury Department to the Department of Justice and consolidated with the Federal Bureau of Investigation (FBI). They argued that the FBN was now more concerned with the enforcement of regulations to prevent illegal sale and use rather than with collecting revenue. Anslinger quickly mobilised his political base to generate opposition at all levels of the US government. The drug industry was quick to throw its weight behind Anslinger, while senators received letters from angry state regulators. The Woman's Christian Temperance Union sent letters to the secretary of the Treasury urging that the FBN 'remain a separate Bureau' within the Treasury Department.[3] Eventually the threat was defused, once again leaving Anslinger safe for the foreseeable future and free to refocus on national and international efforts. In the meantime, issues of international control had taken a backseat to the overarching concern for his bureaucratic survival.

6.3 Control in Germany

At the 1947 CND, the US delegation called the situation in Germany 'unsatisfactory'. The US Zone had instituted strong controls, and US officials worked closely with the German government and police. However, Soviet intransigence had postponed unified control indefinitely.[4] The US highlighted this in UN forums, but the British Zone soon attracted negative attention as the Netherlands, bordering the British Zone, raised serious concerns about smuggling. London acted quickly and by 1949 had appointed a Zone Narcotics Officer mandated to establish 'close liaison' with his US and French counterparts, as well as with authorities in Belgium, Denmark and the Netherlands. Further, specified Dutch officers could pass freely into the zone to cooperate with British authorities. The Netherlands was satisfied, and the situation was defused. Meanwhile, the British government pushed blame onto the East German authorities. They claimed all Western efforts to establish cooperation were ignored, along with all police enquiries into illicit trafficking cases.[5]

Work on a tri-zonal approach continued focusing on creating a Western Germany Narcotics Bureau.[6] In early 1950, the US recommended creating a German Central Narcotics Office covering the Federal Republic. Further, they suggested integrating the Allied Narcotics Officers into one Allied Narcotics Board to supervise the work of the Central Narcotics Office.[7] A West German response to narcotics control was emerging which would thereby take pressure off occupying governments.

6.4 Limitation of Coca Leaf

Following, in part, a drive from the government of Peru, the UN Commission of Inquiry on the Coca Leaf conducted its field research in Peru and Bolivia over the period September to December 1949.[8] Its controversial report concluded that the practice of coca chewing was harmful and should be suppressed. Militating against immediate prohibition, it highlighted a general need to improve socio-economic conditions in areas where it was prevalent and suggested that governments work to prohibit the practice within fifteen years.[9] The march towards the global prohibition of the coca leaf had begun.

In the meantime, the Peruvian CND delegate, Dr Jorge A. Lazarte, with whom many delegations including the US, UK and Canada had formed extremely close relations, had fallen out of favour with his home government and been removed. Peru then sided with Bolivia to strongly challenge the Coca Commission's findings. CND delegations sought to defuse tensions by encouraging dialogue.[10] Sharman and Anslinger were impatient with the fifteen-year timeline and Sharman hoped they would 'cut the Gordian knot immediately'.[11] The UK sought 'a solution which disposes of the matter as soon as possible with the least possible conflict, complication and expense'.[12] By 1951, Bolivia and Peru hardened their stance and sought to bury the report in UN processes.[13] The Secretariat, having spent UN resources on the Commission, was keen to see some conclusion.[14] Control advocates maintained their original strategy, that the Coca Commission should serve as the springboard to incorporating coca production limitation into the Single Convention. The matter was set to drag on.

6.5 Suppressing Opium Smoking in the Colonial Territories

The 1948 CND referred, after a UK amendment, to 'some Far Eastern Territories' failing to meet their obligations around suppressing opium smoking. The UK interpreted this as making a clear distinction between their colonies and others, namely French Indochina, Macao and the Dutch East Indies. The UK was extremely vigilant against any reports which reflected poorly on their colonies. In 1949, Malaya struggled to enforce a prohibition on opium smoking due to political unrest. Singapore, with its estimated 14,000 habitual smokers, reported that the opium situation was 'disturbing', but they avoided enforcing anti-opium laws until the security situation had stabilised. In the meantime, London worked to displace part of the blame to producer countries like China, Siam and Iran for their lack of control.[15]

In August 1950, Thornton, from the Home Office, requested that Consular Officers in South East Asia send secret reports on the opium smoking situation throughout other territories. The Foreign Office torpedoed the idea, concluding that if the CND delegate divulged the information, he could prove 'a liability' given 'the present inflammable state of the Far East'. They argued that the UK should trust that setting a good example would encourage stricter adherence by other signatories.[16] Far from satisfied, Thornton responded that he hoped this 'trust . . . may prove not to be misplaced'.[17]

As the political situation in Burma worsened, it fell entirely off the opium radar as the powers struggled to find a political resolution. With the fall of China, the shift of nationalist Chinese (KMT) troops into the mountain regions laid the seeds of an invigorated illicit opium industry.[18] The UK was concerned to protect their relationship with Burma, while the US aimed to stabilise regional security. Neither had an immediate interest in kicking the hornets' nest of regional opium policy. Meanwhile, the KMT forces began to utilise the ungoverned spaces and opium trade to fund anti-communist insurgency efforts.[19] The KMT quickly gained control of the opium trade in the Shan states, shipping rapidly increasing supplies via Thailand.[20]

Opium had also assumed a particular prominence in the Indochina conflict by 1953. As the UK Legation to Saigon wrote:

> Opium is the most important product of the regions of Laos through which the Vietminh launched their offensive last April and May, and it is in terms of this commodity that the offensive is now being explained on every side. . . . If the Sam Neua region remains in their hands they will retain an assured source of income and further sallies southwards at harvest time, even if no major offensive is launched, will have obvious attractions.[21]

British intelligence also suggested that 'the Vietminh are using some of the raw opium captured in the Laotian campaign' to fund their activities.[22]

6.6 The Emergence of the Red China Conspiracy

The emergence of the People's Republic of China (PRC) regime had enormous implications for the control system. The US and control advocates quickly lost their traditional CND ally to increasing irrelevance. Initial political difficulties centred on having a nationalist Chinese delegate represent China, something the Soviet and Polish delegates raised every year. Soon, however, a much larger issue arose. In 1950, the Chinese Communist regime appeared to re-enter the global export market, offering 500 tons of raw opium to a British firm in Hong Kong. Initially, little was known about the opium, but eventually the UK privately concluded it was collected and warehoused under the previous regime. The PRC appeared to be trying to offload existing stocks and earn some foreign currency in the process.[23]

The 1950 Session urged caution against China rushing back into production given its troublesome history with opium. Control advocates feared it would upend a production limitation agreement.[24] The Board of

Trade in the UK concluded that the opium was unsuitable given that it was double the price of Indian opium. The UK hoped this economic argument would 'avoid any suggestion of political bias' but feared the entire stock would be diverted into the illicit market.[25]

The UK was walking a fine line, as it feared a larger spotlight being thrown on Hong Kong, thereby fuelling anti-colonial sentiments. On the other hand, they were concerned not to further weaken relations with the PRC government. Although it was their 'duty' to inform CND of the matter, the UK delegates were instructed to 'discourage any unnecessary publicity'.[26] As one member of the Foreign Office wrote: '[t]he U.S. Press will be only too pleased to take full advantage of this.'[27] The issue caused the Foreign Office to refocus their sights on drug diplomacy after years of deferring to the Home Office. They highlighted wider 'political repercussions' of unchecked Home Office reports on opium in the Far East and therefore requested greater oversight.[28] The Home Office agreed to forward anything 'liable to have potentially serious political repercussions'.[29]

The US, and Anslinger in particular, who was fresh from his domestic reorganisation battle, seized on these reports to highlight a new international conspiracy that his agency, through the UN, could help thwart. He drew heavily and uncritically on nationalist propaganda, with one report claiming that:

> Opium production and trade have formed an essential part of the Chinese Communists' economic program. Thus during the early 30's ... poppy cultivation and opium smoking were encouraged ... On the other hand, the Chinese Nationalist Government made strenuous efforts for the suppression of opium traffic and smoking.[30]

Anslinger used the 1952 CND Session to castigate the PRC, prompting a furious response from the Soviet Delegate who described Anslinger's statement as 'a planned slander and completely unfounded'. The Soviet delegate then raised US 'aggression' in Korea. Anslinger threatened to call a 'point of order', and the session descended into bickering.[31] Afterwards, the USSR delegate circulated a PRC statement refuting Anslinger's claims and arguing the PRC had pursued strict prohibition. Infuriated, Anslinger spent the next ten months planning a detailed rebuttal to be presented at the 1953 Session.

By 1953 the spectre of a Chinese opium conspiracy loomed large in US drug circles, much as the Japanese spectre had in the 1930s and 40s. Anslinger used it once again to raise drugs as a national security issue, one which only his agency could protect against. He testified to the US Congress that 'efforts to control addiction within Communist China have been feeble and ineffectual' and that they had been carrying on 'Heroin Warfare' against the US. He claimed their goals were 'monetary gain, financing political activities in various countries, and sabotage'. Further, raising the opium danger to US troops in Korea, he told the Senate: 'the communists have planned well and know a well-trained soldier becomes a liability and a security risk from the moment he takes a shot of heroin.'[32] The UK remained deeply sceptical of Anslinger's claims and wanted the issue to quietly die. However, they said little to contest the US claims and instead sought to keep their heads as far below the parapet as possible.[33]

6.7 'Steady as She Goes' at CND

At the 1949 CND Session, the US pursued a policy of continuity with the aim of ensuring speedy progress on the Single Convention. It sought to tee up the 1950 Session for extensive 'study and action', and in 1951 'the Commission could whip the draft convention into its final form' and begin its passage to ECOSOC and ultimately the General Assembly. In the meantime, Anslinger was allowed some leeway to criticise recalcitrant states. He was 'not to criticize publicly ... French Indochina' despite 'retrograde measures' and the re-establishment of the opium monopoly and shops where it was openly sold to registered 'addicts'. He was, however, allowed to continue to draw attention to the situations in Siam, where 'little improvement' had occurred, and Yunnan, as well as to Iran, where the US believed 'approximately 1,300,000 persons are smoking opium daily.'[34]

The UK delegate Thornton enjoyed a relatively subdued 1949 Session and focused on alliance building. He found relations with Anslinger 'remained altogether friendly', but, 'as before', he found Sharman 'rather a handful'. Thornton expressed concerns that 'Anslinger and Sharman ... and others, including the Egyptian, are heads of ... narcotics police forces and see all questions in a single minded way.' This, he noted, was translating into efforts to control all precursors to narcotics: 'it is almost already a struggle to make them keep their clutches off coal tar.'[35]

The UK was also angry that it continued to be criticised for the supposed lack of severity of domestic penalties, by Sharman in particular. Nevertheless, Thornton expected that British public opinion, 'little excited by a drugs menace, would not favour extravagant local penalties to meet a world problem'.[36] This issue pointed to a broader problem which the UK had recognised on several fronts: CND was being used by control advocates to criticise states pursuing different approaches. On the issue of criminal penalties, the UK could handily ignore the complaints of Sharman. In the areas of synthetic drugs and heroin, which touched on strong economic interests, ignoring their pressure was more difficult.

The US and its allies continued to push for strengthening pre-emptive controls on new synthetic drugs. The precedents established around amidone and dolatin assisted them. The Expert Committee on Habit-Forming Drugs of the WHO recommended that any future convention should elaborate pre-emptive controls for compounds similar to amidone and dolantin. The US then passed a CND resolution suggesting all members apply pre-emptive controls on drugs suggested by the Expert Committee.[37]

The UK was deeply suspicious of these efforts. They viewed the 1948 Protocol provisions as sufficient and maintained 'strong reserve' against adding pre-emptive WHO controls to the new Single Convention. UK legislation only allowed control of drugs likely to produce ill effects, and British law was 'strongly suspicious' of a presumption of guilt. UK legal 'realism' sought to balance the danger of an influx of new synthetic drugs, 'mostly of American proprietary', fuelling addiction against the administrative 'nightmare' of scheduling these drugs through Orders in Council.[38]

Highlighting the balancing act for the UK, Thornton wrote:

> If new drugs, devised by our chemical manufacturers, and exported, prove later to be powerful drugs of addiction – as heroin proved to be, although called 'God's own medicine', when invented – our reputation would suffer greatly.[39]

Mitigating against this:

> It is a valuable export trade and if we are to cease exports until ample time has been allowed for a drug to display its vicious characteristics the trade would suffer.[40]

The UK sought to head off this issue by working directly with the Association of British Chemical Manufacturers. Under this approach, scepticism of international interference remained central.[41]

A similar scepticism surrounded heroin. Following a supplementary recommendation to the 1931 Convention, every government was requested to examine the possibility of abolishing or restricting its heroin use. Post-1945, the PCOB had prioritised this, much to the dismay of the UK and others who argued it was 'irreplaceable' for certain uses. By 1949, the UK wrote:

> The [PCOB] made in its this year's report to E.C.O.S.O.C. a considerable song and dance over the countries which had not abolished its use, and notably over two, Finland and Italy, which have greatly increased it.[42]

The UK maintained that the recommendations were 'based on little reality', although acknowledging that over 90 per cent of UK heroin was used for cough mixtures and could be replaced. Their position, therefore, was 'not invulnerable'. London's response was to work with 'non-suppressing countries' including France, Canada and Australia to maintain that heroin was 'irreplaceable'. They were further ill disposed to accept a visit from a WHO expert, saying 'the United Kingdom Government has made its enquiry and is not in the habit of having its word questioned.'[43] Further, as Thornton wrote, 'I should not anticipate a very hearty welcome from medical authorities in this country.'[44]

By 1951, the UK had concluded that the PCOB and WHO desired heroin 'dispensed with altogether'. At CND, opinions remained divided, with the UK, Canada and France on the one side, and the US on the other leading the charge to eradicate it.[45] The heroin issue highlighted the tendency towards mission creep within CND and made the UK increasingly sceptical of accepting any new commitments under the Interim Protocol and eventual Single Convention negotiations.

6.8 Towards Interim Production Control

In 1949, an ad hoc committee began to study an interim production control agreement. It was composed of representatives of the principal opium producing countries, India, Iran, Turkey, the USSR and Yugoslavia. The USSR boycotted the committee, however, while work on the Single Convention was in progress.[46] Key questions for producing countries were: how to carve up the export market, whether to establish complete government monopolies, and the advisability of creating an international purchasing and selling agency.[47] If agreement could be found, control advocates believed that tackling global overproduction was possible, thereby choking off the illicit market. As Anslinger highlighted to CND in 1949,

> For this year the Iranian Government figures the production will be about 1,500 tons. In Turkey the estimate is 439 tons. In one year two countries have approximately between four and five times the medical needs of the world.[48]

Iran and India expressed early support. Turkey quickly set about establishing itself as the heir apparent of the licit market. They compiled extensive statistics for the previous fifteen years and recommended all attendees do likewise, fully aware that most would struggle. Yugoslavia professed an interest in the equitable distribution of the market based on 'a long-term annual average of production'.[49]

Overall, producer states had an economic incentive to try to lock in current market conditions via a global agreement. New synthetics, although vastly oversold by Anslinger, did represent a competitive threat.[50] Similarly, production from poppy straw meant that manufacturers would potentially become far less reliant on traditional producers for raw opium. Lastly, and more immediately, the deterioration of international security had led to opium stockpiling and a spike in demand. This had combined with a number of bad harvests to drive the price up to artificially high levels. A restrictive trade agreement would potentially maintain these high prices and protect against the new threats.

Meanwhile, recalcitrant states like Iran became increasingly dependent on the US for economic aid, which would be jeopardised by continued leakages of their opium into the illicit market. With the death of the Far East monopoly system, Iran had three options: try to lock in a share of the licit market; allow their opium to pile up in warehouses and farmers turn to the illicit market; or ignore negotiations and watch a deterioration of international relations as they were castigated as a narcostate. Their initial effort was towards the first approach.

The key impetus came from the DND and Leon Steinig, who viewed this as his legacy issue. The US was unable to formulate a coherent position. Anslinger doubted a successful outcome but could not afford to interfere at a time of domestic reorganisation threat. The State Department supported the overall process but wanted to avoid souring any producer state relations by exerting pressure or tipping the scales in favour of one over the other. This incoherence between the FBN and State Department saw the US assume the position of interested observer. It offered encouragement when possible and in general professed willingness to accept the economic costs of a successful agreement if it ensured supply reductions.

The UK immediately took a reticent stance. Doubting an agreement could even be reached, in the event that one was, the British expected it to run aground on the rocks of Iranian overproduction. Feasibility aside, the UK's core focus was on economic self-interest. They firstly wanted to protect their role as the world's leading exporter of opium products. Secondly, they wanted to protect their interest as a major consumer through sustaining low prices for NHS medicines. Mitigating their negative attitude, they did not want to appear as subverting the international good out of deference to economic interests. They maintained a low profile and assumed that agreement would stumble on traditional fault lines.

The Committee met in Ankara from 21 November to 7 December 1949. Turkish officials immediately argued that past good performance and the quality of their opium entitled them to the bulk of the licit market. Opium was an important cash crop for their balance of payments with the US, and they intended to yield little except to avoid antagonising Iran if possible as they sought better broader relations.[51] Iran maintained that government budgets would be difficult to sustain without opium revenue and was unwilling to cede the bulk of the global market to Turkey. They demanded a 40 per cent market share and to offload all existing stocks – which were multiples of annual global requirements – preferably to the US for dollars. They also warned of peasant pushback and the need for economic assistance.[52]

India defended their sovereignty and 'quasi-medical' use. They secured an accommodation to count only medical and scientific exports.[53] Yugoslavia was represented by their CND delegate Mr Krasevec, who went out of his way to be cooperative. They sought to maintain their market share at 63 tons per year and publicly support Turkey as part of their broader foreign policy to improve relations. Steinig and the US observer, Mr Merrill, concluded early that the producers did not really want to hammer out an agreement, but instead use them as a means to shift blame to consumers by agreeing unsatisfactory provisions. Steinig used 'every club in the bag' to pressure states and warned of the dangers of failure. Merrill, despite no official role, wielded quiet US leverage, writing: 'I think they were always watching me out of the corner of their eyes, thoroughly aware which side of their bread their opium is spread on.'[54]

States quickly agreed on an international purchasing and selling agency, and negotiations turned to division of the market. In the end, the percentage division for the first 450 tons was: Turkey, 54 per cent; Iran, 26 per cent; Yugoslavia, 14 per cent; India, 7 per cent; others (i.e. the USSR) 4 per cent. An additional excess of 5 per cent would be divided equitably and be used as stocks for the international agency. For amounts in excess of the 450 tons, Turkey would receive a quota of 59 per cent; Iran 30 per cent; India, 7 per cent; others 4 per cent; and none for Yugoslavia, which relinquished its claim as a gesture to Turkey.[55]

With this outcome, the conference exceeded all expectations. Merrill attributed this to the work of Leon Steinig. He suggested the US quickly throw its weight behind the agreement to prevent backsliding. Problems remained, however. It was unlikely the Soviet Union would join, despite provisions made for them. Further, the global licit market was in turmoil following a series of bad harvests. As Merrill pointed out, 'The [Yugoslavians] are now trying to buy opium (!) and the Turks have only stocks of 152 tons and an estimated production for 1949 of 20 or 25 tons! That's only 172.'[56] Nevertheless, member states, and Leon Steinig in particular, pressed on.

Under the agreement, government monopolies would sell their opium to the international Purchasing and Selling Agency operated by the UN, effectively creating an international monopoly. Steinig adamantly maintained the indispensability of this agency, but also its role as a 'precedent' for other dangerous commodities. It was meant as 'an experiment in economic planning' and would, if successful, be incorporated into the Single Convention and potentially other fields beyond drug control.[57]

Major obstacles remained, and Steinig risked overstepping his Secretariat role and even CND's role relative to ECOSOC. Anslinger remained privately cool to the monopoly idea, recognising it would meet headwinds in Washington. The State Department was open to it but suggested that the commercial work be handled by a 'corporation', with interested governments buying shares, and the appointment of a board of directors which could then be tied to the UN via a coordinating authority. Sharman hated the idea, privately mocking at one point that the quota aggregated to 'only 107%'.[58]

The UK openly questioned the 'reality' of the agreement, given the unpredictable impact of synthetics but also the unreliability of producers' statistical returns.[59] UK CND delegate, Mr Hutson, quoted Bismarck's question: 'who is being cheated here?' He went on: 'I approach a subject, on which there has been so much hard lying, with caution.' He wanted to make sure there was no 'hocus-pocus', pointed out it implied economic assistance to Iran but with no authority to do so, and reiterated that the Iranian situation could 'blow the whole thing'. Lastly, he remained unconvinced that the impact of manufacturing from poppy straw had been taken into account. Britain was 'experimenting' with it, and although initially unsuccessful, it could potentially erase a large demand for raw opium. He wrote to Steinig that they would need 'to face the difficulties' head on. Steinig claimed that Hutson's criticisms were not at all 'discouraging, but rather a helpful criticism and commentary', yet he tried to refute each one. Meanwhile, the principal manufacturing and producing countries would meet in Geneva in August 1950 to agree next steps.[60]

In 1950, the UK underwent another change in leadership at the Home Office. Hutson (who had replaced Thornton) left, and Samuel Hoare took his place as the lead CND delegate. Sharman wrote to Anslinger:

> Even if Hoare knows little . . . he is likely to eventually prove a valuable addition to the Commission – a probability which one could never associate with his predecessor.

By mid-1950, Hoare concluded that the monopoly could work in theory, but that its machinery did not seem to have been worked out in detail. He maintained he would wait until the Geneva meetings in August before passing judgement.[61] The hard economic realities were that the UK,

> imports about a quarter of the world requirements of opium, [and] exports about half of this in the form of drugs. This is a valuable export trade, amounting to about £5,000,000 per annum, of which some £50,000 to £70,000 is estimated to be dollar-earning. This trade is conducted not only in competition with other European countries which manufacture drugs from opium, but also . . . with countries such as Hungary, and to some extent Poland, which manufacture drugs, not from opium, but from poppy straw, and can do at far less cost (estimated at 54% less).[62]

Any increase in the price of opium would place British manufacturers at a further disadvantage. Meanwhile, 'A rise of 1% in the cost of raw opium is estimated to increase the cost of the National Health Service [NHS] by $5,000.' The NHS had already witnessed 'unexpectedly high' costs from drugs, and the Treasury had instituted spending controls. They would need very compelling reasons for a rise in costs and a clear sense, not easily justifiable given past failures of Iran, that it would actually control illicit supply. Further, the proposed system would make the UK more dependent on Iranian opium despite its significantly higher cost than Indian opium. The UK position quickly hardened on this point, and although they acknowledged 're-opening of the Ankara quotas would completely wreck' the agreement, they would attempt it.[63]

Further, for the UK, manufacturers would potentially be forced to cover a 10 per cent monopoly overhead cost. They believed that France and the US had more ability to absorb this and might press the UK to sacrifice its commercial interests through appeals to 'the general interests of humanity'. London concluded that they

> cannot afford, at a time when it is still engaged in the effort to bring about a balance between its exports and the imports . . . to agree anything which might imperil, over the next five years, a substantial element in that trade, as well as increase the already heavy cost of the National Health Service.[64]

On top of the UK's commercial concerns, it was slowly becoming clear that the monopoly wheels were coming off. At the Geneva meetings, major obstacles arose. States agreed there would need to be inspections by the international agency, but there was no agreement on their form. More importantly, there was no consensus on how to fix prices. Producers wanted averages of 1947–9, while manufacturers wanted 1937 prices, indexed to staple commodities given that opium prices in 1947–9 were irregularly high. Other disagreements centred on currency options, operating costs, assessing opium quality, overseeing the export of alkaloids from producer countries, and managing competition from poppy straw.

All of these unresolved issues meant that the Geneva meetings ended unsuccessfully, and one member of the US delegation, Charles Dyer, promised 'Never again!' to attend one. Despite the deadlock and Leon Steinig 'trying to proceed with this whole scheme in a very stubborn manner', Anslinger warned Sharman not to 'go too far in raising objections, as we do not wish to give the producing countries a way out now that they have agreed on quotas'. Anslinger wanted to appear supportive in principle and was conscious of the State Department policy to keep the US position 'reserved'.[65]

The Joint Committee of Producers and Manufacturers met again in November 1950. Price remained the key dividing question. To resolve it they formed a subcommittee consisting of Turkey, Yugoslavia, the US and UK, but it quickly became deadlocked. The British delegate wrote: 'The rest of the session was devoted to putting the best face possible upon the failure to agree about anything.' With the Joint Committee having once again failed, CND was forced to take up the matter directly, but there appeared little hope for a changed outcome.[66]

The US entered the 1951 Session of CND conservatively. They produced a back-up plan in case the monopoly negotiations failed, ignored issues around opium smoking in South East Asia, and generally sought to avoid controversy.[67] Privately, they were working to augment their opium stockpiles to cope with the Korean War. The UK commented that US stockpiling 'has left the other manufacturing countries unable to obtain' supplies and 'sent the prices of Iranian opium, the only source left, rocketing'.[68] The French, meanwhile, proposed a global alkaloid monopoly which would divide up the market along current shares. The UK noted this as a 'transparent' effort to establish a cartel of manufacturers and exclude poppy straw alkaloids. This would be to the detriment of consumers facing higher prices and poppy straw producers like Hungary, which would have to abandon production or turn to the illicit market.[69]

Despite an 'exceptionally long' Sixth Session, CND failed to break the deadlock and the monopoly idea was abandoned. To salvage something, states agreed to a French proposal that the principles of the 1931 Convention be applied to opium production as an interim agreement.[70] Steinig, who had been distracted by his role as acting secretary general, rejoined discussions and fought back. Steinig's effort

> to bring the Commission back to a proposal which it had dropped infuriated those delegates who wanted to get on with the French scheme, of whom the most vocal were the French representative, M. Vaille, and the representative of the United States.[71]

The situation escalated to the point where a rupture between the Commission and the Secretariat seemed likely 'unless there is a change either in the representation of certain countries (notably, France, Canada and the United States) or in the directorate of the Division'. The issue was put to a vote and eight members voted to end discussion of the monopoly. Iran and India voted to resume discussions, while three members abstained. Meanwhile, consumer states largely opposed it out of price concerns, with Canada remaining the most militant exponent of free trade.[72]

Peru fretted over the extension of controls to coca production. Mexico opposed any notion of international inspection as an incursion on sovereignty. So too did the Soviet and Polish delegates who also opposed this out of deference to a Single Convention–first policy as well as opposition to the UN undertaking a commercial activity. The UK delegate wrote that US lack of support was 'all important'. The State Department had been largely in favour, while Anslinger had remained personally opposed and had brought them around to his view.[73]

The UK viewed the draft French proposal as containing 'many inconsistences and unworkable provisions' and successfully worked to water it down. The UK pointed out that 'maintenance of free competition in the opium trade must involve over-production' and that:

> The system of estimates and statistics of the 1931 Convention cannot be applied to the production of opium ... drug manufacture can readily be adjusted to meet ... changes in demand, whereas production of opium is inelastic; it depends on harvest and cannot be adjusted after sowing ... [74]

Recognising this distinction, limitation of production was to be achieved by an 'indirect method of limitation of stocks'. A maximum limit of stocks would be set. If a country produced a quantity greater than its export demand, the excess would go into stocks until the maximum was reached. At this point, the PCOB could impose an embargo on exports to deter further overproduction. Even with this compromise, the UK raised objections. Control would merely be a 'statistical control', with the PCOB having no way of determining actual stocks. If a country was accumulating excessive stocks, it could give false statistics, or simply cease buying up domestic opium, thereby leaving it for farmers to 'dispose of' through illicit channels, thus inadvertently fuelling the illicit trade. Further, the UK warned that imposing an embargo on a major producer could have 'disastrous effects' on importers via price spikes and supply shortages.[75]

A 'further objectionable feature' for the UK was that limiting the trade to the four producers risked the formation of a cartel. London pushed for an even more watered-down agreement of statistical reporting, with no attempt to set maximum stocks or provision for an embargo. This received no support, 'no doubt because it would not have had even the appearance of a scheme for limiting production':

> The Commission preferred a scheme which has that appearance, even though no one believes that it will in fact have any important effect upon the present over-production of opium.[76]

The UK delegate abstained from the provisions relating to stocks, the embargo and the four producers but supported the proposal 'in general'. It passed eight to two, with strong US and French support.[77]

As 1952 progressed, the global market became even more confused, but remained a seller's one. The UK believed the Iranian government were purposely understating their stocks in order to keep global prices high. This perception was fuelled by wider UK–Iranian tensions following the nationalisation of the Anglo–Iranian Oil Company by Prime Minister Mossadegh in May 1951. Iran's actions had major implications for Britain's economic position, causing severe disruptions to their balance of payments and highlighting deeper structural weakness in Britain's international position.[78] Iran, meanwhile, was increasingly desperate for foreign currency and sought to offload supplies at the highest possible price. The US government was in the process of stockpiling and was openly willing to purchase all available opium.[79] London was furious that the Iranians had reneged on an agreement to sell opium to a UK firm, Bellairs Atkinson, the previous autumn, presumably, they guessed, out of a desire to sell the opium to the US 'for dollars'.[80]

As matters progressed, the Iranian Monopoly's duplicity caused major headaches for the US in particular and led to an array of unfulfilled arrangements entangling the US government, British firms, courts and even Swiss Banks. One UK official wrote that Iran had shown its 'opportunism and disdain of contractual obligations', as they sought to exploit high international demand by promising their opium to numerous buyers. Next, 'in this ridiculous, but very Persian game was that the Americans tried to get delivery of the opium they had purchased'.[81] The monopoly began to prevaricate. The UK wrote that '[a]nyone with experience of this country would have expected such tactics from the Monopoly, but the Americans seem determined to learn the hard way.' As for the opium situation in Iran, one UK official wrote: 'It is almost impossible to obtain reliable information.' Moreover, official government crops were not believed to represent more than half of the total production, with the excess presumed destined for the illicit market for smoking opium either at home or abroad.[82]

The 1952 Iranian opium saga highlighted continued market volatility. The UN system sought to expand its control of the market at a time when states were simply struggling to ensure that supply met demand. Bluff as they may regarding the impending takeover of synthetics, manufacturing and consumer countries remained dependent on producing countries. This reality was apparent to all involved, as states inched towards an interim agreement and would ultimately help delay a Single Convention for another decade.

6.9 The 1953 Opium Protocol

The UK delegation found the 1953 CND Session 'much more peaceful and good-humoured than in 1952'. Steinig's self-immolation and ignominious removal as head of DND following the collapse of the monopoly negotiations drastically improved Secretariat–CND relations. Gilbert Yates, a former member of the UK civil Service, had replaced him. Although the CND committed itself to moving forward with the Single Convention, a Joint UK–French memorandum confined the session to 'questions of principle and [to] not get involved in detailed drafting'.[83]

The US viewed as 'a very surprising development' the addition of a new Canadian delegate, Mr Kenneth Hossick, 'who was not too well regarded in narcotic circles'. It seemed that Sharman would be replaced at the next session, to the great dismay of Anslinger and the old control advocates. The US warned that Sharman was a vital link given his dual role on the CND and DSB, and his loss to the Commission would 'break the continuity' in relations between the two bodies. Protest as Anslinger may, Sharman's days were numbered.[84]

Illicit traffic discussions proved the highlight of the session and, as the UK described it, 'as usual ... largely sterile'. Anslinger's goals were bilateral. He wanted to defuse tensions with Mexico following 'unkind things said in California ... by highly placed officials' and 'show that our relations with Mexico are still on a high level'. He also maintained pressure on Italy's illicit trade, but his real focus was 'to take a very healthy swing at Red China'.[85] The nationalist Chinese delegate produced a report that infuriated the USSR delegate, who demanded that it and reports from Hong Kong and Japan be struck from the record. The UK tried to mediate, particularly as the Chinese report 'contained many inaccurate statements about Hong Kong and Singapore'. They criticised the Chinese delegate for inaccurate reporting and assured the CND that the Hong Kong report did not in any way reflect on the PRC.[86] Mollified, the USSR withdrew its complaint and tensions 'deflated'. Then Anslinger stepped in, as the UK delegate described it, repeating 'in a desultory and wholly unconvincing manner' the nationalist allegations. Much to London's relief, he took pains to praise British authorities in Hong Kong as 'making diligent efforts' to suppress the traffic from the Chinese mainland. Anslinger labelled the PRC statement of the previous year 'a diatribe of abuse' and claimed:

> the United States is a target of Communist China to be regularly supplied with dollar-earning, health and morale-devastating heroin ... According to reliable information ... financial and economic organs of Red China's Central Regime met behind closed doors in Peiping in early December and decided to expand sales activities abroad this year, primarily in Japan, Southeast countries and the United States.[87]

The UK delegate pointed out that the claims were badly undermined by a recent *London Times* article 'alleging that Chinese Nationalist troops are escorting opium caravans ... estimated to carry 500 kilograms of illicit opium into Thailand every week.' The UK delegate claimed Anslinger's speech was 'answered temperately and effectively' by the USSR delegate, and no further action was taken. Meanwhile, Britain was relieved when fears that the Egyptian delegate would utilise CND to accuse their forces of impeding narcotics control in the Suez Canal zone proved unfounded.[88] These issues together merely served to highlight the further encroachment of geopolitics into illicit traffic discussions and undermine CND's image as a technical and apolitical forum.

Meanwhile, Anslinger received word that certain sections, including members of the PCOB and DSB, were advocating that the Interim Protocol idea be dropped, with relevant parts folded into the Single Convention. Anslinger found the Draft Protocol 'on the whole acceptable' and 'a realistic approach to an urgent problem', and he moved quickly to shore up support and ensure the Protocol Conference went ahead on time. With the monopoly idea dead, the Protocol would operate a 'free order system', allowing market forces to determine prices and manufacturers to choose their opium source. As the UK had pointed out, this would result in continued oversupply, but the US argued the Protocol would finally determine annual global opium requirements and allow some coordination between supply and demand. The PCOB would be key to giving it teeth, by requesting explanations for excessive stocks and imposing embargoes.[89]

Samuel Hoare made clear to Anslinger that the UK 'never had much enthusiasm' for the Protocol, and in a number of key areas the UK and US remained 'at variance'. The US favoured limiting the number of exporters to four, thereby halting poppy proliferation in the future.[90] The UK, strongly supported by Canada, feared a 'trade monopoly' and demanded an open list of producers. The US suggested a compromise of allowing the PCOB to alter the list in response to market changes, but the UK rejected giving the board such 'unprecedented power'.[91]

The UK further opposed limiting government stocks as 'a question of principle' and argued it would have no effect on global overproduction. Instead, it would place unnecessary limits on the sovereign right of governments to determine necessary stocks, 'e.g. for national defence'. Further, Hoare reiterated UK concerns that embargoes could produce supply shortfalls and price spikes. Anslinger became exasperated and pushed the UK to offer 'suggestions' rather than broad criticisms. Hoare responded that 'I very much wish that we could be more constructive' but 'I have no useful suggestions to make.' He argued that setting maximum stocks was 'fallacious, and the fact that we have not been able to suggest a better method does not render us any the less critical of this one.'[92]

The UK delegation entered the 1953 Conference hoping to obtain US and French support to remove the maximum stocks framework. They recognised this would leave the Draft Protocol looking 'even more bare' and that they would need some replacement provisions. The UK suggested 'international inspections' as a means to improving controls within producer countries. The UK did not expect producer countries to go beyond inspection with consent, but this would be 'better than nothing'.[93] The US sought to draw a red line, demanding that denial of a PCOB request would begin an automatic embargo process. Countries, particularly in Latin America, objected to these, unsurprisingly, on grounds of sovereignty.[94]

Morlock, at the State Department, concluded 'that the British Government desires to save its opium and opium alkaloids trade and will use the protocol to that end'. He and Anslinger decided to reject a preliminary conference with the British and instead turn to French delegate Charles Vaille. Vaille and Anslinger did not believe that their maximum stocks proposal would solve global overproduction. However, their goal was to institute systems of national monitoring and control within producer countries and then springboard to production limitations. The key was to 'give power to' the PCOB 'and allow it also to certify (verify) the adequacy of national control'. Vaille agreed that 'the British government will not be of much help to us with this protocol' and would simply throw up new complaints 'ad infinitum'. They decided to forcibly override UK concerns and push through an agreement.[95] What they underestimated was how far UK concerns represented a relatively broad middle ground of opinion which London had in many ways begun to assume a leadership role of.

The Opium Protocol Conference met in May 1953 in New York. Following Vaille's lead, the US and its allies drove through a divisive agreement over all opposition from key manufacturing and producing states.[96] Despite softening many of the provisions they disliked, the UK maintained it provided no 'means by which any substantial limitation of production can be effected'. The agreement also retained a closed list of producers. Instead of four, seven countries – Bulgaria, Greece, India, Iran, the Soviet Union, Turkey and Yugoslavia – could legally export opium. It also included a generous maximum stocks provision set at two years' worth of supplies. The UK maintained it was an unnecessary infringement on national sovereignty and that the PCOB would be unable to uncover excesses as the US and French hoped.[97]

Producers would submit estimates of cultivation areas and amounts harvested, as well as all other relevant statistics around opium production, trade and seizures. The DSB would oversee these estimates and could amend them with the consent of governments concerned. In the case of non-provision, the PCOB would be empowered to generate estimates. It could request an inspection, but only with the consent and collaboration of the government concerned. It could also impose either recommended or mandatory embargoes on the import and export of opium for countries to implement. An embargo could also be imposed on states not parties to the Protocol. States could appeal to an Appeals Committee appointed by the president of the International Court of Justice.[98]

The UK highlighted the provisions for international inspection as potentially having the most impact. However, producers and other states had already rejected them, and they appeared in the final draft thanks only to Vaille's political railroading. The UK argued that altering them to 'any form in which they would meet the objections which have been raised by these countries' would mean losing 'their effectiveness'. The Protocol was acknowledged as an 'interim agreement', administered by the PCOB, pending the Single Convention. Anslinger was quick to highlight that the Protocol finally mandated states to limit all opium use to 'exclusively medical and scientific purposes'. Seeking to galvanise support, he portrayed this as a seismic shift in international control and, as the president of the conference called it, 'the culmination of 44 years of international effort'. Temporary reservations for 'quasi-medical' use for up to fifteen years were made by India and Pakistan. Meanwhile, producers were committed to establishing government monopolies and strictly controlling areas of production. The Protocol also extended controls to the 'inflammatory' issue of poppy straw, mandating production controls and the supply of statistics for the first time.[99]

Initially it received nineteen signatories but required twenty-five ratifications, including three producers and three manufacturers. The Soviet Bloc boycotted the conference and refused to sign, ostensibly out of deference to the Single Convention process. This was spun in the US press as being motivated by deference to the PRC. Whether the Protocol would be ratified by a sufficient number of states remained an open question. The key would be securing producing states, and Anslinger quickly turned to the State Department to begin pressuring Turkey and Iran.[100]

6.10 Conclusion

The rocky road to the 1953 Opium Protocol highlighted the underlying economic and political forces preventing accord. The US and France had expended enormous political capital pushing the agreement through and had alienated many states, most of whom seemed set to reject it. The UK had successfully sat on the sidelines and watched early iterations collapse under their own weight, before becoming a gradually more active opponent. The US and France would now be forced into the background in the coming decade, while the UK took a new invigorated lead as the chief moderate state, pushing through a consensus agreement for the Single Convention as a replacement and successor to the divisive 1953 Opium Protocol.

The Steinig affair had a long-lasting impact on the UN and ushered a 'coming of age' in CND–Secretariat relations. The naturalised US citizen of Jewish Austrian origins who, with the help of Anslinger, had escaped Nazi-occupied Europe and contributed to the survival of the PCOB and DSB in Washington, had drastically overreached in his position as DND director and destroyed his career. Member states would remain vigilant against future technocratic overreach and to ensure that CND remained the driver of policy over the Secretariat.

The UK and US had worked well to quietly kill the monopoly idea. However, London's unsupportive attitude to the Protocol convinced the State Department to turn towards France in order to salvage some international agreement. This coincided with the return of Anslinger to the helm after his focus on domestic survival. The moderate approach taken by the State Department towards the monopoly soon gave way to a reassertive Anslinger. In a repeat of the 1930s, the US took an increasingly aggressive role at CND and was willing to alienate other states to ensure the 1953 Protocol prevailed. This, however, was contingent on maintaining their core ally in France, something which, as we shall see, was unsustainable.

The UK, always distrustful of Vaille's goals and methods, was happy to place itself in opposition to his work. Nevertheless, had the UK taken a less obstructive position regarding the Protocol, resulting in the US concluding they were thwarting any agreement out of deference to pure economic interest, the two may have formed a governing coalition within CND which could have replaced the old Anslinger–Sharman alliance. With Sharman out of the picture and the UK carving out a pragmatic self-interested role, the US turned to Vaille and continued to press ahead with its own prerogatives, ignoring consensus opinion. The opportunity for continued British–US cooperation on this issue was apparent during this time. The eventual failure to realise it would mark a split in relations between the two that would continue over the coming decade, culminating in the US rejecting its own brainchild, the Single Convention, and going to diplomatic war with moderate states.

Ultimately, the Protocol would rise and fall on British–US support. The US, as the single largest market for opium, had killed the opium monopoly by withdrawing its support. Similarly, the 1953 Protocol made it through the conference on the back of the US and guided by French diplomatic manoeuvring. Whether the Protocol would achieve international assent remained an open question. Producers hated the document, moderate states disliked the process that resulted in its creation, and the world's largest exporter of opium products, the UK, remained fundamentally unsupportive. Whether states would unify behind the Protocol or let it die in lieu of the Single Convention would largely be determined by the actions of Britain and the US above all else. It is towards the Single Convention we now turn.

7

From the 1953 Protocol to the 1961 Single Convention

7.1 Introduction

1953–64 represented a period when the international drug system became more polarised. It was also a time when Britain's loss of great power status became increasingly clear. Efforts around the Single Convention ran alongside continuing issues including Sino–US relations in the aftermath of the Korean War; the changing relationship between the British Empire and South-East Asian opium producers; and Anglo–US concerns over the Middle East, particularly Britain's relationship with opium producers in the Baghdad pact before and after the Suez crisis. These issues did not play out in isolation from drug diplomacy, but instead saw much overlap. Furthermore, the role of agency and intra-bureaucratic interaction continued to be a significant determinant of outcomes.

Minor Anglo–American cooperation in the aftermath of the 1953 Opium Conference gave way to divisions leading to an eventual rupture over the Single Convention. There is no overarching economic systemic case for why a '*pax-manufacturica*' or a '*pax-anti-producerica*' did not arise. London certainly would have welcomed it, as would many in the US foreign policy establishment. The explanation, nevertheless, lies with US–UK policy differences – the US pursued a highly restrictive commodity control agreement underpinned by expansive prohibitionist provisions; the UK pursued a consensual and mildly restrictive framework. Further, the breakdown of the US domestic drug consensus and fracturing into different power centres weakened Anslinger's leadership, while he struggled against a backdrop of collapsing personal circumstances and caring for his dying wife.

The US found itself increasingly alone in negotiations. State Department leadership drove a more conciliatory approach towards producers like Iran and Afghanistan. Nevertheless, with Anslinger absent and a lack of institutional knowledge within the State Department, the

US struggled to articulate its position, let alone a grand drug strategy. Anslinger did not help them. He refused to relinquish control and worked remotely to ensure divided US delegations. Often Anslinger circumvented the State Department through allies, particularly France's Charles Vaille. Nevertheless, Anslinger's own hand was weakened by the new DND Director Gilbert Yates, who drove his own vision for the UN system away from the traditionalist power centre around Anslinger, the soon to be absent Sharman, and the highly divisive Vaille. The UK, continuing to carve out a role of quiet, consensual and self-interested diplomacy, found the new environment more conducive to their approach and thus became increasingly assertive.

All of this was cemented by the personal decline of Anslinger. His domestic position never fully recovered from the 1951 reorganisation attempt. Other branches worked assiduously to highlight the flaws in his PRC bashing and to repair relations with Britain and other counterparts. The US domestic addiction terrain also shifted beneath his feet. His traditional constituencies withered, while new, critical, public health constituencies emerged and relished any opportunity to challenge the FBN, its chief and their repressive approach to addiction. A new Whitehouse Executive Committee increased oversight of his agency, while UN processes became so fractured and complex that he could no longer simply run events via his traditional levers. Absent Anslinger, and eventually Vaille, control advocates had no one capable to act as a counterweight to the loud, relentless and disruptive Turkish delegate Dr Majhar Ozkol.[1] In this environment, moderates and consensus-based policy reigned supreme. The real alternate to US leadership remained the UK. London worked with shifting coalitions as needed, while building a moderate bloc of manufacturing states in Europe to help protect shared national interests.

7.2 Beyond the 1953 Protocol

The tumultuous 1953 Conference left drug diplomacy in mild disarray. The US, fearing backsliding, continued to push for signatures of the Protocol. Its Embassies in Tehran and Ankara were asked to pressure the Iranian and Turkish governments.[2] The UK, meanwhile, disliked the Opium Protocol and saw it as a product of Vaille's bullying. They noted in 1954 that 'some delegations had neither forgotten nor forgiven his performance at the Opium conference.'[3] Others viewed the process as dead in the water. Sharman privately remarked that if the single convention was not discussed at all during the 1954 CND Session his 'heart would not be broken'. Sharman also thought memories of Vaille's behaviour could undermine their efforts and hoping 'that Vaille demotes himself from Sergeant Major to Corporal . . . in his arbitrary manner of running things as happened at the Opium Conference'.[4]

Further, the goals for the Single Convention remained unclear. Members of the PCOB and DSB had mixed feelings. They admitted complexity was a downside to the system, but doubted the timing given uncertainties over the impact of synthetic drugs.[5] Most agreed that the PCOB and DSB should be merged into one body – what would become the International Narcotics Control Board (INCB) – but there was no consensus on its functions. Most expected that its role and powers would not be greatly enlarged.[6] Herbert May warned the 'mandatory embargo as applied to opium in the 1953 Protocol would be likely to reduce rather than strengthen the Board's real power, by investing it with an authority which it is unlikely to be able to use effectively.' Regarding production control, May advocated for flexibility, rather than formulae, in determining 'where it considers stocks excessive', pointing out that in 'twenty-six years of the existence of the Board, this power has never been abused'.[7] The INCB Secretariat remained a controversial issue. The DND pushed for control, but some member states, with Leon Steinig's monopoly debacle still fresh in their memories, demanded absolute independence.[8]

Anslinger had clear goals for the Single Convention: incorporate the 1953 Protocol provisions around opium; extend strong production controls to coca and cannabis; expand the mandate of the proposed INCB; and advocate for a strict 'closed institutional' model for treating drug 'addiction'.[9] The UK wanted none of those things and doubted the feasibility of the entire Single Convention project. However, faced with the 1953 Protocol as the alternative, London threw its weight behind the Single Convention and focused on incorporating British interests and goals.

The US, meanwhile, maintained their push for a quick drive towards coca control and the prohibition of coca chewing. On this latter point they met a continued disinterest from the Peruvian delegate who failed to show up for the entire 1953 Session.[10] Neither Peru nor Bolivia submitted any coca production statistics to the PCOB in 1952.[11] Late in 1953, however, the government of Peru signalled it could 'revise' its position on the Coca Commission report.[12] By 1955, both Bolivia and Peru accepted the Commission's findings that coca chewing was injurious to health and were willing to gradually suppress production and consumption.

As states approached the 1955 CND Session, the US over-optimistically noted that 'astonishing progress' had been made over the previous few session with 'no deadlock' on key issues.[13] This statement highlighted the increasing tin ear within US policy circles around actual events in CND.

7.3 Shifting Power and the New Producers Bloc

In 1954, the Turkish CND delegation underwent a change in leadership with the death of the moderate Dr Cemalettin Or.[14] Soon, producing states emerged in a more forceful and coherent bloc, led by the outspoken Turkish delegate Dr Majhar Ozkol whom the UK described as a 'singularly tenacious nuisance'. He hounded manufacturing states about the dangers of synthetic narcotics and pushed for their strict control. Manufacturer bloc disunity increasingly worried the UK delegation, which argued in 1954 that it was 'uncomfortably easy' for producer states to gain a majority through a reliable nucleus of India, Iran, Turkey, Yugoslavia and on occasion Egypt and France (the manufacture of all synthetic drugs was prohibited in France with the exception of pethadine).[15]

Seeking to counter this emerging balance of power, London made initial overtures to the US centred on precursor chemicals. Whereas previous US policy was for strong pre-emptive controls of precursors they increasingly sought to block controls due to global licit opium shortages, increased military demand and pressure from domestic manufacturers not to stifle innovation.[16] London similarly feared pre-emptive controls would stifle innovation, new markets and even the prospect of a more controllable form of pain medicine replacing opium. The Home Office sought Anslinger's support:

> we think that the time has come to take a firm stand against the opium producers' campaign against synthetic drugs and to make it clear that we will not tolerate attempts to draw distinctions which have no medical or scientific foundation.[17]

The Home Office also pointed out that Turkey and Yugoslavia would not have been able to cause such 'mischief' without the support of Vaille. They suggested Anslinger approach Vaille and highlight the dangers to the success of the Single Convention project if manufacturing countries became alienated by anti-synthetic provisions, noting that Vaille was 'far more likely to listen to you than to us'.[18]

Anslinger professed to being 'unalterably opposed' to 'discrimination' in favour of natural opium. He also rolled back on US calls for precursor chemical control, questioning the practicability of available proposals, 'including our own'. The UK concurred, arguing they 'would be wholly impractical and we could not accept it'. Anslinger sought to maintain UK support and keep his ally Vaille out of discussions. He promised the UK, 'we are substantially in accord with your position on synthetics' and privately remarked that the US should 'go along with [the UK] as far as possible'.[19]

Eventually, the issue lost steam. CND became desensitised to Turkish sensationalism, particularly as evidence suggested synthetics made up only a fraction of the illicit trade. As the UK delegate put it, 'the heat which this subject used to generate gradually seems to be dying down.'[20]

Soon after the 1953 Conference, Anslinger's decades-long alliance with Sharman ended. Sharman retired, following a steady decline in his domestic position, and was replaced by Kenneth Hossick, a less substantive delegate who appeared more interested in his personal prestige, leading Anslinger to refer to him to as '[t]hat silly Hossick'.[21] Few in London would miss Sharman. One UK delegate described him as having 'the biased rigidity of a closed mind obsessed with the purely police aspect of the problem'.[22] His ousting was a significant blow to Anslinger, who wrote in 1954 that US efforts were 'injured ... deeply by your decision to retire'.[23] With the full decline of Sharman, Canadian policies moderated sharply, while Ottawa moved quickly towards the UK's moderate bloc.[24]

Anslinger would continue to work with Vaille to push a strict control framework and maintain their 'good custom of being in agreement on everything'.[25] The UK saw Vaille as 'brilliant, dynamic and utterly unscrupulous'.[26] Worsening domestic positions, however, undermined both Anslinger and Vaille's freedom of action and would eventually knock Vaille out altogether. Nevertheless, a more nuanced picture of cooperation emerges when we look to the interactions between the UK and the US in other areas of geopolitics that overlapped with drug diplomacy. It is towards some of these areas which we shall now turn.

7.4 Drug Control in Asia

Following a positive domestic response to his speech at CND in 1953, Anslinger decided to use the PRC conspiracy claim again at the 1954 Session. He laid out details of 'a 20-year plan to finance political activities and spread addiction among free peoples'. The speech was repeated on the floor of the House of Representatives by James E. Van Zandt of

Pennsylvania. Federal Bureau of Investigation (FBI) Director John Edgar Hoover privately dismissed the claims, highlighting that 'no evidence has been found to confirm them.' Anslinger nevertheless sought Japanese support and substantiation. FBN Agent Wayland Speer criticised Japan's 1953 report for failing to sufficiently highlight Communist China as the source of heroin which 'has literally flooded Japan'. The US offered to support Japan's Narcotics Section, sending an observer to the 1954 CND Session, but only 'if he will blast communist China'. Speer had other reasons for the invitation. He wanted to protect the FBN linkage to Japan's Ministry of Welfare and 'prevent other Ministries from gaining a tight hold on narcotics control and narcotic reporting in Japan—as they had before World War II'. Simultaneously, policy transfer from the US continued, as the Japanese Narcotic Section sought to emulate US domestic drug law enforcement techniques and judicial practices.[27]

Many of the seizures that Anslinger attributed to the PRC transhipped through Hong Kong. London was anxious to deflect attention and requested Anslinger to refer to US–Hong Kong anti-trafficking cooperation during the 1954 session. Anslinger obliged, praising Hong Kong authorities for having 'acted vigorously' resulting in 'a noticeable trend towards bypassing this area whenever possible with shipments to other free countries'.[28] The UK was greatly relieved, particularly as a recent Interpol report had criticised Hong Kong. Furthermore, there had been chatter at CND about the 'large number of British ships involved' in recent seizures.[29] The UK delegate speculated that the 'friendly support' from Anslinger who was 'more cooperative than previously' was 'no doubt because of our [own] co-operation'.[30]

UK drug concerns at this time centred on Hong Kong, Singapore and Malaya primarily, while Burma remained in their field of vision. Relations with the nationalist Chinese delegation were strained as they continued to draw unwanted attention to Hong Kong. London saw the nationalists' 1954 report as 'mischief-making' and instructed delegates that it be 'sharply refuted'.[31] The UK steered clear of the conspiracy debate where possible, stating, 'we have no information on the question of complicity of the People's Republic in traffic which is known to be large, though we know that Nationalist forces were engaged in it some time ago.'[32]

The PRC maintained Anslinger's claims were 'slanderous' and 'a fabrication from start to finish'. The State Department became increasingly uneasy. Initially many 'assumed that [Anslinger] has the necessary evidence', but soon internal opposition strengthened. Many questioned whether it would serve 'any constructive purpose' or merely cause 'offense to certain friendly governments', particularly when there was 'no corrobatory information available'. They left it to Anslinger's discretion, and at the 1955 Session he reiterated claims that Communist Chinese was the 'uncontrolled reservoir supplying the world-wide illicit narcotics traffic'.[33]

By the 1956 CND Session, the State Department was rolling back support for the Republic of China. They recognised Formosa's report was 'propagandistic in tone and contains assertions which [are] obviously untrue'. Even Anslinger was critical. The US delegate was authorised to publicly query its factual basis, while maintaining their PRC assertions so as not 'discredit' past US statements. The UK believed the principal source of smuggling to be the Chinese nationalists, particularly the remnants of Chiang Kai-Shek's army around Thailand. The US CND delegates noted that the UK, Canada and others were clearly 'relieved' that the US only gave 'perfunctory support' to Formosa at the 1956 session. Further, they recognised a growing sympathy for inviting a Peking government official as an observer to the CND.[34] The rollback of US support produced a reciprocal cooling of Formosa's support for US goals and thereby weakened another pillar of Anslinger's old CND alliance. As Anslinger's alliance slipped away, the Soviet Union was quickly becoming the swing vote at CND.

London, meanwhile, had accumulated significant intelligence on the illicit traffic in Burma, Cambodia, Thailand and Laos but was unwilling to share it with the UN Illicit Traffic Committee for fear of compromising their sources.[35] This traffic passed through Thailand and on to Hong Kong, Malaya and Singapore, causing considerable embarrassment for authorities. Worse, the UK's own intelligence confirmed Thai assertions that a significant portion originated in the Burmese Shan states, which might 'be the largest source of illicit opium in the world'.[36]

Despite this evidence, the UK maintained strong sympathy for the Burmese authorities.[37] Burma offered no cooperation with CND, refusing even to send an observer until 1960 when one 'put in an appearance' in what the UK would view as an 'encouraging sign'.[38] Nevertheless, the UK's representatives protected them from criticism. For example, even as cannabis seizures on British vessels (originating in Rangoon) began to throw unwanted light on British shipping interests, London remained concerned with deflecting some of Thailand's accusations against Burma.[39] Anslinger's preoccupation with the PRC left Britain free to plead ignorance or agnosticism as to the opium's origin while displacing blame onto Thailand as a transhipment point.[40] UK officials repeatedly castigated Thailand as endemically corrupt and incapable of living up to its international obligations.[41]

Due to reports of large illicit smuggling activities in Thailand, the Thai government were requested to send an observer to the 1956 session. The UK sought US support for its criticisms, but Washington refused. The US delegate was authorised to ask questions, but was warned:

> However serious the opium situation in Thailand appears to be ... the U.S. Representative should bear in mind that Thailand is friendly to the United States. It is desirable to avoid unduly strong charges of laxness on the part of the Thai Government ... which might affect that friendly relationship.[42]

Nevertheless, both the UK and US maintained something of a functional relationship over East and South East Asia in the early 1950s. The US would help overlook British colonial and ex-colonial complications, while London didn't overly challenge the US propaganda campaign against the PRC.

7.5 Drug Diplomacy in the Middle East

In 1955, Iran adopted legislation completely banning opium cultivation. CND delegates viewed questions of economic and technical assistance as 'certain to arise' in the 1956 Session. The US tried to be supportive, noting that the FBN had spent roughly $130,000 a year on overseas illicit traffic operations, giving the US a 'direct financial interest' in efforts to ban production.[43] The issue raised broader complications for US policy but also embarked the UN on a new trajectory of technical assistance in transitioning beyond illicit drug crops.

Many delegations remained sceptical, given past claims, but the US argued Iran was serious this time and, of key importance, the Shah supported the efforts. Further, they warned a lack of UN support would 'play into the hands' of the economic beneficiaries of the opium trade.[44] The US frequently rejected compensating countries to follow their opium commitments, but on other occasions proved willing to dangle technical assistance as a carrot. Now, the State Department saw it as a means to increase influence and encourage control in Iran, but also potentially Thailand and others. Balancing against this, they wished to avoid creating new technical assistance programmes within the UN and pushed instead for earmarking drug funding within existing programmes.

To postpone and deflate the issue in 1956, the US ensured CND pushed it up to ECOSOC. ECOSOC then suggested support come from existing UN technical assistance programmes. The US hoped that this would place them on record as supporting Iran and avoid alienating governments concerned with additional expense and proliferating UN activities, such as the UK. The US delegate noted after the 1956 CND Session that the 'efforts to bring United Nations technical assistance concepts to bear in the field of narcotics control constituted perhaps the most useful work' of the session.[45]

Meanwhile the Anglo–American divergence over the 1953 Protocol's 'closed list' of producers became live over Afghanistan. London had rejected a closed list fearing a cartel of producer states.[46] The US, and particularly Anslinger, was strongly in favour of a small, closed list. The faux 'compromise' in 1953 expanded the list from four to seven but maintained a cap. It included Yugoslavia, Iran, Turkey, India, Bulgaria, Greece and the USSR.

Iran's prohibition decree, however, coincided with an Afghan policy shift. By 1954, Afghanistan was looking to expand its role in the licit opium market. The US Embassy in Kabul reported the government encouraging cultivation and successfully marketed crops to Germany and Italy, along with 'reports of substantial shipments to Russia'.[47] In 1955, Afghanistan asked to join the 1953 Protocol as an official producer. This was despite it having ignored the 1953 Opium Conference and not being a party to the 1925 Opium Convention. Anslinger informed the Afghan delegate that it was too late but that they should join the Protocol, look towards eventual addition to the list and seek technical assistance in the meantime.[48]

The UK foresaw major political complications and hoped to thwart a vote on procedural grounds, specifically that there was no way to amend the list of the 1953 Protocol before it came into force. Should they fail, Mr Green, the UK CND delegate and Home Office bureaucrat, felt the UK should abstain in order to maintain consistency of policy and a sense of equity. The UK had, after all, railed against the closed list and Afghanistan had 'at least as good a claim to be included in the list . . . as Greece'.[49] The Foreign Office took a sharply broader perspective and sought 'the cavalry', or ministerial assistance, in reining in the intransigent Green.[50]

Iran by this point was increasingly acknowledged as making a serious and expensive effort to eradicate their opium trade.[51] Afghan opium 'flooding' in would undermine these efforts.[52] For the UK Foreign

Office, the consequences of anything less than total support for Iran became clear after the 1956 CND, when both the US and UK were believed to have voted in favour of Afghanistan. The US delegation had brokered a compromise resolution, with UK support and French abstention, recognising the justice of the Afghan claim and looking towards including Afghanistan in the list of recognised producers in the Single Convention.[53] Iranian fury soon came to the attention of the UK's secretary of state, who instructed the UK's ECOSOC delegation to try to rehabilitate UK–Iranian relations.[54]

The Foreign Office now worried that a UK abstention would be interpreted as 'support for Afghanistan and her friends ... the Soviet Union'.[55] Above all, the Foreign Office feared that it would cause embarrassment to the secretary of state at the upcoming Baghdad Pact Council and 'might even have a generally adverse effect on the proceedings'.[56] The Baghdad Pact represented the foundation of the UK's Middle East strategy at the time, and anything which threatened it was to be avoided.[57] Furthermore, they thought it 'most important, *particularly at the present time* [emphasis added], to stand loyally by one of our associates in the Bagdad Pact'.[58] This, however, did not sway the Home Office, which refused to change the instruction to Green.[59] They were concerned that a loss of UK credibility would weaken their ability to withstand efforts by France and others to impose stricter controls on synthetics.[60]

Anslinger was implacably opposed to Afghanistan's claim, arguing that there was no need for another producer given global overproduction. Further he pointed to Afghanistan's non-compliance with past agreements and the potential impact on the Iranian illicit market. The State Department sought a middle ground: Afghanistan was free to produce opium under the current system and could continue 'so long as the 1953 Protocol is not operative.' They offered five reasons for US support: to prevent the adverse effects of prohibition on Afghanistan's economy; that the amount produced in Afghanistan was limited and of high quality; the absence of evidence that it was leaking into the illicit traffic; Afghanistan's right to equal treatment; and that crop substitution in Afghanistan was 'not immediately practicable'.[61]

The State Department overruled Anslinger and maintained US policy was to support Afghanistan but would reconsider if evidence 'demonstrated incontrovertibly' negative impacts on Iran.[62] Anslinger set to work uncovering the evidence and raising it at CND. Charles Vaille was similarly opposed, although was unable to throw full French diplomatic weight behind the opposition. He wrote to Anslinger that he was 'desolated by the lamentable attitude' of the State Department and argued it could 'torpedo Iranian resolve' and was capable of 'destroying all that we have difficultly obtained'. He and Anslinger postponed work on the Single Convention and redoubled ratification efforts on the 1953 Protocol, focusing on Turkey, Iran and Greece.[63]

Anslinger privately encouraged Vaille to challenge US policy at the 1956 Session. It took place in Geneva and Anslinger failed to attend, attempting instead to control events via proxies. Vaille led arguments against Afghanistan's admission, while India, seeking a wedge issue between Pakistan and its neighbour, led arguments in favour. Vaille launched a tirade against the US delegation, accusing them of working to increase global overproduction. The US delegate concluded that Vaille and Iran 'had come to some tacit agreement'. When Vaille left, the US delegate demanded correction of the summary record and the remaining French delegate, apparently embarrassed by Vaille's behaviour, quickly agreed.[64]

In the meantime, the UK Foreign Office had gained the upper hand on Green. They discovered that the US delegation remained ambivalent into the 1957 Session and contacted the State Department to express the hope that 'in no circumstances' should the US vote against Iran.[65] The State Department agreed to follow the UK's lead in postponing the issue until the 1958 Session.[66] In the end they were helped by a counterproductive lobbying effort by the Afghan observer which alienated a number of delegations.[67] Anslinger, meanwhile, had ensured new information on the Afghan illicit trade to Iran emerged, causing many to question the accuracy of the Afghan delegate's information.[68]

By 1958, the Afghan issue was resolved through US and DND actions. The head of DND, Gilbert Yates, made a visit to Afghanistan prior to the 1958 CND Session and was expected to recommend technical assistance. Afghanistan had agreed to withdraw its request to be considered a producer, and the US agreed to introduce a CND resolution favouring UN technical assistance. Further, if the 1953 Protocol went into effect, the US promised to give careful consideration to an application by Afghanistan to be included.[69] With this key stumbling block out of the way, forward momentum on the Single Convention once against became possible. The episode nevertheless highlighted continued volatility around the 'closed list' and the danger that the 1953 Protocol and Single Convention project could collapse in the face of national interests.

7.6 Deepening British–US Fault Lines

The early cooperation over Asia suggested an British–US drug alliance was possible during this period, even if it would require substantial compromise and coordination. As time progressed, however, it became less likely as the UK lost faith in the competence of US CND delegations. Policy fault lines between the two states at CND only exacerbated this. Ultimately, these divisions were to widen, as the erratic US performances at the 1957 and 1958 Conferences marked a breaking point in British–US post-war drug diplomacy.

One of the most noticeable divisions emerged over the relocation of the UN Drug Secretariat, DND. A broad UN decentralisation programme planned to move DND to Geneva where the Secretariat of the DSB and PCOB was already set up.[70] Part of the impetus arose from DND efforts to absorb the DSB and PCOB Secretariats.[71] Anslinger had opposed it, but the programme received the unanimous consent from the General Assembly, where the US delegation had remained silent, believing Anslinger's opposing arguments too weak.[72] In 1955, the UK sensed 'agitation' by US domestic groups against the move.[73] They UK entered the 1955 CND prepared to reverse their support should the US raise objections. The US delegation appeared 'divided amongst themselves' and Anslinger failed to raise the matter.[74] Consequently the move was accepted, and the UK considered the issue settled. Further, the UK sought a reputation for thrift at CND and became extremely supportive of the measure once adopted.[75]

Anslinger remained deeply opposed. He feared it would lead to the integration of the secretariats under DND and remove drug control from the New York media spotlight. He mobilised his traditional domestic constituencies, and the issue quickly assumed a narrative of international communist conspiracy. Soon the British Labour Party became implicated. Clement Atlee's visit to China was portrayed as part of a joint British and French 'plot' to encourage Turkey to introduce a resolution recognising Communist China into the UN General Assembly. Soon newspapers reported a conspiracy to remove 'Red China's depravity and its dope running' from the watchful eyes of US politicians and press in New York. The ultimate goal, they argued, was 'a psychological build-up for the recognition and entry of China to the UN'. Anslinger bragged that the New York press had hammered away at the Communist Chinese 'to the point where Chou-En-Lai found it necessary to discuss the situation with Mr. Atlee'. Britain had introduced a resolution to transfer the UN Narcotics Laboratory to Geneva soon after Atlee had come out of that meeting, claiming 'China had clean hands in the narcotic trade'. This played right into Anslinger's narrative.[76]

Ultimately, the State Department refused to push the matter at ECOSOC or the General Assembly, believing that it was not 'important enough to involve US prestige in' either body. Anslinger then failed in his last-ditch appeal to the UN secretary general in 1955 to stop the move.[77] Undaunted, Anslinger maintained his anti-Geneva stance. In 1956, he failed to attend the CND Session in Geneva. The UK privately lamented the loss of the 'firmness' he brought to debates. The State Department told a Foreign Office delegate that the administration was under strong pressure from domestic groups to host CND in New York in 1957 and they had a 'very real need of UK help on this question'.[78] Anslinger got his way and served as chairman for the session but appalled the UK delegation with an incompetent and aggressive performance. He then failed to turn up in Geneva in 1958, where he should have served his second year as chairman. This time, however, his absence was not lamented.[79]

The US then shocked the British by tabling a resolution to hold the 1959 Session in New York. Their justification was a loophole allowing for 'exceptional circumstances'. London called the US resolution 'outrageous' and instructing that it 'be opposed vigorously'. Other CND delegations, however, did not share British concerns about costs and they voted for New York.[80] ECOSOC ultimately rejected the recommendation and the 1959 Commission met in Geneva. Anslinger failed to attend, and the US again tabled a similar resolution which saw the UK as the sole dissenter, and which went on again to fail at ECOSOC.[81] By 1960, the matter appeared to have been dropped. However, by this stage it had become one of a number of divisions between the UK and US delegations. The issue of addiction treatment was another.

As the 1950s progressed, Anslinger's 'closed institution' approach to addiction came under increasing domestic attack. Mounting evidence pointed to the failure of the federal narcotic farms in Lexington and Fort Worth.[82] A new understanding of addiction was emerging among mental health professionals in the US. Many had served in the narcotics farms and watched with dismay as supposed treatment centres were effectively transformed into prisons.[83] Anslinger's domestic 'enemies' looked overseas for counterexamples to the US model. Front and centre was the 'British system'.[84] Continually prodded by US sources on this approach, Anslinger sent a furious letter to his Home Office counterpart.

He chastised the UK for sending encouraging letters to 'eggheads and crackpots in the United States':

> I have tried a number of times to get your people to restrain their remarks to our enemies, and I hope you will see that, in the future, visiting Americans will not be given information which encourages them to attack my Government.[85]

Other Anslinger allies in the US called discussions around the 'British system' 'reminiscent of the Hitler "Big-Lie"'. It was claimed that the British system was not different from the US, except that the UK law allowed for ambulatory maintenance in exceptional cases.[86] The culmination of domestic pushback against Anslinger in the 1950s came with the publication of an interim report by the Joint Committee of the American Bar Association and the American Medical Association. The report called for 'ambulatory treatment'. Anslinger waged a domestic war with its authors and findings.[87] Further, Anslinger sought to muster UN treaty law to defend the 'closed institution' model by enshrining it in the new Single Convention.

The UK viewed itself as having no real 'addiction problem' and sought to avoid internationally imposed responsibilities which would be 'unpalatable' to UK medical professionals.[88] Sometimes this involved the UK just acting disinterested. On one day off from the 1957 Commission, Anslinger organised a trip to an institution for juvenile drug 'addicts'. Instead of attending, Green spent the day writing letters.[89] By 1959, the US and UK remained divided, and the issue would come to a head at the Single Convention Plenipotentiary Conference.[90]

7.7 Towards the Single Convention

As the US entered the 1956 Session, some in the State Department believed the Single Convention drafting process was 'approaching completion'. By the end of the session, it had ground to a 'snail's pace' and became 'so hopelessly snarled in draft' that deferring to a Plenipotentiary Conference seemed the only way forward. Anslinger felt the session became 'badly tangled' in his absence and sought to repair some of the damage. He and Vaille agreed to stall the Single Convention in order to resolve issues around Afghanistan and push for ratification of the 1953 Protocol, writing: 'the Afghan and other situations dictate postponing the Single Convention to a more propitious time. Politics and narcotics should not mix.' He argued against holding an extended CND Session in 1957 in New York on grounds of cost and because 'special consideration of the Single Convention at this time is useless.'[91]

Anslinger's traditional CND alliance structure by this point had largely collapsed. The UK attributed the weakness of the manufacturer bloc to the absence of Anslinger, when in reality changes within the system had created the need for a strategic realignment. The system by the late 1950s was working against manufacturer interests, a situation never envisaged by Anslinger and other post-war framers. Pragmatic states would now fall in behind UK leadership to counter this.

Canada had aligned away from the US towards a pragmatic self-interested position, which placed them as a firm ally of the UK. Vaille continued to buttress Anslinger through French support, and Brazil emerged as a regional pillar for Anslinger and the FBN. However, the US State Department rolled back support for the nationalist Chinese delegation and sought to repair relations with the UK over Hong Kong. In 1956 they wrote to the consulate general in Hong Kong offering 'regrets that erroneous reporting of the United States position at the Commission may have caused embarrassment to Hong Kong Enforcement authorities'.[92] This, in turn, alienated the nationalist delegation and weakened their previously unquestioned support for US positions.

Anslinger calibrated his strategy based on a strong alignment with Vaille, while simultaneously working with the UK to undermine Vaille's efforts on synthetics. However, with Anslinger largely absent from CND sessions during the 1950s, moderate states were increasingly happy to let the 1953 Protocol languish and look towards a watered-down Single Convention. Entering the 1957 Session, both the UK and Canada sought to radically change track. Hossick suggested a UK–Canadian idea to Anslinger that the Secretariat prepare a 'simplified Draft' of principles which could then be refined by a small drafting committee. Anslinger sharply refused, claiming it involved 'a completely new start under a new theory' and would 'lose the value of discussion and decisions on principles of control, over the past several years'.[93]

Meanwhile, DSB elections were set for 1957. The State Department hoped for Herbert May to be re-elected, with indications that Canada would nominate him, and the UK would second.[94] Anslinger had other ideas and quietly worked to secure Vaille's appointment. Anslinger later claimed Herbert May had privately stepped aside at his request, but 'the stupid Canadians put forward his name much to his embarrassment.'[95]

The action triggered diplomatic chaos and talk of high-level resignations.[96] The UK noted angrily that the US delegation stayed silent during the CND discussions 'no doubt due to the influence of Anslinger who [was] known to be personally in favour of Vaille's election.'[97] Tensions continued into ECOSOC. The UK and Canada sought an ECOSOC resolution of censure directed at CND. The US State Department agreed with the UK that it was in 'disregard of [an] ECOSOC recommendation' and privately intimated they were 'upset' by the outcome.[98] Brazil's delegate Mr Pentaedo, secretly prompted by Anslinger, made a strong speech in support of Vaille and CND more broadly.[99] The UK concluded that the speech must have 'been written for him by Mr. Anslinger'.[100] Anslinger's involvement with the scheme, coupled with the increasing incoherence of US policy, contributed significantly to the UK losing faith in the US during 1957 to 1958. After this point, they lost interest in working with the US at CND.

Anslinger later wrote to Pentaedo:

> It was evident to us that the Ottawa-London axis would try to pull others into its orbit to attack the Narcotic Commission for the election of Vaille ... I want you to know that the members of the Commission are grateful for the statement that you made.[101]

The victory was short lived as Vaille was soon removed from the French CND delegation, thereby removing Anslinger's last main ally.[102] Ostensibly, Vaille's removal was the result of a promotion to inspector general for health following the collapse of the Fourth Republic in 1958. Some have suggested it was partly a rebuke for his role in international drug policies and particularly his support of the 1953 Protocol.[103] Thereafter, despite vigorous efforts to steer French drug diplomacy, Vaille failed to convince his superiors nor CND replacement of the Protocol's importance. The French delegation began to deprecate the problem of addiction in France as an issue of 'secondary importance'. For example, they claimed that there were only 295 'addicts', 252 of which used cannabis and were of Algerian-Moroccan descent.[104]

The UK continued to hope for a closer relationship with the US right up to 1957, when they made a final overture to Anslinger. The 1954 Session had provided hope, proving 'the best of the three attended by the present UK representative.' Vaille's chairmanship 'although marred by dishonesty ... was extremely competent' and 'relations with Mr. Anslinger, which have always been friendly at the personal level, were much improved as regards practical co-operation.'[105] The

1955 session turned 'disastrous' for the UK. It was characterised by the emergence of Dr Ozkol of Turkey 'as the energetic, ruthless, unscrupulous and triumphant leader of the opium bloc'. The session 'could have been much worse' but for the UK rallying a moderate bloc, which avoided more objectionable proposals.

Increasingly, the UK viewed CND as being 'heavily weighted with an unscrupulous commercial bloc supported by doctrinaire extremists'.[106] The 1956 Session was 'appallingly wearisome' for the UK and the absence of Anslinger resulting in a 'weak and ineffective' US delegation, meaning that attacks by producers often went unanswered.[107] The UK ended the session with a 'bad row' with Ozkol. India, meanwhile, emerged as a potent moderating force, sponsoring watered-down resolutions on synthetics despite resistance from Vaille. The Soviet delegate spoke only Russian and 'took little part in the debates'. The US pointed out that Ozkol fought, 'sometimes to the point of absurdity' and appeared to throw his weight behind the Single Convention as a means to deflect attention from illicit traffic leakages from Turkey.[108]

The UK delegate, Mr Walker, lamented Anslinger's absence from the 1956 Session, while Canada's representative, Kenneth Hossick, was furious, interpreting it as an overt protest at the removal of CND from New York to Geneva.[109] The UK still held out hopes for closer Anglo–American cooperation, but these were thoroughly dashed during 1957 and 1958. In 1957, the UK Foreign Office sent an overture, forwarding comments on the Draft Single Convention to remind the State Department and Anslinger that US and UK interests 'should be fairly close' on synthetics, although the UK quietly believed that the US had 'wobbled in the past'. They hoped the letter would help keep Anslinger 'on the straight path' with the moderate coalition centred on the Federal Republic of Germany, Switzerland, and Canada. Anslinger was 'always very much a law unto himself and … the State Department either cannot, or does not attempt to keep control of him', but London hoped he could be reined in.[110]

The initial response claimed US positions were being re-examined, and London concluded it did 'not seem to have been a complete waste of time'.[111] The optimism proved short-lived as the 1957 CND assembled in New York under Anslinger's chairmanship. The UK delegation viewed his performance as erratic and incompetent. He 'could never refrain from commenting on the remarks of each speaker' and 'invariably omitted to say whether he was speaking as Chairman or as the US representative'. Further, he made it clear that he had not read certain important documents or grasped important issues and 'frequently disregarded the rules of procedure'. The result was 'superficial' and 'confused' discussions, topped by his inexplicable disruption of Canadian attempts to forward work on the Second Draft of the Single Convention.[112]

With the Afghan issue resolved by 1958 and a keen desire for a treaty basis for the 'closed institution' model in the US, Anslinger worked to put the Single Convention back on track. Further, Iran had acceded to the 1953 Protocol. Vaille and Anslinger now worked to bring in Greece, with the expectation that Yugoslavia would follow.[113] It looked as if a final draft of the Single Convention could be completed at the 1958 Session, ready for a Plenipotentiary Conference. Anslinger hoped to secure ratification of the 1953 Protocol in time to be followed by the ratification of a more extensive and similarly strict Single Convention.

The moderate bloc thwarted these goals at the 1958 Session. His wife's deteriorating health, coupled with numerous domestic challenges, and an unwillingness to lend credibility to the Geneva home for CND meant Anslinger was again absent.[114] The US delegation proved disorganised and erratic. The UK described it as a 'heterogeneous' bunch of FBN bureaucrats and State Department officials who were 'clearly under [his] remote control'. The delegation 'seldom spoke unless it had to' and was at a loss when voting on unforeseen matters. Each delegate was 'watching the others and ... no one dares do anything constructive lest [they] ... incur the wrath of Mr. Anslinger'.

The result was that the US 'took little or no part in helping frustrate moves clearly contrary to its interests, and several times abstained or even voted on the wrong side'. Mr Green of the UK initially feared it was 'likely to go down in history as one of the worst sessions on record' if the Americans did not 'get off their fat bottoms and face their responsibilities'. At one point, France passed a resolution (7–5) to censure West Germany for not controlling the synthetic narcotic normethadone. Worse: 'the USA abstained!'[115] The State Department representative later apologised privately for their error. The Foreign Office labelled it 'something of a shambles' and sought contact with the State Department to see if anything could be done before the session ended.[116]

Anslinger attributed tensions to Mr Green being 'new and sticky' and a '31-year-old, uncured ham' who did not belong at CND. As Anslinger wrote: 'Green (UK), the green delegate who has been giving us trouble throughout the meeting, picking up little details and pieces of lint.' The head of the US delegation Mr Tennyson reported back that the

Canadians and British were giving him a rough time and Anslinger set to work 'preparing some counter measures in cooperation with the Department of State'.[117]

A 'battle' developed over the inclusion of a 'closed institution' provision in the draft Single Convention. The US argued that it was not binding but merely 'a principle'. The UK and Canada pushed back strongly. UK opposition was expected, but the US delegation was 'astonished' with the change in Canadian attitude, which had traditionally 'been similar to ours, that no drug addict could be cured by the ambulatory treatment'. Hossick highlighted sources 'emanating' from the US, suggesting alternatives to the 'closed institution' approach. The US managed to sustain the inclusion of a weak provision when it came to a vote, but the issue appeared set to be reopened at the Plenipotentiary Conference.[118]

The US were also furious about the UK being the only objector to including a provision from the 1912 Convention to cater to other US constitutional concerns. Indicative of the worsening relations, the US delegation held a lunch and dinner for friendly delegations, including France, India, Yugoslavia and Turkey. The US delegation refused to invite the UK or Canadian delegations, claiming Anslinger 'would not have approved any invitation to these groups who had certainly not been helpful to us in any way'.[119]

A 'relatively clean' draft of the Single Convention was finally agreed at the 1958 Session, by including many unresolved minority opinions in footnotes. Deep divisions were merely postponed until the Plenipotentiary Conference. The core disagreements remained between producer and transit countries and 'between different juridical systems'. Whether these issues could be ironed out remained an open question.[120]

The 1959 Session proved 'shorter and less eventful', while Anslinger was again absent.[121] The UK noted that the US delegation was led by a State Department official and proved more competent but 'still failed to show any signs of giving leadership'.[122] Meanwhile, presaging a key feature of the Plenipotentiary Conference, the US delegation noted that on issues pitting manufacturing states against producing states, the Soviet delegation 'usually voted with the latter … to curry their favour'.[123]

Vaille, now removed from the process, professed himself 'extremely pessimistic' and worried that the UK-led bloc, believing 'that the Commerce is too constricted', would push to water down the draft. Anslinger similarly worried that 'the old European block will get together and we may lose many of our gains.' Anslinger was infuriated by the outcomes of the 1959 Session. Without himself or Vaille present to steer the 'rudder', he viewed it as descending into backslapping and lowest common denominator agreements. The US delegation was 'anything but satisfactory' and played an increasingly 'defensive' role. He was outraged by a resolution providing implicit support to ambulatory treatment and labelled it 'one of the most unfortunate statements' ever made by CND. He claimed the US delegation 'must have been absent on that day' and that he would 'be unable to distribute it in this country because it provides a lever for those people who want to create free drug areas'. Anslinger determined to reignite his alliance with Vaille and looked to 'brighter days ahead'.[124]

The 1960 Session proved wholly uneventful. The UK had no expectations from the US and their preparation for the 1961 Plenipotentiaries Conference focused on pushing a fundamental rework of the Third Draft of the Single Convention. They were determined to achieve broad consensus, weaken control provisions and remove elements they found objectionable. The UK was not discriminatory in its means, and was willing to rely on Western European, Asiatic and even Soviet support on areas of overlapping interest. London was even open to reaching out to Latin American countries, which they had previously avoided out of deference to the US sphere of interest. The UK had given up on an Anglo–US cooperative effort and was instead focused on making 'every effort to secure a treaty that the great majority of countries' could accept.[125]

Seeking to regain some initiative at CND, Anslinger, through his agent Siragusa, planned to make an extensive statement on the illicit traffic. The UK continued to downplay it, particularly in the Far East, lest it cause further complications for their colonies. Anslinger wanted to send FBN agents to assist the UK in policing the illicit traffic in Hong Kong and sought to pressure, or embarrass, the UK into inviting him.[126] Siragusa, who served on the Illicit Traffic Committee, felt that UK Representative Green (chair of the Committee) was 'avoiding him'. He believed Green, 'a real sly one', as he apparently knew Siragusa wanted 'to button-hole him about Hong Kong'. Green focused on the State Department side of the US delegation. Siragusa concluded that there was 'a conspiracy to foul' the US statement on Hong Kong and that there was a 'Secretariat-Green-Hossick effort designed to suppress my truthful but perhaps offensive remarks against certain countries – my spotlighting of [the] Hong Kong situation'. Siragusa claimed to Anslinger that he tried to include the remarks regardless of the 'conspiracy', but felt he lacked State Department support, writing,

> I work only for you and the Bureau and I couldn't care less about these State Department men but I am afraid that if I try to double-cross Meyer and slip in some remarks . . . I am certain Chase and Rowell would hit the ceiling and blast you and the Bureau.[127]

Lacking State Department acquiescence, Anslinger and his agents began to look to Japan as a base of operations in the region, claiming '[t]he UK's attitude contradicted their obligations under international treaties respecting the question of cooperation . . . they talk out of both sides of their mouth.'[128] Overall, State Department caution prevailed, as they avoided raising delicate trafficking questions which might bring attention to Chinese nationalist entanglements in the illicit trade. The US also promised France 'not to put them on the spot' over South East Asia.[129]

In the Middle East, Syria and Turkey came to blows over allocating blame on the regional origins of the illicit traffic. The US, meanwhile, described continued Iranian suppression efforts as 'heroic'.[130] It was representative of the session, which became a musical chair, as states shifted blame as source and transit points, ultimately producing no tangible outcomes. Anslinger failed to regain the initiative at CND and instead had to look towards the Single Convention negotiations.

7.8 The Single Convention

The 1961 Plenipotentiaries Conference took place from 24 January to 26 March. It received representatives from seventy countries, but meaningful participation was largely restricted to CND members. Novice delegations were surprised to find representatives tearing up the Third Draft, which had been the culmination of ten years of their own work.[131] The UK noted the US delegation was 'very indifferently represented', while still under the 'remote control' of Anslinger. He was putting in only brief appearances, as his wife's terminal illness meant that he had to commute daily to New York from Washington.[132] The UK saw this leadership void as the reason for the US's failure to secure modifications or retain provisions they hoped for. Had they 'been able to adopt a more flexible attitude' they 'might at least have succeeded in salvaging something from the wreckage'. Despite this, the US signed the convention. Anslinger, however, was far from finished with it.

The UK, on the other hand, saw the Convention as the consolidation they had hoped for with the 'more controversial elements watered down into a generally acceptable form'. They had, further, successfully removed Article 32 dealing with the closed list of producers which had also proved widely unacceptable to other delegates.[133] They had achieved a broad consensus and protected their interests. Vaille, meanwhile, had been unable to rally the French delegation in support of the 1953 Protocol.[134]

The producer bloc entered the Plenipotentiary Conference as the main revisionist force, hoping to weaken many of the main control provisions.[135] Led by the Soviet delegation and facilitated by the moderate bloc, states picked apart the Single Convention. The issue of cannabis produced mixed results. There was unanimous agreement to end cultivation except for industrial purposes, as well as an acknowledgement that small amounts would be allowed for scientific purposes. Given that the plant grew wild, and many nations relied on it for industrial purposes, these were to be explicitly exempted from prohibition. Hungary and other nations pushed back strongly against control of poppy straw, arguing it was an agricultural waste product and 'cannot be regarded as a narcotic'.[136] Producer states ultimately prevailed, thereby weakening its immediate economic threat to traditional opium cultivation.[137]

The Soviet bloc worked with manufacturing states, including Switzerland, Canada and the UK, to remove the 'closed list'.[138] The new International Narcotics Control Board (INCB) was expanded to eleven members, with some move towards fusing the CND and INCB Secretariats, although the latter remained purposely vague. The Control Board maintained the right to recommend an embargo, which the US pointed out was 'considerably weaker' than the mandatory embargo provision in the 1953 Protocol. Parties would furnish estimates for requirements and exports and would need to remain within these estimates. INCB could establish estimates for any state which failed to supply them, including non-parties. The US noted that the provisions around estimates and statistics were 'virtually the same as the requirements in the existing treaties', although wide reservation provisions threatened to undermine these. The scheduling system, expanding on the two Schedules of the 1931 Convention, now included four under the same principle of linking degrees of control to the drug's believed 'addicting liability' versus therapeutic benefit ratio.[139]

Parties were permitted reservations around maintaining existing opium smokers in their territories, with no new registration allowed after 1964. Opium eating, or quasi-medical use, was to be abolished within fifteen years of the Convention coming into force. Parties were to establish national agencies to collect opium crops, and cultivation would be restricted to those licensed by the agency. All countries which produced opium for ten years prior to January 1961 could continue to produce opium. Further, any country could produce and export up to 5 tons annually simply by notifying INCB. A country wishing to export more than 5 tons had to notify ECOSOC, which could either approve or simply recommend against it. The US pointed out that this was a 'an entirely different concept' of production limitation than in the 1953 Protocol and was instead,

> a compromise provision resulting from the insistence of the Soviet Bloc, countries in the British Commonwealth, and some African countries that the new countries be permitted to produce and export opium if they so desire.[140]

The Convention recommended that parties prohibit cultivation if they considered it the most adequate method to prevent diversions into the illicit traffic. The US viewed this as providing a 'constitutional basis' for the Opium Poppy Control Act enacted by the US Congress in 1942 should it be challenged in the federal courts.[141] The 1936 Illicit Traffic Convention, which had been poorly subscribed, was the only previous convention not incorporated into the Single Convention. Instead, it included a weak and 'tenuous recommendatory type provision' on penalties for traffickers and extradition. It was due to the weakness of this provision that many states already parties to the 1936 Convention demanded the convention be kept in force.[142]

The Single Convention controlled coca cultivation under the same mechanisms as opium cultivation, while it included a special provision to protect the Coca Cola Company's access to non-alkaloid coca leaves used for flavouring. Meanwhile, states permitting chewing of coca leaf agreed to abolish the practice within twenty-five years of the Convention coming into force. Similar provisions applied to cannabis, with the exception of cannabis for industrial purposes (fibre and seed) or horticultural purposes.[143]

Driven by Soviet demands, reservations were permitted to specified articles around the application of the system of estimates and statistics. Reservations to other articles could be made with the support of two-thirds of ratified states. The US noted that no reservations were permitted to the 1953 Protocol, barring provisional reservations around opium smoking and eating as well as coca leaf chewing.[144]

The US had squeezed language around compulsory treatment in a 'closed institution' into the third draft. In negotiations, this was strongly watered down so as to recommend, for those with serious problems, to provide adequate treatment facilities, if they had the economic means to do so. Anslinger viewed this as having 'no value'. In particular, he blamed the Holy See, which raised objection to the words 'civil commitment' as Anslinger commented, 'due to their fears that this would be used against the Cardinals and Bishops in the Iron Curtain countries'. He continued: 'I don't think the Communists need anything like this if they want to throw somebody in jail.' He was also furious that the 'Holy See Delegation sat there for nine weeks not uttering a word and when they had something to say didn't have the common decency to consult us.'[145]

Anslinger wrote to Vaille on 3 March, 'the Soviet bloc has just about destroyed the Single Convention. They have won on nearly every point.' The closed list would be supplanted by an amendment, 'peddled by Canada', allowing any country to export up to 5 tons without notifying the INCB. Vaille described it as a 'disaster'. Both argued the open list of producers would create an open global market, drive up supplies, down prices and potentially flood the illicit market. Overall, they believed it 'set back international control of narcotics fifty years'.[146]

Gilbert Yates and the DND secretariat argued that '" something" is better than "nothing"'. Anslinger argued that this 'something may even be worse than the nothing'.[147] As the Conference drew to a close the US dug in its heels around reservations but had not yet come to the point of open intransigence. Anslinger publicly professed willingness to allow some reservations, to satisfy the Soviets, provided they did not 'open the floodgates'. He even professed some propaganda benefit in having the Soviets on record as opposing certain provisions via reservations. By the 18th of March Anslinger left the Conference giving the impression he would push the US towards signature. He argued he needed to place the final document before the President's Committee on Narcotics and secure their ascent before it could be sent on to Congress.[148] In reality Anslinger had already turned on the convention:

> We worked twelve years to consolidate all the treaties and protocols. Unfortunately the political situation was not such as to create an atmosphere for objective negotiation. Consequently, the Single Convention, although adopted, was in my opinion laid to rest by the Soviet bloc, the British Commonwealth, and the Holy See.[149]

The US gave two key reasons for opposition: the production limitation provisions and the permissible reservations around the system of estimates. William McAllister speculates that a key reason for Anslinger's rejection of the Single Convention was the absence of a provision similar to that in the 1931 Convention mandating a separate government administration to oversee narcotics. McAllister argues that Anslinger required this to justify his agency's position within the US Government. This argument seems uncompelling in comparison to the issues Anslinger publicly and privately claimed drove his rejection – the lax production limitation provisions and the loose reservation provisions.[150] The US argued the reservations, if applied to various aspects of the INCB's work, would result in the Board not having any authority to regulate the market.[151] They went on, 'the estimates and statistics system of the 1931 Convention had been destroyed. Any party . . . could by reservation prevent examination of its statistics.'[152]

Anslinger set to work securing the support of senators and pharmaceutical interests. Senator Homer Copehart agreed with Anslinger's reading and promised to reject the Convention if Anslinger signed it and offered it to the Senate for confirmation:

> far from strengthening international control . . . [it] could become the means of flooding countries . . . with large amounts of addicting drugs. I am particularly concerned . . . because I am informed that it was at the insistence of the Soviet bloc . . . that certain fundamental controls . . . have been weakened and can be destroyed . . . [A]s is well recognized, traffic in addicting drugs has been an insidious tool in the cold war for weakening the moral fiber and physical well-being of people throughout the world.[153]

The pharmaceutical sector warned the new INCB 'could be ignored and flouted with impunity'. Despite his domestic lobbying efforts, Anslinger found the US ECOSOC delegation 'solidly against me and want the treaty'.[154] Holding the domestic line while caring for his dying wife, his efforts received a major boost when Senate Foreign Relations Committee Member Senator Alexander Wiley pushed the State Department to pressure Turkey and Greece and ensure no encouragement was given to the Single Convention.[155]

As one Treasury official wrote, however, despite a clear US position 'the Department of State people at the working level were not cooperating in the maintenance of that position.' The State Department responded that the Treasury wanted to play the policy in 'high key', while the State Department wanted to play it in 'low key' on the assumption that the Single Convention would fail on its own. Further the State Department criticised the handling of the 1961 Plenipotentiary Conference, complaining that the US delegation had 'completely lost control of the situation' and 'failed to line up the necessary votes'. They made clear that the matter would not receive major attention at the General Assembly level, where they privileged 'political' over 'technical' issues.[156]

The UK Embassy in Washington had gained the impression that the State Department agreed with the UK but that it had been sidelined by the FBN.[157] The UK could not understand how Anslinger expected the Protocol to function given the widespread disapproval. Even if he succeeded it would simply become a 'lame duck', and they could not understand why Anslinger would want to 'bring discredit' on the international machinery 'which up to now had worked very well'.[158] They soon viewed their role as not only salvaging the Single Convention but also the international control system itself.

Of key importance to Anslinger was the recognition that he could receive significant blowback from his traditional domestic constituencies. Even before the Conference had closed, Hearst Papers wrote editorials blasting the outcome as a Soviet plot to flood the world with opium and pointing out that the lead Soviet delegate had a history of espionage.[159] Other constituencies, such as the Women's Christian Temperance Movement, soon followed suit. Anslinger had lost control of the international negotiating process. He was now unhappy with the provisions of the agreement and felt he had little choice but to try to torpedo it. Green for the UK, with US views now clearly elaborated, found little to be gained by further arguing.[160] He sought to downplay US dismay as far as possible to allow time for the Convention to come into force.

7.9 The Rushes to Ratify

Anslinger gambled that ratification by another producer would bring the 1953 Protocol into force and indefinitely postpone the Single Convention. He began to secretly lobby the Greek and Turkish governments, sending a mission to both countries in 1962.[161] In same year the US finally made public their opposition to the Single Convention, asking that the 1953 Protocol should be given 'at least five years' to prove itself effective. They were willing to make some amendments, for example eliminating local inquiry and mandatory embargo provisions but maintained the 'closed list' was 'the very essence of the Protocol'. They admitted that only one country might become the sole source of exportable opium, but this 'might not be a bad thing' or that no opium might be available at all, and therefore steps should be made available to ensure a supply in such a situation.[162]

Turkey, and its traditional US 'stumbling block' Dr Ozkol, sought to delay US pressure until after the next CND meeting. Anslinger ignored this and turned to Greece for 'possible quicker action'.[163] Greece was sternly reminded that the international community had included them in the 1953 Protocol 'closed list', yet Greece did nothing to ratify it. Confronted with direct US pressure, Greece professed displeasure with the Single Convention and promised to look again at ratifying the 1953 Protocol. As one US team member wrote of the new Greek representative,

> Prof. Tsatsas, in our opinion, represents a breaking up of the so-called "Balkan Bloc." ... Greece, Turkey and Yugoslavia have worked closely together over the past few years. We have seen undue influence exerted by Mr. Ozkol of Turkey ... and to a lesser extent, Nicolic of Yugoslavia.[164]

Soon after leaving Greece, the US team were 'confident' of a quick ratification despite the political difficulties which had 'paralyzed' the Greek Parliament.[165] Soon thereafter, they received word the Greek government had taken action to ratify the 1953 Protocol. One of the US team members signed off, '[e]ven if the Greek Parliament has not yet acted, I believe I can say ... "Mission Accomplished".'[166]

At the 1962 CND, Greece announced its intention to ratify the 1953 Opium Protocol. The US delegation reported that the UK and Canada responded with 'an angry and unremitting attack' on Greece. With only the US and Egypt offering support, the Greek delegate buckled under the British–Canadian onslaught and also vaguely committed to eventual ratification of the Single Convention. Soon after Greece asked for US support in becoming a member of ECOSOC, something 'obviously asked as a return favour for ratification of the [Opium Protocol]'. Anslinger immediately began work to oblige.[167] The US continued a major diplomatic offensive through 1962 with extensive shuttle diplomacy and utilising their embassies to undermine the Single Convention. Many governments professed sympathy but few expressed willingness to change their position, and the US seemed unlikely to arrest the trend. India summed up the views of many, claiming that although it supported stricter provisions in the 1961 Convention, it attached greater importance to securing universal adherence.[168]

The 1953 Opium Protocol came into force on 8 March 963. Anslinger recognised this would force Turkey into ratification 'as they have enormous stocks and the only manufacturing customer able to buy will be the UK'.[169] Turkey soon moved towards ratification, citing 'disappointing' opium sales as the main driver and the hope that it would result in preferential access of exports to the US market.[170] On 15 July Turkey ratified the Protocol.[171] However, the Greek announcement had also accelerated efforts to bring the Single Convention into force. It had become apparent that the 1953 Protocol would give India an effective monopoly on licit opium production to parties of the Protocol. The UK and Canada both stated their intent to ratify the Singe Convention as soon as requisite domestic legislation could be passed. The Netherlands, Yugoslavia, India, Switzerland, Morocco and Poland all spoke in favour of the Convention and the Afghan observer described it as an achievement for the broader United Nations. CND also passed a resolution urging ECOSOC to invite governments to ratify the Single Convention.[172] On 13 November 1964, Kenya became the fortieth signatory to accede, thereby bringing it into force one month later.[173]

7.10 Conclusion

Anslinger's strategy had failed. The 1953 Protocol had come into force but had failed to stop the Single Convention, which superseded it. The US would continue to boycott the Convention for several years, eventually ratifying in 1967 following Anslinger's retirement. A decade since the 1953 Opium Conference, the US was entirely isolated in the field of international narcotics control. The UK on the other hand was firmly nestled within the new system, while the Anglo–US drug relationship was, by this stage, severely weakened, tense and distant.

The UK was hoping for broad accord and to protect key national interests. They initially looked towards an American led anti-producer front. When this failed to emerge, the UK began building its own eclectic coalition, encompassing Western European states and the moderate Indian delegation. The UK and India eventually worked closely to find a middle ground between hard-line producers, manufacturers and stringent control advocates.

Anslinger was hoping to sustain a crumbling US drug consensus in the face of collapsing alliances and shifting systemic power structures. His leadership undermined the formulation of a coherent US policy, prevented flexibility in the face of changed circumstances and stopped the emergence of cooperation with the pragmatic UK, much to the dismay of the State Department. US and UK interests diverged somewhat, but some degree of negotiation and nurturing could have potentially produced a governing alliance, instead of a breakdown in relations. As a result,

Anslinger consigned the US to a unilateral approach followed by a period of isolation. Further, Anslinger failed to achieve most of his goals during this period.

The battle between the 1953 Protocol and the 1961 Single Convention highlighted the entrenched divisions within the system as well as changed political realities. On the one side was the US, using all diplomatic levers possible and advocating for a strict document which would squeeze licit supplies while furthering a prohibitionist model internationally. On the other side were producer states, whose economic interests were tied to avoiding new domestic control obligations, levelling the international regulatory structure, maintaining relatively open markets and shifting the regulatory burden towards synthetics and poppy straw manufacturing. They allied with hard-line non-interventionist states such as the Soviet Bloc, Latin American countries such as Mexico, and postcolonial states in Africa which desired the freedom to pursue self-sufficiency in pain medicines and potentially develop export markets later. The UK remained in the middle, triangulating between these groups to help secure its national political and economic self-interests. The UK vision eventually won given the relatively easy sell of the Single Convention over the 1953 Protocol.

The Single Convention battle also highlighted the internal rifts within the US government, between pragmatists in the State Department and hard-line control advocates in the Treasury Department. The latter were able to mobilise powerful congressional actors and arouse strong public opinion to force the State Department to take an active stand against a consensus-based international framework. The State Department reluctantly acquiesced. Single Convention politics did not seep into General Assembly politics, however. Driving Anslinger and US hard-liners were a variety of interests, including bureaucratic self-interest, a desire to maintain prohibitionist domestic constituencies, as well as a genuine belief in the importance of their efforts. Further, personal and diplomatic prestige played an important part, particularly for Anslinger. Coming to the end of his career, he had no desire to see international control efforts, as he saw it, fizzle out on his watch.

However, none of these factors could mitigate against the fact that Anslinger had lost control of domestic and international processes. He proved unable to dictate the direction of negotiations. When they failed to progress according to his wishes, he spent the last of his political capital trying to railroad through an unpopular agreement. His failure reflected a broader shift in international drug diplomacy. The

'Gentlemen's Club' of old had been replaced by a complex international framework with multiple power centres and an array of national interests expressed in a more self-assured manner. Traditional actors had lost the initiative, and the British approach, based on consensus documents and a belief in relatively light-touch global regulation, won the day.

As throughout the previous five decades, the US and UK took different approaches to international drug control. The UK represented a pragmatic strand that sought to make accommodations with local conditions and hurdles to control. The US maintained an aggressive diplomatic stance based on a firm belief in prohibition, policing and control to surmount all obstacles. Increasingly, however, local and regional accommodations showed the US consistently willing to subvert the narcotics agenda when national interests demanded, but the outward expression of US policy never deviated. The US favoured prohibition as a 'one-size-fits-all' global policy. The UK sought a regulatory compromise that maintained this issue below the radar; highlighted the UK as a good global citizen; and prevented an unchecked drug commodity market. Within these approaches there was much overlap between Britain and the US. When the two worked to exploit these overlaps, namely around the creation of international regulations, forward political progress was possible. When the two focused on their differences, namely around the severity of regulations and the inculcation of the prohibitionist model at the international level, competition and political breakdown often ensued. The battle over the Single Convention was the clearest example of this.

8

Assessing the Legal Legacy of the Single Convention

8.1 Introduction

The passage of the Single Convention represented a high-water mark in the international regulatory system. While it contained little in terms of innovation, it streamlined the complex array of drug treaties, while moving the terrain of control forward marginally. It essentially solidified an economic regulatory framework for a global licit commodity market in listed drugs. To enforce this market, it mandated certain action around controlling and prohibiting non-medical production and manufacturing. Key questions around dealing with 'addiction' and suppressing non-medical consumption were left largely unanswered. Control advocates believed that effective regulation of the licit market would squeeze out illicit supplies, leaving a relatively minor role for prohibitionist aspects and police enforcement. Time would prove this belief misjudged. When the failures of the regulatory approach to quell the illicit market became apparent, international policy path determinacy fuelled a commensurate growth in enforcement efforts, thereby creating the modern 'war on drugs'.

The US may have lost the battle around the Single Convention and control of the system in the 1960s, but they would enter the 1970s ready to refight many of these battles, beginning with the declaration of the 'war of drugs' and an aggressive new round of bilateral drug diplomacy. Ultimately the 'war on drugs' was not an inevitable outgrowth of these documents, but instead represented a specific set of interpretations, bureaucratic and normative trajectories and member state implementations. For example, by the 1990s, INCB would assume a more enforcement-oriented and arguably political organisation than had ever been envisioned by the drafters of the Single Convention.[1] That is, except for the US and its allies which, under Anslinger, had pushed for CND to be a small technocratic committee empowered to chastise and challenge states parties.

Moderate and non-interventionist architects of control had pushed back strongly against the idea that INCB or its predecessors, PCOB and DSB, should do anything but collect, organise and report on statistics. It is through the flexible evolution and interpretation of such terms as 'quasi-judicial', something originally meant to highlight its independence from the League of Nations, that an INCB self-conception as the 'guardian' of the international conventions emerged. These sorts of historical nuances are too often lost in renderings of the UN drug control system which attempt to reverse-engineer the story by reading the contemporary political contours. This work has self-consciously served as a counterweight to contemporary analyses which draw on a selective reading of history to fit an analytically neat conception of the system. It was, first and foremost, a negotiated multilateral outcome, rather than a US hegemonic imposition.

As a deep reading of primary sources highlights, the system was not legally destined to adopt the drug war mantle ascribed to it in recent decades. It is also not determined to continue as a bastion of repressive international policies without specific legal redrafting. The Single Convention and subsequent treaties, building on a legacy of past conventions, consensus policymaking and deeply divergent national conceptions, are the legal foundation of a system of controls which evolved over the decades prior and hence. It was not the sole determinant of drug policies globally. It was a legal enabler, but it relied on member state interest and implementation.

The official Convention Commentary highlights,

> the Single Convention provides ... two basic features: limitation of narcotics supplies of each country and territory to the quantities that it needs for medical and scientific purposes, and authorization of each form of participation in the drug economy, that is, licensing of producers, manufacturers and traders, governmental authorizations of each import and export, and the requirement of medical prescriptions for consumption.[2]

Beyond this, key questions of how to achieve that goal remain an area of conflicting and competing aims, policy flexibility, legal overlap, resourcing constraints and policy prioritisation. Historians William McAllister and Joseph Spillane well define the issue of global regulation of drugs:

> The roots of the modern drug regulatory apparatus stem from late 19th century efforts to define the boundaries of appropriate sale and use of

> drug products … The central task was to find ways of balancing negative effects (toxicity, addiction) with positive effects (therapeutic benefit, pain relief).[3]

This book highlights dual strands of international drug control: regulations and prohibitions. Each was an essential feature of the other, as in all regulatory systems. European states tended to favour regulatory models, underpinned by recourse to prohibitions, particularly within their colonies. The US tended to favour strict prohibitionist approaches underpinned by rigid repression. These divergent worldviews melded through tense international negotiations in the first half of the century, despite initially torpedoing consensus. The US walked out of the 1925 Conference and ceased effective cooperation with the 1936 Plenipotentiary Conference. Conflicting economic interests around regulating global trade patterns provided further obstacles but also, ultimately, the clearest negotiating terrain. Therefore, the construction of a regulatory system managing the trade and guiding national regulation of listed substances was pursued with vigour and ultimately success. The Single Convention was the legal culmination of this early story.

8.2 The Contemporary Governance System

The contemporary system stands on three international drug conventions: the 1961 Single Convention on Narcotic Drugs (as amended by the 1972 Protocol), the 1971 Convention on Psychotropic Substances, and the 1988 United Nations Convention against Illicit Traffic in Narcotic Drugs and Psychotropic Substances. It is overseen by the UN CND, as the political decision-making body. Its implementation and monitoring of compliance is supported by INCB. The system also has its own Drug Secretariat, currently the United Nations Office on Drugs and Crime (UNODC). Further, WHO operates as a supportive technocratic body, albeit in a central mechanism of providing expert guidance on substances and their suitability for control.

At its core is the 'system of estimates' whereby member states predict and declare their demand and eventual consumption to INCB. This is further underpinned by the 'system of scheduling', the categorisation of drugs according to their supposed utility, medical value, potential harm and risk of abuse. This lists substances in categories which require specific regulatory controls by member states. Ultimately, member states adopted an indirect system of control which tracks key parts of the trade, such as production, transit, manufacturing, distribution and the creation of estimates for domestic demand. By comparing these estimates with actual market outcomes, states hoped to limit illicit market leakages.[4]

8.3 The Scheduling System under the Single Convention

The Single Convention consists of four Schedules. Schedule I corresponded to Group I of the 1931 Convention and the 1948 Protocol. The 1931 Convention had divided Group I into subgroups, both subject to the same regulatory regime, (a), drugs 'capable of producing addiction', and (b), non-addictive drugs convertible into drugs capable of producing addiction that were not much used in medical practice.[5] Group II constituted convertible drugs that were widely used in medicine. The 1948 Protocol, however, did not differentiate between subgroups (a) and (b).[6] Drugs under this Schedule I are under the 'standard regime' of the convention. The principle features are

> Limitation to medical and scientific purposes of all phases of narcotics trade (manufacture, domestic trade, both wholesale and retail, and international trade) in, and possession and use of, drugs; requirement of governmental authorization (licensing or state ownership) of participation in any phase of the narcotics trade and of a specific authorization (import and export authorization) of each individual international transaction; obligation of all participants in the narcotics trade to keep detailed records of their transactions in drugs; requirements of a medical prescription for the supply or dispensation of drugs to individuals; and a system of limiting the quantities of drugs available, by manufacture or import or both, in each country and territory to those needed for medical and scientific purposes.[7]

States parties have to formally authorise participation in the domestic trade via 'licensing or state ownership'. Further, they are obliged to issue specific import and exports authorisations for international transaction; keep detailed records; provide medical prescriptions for dispensation to individuals; and overall limit drugs available by manufacture or import to medical and scientific purposes.[8] Production, that is, harvesting opium, coca leaves, cannabis and cannabis resin, is limited *in principle* but is not part of the standard regime.[9] Some drugs are maintained in specific regimes on top of Schedule I, namely, opium, coca leaf, cannabis and cannabis resin. Some included varying 'transitional' periods of control.[10]

Drugs under Schedule II have many overlapping controls with Schedule I, with certain exceptions. No drug in Schedule II can be listed in Schedule IV. Schedule II corresponds to Group II of the 1931 Convention and

1948 Protocol but were under 'a considerably stricter regime'. Group II of the 1931 Convention contained drugs 'considered not to be capable by themselves of producing "addiction", but to be convertible into such drugs, and which are widely used in medicine'.[11] This reflected the desire in the 1920s and 30s to privilege certain types of manufactured opiates, such as codeine, which were viewed as 'slightly addiction-producing' and thereby in Group II (b) 'not because of this property, but because of its capacity to be converted into "addiction" producing drugs'.[12]

Group II had thereby been 'exempted from several controls' applicable to Group I, ostensibly 'in order not to place too great a burden on medical practitioners, retail pharmacists and patients'.[13] Retail distributors did not require a licence or to keep records of transactions; medical prescription were not required; governments did not have to furnish quarterly import and export statistics, only annual ones, and did not have to report on consumption. Estimates and final statistics could vary to a much wider degree than those under Group I. Even if requested to explain these estimates to PCOB, governments could limit their reply to a 'summary statement'. Further, preparations 'adapted to a normal therapeutic use' were exempted from the administrative controls under the 1925 Convention, in particular the import certificate and export authorisation system.[14]

As such, prior to the Single Convention, Group II were 'exempted from control as regards both internal distribution (wholesale and retail) and international trade'. That is, 'requirements of licensing, import and export authorization, statistical reporting, record keeping, medical prescription, limitation of trade and use to medical and scientific purposes'.[15] The Single Convention changed this by subjecting them to the same controls as Schedule I, with a few exceptions. Governments are not bound to prevent their accumulation by retail distributors in excess of quantities needed for regular business conduct; medical prescriptions to individuals are not obligatory; labelling is not required to show the 'exact content by weight or percentage'. Meanwhile, no express privileging occurs for preparations 'adapted to a normal therapeutic use' within Schedule II, 'but the same effect is obtained by including in Schedule III preparations of drugs in Schedule II which, as defined in that Schedule, are in fact "adapted to a normal therapeutic use".'[16]

Unlike Group II, Schedule II of the Single Convention does require a licence for retail trade or distribution, except when carried out by a state enterprise. It also extends the scope of control beyond just manufacture, to a general 'control under licence' principle for all involved in the trade. Further, it more strictly controls drugs such as codeine and ethylmorphine and requires submission of statistics on consumption as well as quarterly statistics on imports and exports.[17] This meant that INCB, under Schedule II (unlike PCOB under Group II, which only received annual statistics), could technically order a discontinuation of exports to any country or territory in the current year if it learned from quarterly statistics that the exports would breach its import limits. Meanwhile, under the Single Convention, 'licensed drug manufacturers must obtain periodical permits specifying the kinds and amounts of drugs which they are entitled to make.' This is to allow governments to assign quotas and prevent excessive manufacturing above their national limits.[18]

Schedule III 'contains preparations which enjoy a privileged position under the Single Convention, i.e. are subject to a less strict regime than other preparations'.[19] These corresponded to 'exempted preparations' under the 1931 Convention which did not require export authorisation for specific 'exempted preparations'.[20] The Single Convention again imposes a 'considerably stricter regime' and reduces the number of exempted substances. Further, it got rid of the term 'adapted to a normal therapeutic use'. Schedule III includes preparations of all drugs in Schedule II. Preparations in Schedule III are subject to the same control as Schedule II, with the exception that the import certificate and export authorisation system does not apply. Further, although drugs utilised in their preparation must be reported to INCB, estimates and statistical returns did not need to contain information on preparations in Schedule III. Of course, national governments explicitly retained the right to adopt 'more strict or severe' measures than those outlined.[21]

As the Technical Committee of the 1961 Plenipotentiary Conference highlighted, Schedule III targets preparations which,

(a) Are intended for legitimate medical use; and
(b) Have a specified drug content and are compounded with one or more ingredients in such a way that the preparation has no, or negligible risk of abuse, and in such a way that the drug cannot be recovered by readily applicable means or in yield which would constitute a risk to public health.[22]

In general, Schedule III enables a lessening of regulatory burdens to the point that it provides an 'exemption in order to facilitate wide-spread consumption without medical supervision'. However, the burden is against inclusion in Schedule III, with the Commentary highlighting that '[i]nclusion of a preparation in Schedule III is not favoured by the spirit of the Single Convention.'[23]

Schedule IV remains a widely misunderstood regime within the Convention. All drugs in Schedule IV are, by definition, also in Schedule I. Schedule IV provides supplementary regulatory guidance whereby (a) parties evaluate whether the listed drugs are particularly dangerous as to require "special measures of control" and (b) decide whether to prohibit production, manufacture, export and import of, trade in and possession or use, except for medical and scientific research, 'if in its opinion the prevailing conditions in its country render it the most appropriate means of protecting public health and welfare'.[24] As such, the prerogative rests firmly with member states, and Schedule IV serves as an indicative framework, rather than a binding regulatory one. Indeed, the Commentary set a subjective and low test, "[i]f a Party believed ... that special measures were required, but refused to adopt them ... it would not be acting in good faith and thus would violate its obligation.'[25] Whether a Party's opinion was legitimate, meanwhile, 'could not be challenged by any other Party'.[26]

The Schedule IV legal compromise represents an early and vital internal flexibility. Indeed, the Commentary goes into great length to address the 'controversial question' of mandatory prohibitions. There was no consensus at the 1961 Conference as to whether prohibitions on drugs such as cannabis, cannabis resin, desomorphine, heroin and ketobemidone should be mandatory or only recommended. As the Commentary highlights, '[t]his was a continuation of a long-lasting international controversy regarding the usefulness of prohibiting particularly dangerous drugs without therapeutic properties not obtainable from other less dangerous substances.'[27] Early battles in the League OAC had centred on whether to ban heroin. Compromises enabled prohibitions on certain types of trade in heroin, but national regulatory sovereignty prevailed, based on 'the belief that the decision regarding prohibition should be left to the judgement of each Government, and that international organs should limit themselves to recommending prohibitions where advisable but should not be authorised to prescribe it in a mandatory manner'. Article 2, para. 5 of the Single Convention 'constitutes a compromise which leave prohibition to the *judgement*, though theoretically not to the *discretion*, of each party'.[28]

8.4 The (Re)Scheduling Process

The 1925, 1931 Treaties and the 1948 Protocol included procedures for adding substances. For example, the 1925 Convention, as amended by the 1946 Protocol, authorised the WHO 'to extend its application to "any narcotic drugs" which it found to be "liable to similar abuse and productive of similar ill effects as the substances" to which Chapter III of the Convention applied (i.e., similar to those of medicinal opium, cocaine, ecgonine, morphine, heroin and galenical preparations (extracts and tinctures) of Indian hemp (cannabis))'.[29] The Single Convention followed in this lineage, established a relatively open and flexible system for scheduling and rescheduling drugs. Under Article 3, WHO or state parties can initiate the scheduling process, while CND has the authority to decide whether to place, remove or change the scope of controls on any given substance. WHO has wide discretion in selecting the schedule and is guided both by the need to protect 'public health' from addiction and to ensure accessibility for medical and scientific needs.[30] CND decides whether a substance is to be placed under international control but can only take a positive decision in accordance with the recommendation of WHO, except where it decides to reject a recommendation for simultaneous inclusion under Schedule IV. CND is to be guided by the pharmacological and chemical findings of WHO, and in cases where it does not accept them, it should be guided by 'considerations such as those of an administrative or social nature'. CND cannot unilaterally decide to extend control to a substance if WHO has not recommended to do it.[31]

The Single Convention took over many of the procedures of previous conventions but also differed in a number of areas.[32] As under all three previous treaties, control could only be extended to drugs 'liable to the *same* kind of abuse and productive of the *same* kind of harmful effects as the drugs already under control'.[33] Control can be extended 'to a substance of any chemical structure whatsoever'.[34] The Convention allows CND to recommend control 'pending the outcome of the procedure on the control status', in effect granting the capability of emergency control.[35] Further, the Single Convention allows decisions 'exempting preparations from measures of control'.[36] The UN Office of Legal Affairs quickly determined that barbiturates, tranquillisers and amphetamines lay beyond the regulatory scope of the Single Convention, despite the similarity of effects of amphetamines to cocaine and barbiturates and tranquillisers to morphine. Although a simple agreement among parties could expand the application of the Single Convention to these drugs, myriad political and economic divisions prevented it and set the stage for an entirely separate convention, the 1971 Convention on Psychotropic Substances.[37]

8.5 Scheduling and Control under the 1971 Convention

The 1971 Convention of Psychotropic Substance, or Vienna Convention, dealt with the emergence of 'psychotropic substances'. As with the Single Convention, these are substances legally defined in terms of their scheduling, in this case, 'any substance, natural or synthetic, or any natural material in Schedule I, II, III or IV'.[38] The Vienna Convention also has four schedules that can, like the Single Convention, be amended 'by a different and simpler procedure than the revision of other parts of the treaty' and thereby 'may impose on Parties additional obligations without their consent'. Unlike the Single Convention, the Vienna Convention does, in some cases, apply provisions to less strict regimes which do not also apply to the more strict regimes.[39]

Changes in Schedules 'is patterned after the Single Convention', requiring action by both WHO and CND.[40] However, unlike the Single Convention, CND may 'place that substance under a particular control regime, change its regime, or free it from control, even if its action is not in accord with [WHO's] recommendation'.[41] However, CND cannot place under control 'an uncontrolled substance which [WHO] has not found to have the properties defined in article 2 . . . or refuse to free such a substance from control'.[42] It can also not place in Schedule I 'or refuse to delete from that Schedule a substance which the [WHO] has found to have more than a "very limited" therapeutic usefulness'.[43] As such, a safeguard against a political decision is built in, whereby the power of CND is checked by WHO.

The Single Convention allows CND to control precursors of controlled drugs, that is, 'substances "convertible" into controlled drugs'.[44] CND has no such authority under the Vienna Convention. Further, the Vienna Convention does not allow temporary binding emergency scheduling measures.[45] Decisions to change Schedules requires a two-thirds majority of total membership as opposed to a simple majority under the Single Convention.[46] Although both Conventions include the right of appeal to ECOSOC against rescheduling decisions, the Vienna Convention also includes 'the right to refuse to carry out some of the control measures' required by scheduling a new substance or by transference from a less strict to a stricter regime.[47] Overall,

> As regards the question whether a substance should be controlled or in which Schedule a substance should be placed, WHO has very wide discretion in making its recommendations, as [CND] has in making its decisions.[48]

In preparation for the Plenipotentiary Conference, the WHO Expert Committee drew up a list of substances to be included. All but one of the substances recommended were placed in the corresponding schedules suggested, while some substances recommended for scheduling were not included. The 'considerations' which guided WHO and established the basis for future scheduling were,

> For inclusion in Group (a) which became **Schedule I** of the Vienna Convention: Substances whose liability to abuse constitutes an especially serious risk to public health and which have a very limited, if any, therapeutic usefulness.
>
> For inclusion in Group (b.1) which became **Schedule II**: Substances whose liability to abuse constitutes a substantial risk to public health and which have little to moderate therapeutic usefulness.
>
> For inclusion in Group (b.2) which became **Schedule III**: Substances whose liability to abuse constitutes a substantial risk to public health and which have moderate to great therapeutic usefulness.
>
> For inclusion in Group (c) which became **Schedule IV**: Substances whose liability to abuse constitutes a smaller but still significant risk to public health and which have a therapeutic usefulness form little to great.[49]

Meanwhile, tobacco and alcohol were discussed at the 1971 Conference and explicitly considered inappropriate for international control for reasons that appears to strain both logic and consistency yet were parroted by the Commentary. With the conclusion of the Vienna Convention, the control system was rounded off to enable controls of a much wider variety of drugs than the Single Convention alone, although under a somewhat less strict regime. With the regulatory framework agreed against a backdrop of growing illicit consumption and trade, international discussions almost invariably turned to enforcement measures against illicit trafficking activities.

8.6 The 1988 Convention against Illicit Traffic in Narcotic Drugs and Psychotropic Substances

Latin American governments provided the key impetus for the next drug Convention. Struggling to overcome the growing power of illicit drug actors, they sought some way to displace the burden to the UN and other member states. This began with the Quito Declaration against Traffic in Narcotic Drugs to the UN General Assembly in 1984. Signed by Bolivia, Colombia, Ecuador, Nicaragua, Peru and Venezuela, it called for, among other measures, drug trafficking to be treated as a crime against humanity.[50] Facing domestic opposition and weak state apparatus, policy displacement to the UN appeared a logical choice and could help shore up regional enforcement capabilities. The Quito Declaration was followed in quick succession by the 1985 New York Declaration against Drug Trafficking and the Illicit Use of Drugs, submitted to the UN by Argentina, Bolivia, Brazil, Ecuador, Peru and Venezuela.[51] While Latin American suggestions to expand the jurisdiction of the International Court of Justice (ICJ) and to treat drug trafficking as a crime against humanity were rebuffed by less affected and non-interventionist states, a convention became widely seen as the means to address the problem[52]

Governments enumerated fourteen elements for the convention. These included a focus on asset seizure, extradition, control of precursor chemicals, intelligence sharing, and all activities related to trafficking, including 'crop substitution'.[53] Latin American governments, meanwhile, move from secondary actors to key proponents of transnational legal developments in the field.

The 1988 Convention, widely viewed as the most 'prohibitionist' convention, enshrined two major innovations. First, it created mechanisms to 'monitor certain substances, including precursors, chemicals and solvents, which are used in the manufacture of narcotic drugs and psychotropic substances'.[54] Secondly, as UNODC writes,

> it was designed to hit drug traffickers where it hurts them most: by depriving them of financial gains and freedom of movement, extending the scope of control to measures to prevent money laundering and facilitate the tracing, freezing and confiscation of proceeds from drug trafficking.[55]

The Convention added few substantive regulatory parameters, other than solidifying a criminalisation paradigm around the non-medical and non-scientific trade. It also included a specific paragraph dealing with 'personal consumption contrary to the provisions of the 1961 Convention ... or the 1971 Convention'.[56] The Commentary acknowledged this as a 'controversial matter' even at the time and ultimately goes on to highlight that it,

> reflects a compromise on a number of points ... First ... the safeguard clause referring to constitutional principles and the basic concepts of a party's legal system ... Secondly, the final words requiring the conduct to be 'contrary to the provisions of' the earlier conventions. This could be

> interpreted as enabling the parties to retain the stance that they adopted regarding the interpretation of those earlier texts.[57]

Ultimately, while the 1988 Convention appeared to appease those calling for criminalisation of consumption, it provided sufficient interpretive flexibility for dissenting states.

8.7 From 1988 to 2021

From 1988 to 2008, the UN drug control system appeared to operate on a form of institutional autopilot. The momentum towards increasing system enforcement reached a pinnacle during the UN General Assembly Special Session (UNGASS) on the World Drug Problem in 1998 which ran under the banner, 'A drug free world – We can do it!' Beneath this seeming autopilot, national and international policy approaches were, however, subtly diverging.

This quiet tidal shift became visible in the first two decades of the 2000s, birthing a tumultuous period for the system. For decades, public health–focused critics advocated a far greater emphasis on harm reduction–based approaches. They drove local and national policy changes, while working to build a coalition at the international level to carve out new space for public health and human rights–based drug policies. These successes coalesced with major geopolitical and normative shifts. For example, In Latin America, US President Barack Obama worked to repair regional relations through a shift towards a more consensual multilateral approach. This coincided with a series of fiscal crises throughout the US and overseas deriving from the 2007–2008 financial crisis, which forced local and national governments to re-examine their drug war policies. As part of this, cannabis legalisation came firmly onto policy agendas.[58]

The Latin American Commission on Drugs and Democracy, a high-profile collection of former presidents and leaders, challenging the war on drugs.[59] This was followed by the 2011 Global Commission on Drug Policy report arguing for 'not just alternatives to incarceration and greater emphasis on public health approaches to drug use, but also decriminalization and experiments in legal regulation'.[60] Soon, sitting world leaders, including in Colombia and Mexico, joined the chorus. In 2012, President Santos of Colombia wrote,

> The Colombian Government strongly believes that the time has come to take a fresh look and we invite world leaders, scientists and experts to start

> an open, serious and honest debate about this war. The time has come to think outside the box. Our invitation is to dutifully study new formulas and approaches screened through an academic, scientific and non-politicised lens, because this war has proven to be extremely challenging and oftentimes, highly frustrating. This is a global problem that demands a global solution, and therefore a new international consensus is needed.[61]

Stalwart proponents of the system began to openly challenge its core tenets. Meanwhile, the US government tacitly enabled this dialogue, often against the more hawkish elements within its own administration. In 2012, Vice President Joe Biden declared the debate on drug war orthodoxy as 'totally legitimate', paving the way for a more substantial regional dialogue.[62] The Organization of American State (OAS) moved into the policy discussion, producing the report *Scenarios for the Drug Problem in the Americas, 2013–2025.*[63] Alongside this, Uruguay, Colorado and Washington State moved ahead with cannabis legalisation. Again, the Obama administration's drug war scepticism won out, producing an accommodationist federal response. This forced the US State Department to seek accommodation with the UN drug conventions, arguing for treaty flexibility and the reality that 'some countries will have have very strict drug approaches; other countries will legalize entire categories of drugs.'[64]

To some degree, this controversial US response, which I have termed the 'Brownfield doctrine', was not just about squaring a complex US federal legal accommodation with international law.[65] It effectively opened the door for Latin American governments to walk through, perhaps recognising that few if any would. None did. Instead, the pursuit of consensus continued via the UN and an expansive, but hardly radical, UNGASS strategic review process and 2016 Outcome Document.[66] Many civil society actors maintained the possibility of radical systemic change but were widely disappointed with the immediate UNGASS 2016 outcome.[67] Most, however, eventually came to recognise the incremental victories within UNGASS 2016.[68]

Many core tenets of the control system had been challenged. Ultimately, member states chose to openly ignore parts of the treaties related to prohibitions on cannabis through recourse to treaty 'flexibilities'. Still, the core structural foundation held. While increasingly peripheral elements of the control system bent, and in some case broke, the structure of the regulated global market retained clear functional utility for states. The desire for certainty, a level playing field of global regulations, and the imperative of maintaining a century-old system of international cooperation drastically outweighed internal divisions and tensions around specific substances, enforcement models and diverging visions of public health–based drug policies. Many reformists maintain the system is undergoing a long existential crisis that must either force deep structural reform, or even face collapse.[69] Others have argued that the system is merely undergoing a new period of prolonged dissensus, not dissimilar to the 1930s and 50s. Provided the functional utility of the regulatory core holds for a majority of member states, as it seems to have, the latter school argues the system will likely adapt, survive and simply become more complex.[70]

8.8 Conclusion

As the system progresses through its second century, its core regulatory tenets, birthed at a time when drug dependence was little understood and the enormous future impacts of illicit markets hardly imagined, remain the foundation for global drug policies. The Single Convention had given coherence and permanence to the complex and iterative framework developed from the 1909 Shanghai Commission onwards. By the coming into force of the Single Convention, the UN CND was the unrivalled home of multilateral drug issues and would only solidify this grasp in the coming decades. The Vienna Convention represented a furtherance of the system to incorporate new drugs and drug issues, albeit under a more limited and malleable control framework. The 1988 Convention represented, in some ways, a logical conclusion of this process. The weaknesses of the supply-centric model and repressive prohibitionist strategies were readily apparent to many governments as early as the 1930s. However, the direction of control was set within a regulatory system within which all states assumed a responsibility for enforcement and adherence. As illicit markets expanded and spiralled in the 1960s and 70s, countries buckling under the pressure of narcotrafficking and narco-fuelled insurgencies sought greater international cooperation to help them fight what was quickly becoming a global war. This dovetailed with the escalating US-led 'war on drugs' and its related 'war on crime' of the 1980s and 90s.

By the 2000s, impatience with the enforcement-led prohibitionist approach led to open divergences in the previous overtly consensus-oriented system. European governments became increasingly focused on public health–based approaches and recoiled from the aggressive militarism of the drug wars, preferring instead to focus on issues of development and governance. Latin American governments were more willing and able to challenge the basis of policies which imposed a disproportionate impact on them. The complex interplay between the politics of the war on terror, the heaving fiscal crises of the late 2000s, and the emergence of racial and social justice politics which pointed to the deep and scarring impacts of the war on drugs, coalesced to crack the consensus around repressive drug policies. Moreover, these policies were not seen as working. Supply continued unabated, albeit in shifting forms, while public health–based approaches, previously seen as at odds with the system, were demonstrating some of the only clear examples of policy success. States proved increasingly willing to countenance a shift in normative and policy emphasis in the lead-up to UNGASS 2016. Merging these reformist views with the visions of the system's many conservative proponents ultimately produced a policy widening and the onset of a more flexible approach to the peripheral elements of the system, while maintaining the regulatory core of the Single Convention, the Vienna Convention and the 1988 Convention. This process of system adaptation remains an ongoing phenomenon.

9

Conclusion: UN Drug Control in the Twenty-First Century

Towards a Regime Complex?

9.1 Introduction

At the outbreak of war in 1939, the survival of international drug control efforts was by no means assured. Through a mixture of Anglo–American cooperation, underpinned by US leadership, the technical aspects of the system survived by moving operations to Washington, ready to be co-opted into a post-war framework. The shape of this framework would be determined by a continuation of the normative, economic and political battles that had frequently stalled control efforts over the previous decades. These battles placed control advocate states on the one side and producer states on the other. In the middle were manufacturing and, to a lesser degree, consuming states. The US epitomised the control advocate perspective, seeking to create a strong international framework for shrinking global drug markets, both licit and illicit. The UK represented the regulatory strand which sought to protect economic and political interests while supporting international cooperative efforts around the core normative goals of the system: reducing the 'abuse' of 'dangerous drugs'. The system which emerged under the 1961 Single Convention was ultimately an accommodation between the US and UK approaches: a relatively weak regulatory system, underpinned by prohibitionist aspects. How these prohibitionist aspects would be implemented would be a key question for the control system over the coming decades.

The 1961 Convention created a mixed system, based on strong normative goals and trajectories but underpinned by relatively weak enforcement mechanisms and production controls. The US had sought an agreement to squeeze the global opium market. The UK sought one to regulate it. In the end the UK won, and this victory became enshrined in the Single Convention. Ultimately, the UK had relied on various coalitions of states to achieve this, highlighting their central role as pragmatist-in-chief within the system, which can be traced back to its origins at the turn of the twentieth century. The UK consistently charted a middle course between the hard-line prohibitionism of the US on the one hand and the economic self-interest of producer states and non-interventionist impulses of other groups such as the Soviet Bloc on the other hand.

The 'war on drugs' was not a creation of any UN framework or treaty. It was certainly facilitated by the UN and the international drug control system, but it represented a far more complex phenomenon, driven by a mixture of national, bilateral, regional and international efforts. Rolling them back will, therefore, be far more complex than reforming one multilateral treaty framework. This book contributes to current debates by highlighting the role of competing strategic visions in driving international efforts and the evolution of member states' engagement with, and understanding of, the UN system's mission. It demonstrates that interpretation and implementation of the system's strategy, goals, metrics and outcomes have shifted in the past, within the same treaty framework. Meanwhile, this book highlights routes to effecting these changes by pointing to the role of individual agency, economic interests, political narrative and social forces in driving the international control system and shaping its sense of mission and, eventually, reforms.

9.2 Foreign Policy and the Drug Wars

International control was as much a battle fought at the local, national and regional levels as the multilateral ones. While battles on the overarching sense of 'mission' and other grand narratives were shaped in the halls of the UN, member states pursued wildly differing implementations. Some, such as the US, sought to export their visions to other states. Others, such as Britain, had blamed their inability to institute effective commodity controls in their colonies on weaknesses in neighbouring territories. Others still, saw the international system as a mechanism to outsource control efforts to producer and transit countries. The inability of control advocates to secure effective cooperation from states like Afghanistan, Burma and (initially) Iran presaged the deeper battles that were to follow around implementation. It was one thing to make broad international commitments. It was quite another to implement them in the face of hard economic, political, social and other governing realities.

The 1939–72 period highlights the extent to which perceptions and politics frequently mattered more than facts within the control system.

Further, it highlighted the consistent utilisation of the drug issue as a stick to beat foreign policy opponents, despite facts on the ground. The case of wartime Japan remains debatable, but in the case of Communist China, Anslinger fabricated an opium conspiracy exactly when the PRC was undertaking one of the most extensive eradication campaigns in human history – at an incalculable human cost. Latin America was a case of the US turning its attention to its regional neighbour when efforts to interfere with countries further overseas stalled. The Middle East represented a veritable game of musical chairs of blame displacement, while Britain was only too happy to displace blame onto Thailand and Iran when useful. Asia, more broadly, saw Britain and other colonial powers pursue essentially pragmatic policies in the dying days of the opium monopolies, only to be castigated as protecting naked economic self-interest. The monopoly system had enabled effective management of the issue from their perspective. When it was removed, governance became more difficult and saw countries like Britain displace blame onto their neighbours, as in the case of Thailand.

Drug diplomacy also operated within a broader framework of international relations. Foreign policy concerns complicated drug diplomacy and vice versa. For example, within UK policy formulation we have seen that struggles between the Home Office and Foreign Office over the issue resulted in occasional mild blow-ups. Although often quickly defused, these episodes highlighted the complications for broader foreign policy concerns – for example when Afghanistan sought to join the 1953 Protocol's list of recognised producers. The US meanwhile saw a similar dance between Anslinger and the State Department. Anslinger's penchant for cowboy diplomacy ran at full throttle during World War II. He continued his bilateral efforts into peacetime via his overseas agents and attempted to use the UN as his bully pulpit. Nevertheless, the State Department wielded an effective means of oversight via ECOSOC and eventually weakened Anslinger's control of CND.

Meanwhile, Anslinger had a tremendous knack for blending drug policy into foreign policy concerns. For example, his use of Japan, the Four Freedoms, anti-colonialism, Communist China, and the Soviet Union, and his circumventing of the State Department's concerns at a number of junctures. In the 1960s, the latter had no desire to challenge the Single Convention but watched as the domestic ground shifted and forced them into pursuing Anslinger's revisionist stance. The UK, on the other hand, had a general desire to keep drug policy separated from broader foreign policy issues. London relished highlighting drug control as a shining example of international cooperation despite the insipid hollowing out of other international institutions by Cold War dynamics. Moreover, the UK threw up the sandbags any time drug policy risked encroaching on colonial, regional or other economic interests. Anslinger was well aware of these UK concerns and was more than happy to exploit or accommodate them depending on how it would support his domestic or international agenda, for example overlooking the illicit trade in Hong Kong in the 1950s or later linking London to supposed PRC diplomatic conspiracies.

Regarding production control, the US attitude remained that the lower the number of producers and thereby licit opium production, the lower the risk of illicit market development. They remained laser-focused on perceived global overproduction and the need to suppress it at all costs via regulations, prohibitions and strict police enforcement. All control efforts over this period were therefore to be geared towards producing less opium. This was the prohibitionist strand of the system. The UK was more concerned with consensus, market protection and a minimisation of regulatory costs. They sought a regulated framework that could point towards abuses and inadequate controls. They were less concerned about the scale of the market but were happy to highlight regulatory weaknesses, provided the costs of correcting those weaknesses were born by other states. This was the regulatory strand of the system. Opium and to a far lesser extent cocaine were the main focuses. The controls created for these substances were extended onto synthetics, cannabis and other drugs, but the thrust of international efforts remained heavily focused on opium and cocaine. Cannabis and coca leaf generated strong interest but proved expendable in the short-term out of deference to broader opium control, for example, the US preferring the 1953 Protocol to the 1961 Convention.

With their victory over the US, the British-led vision for regulation can also be said to have won. Nevertheless, the prohibitionist aspects built into the system by hard-line states would be strengthened going forward, via aggressive US drug diplomacy, funding initiatives and the solidification of international prohibitionist norms to help create the modern 'war on drugs'. Despite this implementation, the system remained fundamentally one of regulation, underpinned by prohibitionist aspects. The core remained focused on the consensus vision of regulating the flow of 'licit' or 'ethical' narcotics and minimising their leakage into the illicit market.[1]

Later, the US would re-engage and ratify the Single Convention in 1967 and use the framework provided under the Single Convention to help rally states towards a repressive prohibitionist model. Yet the system was ultimately one that had many possible alternative outcomes and directions. When the Single Convention came into force, it could have continued down the path towards regulation and heavy subjugation to other economic and foreign policy concerns. Alternatively, it could become oriented towards eradicating certain types of substances and practices via the proliferation of repressive prohibitionist models around the globe and the diffusion of police enforcement efforts. The policy and bureaucratic trajectories pushed towards the prohibitionist aspects, particularly when the US provided leadership, but the system itself was malleable.

9.3 The Geopolitical Economy of Control

International drug diplomacy up until 1967 witnessed much overlap and division. The overlap was around the pursuit of a global regulatory framework for 'dangerous drugs' internationally. The division was around the frontier and peripheral aspects of this; namely, where to draw the line between licit and illicit consumption; how tightly to restrict, regulate and prohibit global supplies; how much interference in national affairs to allow international organisations; and how to deal with existing drug consuming populations. In a broader sense, however, it was a question of expectations.

The UK, representing moderate states, viewed the end point of the international control system as facilitating better international management of drugs but also serving as a beacon towards broader international cooperation. It would inevitably provide an imperfect response to an insoluble issue. Nevertheless, it could help states mitigate the problems associated with drugs; minimise cross border disagreements as states dealt with licit and illicit commodity flows; breed new areas of international cooperation; and minimise the risks for their own bilateral and colonial relations deriving from the drug issue. More broadly, it allowed for discussion and action around the most poignant drug issues while establishing a normative framework and international direction of travel towards a world without drug 'abuse'. In this latter sense, Britain had minimal expectations that the international community would ever reach that destination, but it was the defusing of potential international tensions that was key. John Strang and Michael Gossop's description of the 'British System' of domestic control seems apt for British international drug policy: 'the quintessential characteristic ... [is] its lack of rigid form and hence its potentially greater capacity to be intuitively reactive to changed circumstances.'[2]

For the US, the system offered hope for an international framework for genuinely achieving a world without drug 'abuse'. Time and again, public expressions and policy formulations were based on this principle. Whether it was speeches in the Houses of Congress highlighting that the struggle for drug control was akin to the efforts to end slavery, or the State Department repeatedly stating in public that a solution to the global drug problem was within reach. Under the US approach, the problem was soluble if all states pursued the US formula of strict regulations, prohibitions and repression. Political will was the key ingredient, a mechanism to chastise recalcitrant or failing states and a forum to disseminate their one-size-fits-all model based on policing, enforcement and the 'closed institution' approach to addiction.

Where US and moderate visions overlapped, cooperation and forward political progress was possible. When the two were unable to overcome their divisions, competition and international political breakdowns emerged. The battle over the Single Convention represented the greatest example of this, highlighting not only core drug interests, but also the role of agency, social forces, and deeper economic and political interests in sustaining cooperation. The breakdown arose from a divergence of interests that had their origins in different historical approach to narcotics control. This, however, was fatally worsened by strategic ineptitude and poor US leadership under Harry Anslinger.

The historical approaches of the UK and US, in particular, to narcotics control solidified and developed around the turn of the twentieth century. The US was driven by a moralistic and self-interested belief in prohibition and 'control at the source'. This was, under the US conception, to be effected by suppression at all points in the supply chain via regulation of medical and scientific usage, strict prohibitions around non-medical and non-scientific consumption enforced by uniform legislation and policing globally, and the mandatory 'closed institution' approach to drug 'addiction'.

The UK on the other hand was driven by more practical and similarly self-interested concerns. Initially, they walked a balancing act between maintaining colonial opium monopolies and avoiding the imposition of strict prohibition in their colonies given the expected practical and monetary difficulties. Mitigating this was the desire to encourage US interest in international cooperation around drugs. The UK believed that the US involvement with the League of Nations drug control system could spill over into other areas of international cooperation. The convergence of these goals with US moderation in the early 1930s witnessed the creation of international manufacturing regulations via the system of estimates.

The divergence between the US and UK over the continuation of opium smoking and the opium monopolies returned to fuel League OAC tensions and helped prevent any production limitation agreement. World War II altered the dynamics of this previous obstacle. Further, it highlighted the central role of agency in driving the drug issue forward. Without Anslinger's leadership, the resolution of the UK, Dutch and French colonial question was unforeseeable. With the shift, European powers furthered their commitment to end the opium monopolies, albeit imperfectly, and the move towards decolonisation lessened this as an issue of transatlantic division.

The post-war period offered the prospect of a new Anglo–American drug alliance. The UK toughened its supply-centric stance against certain Asian powers, notably Thailand, and sought to demonstrate its commitment to regulation via cooperation with the US on Germany. Nevertheless, both cases further demonstrated that the UK was willing to support US control interventionism only when it gelled with broader geopolitical interests. Further, with its domestic economic and balance of payments situation worsening, the UK was vigilant against any regulations that might adversely affect its drug manufacturing sector or raise costs for its National Health Service. Meanwhile, witnessing the tendency towards mission creep, the UK tried to dig in its heels and prevent international bodies appropriating new powers of oversight or intervention.

The US, meanwhile, emerging from the war with a new international leadership role was forced to temper some of its drug policy goals to broader geopolitical interests. Their public narrative, driven by Anslinger but increasingly softened by the State Department, remained one of strict global drug controls via the diffusion of political will, uniform legislation, police enforcement and a desire to strengthen CND's oversight of national policy implementation. The US drug control lobby, represented by groups such as the Women's Christian Temperance Union, retained an extremely important role in policy formulation and a formidable 'army' for Anslinger, as demonstrated by the failed reorganisation efforts against the FBN in the 1940s and 50s. No such lobby emerged in the UK, and policy remained fundamentally driven by technocratic concerns, bureaucratic turf battles and tempered by some domestic medical and economic constituencies.

The relationship between the FBN and the State Department would ultimately determine the shape of US post-war drug diplomacy. Anslinger's relatively close relationship with George Morlock, the State Department's lead on narcotics and core inner circle ally, helped smooth the process. Nevertheless, the State Department, having spent significant political capital on the Judd Resolution, pushed drug control down their UNO creation priority list, cutting Anslinger out of the process and trying to outsource diplomatic heavy lifting on the drug issue to the UK and China. This facilitated a relatively consensual multilateral period beginning with the creation of CND and culminating in the rapid passage of the 1948 Protocol. The loss of Morlock in the 1950s led to a further decline in State Department interest. Anslinger initially countered by linking the narcotics issue within the 'red-baiting' of the McCarthy Era, inventing a PRC conspiracy to destroy the West with opium and earn foreign exchange. The State Department soon tired of this narrative and limited Anslinger's scope to leverage UN forums.

Anslinger's overreach laid bare his failure to make CND an enforcement body in which member states would be openly chastised. The State Department, initially reliant on ECOSOC to defuse CND-generated tensions, withdrew support at CND the moment US statements were seen to impede broader US diplomatic strategy. Anslinger had used Iran, Mexico, Indochina, Thailand, India and China, among others at various times, as test cases for the interventionist capability of CND. The State Department torpedoed each of these in turn.

CND had become far more activist and interventionist than may have been the case without Anslinger's sustained leadership efforts. Ultimately, however, reticence of key member states, such as the UK, and a lack of State Department support prevented it attaining the enforcement body status that Anslinger and US drug control lobbyists desired. By the end of the 1950s, it appeared to have adopted the previous League OAC tendency towards backslapping and serving as a talking shop. The State Department eventually supported the Single Convention as a moderate international agreement which would strengthen relations in other fields. They were overruled, however, as Anslinger secured the support of his traditional constituencies and key US senators.

In the 1950s and 60s, states held differing visions for international production limitation and the expansion of prohibitionist obligations. US CND delegations, when led by Anslinger, continued the World War II inner circle agenda and generally sought to strengthen CND. They continued to push for mandatory inspections; trade embargo provisions;

internationally driven decisions around which drugs would be permitted and prohibited (most notably around heroin); mandating exactly how states should deal with addiction and drug traffickers. At the other end of the spectrum were Soviet Bloc states which championed non-interference. Many Latin American and newly emergent nations were similarly keen to prevent external interference. Further, newer states were unwilling to lock in an agreement that forever barred them from involvement in the licit trade and make them dependent on a small number of producer and manufacturing countries for their medicines.

By the 1950s, the UK was on alert against further encroachment on national sovereignty, whether commercial or criminal. Further, they wished to maintain good relations with soon-to-be or already former colonies and professed sympathy with demands for equality of national opportunity in the field around opium production and even manufacture. Further, allowing an open list of producer states meshed extremely well with the UK's economic interests of ensuring cheap opium supplies for their manufacturing sector, thereby helping their balance of payments position and NHS. They flatly rejected US calls for a 'closed institutional' model of treatment. On the other hand, the UK sought accommodations, willing to subsume certain national prerogatives to produce accord.

The US and UK also had important overlapping interests, namely their large pharmaceutical sectors and a desire to ensure equality of treatment of synthetic narcotics relative to natural opiates. Had they worked to overcome their differences, a more harmonious transatlantic diplomatic process might have ensued. Ultimately, this was made impossible by the leadership of Harry Anslinger. His attempt to retain control of CND, despite absenteeism, a weakened domestic position and personal complications, ensured divided and incompetent US delegations which failed to elaborate and advocate US interests. Ultimately, the UK retained its red lines around the NHS, drug manufacturers and treatment. The US ultimately failed to secure a strict agreement and sought to roll back control efforts to the 1953 Protocol, something completely undesirable to the majority of states.

Had Anslinger, at times, adopted a more moderate and engaged approach, the US would not have become isolated to the extent that it did, nor perhaps would it have failed so extensively to achieve its desired ends around the 1961 Convention. Part of this unwillingness derived his strategic failure to recognise the changed politics of the system. Part stemmed from his fear of alienating his core domestic constituencies and Congressional support base in Washington by advocating for a retrograde document. When he failed to secure his desired ends in the Single Convention, he ultimately chose to sacrifice it, portraying it as part communist conspiracy and part economic self-interest in the face of US control efforts. Ultimately, he felt that the 1953 Protocol would serve as a better opium control arrangement which could then be extended to cannabis and coca controls.

The UK had by the mid-1950s given up on accommodating the erratic, often incompetent and unpredictable US delegations and sought, quite successfully, to protect its own interests. It had been reticent to see the production limitation agreement reach fruition under the 1953 Opium Protocol, given recent opium market fluctuations and other economic concerns. When faced with that unsatisfactory document and producer states' efforts to undermine synthetic narcotics, the UK forged ahead with the Single Convention, driving it in a more moderate and acceptable direction with the aim of replacing the 1953 Protocol. Furthermore, evidence suggests that the US's own State Department retained a closer affinity to the UK's approach than to Anslinger's, but ultimately, through a mixture of bureaucratic outmanoeuvring and a need to placate domestic anti-opium concerns, were reluctantly forced to tow Anslinger's line.

The Anglo–American breakdown, therefore, was ultimately the result of interests and leadership. Had a more effective leadership reigned within the FBN during the 1950s or had policy been more clearly in the hands of the State Department, the outcome around the Single Convention might have been significantly different. On the other hand, without the US pushing the envelope on the issue over the previous six decades, it is unlikely that the CND would have emerged in the form that it did, even if that did not reflect US desires for an international enforcement body with strong oversight of national policies. The US would spend the next half-century utilising and evolving CND into an enforcement body via mild treaty reforms, funding initiatives and aggressive bilateral diplomacy, but this was a far from inevitable outgrowth of the 1961 Convention.

9.4 Towards a New Understanding of Global Drug Governance

Policy analyses of international drug control remain dominated by an international relations theoretical focus. Further, this focus is limited to a largely 'orthodox' interpretative school which portrays drug control in analytically parsimonious terms. The drug control system, or 'global drug prohibition regime' was, the orthodox interpretation holds, a US creation foisted upon the rest of the world through US hegemony. The contemporary extrapolation is that a decline of US hegemony has provoked and will continue to provoke a crisis within the system.[3] However, as more recent revisionist analyses have highlighted, this orthodox analysis fails to take account of the historical nuances of the system, such as those highlighted in this book, and ignores the broader experience and analyses of global regimes and governance architectures.

Orthodox analyses date to the prohibition regime conception first outlined by Ethan Nadelmann is his groundbreaking 1991 article.[4] The foundational principle has developed that the US created a robust prohibition regime via the League of Nations and subsequently the UN.[5] This analysis was furthered in a strongly deterministic manner by David Bewley-Taylor who came to represent the core proponent of the orthodox approach.[6] Revisionist, 'pluralist' scholars increasingly challenge this conception and in many ways work to de-exceptionalise drug control, placing it within the context of other international governance trends and regimes. They thereby suggest that the tensions within international drug policy debates mirror those found in other areas of global governance.[7]

Pluralist scholars point to a lack of historiographical rigor or grounding within orthodox analyses. Instead, they suggest orthodox scholars seek to simplify the historical reality of the system to enable a politically parsimonious explanation of its recent fragmentation. The result, as I have written elsewhere, 'was historical narrative being reverse engineered from policy tropes which were largely US-centric and lacking in fine grained political economy and diplomatic historical analysis of the processes that led to the creation of the system'.[8] Aside from the historical broadsides on the foundations of the orthodox approach, their conclusions, namely that declining US hegemony would inevitably produce cascading crises, have been weakened by actual outcomes. First, despite a prolonged challenge to US hegemony, both within the UN and the drug control system, no discernible risk of collapse is apparent. Indeed, fragmentation has merely provoked a rise of other conservative states, such as Russia and China, eager to take the US's lead on global drug control. Further, far from a normative unravelling within the system, a policy spectrum widening has been more clearly observed. States which wish to liberalise their approaches are doing so. Those that wish to pursue hard repressive models likewise feel unconstrained by broader norms of international law. Neither conservative nor reformist states appear to act out of deference to the UN drug control treaties but their own national visions.[9]

Second, these rigid orthodox analyses, characterising drug control as a uniform 'straitjacket', show little attempt to locate the drug control system within broader international trends, regulatory systems or regimes. Under the orthodox conception, only by challenging the firm and immutable limits of the regime's 'legal latitude' can any meaningful systemic policy change occur. They Aruge that the system has 'finite flexibilities' which member states cannot adjust without foundational and textual legal reforms.[10] Pluralists offer an alternative viewpoint based on historical contingency, complexity and thereby wider conceptions of flexibility within the system. As I have written elsewhere, '[w]hat becomes clear when one de-exceptionalizes the issue is that the tensions within international drug policy debates, such as cannabis legalisation, mirror those found in other areas of global governance.'[11]

Contemporary drug diplomacy analyses can, therefore, now be divided between two schools: regime 'integrationists' and system 'pluralists'. Further, the integrationist approach is subdivided among reformists and conservatives. Reform integrationists subscribe strongly to the orthodox analyses of a US hegemonic prohibition regime, irreconcilable with emerging national policy pluralism. Accepting treaty 'flexibilities' under this reading, particularly around cannabis legalisation, is a legal fiction which can only postpone radical systemic change, or indeed serves to threaten the foundations of international law. Conservatives integrationists, meanwhile, echo this legal certitude but differ on end points. Russia, China, Egypt and others seek to increase states' repressive policy orientation. System pluralists, on the other hand, argue from a position of historical regulatory complexity. They highlight a pragmatic utility of, and broad international precedents for, a less integrated system as policies develop at local levels and thereby expand the global evidence base.[12]

9.5 Drug Control, Global Governance and International Law

Broad analyses of the 'fragmentation' of 'governance architectures' have yet to be applied rigorously to the field of drug control. What becomes clear when one de-exceptionalises the issue is that the tensions within international drug policy debates mirror those found in other areas of global governance and international law. For example, scholars have pointed to a broad battle between those advocating greater 'diversity' of policy as a means to enable international progress vs those arguing for the pursuit of integrated governance architectures.[13] A similar story can be found in the recent history of UNGASS, where reform voices divided among what this book has described as reform integrationists and reform pluralists. The former argued that acceptance of diversity or 'flexibility', was a threat to the reintegration of an apparently collapsing control system under a more progressive 'regime'.[14] Pluralists argued that fragmentation and 'flexibility' would enable the creation of new policies at local and national levels which could then percolate back up to the international level.[15]

Synthesising these pluralists' insights, de-exceptionalising the fragmentation within drug control, and applying a more complex 'global architecture framework' allows, as Bierman et al. highlight, for the analysis of situations of both synergy and conflict between different regimes or other types of institutions across a given issue area. It also allows us to study synergy and conflict between the overarching norms and principles that govern these interactions.[16] They continue:

> High degrees of fragmentation are a frequent characteristic of global governance architectures ... Many policy domains are instead marked by a patchwork of international institutions that are different in their character (organizations, regimes, and implicit norms), their constituencies (public and private), their spatial scope (from bilateral to global), and their subject matter (from specific policy fields to universal concerns).[17]

Meanwhile, the concept of fragmentation is well developed within international law studies. Wilfred Jenks wrote in the 1950s of international law emerging as varied 'municipal' law systems, without a clear overarching legislative body. He suggested this argued for an adjudication system to deal not just with interstate legal rivalries but the conflicts between various treaty regimes.[18] His analysis proved prescient of international regime proliferation, with the twentieth century seeing over 50,000 treaties registered with the UN and thousands of other open multilateral treaties.[19]

Further, scholars have pointed to the sociological phenomenon of 'functional differentiation'. This process fuels complexity and specialisation in international society, leading to ever more diverse constellations of treaty regimes, interstate interests, civil society groups and institutional interests. As Koskenniemi writes, fragmentation has been 'accompanied by the emergence of specialized and (relatively) autonomous rules or rule-complexes, legal institutions and spheres of legal practice'.[20] Thus, recognition of treaty overlaps and interrelation is not a new phenomenon within international law more broadly but has only recently even begun to be applied to international drug control.[21]

Legal scholarship long ago escaped dichotomous ideals of uniformity and coherence. Indeed, critics highlight that these ideas initially helped obscure key power relations and normative assumptions within competing international law projects.[22] Cogan et al. highlight that legal fragmentation itself 'has a politics' in that it is 'the language in which competing groups argue about their relative power and the differing policies they seek to promote'.[23] They continue that during the post–Cold War battle between uniformity and fragmentation,

> Conservatives (meaning those who sought to maintain some imagined uniform general international law) have clearly lost. Indeed, they really had no chance. The facts had changed, and new legal regimes were required in order to solve new problems. In a decentralized system like that of international law fragmentation, and its institutional counterpart 'proliferation', were (and are) inevitable.[24]

More optimistic scholars foresee an international legal order that resembles the 'messy, porous, multiple-value and constituency politics of democratic pluralism', but is 'underpinned by a more absolutist baseline commitment to the preservation of the human'.[25] This point brings us into a well-defined field of study within the application of Western law to old colonial territories, but one which has remained relatively under developed in an international architecture context: 'legal pluralism'.[26] Sally Engle Merry defined legal pluralism as 'a situation in which two or more legal systems coexist in the same social field'.[27] In a similar vein, embryonic drug law discussions suggest adaptive approaches based on hierarchies of legal instruments, for example, some analyses have pointed to the subservience of UN drug treaties to the UN Charter,[28] the latter thereby seemingly providing a check on human rights–degrading responses to drug control.

Nico Krisch, meanwhile, divides recent debates over 'postnational law' into two key approaches: constitutionalism and pluralism. The former, he writes, 'is directed at a political order comprehensively shaped by law, one in which politics, passions, and power are tamed by the particular rationality of the legal system' and it ultimately aspires to 'a framework that determines how political actors can pursue their causes'.[29] However, Krisch dismisses the constitutionalist approach as placing too great a transformational burden on postnational institutions and society. Lighter approaches to constitutionalism, pervasive and perhaps more realistic, ultimately, he suggests, don't come sufficiently close to meeting the constitutionalists' goals.[30]

Krisch instead suggests a 'pluralist' reconceptualisation of a postnational order, 'characterized by a multiplicity of legal sub-orders, not connected through an overarching frame but interacting in often political modes'.[31] He points to numerous possible examples of regional and global governance, for example the UN sanctions and human rights regimes as well as the regime complexes around international trade, environment and food safety.[32] He also points to a 'normative appeal' to this kind of pluralism:

> By reflecting diverging views on the right scope of the polity, it respects individuals' autonomy and their right to shape their political order, thus furthering democratic values. By leaving relations between different layers of law unsettled, it allows for contestation and adaptation which helps to stabilize postnational governance and remedy power imbalances in its initial design.[33]

Or to frame it in legal harm reduction terms, as Eileen Denza writes,

> So long as national constitutions reflect the history and identity of independent states, and so long as international law itself remains in general non-intrusive as to how it is applied and enforced at national level, there will be infinite variety in national legal systems, and as such, attempts to manage the interrelation of national and international law should focus on approaches conducive to the 'avoidance of conflict'.[34]

The International Law Commission has similarly sought to address some of these issues directly, particularly, 'the splitting up of the law into highly specialized "boxes" that claim relative autonomy from each other and from the general law'.[35] More recent and optimistic scholarship has spoken of a 'refinement on international law' moving into a post-fragmentation period which has incorporated the lessons of fragmentation.[36] As Anne Peters argues, 'new techniques' and 'procedural phenomena' have enabled a greater scope for pluralism, contestation and politicisation within the development of international law.[37] Indeed, a number of works now speak of the 'integrationist forces of Fragmentation'.[38]

9.6 Envisioning the Regime Complex

In a 1982 article, Stephen Krasner articulated a dominant 'modified structural' realist paradigm for international relations theory. This paradigm accepted the orthodox structural realist premise of an international system comprising 'functionally symmetrical, power-maximizing states acting in an anarchic environment'.[39] But, he argued, 'they maintain that under certain restrictive conditions involving the failure of individual action to secure Pareto-optimal outcomes, international regimes may have a significant impact even in an anarchic world.'[40] Thus, the institutionalism inherent in regime theories could coexist with the institutional scepticism of realist scholarship, through this functionalist theoretical bridge. On this point neo-realists, neoliberals and constructivists converged in the 1980s on a relatively consensus definition of regimes.[41] This was ultimately the definition elaborated by Krasner as 'sets of implicit or explicit principles, norms, rules, and decision-making procedures around which actors' expectations converge in a given area of international relations'.[42]

The study of regimes continued along various strands, coinciding with scholars' overarching theoretical frameworks. Neorealists placed a significantly greater emphasis on the role of power and power asymmetries in the formation and operation of regimes.[43] Meanwhile, neoliberals and constructivists developed regime theories derived from their own foundational assumptions. The former emphasised rule-based institutional governance as a mechanism to enable cooperation to overcome suboptimal outcomes. The latter maintained a focus on the subjectivity of norms and principles in the process of regime formation and development.[44] Ultimately, there has been a broad absence of neoliberal institutional or constructivist approaches to evaluating and defining the international drug control system. My work probably comes closest to a neoliberal framework in advocating a strongly functionalist understanding of its evolution and continuation underpinned by a more explicitly historical-constructivist analysis of the roles of state interests and individuals, such as this book provides.[45]

As Colgan et al. write, 'robust regimes' emerge where there are low conflicts of interest and high concentrations of power.[46] Orthodox drug prohibition regime theories are predicated on such a conception. Namely, that the US represented the hegemon, providing stability, leverage and the diplomatic initiatives necessary for the production of a coherent prohibition regime.[47] Under this conception, colonial, transitioning and postcolonial states emerge as rule-takers, beholden to US power and its ideological pursuit of an interventionist 'war on drugs'. Further, European states are represented as relatively passive followers of the US system. As highlighted, historiography over the past three decades sheds a more complicating light. For a start, US hegemony represented a relatively delayed structural development. The US was not even a member of the League of Nations; European states were more activist participants than earlier US-focused historiography gave credit to;[48] modern drug prohibitions did not originate in the US but in Asia;[49]

decolonisation agendas often buttressed and drove prohibitions rather than passively inculcating them;[50] the Cold War and the realities of bipolarity acted as a fundamental constraint on US hegemony and the UN system's ability to pursue US grand visions.[51] The analytic simplicity of the US-led global drug prohibition regime narrative does not, it seems, stand up to empirical evaluation.

The drug control system itself in fact closely reflects the definition of a regime complex suggested by Raustiala and Victor. Namely, it represented 'an array of partially overlapping and non-hierarchical institutions governing a particular issue area'.[52] Initially, the treaty technical bodies, the PCOB and DSB, were purposely divided based on a desire to prevent a centralisation of mandates and bureaucratic control.[53] Ultimately, these were united under the INCB, but a division of power persists, with varying overlapping mandates with CND, UNODC and WHO. Some states, particularly the US, were early advocates for a unified control apparatus under the oversight of a strong single semi-judicial body. However, member states coalesced around a fragmented system with siloed, competing and occasionally unclear mandates to ensure no preponderance of institutional power which could ultimately threaten or supplant national prerogatives.[54] The contemporary UN drug control system reflects this historical reality.

Again, drug control is not unique.[55] Muzaka examines how the intellectual property regime became 'complex', writing that '[i]ntellectual property rights (IPRs) have been contested since their early beginnings', while contestation of key issues, present since the outset, have become more 'intense' and 'global' in recent decades.[56] Although the IPRs regime attempted consolidation in the 1990s under a legally binding WTO dispute resolution mechanism, Muzaka contends that the unresolved tensions persisted. Kolgane et al. go further, claiming that the attempts to enforce a one-size-fits-all model in fact helped make the underlying tensions 'more problematic, obvious and acute'.[57] The result has been the proliferation of overlapping and intersecting regimes meaning,

> IP norms and rules emanate from many other sites, such as the WTO, various human rights bodies (e.g. ECOSOC and CHR), the World Health Organization (WHO), several bilateral free trade agreements (FTAs), the UN Industrial Development Organization (UNIDO), the Convention on Biodiversity (CBD) and even UNESCO. In other words, regimes not previously concerned with intellectual property are now overlapping with each other in this issue-area.[58]

The recent history of drug control again resonates deeply. For example, the UNGASS 2016 witnessed an unprecedented engagement by other UN agencies and bodies.[59] Similarly, the attempt to enforce uniformity perversely exacerbated centrifugal forces. As the early examples of cannabis regulatory fragmentation became apparent in the late 2000s, conservative elements within INCB sought to intervene. The president of INCB at the time, Raymond Yans, directly challenged Uruguay's decision to legalise cannabis, famously referring to the country as 'pirates'. Uruguay portrayed INCB as pursuing the US's drug control agenda while seeming to ignore state-level cannabis legalisation in the US.[60] Alongside damage to its perceived impartiality, its lack of enforcement capability was made overt. Steering clear of the diplomatic pitfalls of the issue, UNODC adopted a relatively agnostic position. Amid leaked reports of rising tensions within its membership,[61] INCB soon followed suit, choosing to veil criticisms within broad diplomatic language and avoiding further direct confrontations with member states.

How then to bridge the gap between pluralists and integrationists on drug control? Both largely agree on the need for some functional rules-based framework for the control of drugs and indeed control of state actions implementing drug control. On what those rules should be and how they are to be interpreted, there is wide divergence, in many cases unbridgeable. Kuyper suggests that the process of fragmentation and regime complexity should be viewed as a mechanism to effect the 'democratization' of the global system.[62] He argues, in terms resonant with drug policy debates, that '[b]ecause each issue-area of world politics is distinct, we require tailor-made (as opposed to one-size-fits-all) responses to the global democratic deficit.'[63] He enumerates a fundamental set of normative standards which must be 'more or less satisfied', specifically 'equal participation, accountability, and institutional revisability'.[64]

Within this context, assuming increased devolution and pluralism in drug control as our starting point seems logical for enabling reform, for a number of reasons. First, the CND operates heavily as a consensus system. The belief in oppositional politics to change this was perhaps shown to be wanting in the 'reform optimist' disappointment at UNGASS 2016.[65] Adapting the thesis put forward by Muzaka in the case of IPRs, dissatisfied state and non-state actors are currently attempting to reframe drug control through linking it to other issue areas and regimes.[66] Helfer explains this as a process of 'regime shifting', whereby actors seek out regimes where they have greater bargaining power.[67] Human rights actors push Geneva to assume a greater role. Development practitioners looks to New York and Washington DC. UNODC, meanwhile, fights to retain the primacy of Vienna.

Simultaneously, we can look to regime 'linkages' as a key modality of both change and continuity. These linkages are the connective tissue within regimes. They also define the natural limits of institutions and regimes within a complex and are the subject of reconceptualisation and renegotiation over time. These linkages, as Kuyper highlights, despite a member state–centrism of many critical drug regime analyses, are particularly susceptible to the influence of non-state actors.[68] Meanwhile, incorporating Keohane and Victor's spectrum approach to regime integration,[69] we can perhaps expect to find drug control moving down the spectrum of legal integration towards greater complexity, devolution and diversity as regime shifting and legal fragmentation take their effect. Whether this process itself sows the seeds for eventual reintegration remains to be seen.

9.7 Conclusion

The architecture of drug control lives not in reductionist frameworks of understanding state actions, limitations and flexibilities. The UN drug control system was constructed on a complex suite of treaties, ambiguities, uncertainties, lagged policy reactions and various other diluting factors. The fragmentation, almost universally acknowledged, of recent years is simply a continuation of the fissures that long underpinned the drug control system and indeed many other international regime systems. In many ways, it is a product of the congestion of international treaty regimes, widely cited and analysed from the 1970s and integrated into the regime literature beginning in the 1990s, and then more systematically analysed with the coalescence around the regime complex formulation.[70]

The next step will be to analyse the ways in which shifting governmental, non-governmental, institutional and regime alliances and constellations can and likely will impact the field of drug control, from international fora, down to the most micro level of communities engaged in trading internationally regulated commodities under a regime complex. As rules become less dichotomous, as interpretations become more varied, and as the instrumental tools for implementing policy choices become more and more contingent on regimes and legal orthodoxies that have little or no relation to the drug control system which originated them, the complexity of policies will become more apparent and ubiquitous. Predictions on this front will be the remit of future research.

This chapter merely resolves to make the conceptual leap to a new interpretive framework for drug control globally and its interaction with local politics and policies.

This book has sought to provide an exhaustive account of the creation of the UN drug control system through the coming into force of the 1961 Single Convention on Narcotic Drugs. The limitations herein are a product of the reliance on Anglo–American and UN archival sources. As such, it inevitably falls short of its goal. Nevertheless, it offers clear avenues for future historical research agendas. Disaggregating from the parsimony of US-centric analyses promises a rich historical endeavour for years to come. Understanding the various national interests, diplomatic contours and domestic political alignments fuelling the drive towards an international drug control system will greatly extend our understanding of the system itself and how drug control can, and likely will, evolve into the future.

The preceding chapters have argued that the outcomes of international drug control efforts, between the partial collapse of the League of Nations system in 1939 and the coming into force of the Single Convention in 1964, derived from a triangulation of three international drug control blocs. These were: control-advocate states, led by the US; producing states and their non-interventionist allies, led by Turkey and the Soviet Union; and moderate manufacturing and consuming countries, led by the UK. In this triangulation process, the UK and US remained the lead international actors and represented the two core policy strands within the system: regulations and prohibitions respectively. These strands overlapped around creating a global regulatory system for managing the international trade in 'dangerous drugs'. They diverged around the peripheral or frontier aspects of this system; namely, where to draw the line between licit and illicit consumption; how tightly to restrict, regulate and prohibit global production; how much national oversight and domestic interference to allow international organisations; and how to deal with existing drug-consuming populations.

When policy interests sufficiently overlapped, and when transatlantic coalitions consciously worked together, international political progress was possible. Where the two diverged – around US demands for strict adherence to prohibitionist principles; overly restricting manufacturers' abilities to procure raw materials; or accepting national obligations for a repressive 'closed institutional' model of dealing with 'addiction' – political momentum generally stalled. Finally, this book argues that the 1961 Single Convention was ultimately a compromise, a regulatory system with prohibitionist aspects. However, in the short term, the Single Convention represented a victory for the regulatory strand and UK-led coalitions over the US-led prohibitionist strand. It highlights that by the 1970s, the US approach once again gained predominance and the system became asymmetrically focused on its prohibitionist strand, perhaps most visibly demonstrated by President Nixon's declaration of a 'war on drugs'.

It has concluded by examining the legal implications of the Single Convention and its continued impact on policy debates. It has charted a new course in drug policy analysis, examining the recent trends of system fragmentation and the emergence of a drug control regime complex. With the onset of cannabis legalisation around the world and other forms of policy fragmentation, the system continues to sail into uncharted territory. As states grow more adventurous and vocal in their search for alternatives, this work highlights that it is vital to return to the history of the current regulatory system and better evaluate the normative, geopolitical, political and socio-economic conditions which produced its regulatory underpinnings.

Six decades on from the 1961 Plenipotentiary Conference, the key questions of international drug control have only grown in scale and prominence. A more thorough understanding of the control system that member states have inherited and the failings and limitations therein, as well as the possibilities of cooperation and consensus will undoubtedly help member states as they seek to chart the next century. The goal of a 'drug-free world' has undoubtedly been shown as a weak and simplistic strategic goal for a complex global phenomenon. Better managing and regulating licit and illicit drug markets will be key to move beyond the many failures of the 'war on drugs' era and establish a future of drug policy grounded in UN principles of cooperation, pragmatism, rule of law, socio-economic development and human rights.

NOTES

Introduction

1 Kettil Bruun, Lynn Pan and Ingemar Rexed, *The Gentlemen's Club: International Control of Drugs and Alcohol* (Chicago, IL: University of Chicago Press, 1975).
2 Statement by Harry Anslinger to 20th Session of CND, on the Review of the Commission's Work During its First Twenty Years, 16 December 1965, FBNA/ACC170–74-5/Box124/File1230–1, United Nations 20th Session (1965).
3 'Ethical' description comes from: William B. McAllister, 'Reflections on a Century of International Drug Control' (London: The London School of Economics, October 2012), 13, https://eprints.lse.ac.uk/47122/1/Governing%20the%20global%20drug%20wars%28published%29.pdf.
4 See for example: John C. McWilliams, *The Protectors: Harry J. Anslinger and the Federal Bureau of Narcotics, 1930–1962* (Newark: University of Delaware Press, 1990), 86–7.
5 McAllister, *Drug Diplomacy in the Twentieth Century: An International History.*
6 Ibid.
7 David R. Bewley-Taylor, *International Drug Control: Consensus Fractured* (Cambridge: Cambridge University Press, 2012).
8 John Collins, 'Rethinking "Flexibilities" in the International Drug Control System—Potential, Precedents and Models for Reforms', *International Journal of Drug Policy* 60 (2018): 107–14.
9 John Collins, 'Evaluating Trends and Stakeholders in the International Drug Control Regime Complex', *International Journal of Drug Policy* 90 (1 April 2021): 103060, https://doi.org/10.1016/j.drugpo.2020.103060.
10 Richard Lines, *Drug Control and Human Rights in International Law* (Cambridge: Cambridge University Press, 2017), https://books.google.co.uk/books?id=zNqiDgAAQBAJ.
11 Arnold H. Taylor, *American Diplomacy and the Narcotics Traffic, 1900–1939: A Study in International Humanitarian Reform* (Durham, NC: Duke University Press, 1969).
12 Bruun, Pan and Rexed, *The Gentlemen's Club: International Control of Drugs and Alcohol.*
13 William O. Walker III, 'Bibliographic Essay', in *Drug Control Policy: Essays in Historical and Comparative Perspective*, ed. William O. Walker III (Pennsylvania State University Press, 1992), 170.
14 McAllister, *Drug Diplomacy in the Twentieth Century: An International History.*

15 John Collins, 'Breaking the Monopoly System: American Influence on the British Decision to Prohibit Opium Smoking and End Its Asian Monopolies, 1939–1945', *International History Review* 39, no. 5 (February 2017): 770–90.

16 Virginia Berridge, *Opium and the People: Opiate Use and Drug Control Policy in Nineteenth and Early Twentieth Century England* (London: Free Association Books, 1999), xxix.

17 Isaac Campos, *Home Grown: Marijuana and the Origins of Mexico's War on Drugs* (University of North Carolina Press, 2012); Paul Gootenberg, *Andean Cocaine: The Making of a Global Drug: The Making of a Global Drug* (University of North Carolina Press, 2009).

18 James H. Mills, 'Cocaine and the British Empire: The Drug and the Diplomats at the Hague Opium Conference, 1911–12', *The Journal of Imperial and Commonwealth History* 42, no. 3 (2014): 400–19.

19 James H. Mills, *Cannabis Britannica: Empire, Trade, and Prohibition 1800–1928: Empire, Trade, and Prohibition 1800–1928* (Oxford: Oxford University Press, 2003); James H. Mills, *Cannabis Nation: Control and Consumption in Britain, 1928–2008* (Oxford: Oxford University Press, 2012).

20 James Windle, 'How the East Influenced Drug Prohibition', *The International History Review* 35, no. 5 (October 2013): 1185–99.

21 Collins, 'Breaking the Monopoly System: American Influence on the British Decision to Prohibit Opium Smoking and End Its Asian Monopolies, 1939–1945',

22 John Collins, 'War, Decolonisation and The Birth of the Illicit Opium Trade in Burma', in *Historical Perspectives on Organised Crime and Terrorism*, ed. James Windle et al. (Oxfordshire: Routledge, 2017).

23 John Collins, 'Imperial Drug Economies, Development, and the Search for Alternatives in Asia, from Colonialism to Decolonisation', *Drug Policies and Development*, 27 August 2020, 43–63, https://doi.org/10.1163/9789004440494_004.

24 Carl A. Trocki, *Opium, Empire and the Global Political Economy: A Study of the Asian Opium Trade, 1750–1950* (Oxfordshire: Routledge, 1999).

25 William O. Walker III, *Opium and Foreign Policy: The Anglo-American Search for Order in Asia, 1912–1954* (Chapel Hill: University of North Carolina Press, 1991).

26 Bradley Hansen, 'Learning to Tax: The Political Economy of the Opium Trade in Iran, 1921–1941', *The Journal of Economic History* 61, no. 1 (1 March 2001): 95–113.

27 Maziyar Ghiabi, *Drugs Politics: Managing Disorder in the Islamic Republic of Iran* (Cambridge: Cambridge University Press, 2019), https://books.google.be/books?id=HoOWDwAAQBAJ.

28 J. T. Bradford, *Poppies, Politics, and Power: Afghanistan and the Global History of Drugs and Diplomacy* (Ithaca: Cornell University Press, 2019), https://books.google.co.uk/books?id=iapzDwAAQBAJ.

29 Ethan A. Nadelmann, 'Global Prohibition Regimes: The Evolution of Norms in International Society', *International Organization* 44, no. 4 (1 October 1990): 479–526.

30 Bewley-Taylor, *The United States and International Drug Control, 1909–1997* (London: Continuum, 1999); Mandy Bentham's book, is one of a number of other books that approaches the subject from the international relations discipline: Mandy Bentham, *The Politics of Drug Control* (New York: Macmillan, 1998).

31 Bruun, Pan and Rexed, *The Gentlemen's Club: International Control of Drugs and Alcohol.*
32 Bewley-Taylor, *The United States and International Drug Control, 1909–1997*, 210.
33 Virginia Berridge, 'Illicit Drugs and Internationalism: The Forgotten Dimension', *Medical History* 2, no. 45 (2001): 282–88.
34 Bewley-Taylor, *International Drug Control: Consensus Fractured.*
35 Bruun, Pan and Rexed, *The Gentlemen's Club: International Control of Drugs and Alcohol.*
36 H. Richard Friman, *NarcoDiplomacy: Exporting the U.S. War on Drugs* (Ithaca: Cornell University Press, 1996).
37 Kal Raustiala and David G. Victor, 'The Regime Complex for Plant Genetic Resources', *International Organization* 58, no. 2 (2004): 279, https://doi.org/10.1017/S0020818304582036.
38 Jonathan W. Kuyper, 'Global Democratization and International Regime Complexity', *European Journal of International Relations* 20, no. 3 (2014): 620–46, https://doi.org/10.1177/1354066113497492.
39 Frank Biermann et al., 'The Fragmentation of Global Governance Architectures: A Framework for Analysis', *Global Environmental Politics* 9, no. 4 (2009): 14–40, https://doi.org/10.1162/glep.2009.9.4.14.

Chapter 1

1 David Courtwright, 'A Short History of Drug Policy or Why We Make War on Some Drugs but Not on Others', in *Governing the Global Drug Wars*, ed. John Collins (London: LSE IDEAS, 2012), https://eprints.lse.ac.uk/47122/1/Governing%20the%20global%20drug%20wars%28published%29.pdf.
2 Joseph Spillane and William B. Mcallister, 'Keeping the Lid on: A Century of Drug Regulation and Control', *Drug and Alcohol Dependence* 70, no. 3 (2003): S. 6, https://doi.org/10.1016/S0376-8716(03)00096-6.
3 Trocki, *Opium, Empire and the Global Political Economy: A Study of the Asian Opium Trade, 1750–1950.*
4 David Bello, 'The Venomous Course of Southwestern Opium: Qing Prohibition in Yunnan, Sichuan, and Guizhou in the Early Nineteenth Century', *The Journal of Asian Studies* 62, no. 4 (2003): 1109–42, https://doi.org/10.2307/3591761.
5 Courtwright, 'A Short History of Drug Policy or Why We Make War on Some Drugs but Not on Others'.
6 Trocki, *Opium, Empire and the Global Political Economy: A Study of the Asian Opium Trade, 1750–1950.*
7 Bello, 'The Venomous Course of Southwestern Opium', 1134.
8 Ibid.
9 Pierre-Arnaud Chouvy, 'Drug Trafficking in and out of the Golden Triangle', in *An Atlas of Trafficking in Southeast Asia: The Illegal Trade in Arms, Drugs, People, Counterfeit Goods and Natural Resources in Mainland* (IB Tauris, 2013), 1–32, https://hal.archives-ouvertes.fr/hal-01050968; Carl A. Trocki, 'Opium and the Beginnings of Chinese Capitalism in Southeast Asia', *Journal of Southeast Asian Studies* 33, no. 2 (2002): 297–314, https://doi.org/10.1017/S0022463402000152.
10 Trocki, 'Opium and the Beginnings of Chinese Capitalism in Southeast Asia', 297.
11 Ibid., 297–8.

12 Rachel Kranton and Anand V. Swamy, 'Contracts, Hold-Up, and Exports: Textiles and Opium in Colonial India', *American Economic Review* 98, no. 3 (1 June 2008): 967–90, https://doi.org/10.1257/aer.98.3.967.
13 Trocki, 'Opium and the Beginnings of Chinese Capitalism in Southeast Asia'.
14 John F. Richards, 'Opium and the British Indian Empire: The Royal Commission of 1895', *Modern Asian Studies* 36, no. 2 (2002): 375–420, https://doi.org/10.1017/S0026749X02002044.
15 Collins, 'Imperial Drug Economies, Development, and the Search for Alternatives in Asia, from Colonialism to Decolonisation'.
16 Trocki, 'Opium and the Beginnings of Chinese Capitalism in Southeast Asia', 299–300.
17 Richards, 'Opium and the British Indian Empire'.
18 Ibid.
19 Collins, 'Imperial Drug Economies, Development, and the Search for Alternatives in Asia, from Colonialism to Decolonisation.'
20 Ibid.
21 H. Wayne Morgan, *Drugs in America: A Social History, 1800–1980* (Syracuse University Press, 1981), 43.
22 Douglas Clark Kinder, 'Shutting Out the Evil: Nativism and Narcotics Control in the United States', in *Drug Control Policy: Essays in Historical Comparative Perspective*, ed. William O. Walker III (Pennsylvania State University Press, 1992).
23 Taylor, *American Diplomacy and the Narcotics Traffic, 1900–1939: A Study in International Humanitarian Reform*, 20–46.
24 Kathryn Meyer and Terry M. Parssinen, *Webs of Smoke: Smugglers, Warlords, Spies, and the History of the International Drug Trade* (Oxford: Rowman & Littlefield, 2002), 41.
25 David F. Musto, *The American Disease: Origins of Narcotic Control*, 3rd ed. (London: Oxford University Press, 1999), 30; S. D Stein, *International Diplomacy, State Administrators, and Narcotics Control: The Origins of a Social Problem* (Aldershot: Gower, 1985), 27–49.
26 See: Morgan, *Drugs in America: A Social History, 1800–1980*, 44–117; Musto, *The American Disease: Origins of Narcotic Control*, 1–23.
27 McAllister, *Drug Diplomacy in the Twentieth Century: An International History*, 27.
28 Ibid., 24; 28–30.
29 Ibid., 30–1; James H. Mills has in a revisionist reading of the 1912 Convention, suggests that Britain's role in driving control efforts may be underestimated. Mills, 'Cocaine and the British Empire: The Drug and the Diplomats at the Hague Opium Conference, 1911–12'.
30 'The Hague International Opium Convention' (The Hague, 1912).
31 Berridge, *Opium and the People: Opiate Use and Drug Control Policy in Nineteenth and Early Twentieth Century England*, 258–9.
32 Taylor, *American Diplomacy and the Narcotics Traffic, 1900–1939: A Study in International Humanitarian Reform*, 141–4.
33 Treaty Preamble quoted in: Bruun, Pan and Rexed, *The Gentlemen's Club: International Control of Drugs and Alcohol*, 38.
34 McAllister, *Drug Diplomacy in the Twentieth Century: An International History*, 37, 50–3.

35 Meyer and Parssinen, *Webs of Smoke: Smugglers, Warlords, Spies, and the History of the International Drug Trade*, 68.
36 Ibid., 67–72. McAllister, *Drug Diplomacy in the Twentieth Century: An International History*, 61–3.
37 Quoted in: Meyer and Parssinen, *Webs of Smoke: Smugglers, Warlords, Spies, and the History of the International Drug Trade*, 68–9.
38 Letizia Paoli, Victoria A. Greenfield, and Peter Reuter, *The World Heroin Market: Can Supply Be Cut?* (Oxford University Press, 2009), 16.
39 Meyer and Parssinen, *Webs of Smoke: Smugglers, Warlords, Spies, and the History of the International Drug Trade*, 68–9.
40 Quoted in ibid., 71.
41 Meyer and Parsinnen describe the policy as a 'masterpiece of hyocricy'. Ibid., 71.
42 McAllister, *Drug Diplomacy in the Twentieth Century: An International History*, 67–74.
43 Ibid., 76–7; Bruun, Pan and Rexed, *The Gentlemen's Club: International Control of Drugs and Alcohol*, 14.
44 McWilliams, *The Protectors: Harry J. Anslinger and the Federal Bureau of Narcotics, 1930–1962*, 31–3, 44; McAllister, *Drug Diplomacy in the Twentieth Century: An International History*, 89.
45 See for example: McWilliams, *The Protectors: Harry J. Anslinger and the Federal Bureau of Narcotics, 1930–1962*, 86–7.
46 Douglas Kinder was the first to apply the term 'bureaucratic entrepreneur' to Anslinger. Douglas Clark Kinder, 'Bureaucratic Cold Warrior: Harry J. Anslinger and Illicit Narcotics Traffic', *Pacific Historical Review* 50, no. 2 (1 May 1981): 169–91. The term 'moral entrepreneur' was coined by Howard Becker. Howard Saul Becker, *Outsiders: Studies in the Sociology of Deviance* (Free Press, 1997).
47 McAllister, *Drug Diplomacy in the Twentieth Century: An International History*, 89–91.
48 Walker III, *Opium and Foreign Policy: The Anglo-American Search for Order in Asia, 1912–1954*, 57.
49 McAllister, *Drug Diplomacy in the Twentieth Century: An International History*, 110.
50 Ibid., 95–6.
51 Ibid., 101.
52 Ibid., 100.
53 Robert Maule, 'British Policy Discussions on the Opium Question in the Federated Shan States, 1937–1948', *Journal of Southeast Asian Studies* 33, no. 2 (June 2002): 203–24; Robert Maule, 'The Opium Question in the Federated Shan States, 1931–36: British Policy Discussions and Scandal', *Journal of Southeast Asian Studies* 23, no. 1 (March 1992): 14–36.
54 McAllister, *Drug Diplomacy in the Twentieth Century: An International History*, 106–9.
55 Department of State Press Release, Weekly Issue No. 111, Publication No. 256, pp. 444–6 quoted in Memo: The Problem of Prepared Opium, 23 March 1943, FBNA/ACC170-74-5/Box124/File1230-A, Postwar Narcotics Problems #1.
56 McAllister, *Drug Diplomacy in the Twentieth Century: An International History*, 112–14; Alan A. Block, 'European Drug Traffic and Traffickers between the Wars:

The Policy of Suppression and Its Consequences', *Journal of Social History* 23, no. 2 (1 December 1989): 315–37.

57 McAllister, *Drug Diplomacy in the Twentieth Century: An International History*, 123.

58 The typology of control advocates, producer states, manufacturing states and consumer states is derived from: McAllister, *Drug Diplomacy in the Twentieth Century: An International History.*

59 Ibid., 127.

Chapter 2

1 FPA Memo: 'Control of Opium and Other Dangerous Drugs…', December 1944; Numerous references to perceived politicization of OAC in: FBNA/ACC170–74-5/Box120/File1230–1, [UNO] #1 (1939–45); Extract from: Acting Sec-Gen Report on the Work of the league 1941–1942, FBNA/ACC170–74-12/Box171/File 1230-8, PCOB (1940–67); Makins to Chatterjee, 11 September 1940, PRO, FO371/24749.

2 Quoted in Renborg memo: 'Note on the Importance of the Estimate System…', 6 July 1942, FBNA/ACC170–74-12/Box171/File1230–8, DSB (1940–67).

3 McAllister, *Drug Diplomacy in the Twentieth Century: An International History*, 136.

4 Anslinger to Sharman, 6 August 1940, FBNA/ACC170–74-12/Box152/File0660 Canada I (1929–41).

5 McAllister, *Drug Diplomacy in the Twentieth Century: An International History*, 137–40.

6 Ibid.

7 to May, 10 October 1940, FBNA/ACC170–74-12/Box171/File1230–2, PCOB (1939–48).

8 FO to Kelly (Berne), 7 August 1940, BNA-FO371/24749; File Minutes, 3 April 1942, Proposed Meeting of the PCOB, BNA-FO371/28075.

9 See files 'Position of the [PCOB]', July–November 1940, BNA-FO371/24749.

10 McAllister, *Drug Diplomacy in the Twentieth Century: An International History.*

11 McAllister, 'Reflections on a Century of International Drug Control', 11.

12 Moorhead to Gavrilovitch, 6 March 1946, FBNA/ACC170–74-5/Box120/File1230–1 [UNO] #3 (1946).

13 Mona Yung-Ning Hoo, *Painting the Shadows: The Extraordinary Life of Victor Hoo* (London: Eldridge and Co., 1998).

14 McAllister, *Drug Diplomacy in the Twentieth Century: An International History*, 90.

15 Ibid., 138 & 149.

16 Lothian to FO, 5 September 1940; Chatterjee to Makins, 3 September 1940; Makins to Chatterjee, 11 September 1940; Makins to Chatterjee, 25 September 1940, BNA-FO371/24749.

17 Gaston to Morgenthau, 19 September 1940; Hart to Weddell, November 1940; further correspondence: FBNA/ACC170–74–12/Box171/File1230–2 PCOB (1939–48).

18 Memorandum: 'Activities of the [PCOB]', 15 March 1941; Herbert May to Anslinger 26 June 1941; numerous files in FBNA/ACC170–74-12/Box171/File1230–2 PCOB (1939–48).

19 See extensive documentation in FBNA/ACC170–74-12/Box171/File1230–8 DSB (1940–67); FBNA/ACC170–74-12/Box171/File1230–2 PCOB (1939–48).
20 Felkin to Anslinger, 28 August 1941, FBNA/ACC170–74-12/Box171/File1230–2 PCOB (1939–48).
21 Anslinger to Felkin, 12 February 1943, FBNA/ACC170–74-12/Box171/File1230–2 PCOB (1939–48).
22 'The Reminiscences of Herbert L. May', in *Oral History Research Office* (New York: Butler Library, Columbia University, 1951), p. 85.
23 Report on the Work of the league 1941–1942, FBNA/ACC170–74-12/Box171/File1230–8, PCOB (1940–67).
24 Delevingne to Renborg, 16 February 1942, FBNA/ACC170–74-12/Box171/File1230–8, DSB (1940–67).
25 Treasury Dept. to State Dept., 14 June 1940; Report on the Work of the league 1941–1942, FBNA/ACC170–74-12/Box171/File1230–8, PCOB (1940–67).
26 Bertil Renborg: Note on the Possibility of Using International Control of Narcotic Drugs as a Means of Preventing Aggression, FBNA/ACC170–74-5/Box120/File1230–1 [UNO] #2 (August–October 1945); McAllister, *Drug Diplomacy in the Twentieth Century: An International History*, 145–9.
27 State Department Aide Memoire, 21 September 1943, PRO, FO371/34545; numerous documents in FBNA/ACC170–71-A-3554/Box20/File0660, Japan (1934–46) & Japan Postwar (1945).
28 Meyer and Parssinen, *Webs of Smoke: Smugglers, Warlords, Spies, and the History of the International Drug Trade*, 280.
29 US Treasury Dept. Press Release, 26 January 1942, FBNA/ACC170–75-17/Box86, Miscellaneous File 1910 Hiscock #1.
30 Morgan, *Drugs in America: A Social History, 1800–1980*, 108–9.
31 Berridge, *Opium and the People: Opiate Use and Drug Control Policy in Nineteenth and Early Twentieth Century England*, 262.
32 For example see: George White to Anslinger, 6 January 1943; numerous documents, FBNA/ACC170–71-A-3554/Box18/File0660, Iran (1941–5).
33 Wright to Clarke, 6 October 1943, BNA-FO371/34545.
34 McAllister, *Drug Diplomacy in the Twentieth Century: An International History*, 132.
35 Anslinger to Sharman, 6 August 1940, FBNA/ACC170–74-12/Box152/File0660 Canada I (1929–41).
36 McAllister, *Drug Diplomacy in the Twentieth Century: An International History*, 144–5.
37 For example see Sharman Memorandum: Re. Supply of Narcotics from Great Britain to Canada, 28 June 1944, FBNA/ACC170–74-12/Box152/File0660, Canada II (1942–5).
38 Chest kilogram metric from: Timothy Brook, 'Opium and Collaboration in Central China 1938–1940', in *Opium Regimes: China, Britain, and Japan, 1839 – 1952*, ed. Timothy Brook and Bob Tadashi Wakabayashi (Berkeley: University of California Press, 2000), 328.
39 Blaxter to Thornton, 27 April 1940; Letter to Thornton, 15 May 1940, BNA-FO371/24748.
40 Note on Nemazi Family, 18 June 1940, FO371/24748.
41 Ronson to Henniker, 23 September 1940, BNA-FO371/24748.

42 Talbot's Minute, 9 October 1940; Minutes, 14 October 1940, File: Purchase of Opium from Iran, BNA-FO371/24748.
43 Singapore to Loyd, 10 August 1940; CO to Straits Settlements, 23 November 1940, BNA-FO371/24749.
44 FO to Messrs. Bellairs Atkinson, 28 January 1941, BNA-FO371/24749.
45 Quote in IOC (54)84, 19 June 1954, BNA-CAB134/958.
46 McAllister, *Drug Diplomacy in the Twentieth Century: An International History*, 94.
47 Sharman to Anslinger, 3 May 1943, FBNA/ACC170–74-12/Box152/File0660, Canada II (1942–5).
48 Sharman to Anslinger, 29 July 1940, FBNA/ACC170–74-12/Box152/File0660, Canada I (1929–41).
49 Col. Sharman's Circular to Licensed Narcotic Wholesales, 14 September 1939; Sharman to Anslinger, 20 July 1940; Anslinger to Sharman, 6 August 1940, FBNA/ACC170–74-12/Box152/File0660, Canada I (1929–41).
50 Anslinger to Coles, 21 June 1939; Coles to Anslinger, 11 July 1939; Thornton to Anslinger, 19 October 1939; Anslinger to Thornton, 4 November 1939, FBNA/ACC170–71-A-3554/Box18/File0660, England (1928–42).
51 Note attached to: 'Drug Prescription Betrays Doctor as an Addict', *The Daily Express*, 12 January 1940; numerous press clippings; US Consulate to Secretary of State, Subject: 'Liverpool as a Port of Transfer for Opium Smuggling', 26 May 1942; Anslinger to Thornton, 21 October 1942, FBNA/ACC170–71-A-3554/Box18/File0660, England (1928–42).
52 Memo: The Problem of Prepared Opium, 23 March 1943, FBNA/ACC170–74-5/Box124/File1230-A, Postwar Narcotics Problems #1.
53 [LON] 1751(f), 22 April 1939; [LON] O.C.1753(c), 20 February 1939; [LON] C.C.1792, 17 September 1940, quoted in Memo: The Problem of Prepared Opium, 23 March 1943, FBNA/ACC170–74-5/Box124/File1230-A, Postwar Narcotics Problems #1.
54 Sharman to Asnlinger, 5 September 1942, FBNA/ACC170–74-5/Box124/File1230-A, Postwar Narcotics Problems #1.
55 [LON] C.635.H.254.1930.XI, November 1930, Vol. I, P. 37. Quoted in Memo: The Problem of Prepared Opium, 23 March 1943; Memo: The Problem of Prepared Opium, 23 March 1943, FBNA/ACC170–74-5/Box124/File1230-A, Postwar Narcotics Problems #1.
56 For a discussion of this phenomenon see: Meyer and Parssinen, *Webs of Smoke: Smugglers, Warlords, Spies, and the History of the International Drug Trade*, 12.
57 Yongming Zhou, *Anti-Drug Crusades in Twentieth-Century China: Nationalism, History, and State Building* (Oxford: Rowman & Littlefield, 1999), 80–4.
58 Memo: The Problem of Prepared Opium, 23 March 1943, FBNA/ACC170–74-5/Box124/File1230-A, Postwar Narcotics Problems #1.
59 See extensive US FBN files: FBNA/ACC170–71-A-3554/Box16/File0660, China Folders 14–18 (1936–46); For British accounts see: BNA-FO371/34546.
60 Renborg to Sharman, 29 July 1942; Sharman to Renborg, 1 August 1942; Morlock to Anslinger, 6 August 1942, FBNA/ACC170–74-5/Box124/File1230-A, Postwar Narcotics Problems #2.
61 Sharman to Anslinger, 6 July 1942; Delevingne to May, 25 April, 1942; Anslinger to Sharman, 1 July 1942, FBNA/ACC170–74-5/Box124/File1230-A, Postwar Narcotics Problems #1.

62 Anslinger to Sharman, 2 September 1942, FBNA/ACC170–74-5/Box124/File1230-A, Postwar Narcotics Problems #1.
63 Sharman to Anslinger, 5 September 1942; Morlock to Anslinger, 11 September 1942; Anslinger to Chamberlain, 3 October 1942, FBNA/ACC170–74-5/Box124/File1230-A, Postwar Narcotics Problems #1.
64 Renborg to Anslinger, 28 December 1942, FBNA/ACC170–74-5/Box124/File1230-A, Postwar Narcotics Problems #1.
65 Renborg Memorandum Concerning Presparation for the Post-War Period, August 1942, FBNA/ACC170–74-5/Box124/File1230-A, Postwar Narcotics Problems #1.
66 Anslinger to Renborg, 21 December 1942, FBNA/ACC170–74-5/Box124/File1230-A, Postwar Narcotics Problems #1.
67 Sharman to Renborg, 4 January 1943; Renborg to Anslinger, 18 January 1943; Renborg to Sharman, 18 January 1943; Sharman to Anslinger, 21 January 1943, FBNA/ACC170–74-5/Box124/File1230-A, Postwar Narcotics Problems #1.
68 Collins, 'Breaking the Monopoly System: American Influence on the British Decision to Prohibit Opium Smoking and End Its Asian Monopolies, 1939–1945'.
69 'Meeting in the Office of the Commissioner of Narcotics', 4 December 1942, FBNA/ACC170–74-5/Box124/File1230-A, Postwar Narcotics Problems #1.
70 Memo: Meeting in the Office of the Commissioner of Narcotics, 13 January 1943; Sharman to Anslinger, 24 December 1942; Chamberlain to Dixon, 7 January 1943; Anslinger to Sharman, 8 February 1943, FBNA/ACC170–74-5/Box124/File1230-A, Postwar Narcotics Problems #1.
71 Minister Plenipotentiary to Anslinger, 12 March 1943, FBNA/ACC170–74-5/Box124/File1230-A, Postwar Narcotics Problems #1.
72 Williams (FO) to Harris (HO), 18 Febraury 1943, BNA-FO371/34545.
73 Delevingne to Harris (HO), 28 February 1943, BNA-FO371/34545.
74 FO to Halifax, 4 March 1943, BNA-FO371/34545.
75 Gater (CO) to Harris (HO), 6 April 1943, BNA-FO371/34545.
76 Williams' minute, File: Minutes of Informal Meeting of the [FPA], 25 May 1943, BNA-FO371/34545.
77 Minutes of Meeting in the Office of the Commissioner of Narcotics, 17 March 1943, BNA-FO371/34545.
78 Ibid.
79 Draft: Hamilton to Dr. Thompson, 8 March 1943; Morlock to Anslinger, 25 March 1943; Hamilton to Dr. Thomson, 20 March 1943, FBNA/ACC170–74-5/Box124/File1230-A, Postwar Narcotics Problems #1.
80 McAllister, *Drug Diplomacy in the Twentieth Century: An International History*, 150–1.
81 Townsend Hoopes and Douglas Brinkley, *Franklin Delano Roosevelt and the Creation of the U.N.* (Yale University Press, 1997), 65–7.
82 Halifax to Anthony Eden (FO), 26 April 1943, BNA-FO371/34545.
83 Scott's Minute; Minute, File: Minutes of Informal Meeting of the [FPA], 26 May 1943, BNA-FO371/34545.
84 'The Fight Against Opium and the System of a Government-Monopoly' from DeKat Angelino, *Colonial Policy*, Vol. II, in FBNA/ACC170–74-5/Box124/File1230-A, Postwar Narcotics BNAblems #1.
85 Anslinger note attached to DeKat Angelino, *Colonial Policy*, Vol. II, FBNA/ACC170–74-5/Box124/File1230-A, Postwar Narcotics Problems #1.

86 Ibid.; Moorhead memo, 14 June 1943, FBNA/ACC170–74-5/Box124/File1230-A, Postwar Narcotics Problems #1.

87 Roberts to Under-Secretary of State, 15 June 1943, BNA-FO371/34545.

88 Roberts' minute, File: Minutes of Informal Meeting of the [FPA], 25 May 1943; Paskin (CO) to FO, 16 June 1943, BNA-FO371/34545.

89 FO to Washington Embassy, 2 November 1943, BNA-FO371/34546.

90 Ibid.

91 Harold H. Traver, 'Colonial Relations and Opium Control Policy in Hong Kong, 1841–1945', in *Drugs, Law, and the State*, ed. Harold H. Traver and Mark S. Gaylord (New Brunswick: Transaction Publishers, 1992), 143–4.

92 Minutes of the Thirty-Third Meeting of the Inter-Departmental Opium Committee, 7 September 1943, BNA-FO371/34545.

93 Secretary of State to Government of India, 25 October 1943, BNA-FO371/34546.

94 For example see, Delevingne to Reynolds, 25 October 1943, BNA-FO371/34546; Parliamentary Question and Answer, 10 November 1943, BNA-FO371/34546.

95 Wright to Clarke, 6 October 1943, BNA-FO371/34545.

96 Tomkins to Williams, 12 April 1944, BNA-FO371/39366.

97 Tomkins to Williams, October 1943, BNA-FO371/34546.

98 Minutes of the Thirty-Fourth Meeting of [IOC], 27 October 1943; Minutes of the Thirty-Third Meeting of [IOC], 7 September 1943, BNA-FO371/34545.

99 'Remarks by Congressman Carroll Reece', 7 July 1943; Carroll Reece to Anslinger, 4 September 1943; Anslinger to Carroll Reece, 16 September 1943; Telegram from American Embassy, Chungking to State Department, 10 August 1943; FPA to Mr. Paton, 19 August 1943; Moorhead to Anslinger, 18 August 1943, FBNA/ACC170–74-5/Box124/File1230-A, [LON] Postwar Narcotics Problem #2 (1942–3).

100 War Secretary Stimson to Treasury Secretary Morgenthau, 11 August 1943, FBNA/ACC170–74-5/Box124/File1230-A, [LON] Postwar Narcotics Problem #2 (1942–3).

101 Helen Howell Moorhead to Anslinger, 18 August 1943; Anslinger to Dr. Hoo, 13 August 1943, FBNA/ACC170–74-5/Box124/File1230-A, [LON] Postwar Narcotics Problem #2 (1942–3).

102 State Department Aide-memoire, 21 September 1943, BNA-FO371/34545.

103 Wright (Washington Embassy) to Clarke (FO), 6 October 1943, BNA-FO371/34545.

104 See BNA-FO371/34546.

105 McAllister, *Drug Diplomacy in the Twentieth Century: An International History*, 151.

106 Walker III, *Opium and Foreign Policy: The Anglo-American Search for Order in Asia, 1912–1954*, 153–7.

107 Dudley Minute, File: Control of opium in Far Eastern Territories freed from Japanese occupation, 18 October 1943, BNA-FO371/34545. Also numerous documents in BNA-FO371/34546.

108 Sharman to Anslinger, 18 September 1943, FBNA/ACC170–74-5/Box124/File1230-A, [LON] Postwar Narcotics Problem #2 (1942–3).

109 Anslinger Note, 4 October 1943, FBNA/ACC170–74-5/Box124/File1230-A, [LON] Postwar Narcotics Problem #2 (1942–3).

110 Opium smoking, Far Eastern Territories, 10 November 1943; Statement by Acting Secretary of State, 10 November 1943, BNA-FO371/34546.
111 Wright to Anslinger, 17 November 1943; 'Opium Control', *The Washington Post*, 14 December 1943, FBNA/ACC170-74-5/Box124/File1230-A, [LON] Postwar Narcotics Problem #2 (1942–3); Minutes, 29 December 1943, File: Chinese reactions to [HMG] Decision. . ., BNA-FO371/34546.
112 'The Trade in Opium', The Times, 26 November 1943; Congressional Record: Remarks of Rep. Carroll Reece, in House of Representatives, 2 Decemeber 1943, FBNA/ACC170-74-5/Box124/File1230-A, [LON] Postwar Narcotics Problem #2 (1942–3).
113 'China Hails British, Netherlands Statement on Opium,' 24 November 1943, BNA-FO371/34546.
114 'A Ban on Opium', Letter to the Editor of *The Times*, 11 December 1943; 'Opium Traffic in the Far East', *The Lancet*, 18 December 1943, FBNA/ACC170-74-5/Box124/File1230-A, [LON] Postwar Narcotics Problem #2 (1942–3).
115 McAllister, *Drug Diplomacy in the Twentieth Century: An International History*, 152.
116 Art 3(a), 'The Hague International Opium Convention' (The Hague, 1912).
117 Taylor, *American Diplomacy and the Narcotics Traffic, 1900–1939: A Study in International Humanitarian Reform*, 306.
118 Hansen, 'Learning to Tax: The Political Economy of the Opium Trade in Iran, 1921–1941.'
119 Alfred W. McCoy, *The Politics of Heroin: CIA Complicity in the Global Drug Trade, Afghanistan, Southeast Asia, Central America, Colombia*, 3rd ed. (Brooklyn, NY: Lawrence Hill Books, 2003), 468.
120 Friman, *NarcoDiplomacy: Exporting the U.S. War on Drugs*, 43.
121 'Opium trade is Hit', St Louis Post Dispatch, 3 September 1941; Secretary of State to Customs Agency Service, 21 October 1941; American Consul Teheran, 27 February 1942, FBNA/ACC170-71-A-3554/Box18/File0660 Iran (1941–5); Hansen, 'Learning to Tax: The Political Economy of the Opium Trade in Iran, 1921–1941', 107.
122 McAllister, *Drug Diplomacy in the Twentieth Century: An International History*, 148.
123 Saleh to Anslinger, 27 March 1942; Opium Prices in Iran, Quarter ended 31 December 1942, Berle to Dreyfus, 6 March 1943; Draft Memorandum (undated), FBNA/ACC170-71-A-3554/Box18/File0660, Iran (1941–5);
124 Memoradum: Trade Agreement with Iran, by George Morlock, 1 April 1942, FBNA/ACC170-74-12/Box142/File0480-172, Opium Reserves, Iranian Opium (1941–5).
125 For example see Memorandum of Conversation: Importation of Iranian Opium, 14 September 1942; Draft note to Secretary of State, September 26 1942; Morlock to Anslinger, 5 October 1942, FBNA/ACC170-74-12/Box142/File0480-172, Opium Reserves, Iranian Opium (1941–5).
126 Thornton to Williams, 6 April 1943; Minutes, 13 & 15 April 1943, File: Traffic in Persian Opium; Williams to Thornton, 17 April 1943, BNA-FO371/34541.
127 Trade Agreement between the US and Iran Signed 8 April 1943. Press Release, FBNA/ACC170-71-A-3554/Box18/File0660 Iran (1941–5); http://history.house.gov/HistoricalHighlight/Detail/36918.

128 Cordell Hull to Mohammed Shayesteh, 8 April 1943; Herbert Gaston to Henry Stimson, 21 December 1943, FBNA/ACC170-71-A-3554/Box18/File0660 Iran (1941–5).

129 Paraphrase of telegram from US Legation, Tehran, 14 October 1941; State Department to FBN, 20 October 1941; Engert to Secretary of State, 19 December 1942; State to Legation Kabul, 21 January 1943; Note of telephone call, 12 October 1943; State to American Minister Kabul, 22 January 1944, FBNA/ACC170-74-12/Box151/File0660, Afghanistan (1929–68).

130 He eventually wrote a book about his years of service in Egypt. Thomas Russell, *Egyptian Service: 1902–1946* (Murray, 1949).

131 Compilation of news clippings; use of term 'drug habit' in Russell Pasha to Anslinger, 23 June 1943, FBNA/ACC170-71-A-3554/Box16/File0660, Egypt (1940–5).

132 Russell Pasha to Anslinger, 7 September 1941; Anslinger to Russell Pasha, 23 June 1941, FBNA/ACC170-71-A-3554/Box16/File0660, Egypt (1940–5). Correspondence in FBNA/ACC170-73-1/Box45/File0145, Mrs. Corinna Lindon Smith (1940–58).

133 'War Deals Death Blow at Drug Traffickers', Egyptian Mail, 12 February 1941; Russell Pasha to Renborg, 24 March 1942, FBNA; Russell Pasha to Anslinger, 7 September 1941; Russell Pasha to H.E. Hussein Sirry Pasha, 16 November 1941; FBNA/ACC170-71-A-3554/Box16/File0660, Egypt (1940–5).

134 Ibid.

135 Anslinger and Gaston Notes attached to Russell Pasha to Anslinger, 24 March 1942; Gaston to Morlock, 30 April 1942; Memorandum of Conversation between Morlock and Saleh, 19 September 1942, FBNA/ACC170-74-12/Box142/File0480-172, Opium Reserves, Iranian Opium (1941–5).

136 Russell Pasha to Anslinger, 25 July 1942, FBNA/ACC170-71-A-3554/Box16/File0660, Egypt (1940–5).

137 Russell Pasha to Shone, 26 December 1943, BNA-FO371/39364.

138 Williams (FO) to Harris (HO), 19 January 1944; Reynolds (HO) to Williams (FO), 3 February 1944, BNA-FO371/39364.

139 See clippings in: Drug Traffic in Egypt, 24 April 1944, BNA-FO371/39364; Russell Pasha to Anslinger, 25 July 1942; Anslinger to Russell Pasha, 3 March 1944, FBNA/ACC170-71-A-3554/Box16/File0660, Egypt (1940–5); Russell Pasha to H.E. Faud Serag El Din Pasha, 22 April 1944, BNA-FO371/39364.

140 Ibid.

141 Ibid.

142 Sharman to Anslinger, 10 October 1943, FBNA/ACC170-74-12/Box152/File0660, Canada II (1942–5); Anslinger to Thornton, 2 March 1944; Sharman to Thornton, April 1944; Anslinger to Sharman, 18 April 1944, FBNA/ACC170-71-A-3554/Box18/File0660, England (1943–50). Sharman to Anslinger, 5 April 1944, FBNA/ACC170-71-A-3554/Box18/File0660, England (1928–42).

143 Sharman to Anslinger, 15 April 1944; Anslinger to Sharman, 18 April 1944; Sharman to Anslinger, 5 April 1944; Anslinger to Sharman, 18 April 1944; Anslinger to Sharman, 9 August 1944; FBNA/ACC170-71-A-3554/Box18/File0660, England (1943–50).

144 Anslinger to Thornton, August 10 1944, FBNA/ACC170–71-A-3554/Box18/File0660, England (1943–50); 'Open scandal' quote in: US Treasury Dept. Press Release, 26 January 1942, FBNA/ACC170–75-17/Box 86/File1910, Hiscock #1.
145 Col. Sharman's Memorandum: Re. Supply of Narcotics from Great Britain to Canada, 28 June 1944, FBNA/ACC170–74-12/Box152/File0660, Canada II (1942–5).
146 Anslinger to Sharman, 1 September 1943; Anslinger to Sharman, 23 July 1942; Sharman to Anslinger, 28 July 1942, FBNA/ACC170–74-12/Box152/File0660, Canada II (1942–5).
147 Ministry of Foreign Affairs of Brazil, Quoted in: Anslinger to Sharman, 27 July 1944, FBNA/ACC170–74-12/Box152/File0660, Canada II (1942–5).
148 Sharman to Anslinger, 28 July 1942; Col. Sharman's Memorandum: Re. Supply of Narcotics from Great Britain to Canada, 28 June 1944, FBNA/ACC170–74-12/Box152/File0660, Canada II (1942–5); Morlock to Anslinger, 14 April 1944; Sharman to Anslinger 27 May 1944, FBNA/ACC170–74-5/Box120/File1230–1 [UNO] #1 (1939–45).
149 PCOB quote in: Col. Sharman's Memorandum: Re. Supply of Narcotics from Great Britain to Canada, 28 June 1944, FBNA/ACC170–74-12/Box152/File0660, Canada II (1942–5).
150 Clutterbuck to Hudd, 18 November 1944; Sharman Memorandum: Re. Narcotic Supplies . . ., London, 3 December 1944, FBNA/ACC170–74-12/Box152/File0660, Canada II (1942–5).
151 Thornton to Anslinger, 3 October 1944, FBNA/ACC170–71-A-3554/Box18/File0660, England (1943–50).
152 Coles to Anslinger, 25 October 1945; Anslinger to Coles, 14 November 1946, FBNA/ACC170–71-A-3554/Box18/File0660, England (1943–1950).
153 Hudson Minute, File: Suppression of opium smoking, 13 March 1944, BNA-FO371/39366.
154 British Aide-Memoire to US Government, October 1943, FBNA/ACC170–74-5/Box124/File1230-A, [LON] Postwar Narcotics Problem #2 (1942-3).
155 Minutes of the Thirty-Fourth Meeting of IOC, 27 October 1943, BNA-FO371/34545.
156 FO to Washington Embassy, 30 October 1943, BNA-FO371/34546.
157 Drawn from: Report . . . opium problem in Burma, 30 November 1943, BNA-FO370/39366.
158 Drawn from: Report . . . opium problem in Burma, 30 November 1943, BNA-FO370/39366.
159 LBO to Taylor, January 1944, BNA-FO371/39366.
160 Lindsay Minute, Notes on Policy of Opium Prohibition in Burma, January 1944; Letter, Lindsay to McGuire, 27 November 1943, BNA-FO371/39366.
161 Williams' Minute, 7 February 1944; Scott Minute, 14 February 1944, BNA-FO371/39366.
162 Williams to Taylor, 8 March 1944, BNA-FO371/39366.
163 Wright to Anslinger, 17 November 1943, FBNA/ACC170–74-5/Box124/File1230-A, [LON] Postwar Narcotics Problem #2 (1942–3).
164 Drawn from: Congressional Record No. 33, 21 Febrary 1944, BNA-FO371/39366.

165 Lee Edwards, *Missionary for Freedom: The Life and Times of Walter Judd* (Paragon House, 1990); Gao Yanli, 'Judd's China: A Missionary Congressman and US-China Policy', *Journal of Modern Chinese History* 2, no. 2 (December 2008): 197–219.

166 William B. McAllister, 'A Limited Enterprise: The History of International Efforts to Control Drugs in the Twentieth Century' (PhD Dissertation, Virginia, University of Virginia, 1996), 269–71.

167 Drawn from: Congressional Record No. 33, 21 Febrary 1944, BNA-FO371/39366.

168 Taylor to Williams, 12 March 1944, BNA-FO371/39366.

169 WO to SACEA, 21 February 1944, BNA-FO371/39366.

170 Roberts to Wright, 23 March 1944, BNA-FO371/39366.

171 Halifax to Sir. Cadogan, 17 April 1944, BNA-FO371/39366.

172 Harrison to Taylor, 1 May 1944, BNA-FO371/39366.

173 Taylor to Harrison, 10 May 1944; Reay Minutes, 14 & 21 May 1944, File: Control of Opium Smoking in Burma, BNA-FO371/39366.

174 Morlock to Anslinger, 14 April 1944, FBNA/ACC170–74-5/Box120/File1230–1 [UNO] #1 (1939–45).

175 The impact of the Judd Resolution has been dramatically understated in existing historiography. Most have largely overlooked it. William O. Walker mentions it in passing and that the UK found it an annoyance. William O. Walker III, ed., *Drug Control Policy: Essays in Historical and Comparative Perspective* (Pennsylvania State University Press, 1992), 163. William McAllister, in an early work, acknowledges it as an example of Congressional action then utilised by the State Department, McAllister, 'A Limited Enterprise: The History of International Efforts to Control Drugs in the Twentieth Century', 270. He omits mention of the resolution in his later text McAllister, *Drug Diplomacy in the Twentieth Century: An International History*.

176 HR 241, June 8 1944, BNA-FO371/40503.

177 Press Statement by Secretary of State, July 3 1944, BNA-FO, 371/40503.

178 See File: Suppression of opium smoking. . ., C 4781, April 1944, BNA-FO371/39366.

179 Gaston to Bloom, 13 May 1944, BNA-FO371/40503.

180 Stimson to Bloom, May 1944, BNA-FO371/40503.

181 Hudson Minute, File: Suppression of opium smoking, 13 March 1944, BNA-FO371/39366.

182 Excerpt, Chungking to State Department, 8 July 1943; Memo: Rice to Gauss, 23 February 1944; Report, Chungking, 30 October 1943; Excerpt from Report, re. Chungking Embassy official's trip. . ., 18 January 1944, FBNA/ACC170–71-A-3554/Box16/File0660, China #18 (1942–6).

183 'Chang Reiterates Decision to Wipe out Drug in Opium Suppression Day Message', Chinese News Service, NYC, 3 June 1944; *New York Times* Article and Herbert Gaston's note attached, 29 July 1944, Report on Opium Smoking in Chengtu, December 1944, FBNA/ACC170–71-A-3554/Box16/File0660, China #18 (1942–6).

184 Memo by Wallinger, forwarded by Washington DC Embassy to State Dept., 28 March 1945, FBNA/ACC170–71-A-3554/Box16/File0660, China #18 (1942–6).

185 State Department Memorandum for British Government, September 1944, BNA-FO371/40503.
186 Gallman to Sterndale-Bennett, 8 September 1944, BNA-FO371/40503.
187 State Department Memorandum for British Government, September 1944, BNA-FO371/40503.
188 Quoted in Pethick-Lawrence to Noel Baker, 25 January 1946, BNA-FO371/57108.
189 State Department Memorandum for British Government, September 1944, BNA-FO371/40503.
190 Ibid.
191 Moorhead to Anslinger, 10 November 1944, FBNA/ACC170–74-5/Box120/File1230–1 [UNO] #1 (1945).
192 Opium Prices in Iran – Quarter Ended March 31, 1944; White to Anslinger, 29 June 1944, FBNA/ACC170–71-A-3554/Box18/File0660, Iran (1941–5).
193 Opium Prices in Iran – Quarter Ended June 30, 1944, FBNA/ACC170–71-A-3554/Box18/File0660, Iran (1941–5).
194 Memorandum to Government of Iran, September 1944, BNA-FO371/40503; State Department to Morris, 23 October 1944, FBNA/ACC170–71-A-3554/Box18/File0660, Iran (1941–5).
195 Opium Prices in Iran – Quarter ended September 30, 1944, FBNA/ACC170–71-A-3554/Box18/File0660, Iran (1941–5).
196 State Department to American Minister Kabul, 22 January 1944, FBNA/ACC170–74-12/Box151/File0660, Afghanistan (1929–68).
197 Rep. Judd Remarks, House of Representatives, 5 December 1944; Department of State Press Release, 20 November 1944; Afghan MFA to US Minister Kabul, 11 November 1944, FBNA/ACC170–74-12/Box151/File0660, Afghanistan (1929–68).
198 'Judd Fearful of Iran as Center for Narcotics', *The Evening Star*, Washington, 26 November 1944, FBNA/ACC170–71-A-3554/Box18/File0660, Iran (1941–5).
199 Statement from SACSEA, May 6 1944, Enclosed in Letter Taylor to Marrison, 14 August 1944, BNA-FO371/40510.
200 Paskin to Hone, 21 September 1944, BNA-FO371/40510.
201 Annan to Taylor, 13 October 1944, BNA-FO371/40510.
202 Mountbatten to Amery, 21 August 1944, BNA-FO371/40510.
203 Munster to Mountbatten, 13 September 1944, BNA-FO371/40510.
204 Ibid.
205 Mountbatten to Under Secretary of State, 12 October 1944, BNA-FO371/40510.
206 Amery to Mountbatten, 1 January 1945, BNA-FO371/40510.
207 Annan to Logan, 12 February 1945; Memo re. Opium in Burma, BNA-FO371/50654.
208 See numerous minutes and letters in file: Draft Directive on Dangerous Drugs for Commanders in S.E. Asia Command and S.W. Pacific Command, September 1944–March 1945, BNA-FO371/40510.
209 Halifax to FO, 31 March 1945, BNA-FO371/50654.
210 Annan to Logan, 11 April 1945, BNA-FO371/50654.
211 Mabbott Minute, 22 May 1945, File: Opium Policy in Burma, BNA-FO371/50654.
212 Owen to Annan, 30 December 1944; Owen Minute, File: Proposed Measures for Suppressing Opium Traffic, 30 December 1944, BNA-FO371/40503.
213 Memorandum on the Opium Traffic, 2 August 1945, BNA-FO371/50654.

214 State Department Note from the United States Government on Opium Policy in Burma, 8 August 1945, BNA-FO371/50654.
215 Mabbott to Reynolds, 31 August 1946, BNA-FO371/50654.
216 [FPA] Memorandum on Control of Opium and Other Dangerous Drugs Under a New General International Organization, December 1944, FBNA/ACC170–74-5/Box120/File1230–1 [UNO] #1 (1939–45).

Chapter 3

1 Sean Greenwood, *Britain and the Cold War, 1945–1991* (St. Martin's Press, 2000).
2 Bertil Renborg: Note on the post-war organization of international drug control, September 1944, BNA-HO 45-23162.
3 Ibid.
4 Ibid.
5 Bertil A. Renborg, 'The Grand Old Men of the League of Notions', *United Nations Bulletin on Narcotics* (1964). www.unodc.org/unodc/en/data-and-analysis/bulletin/bulletin_1964-01-01_4_page002.html
6 PCOB Report, 'Pre-War Production and Distribution of Narcotic Drugs and Their Raw Materials', *Opium and Other Dangerous Drugs*, XI.1 ([LON], 1944), 7, FBNA/ACC170–74-5/Box120/File1230–1, UN 1st Session (Jan 1946–Dec 1946).
7 Ibid.
8 League OAC Report to the Council, 12 June 1939, FBNA/ACC170–74-5/Box120/File1230–1 [UNO] #1 (1945).
9 Ibid.
10 Ibid.
11 Ibid.
12 Ibid.
13 Drawn from: Memo, January 1946, FBNA/ACC170–74-5/Box120/File1230–1, UN 1st Session (Jan 1946–Dec 1946).
14 William B. McAllister, 'Reflections on a Century of International Drug Control', ed. John Collins, *Governing the Global Drug Wars*, LSE IDEAS Special Reports, October 2012, 10.
15 Bertil Renborg: Note on the post-war organization of international drug control, September 1944, BNA-HO 45/23162.
16 Anslinger to Werner Thomas, 15 May 1941, FBNA/ACC/170-74-12/Box152/File0660 Germany #12 (1932–59).
17 Sharman to Anslinger, 4 November 1941, FBNA/ACC170–74-12/Box 152/File0660, Canada I (1929–41).
18 Quote: Sharman to Anslinger, 24 October 1944, FBNA/ACC/170-74-5/Box 120/File 1230-1, [UNO] #1 (1945).
19 Moorhead to Delevingne, 16 August 1942, FBNA/ACC170–74-12/Box171/File1230–2, PCOB (1939–48); Makins Minute, File: United States Censorship of Opium Returns, 10 July 1942, BNA-FO371/31066.
20 Moorhead to Delevingne, 16 August 1942, FBNA/ACC170–74-12/Box171/File1230–2, PCOB (1939–48).
21 Ibid.

22 Memorandum of Conversation between Anslinger and Sharman, 27 July 1942; Moorhead to Delevingne, 16 August 1942, FBNA/ACC170-74-12/Box171/File1230-2 PCOB (1939–48).
23 Morlock note to Anslinger, 6 February 1942; Sharman to Anslinger, 13 February 1942; Anslinger to Sharman, 17 February 1942, FBNA/ACC170-74-5/Box124/File1230-A, Postwar Narcotics Problems #1.
24 Paraphrase of telegram from American Embassy to State Department, 19 April 1944, FBNA/ACC170-74-5/Box120/File1230-1 [UNO] #1 (1939–45).
25 Renborg to Reynolds, 6 February 1945, BNA-HO 45/23162.
26 Drawn from: Bertil Renborg: Note on the post-war organization of international drug control, September 1944, BNA-HO 45/23162.
27 See numerous documents in FBNA/ACC170-74-5/Box120/File1230-1 [UNO] #1 (1945).
28 Sharman to Anslinger, 3 June 1944; Anslinger to Sharman, 14 June 1944, FBNA/ACC170-74-5/Box120/File1230-1 [UNO] #1 (1945).
29 Sharman to Anslinger, 27 May 1944; Memorandum of Conversations, 13 April 1944, FBNA/ACC170-74-5/Box120/File1230-1 [UNO] #1 (1945).
30 Sharman to Anslinger, 24 October 1944; Sharman to Anslinger, 3 June 1944, FBNA/ACC170-74-5/Box120/File1230-1 [UNO] #1 (1945).
31 Sharman to Hume Wrong, 28 July 1944; Moorhead Memo, undated; May to Anslinger, 24 June 1944, FBNA/ACC170-74-5/Box120/File1230-1 [UNO] #1 (1945).
32 Ibid.
33 Anslinger to Sharman, 14 June 1944; Sharman to Hume Wrong, 28 July 1944, FBNA/ACC170-74-5/Box120/File1230-1 [UNO] #1 (1945).
34 Sharman to Wrong, 22 June 1944, FBNA/ACC170-74-5/Box120/File1230-1 [UNO] #1 (1945).
35 Memorandum of Conversation, 18 October 1944; Wrong to Sharman, 26 July 1944; Sharman to Anslinger, 24 October 1944, FBNA/ACC170-74-5/Box120/File1230-1 [UNO] #1 (1945).
36 Moorhead to Anslinger, 15 June 1944, FBNA/ACC170-74-5/Box120/File1230-1 [UNO] #1 (1945).
37 Renborg to Morlock, 3 October 1944; Anslinger to Sharman, 19 October 1944, FBNA/ACC170-74-5/Box120/File1230-1 [UNO] #1 (1945).
38 Sharman to Anslinger, 24 October 1944, FBNA/ACC170-74-5/Box120/File1230-1 [UNO] #1 (1945).
39 Ibid.
40 Morlock Memo: Integration … Narcotics into the [UNO], undated; Moorhead to Morlock, 2 November 1944; Memorandum of Conversation: Integration of Opium Work in the [UNO], 15 November 1944, FBNA/ACC170-74-5/Box120/File1230-1 [UNO] #1 (1945).
41 FPA Memo: Control of Opium … under a New General International Organization, 27 December 1944; Moorhead memorandum of Interview with Pasvolsky, 9 November 1944, FBNA/ACC170-74-5/Box120/File1230-1 [UNO] #1 (1945).
42 Quoted in: Greenwood, *Britain and the Cold War, 1945–1991*, 8.
43 Hoopes and Brinkley, *Franklin Delano Roosevelt and the Creation of the U.N.*, 185.

44 Quoted in Memorandum: Relationship of Drug Control Bodies to the United Nations: Summary Recommendations, 17 September 1945, FBNA/ACC170–74-5/Box120/File1230–1 [UNO] #1 (1945).
45 Anslinger to Sharman, 20 September 1945, FBNA/ACC170–74-5/Box120/File1230–1 [UNO] #1 (1945).
46 Anslinger to Felkin, 18 September 1945, FBNA/ACC170–74-5/Box120/File1230–1 [UNO] #2 (1945).
47 Sharman to Anslinger, 22 September 1945; Delevingne to Moorhead, 23 September 1945, FBNA/ACC170–74-5/Box120/File1230–1 [UNO] #1 (1945).
48 Felkin to Anslinger, 8 October 1945, FBNA/ACC170–74-5/Box17/File0660, Post War Germany (1945).
49 'WCTU Urges Control of Opium Continues', *Newark News*, 12 October 1945; Hearst Press Editorials in FBNA/ACC170–74-5/Box120/File1230–1 [UNO] #1 (1945).
50 Anslinger to Hoo, 19 September 1945, FBNA/ACC170–74-5/Box120/File1230–1 [UNO] #1 (1945).
51 Anslinger: Draft Memo to US Rep., August 1945; Sharman to Anslinger, 18 August 1945, FBNA/ACC170–74-5/Box120/File1230–1 [UNO] #2 (1945).
52 Renborg to Morlock, 7 November 1945; Sharman to Anslinger, 1 December 1945, FBNA/ACC170–74-5/Box120/File1230–1 [UNO] #2 (1945).
53 For discussions of Renborg's suspected 'pro-Nazi' attitude see: File U3718, 12 March 1946, BNA-FO371/57108.
54 Minute, 'Narcotics Commission', 26 March, 1946; Noel-Baker to Henderson, 3 April 1946; Minutes, 26 March, 8 May, 1946, BNA-FO371/57108.
55 Sharman to Anslinger, 27 May 1944, FBNA/ACC170–74-5/Box120/File1230–1 [UNO] #1 (1945).
56 HO Memo: International Control of the Drug Traffic, 26 October 1945, BNA-CO 323-1885-6.
57 File Minute, 19 November 1945; Noel-Baker to Chuter, 15 October 1945; Minutes of the Thirty-Ninth Meeting of [IOC], 21 November 1945, BNA-CO 323-1885-6.
58 File Minute 2, 19 November 1945; Chuter Ede to Noel-Baker, 31 October 1945; Minutes of the Thirty-Ninth Meeting of [IOC], 21 November 1945; Draft Recommendation for Submission to Committee 7 ([LON]), 21 November 1945; Logan to Acheson, 14 December 1945, BNA-CO 323-1885-6.
59 Minutes of the Fortieth Meeting of [IOC], 18 January 1946; File Minute, 19 January 1946, BNA-CO 323-1885-6.
60 File Minute, 19 January 1946, BNA-CO 323-1885-6.
61 Moorhead to Anslinger, 28 August 1945; Moorhead Memo, December, FBNA/ACC170–74-5/Box120/File1230–1 [UNO] #2 (1945).
62 Morlock to Anslinger, 5 November 1945; Anslinger to hoo, 9 November 1945; Anslinger note attached to US London Embassy to Secretary of State, 10 November 1945, FBNA/ACC170–74-5/Box120/File1230–1 [UNO] #2 (1945).
63 Anslinger to Hoo, 10 October 1945, FBNA/ACC170–74-5/Box120/File1230–1 [UNO] #1 (1945).
64 Anslinger to Hoo, 9 November 1945, FBNA/ACC170–74-5/Box120/File1230–1 [UNO] #2 (1945).
65 Excerpt from Telegram to American Embassy, London, 21 November 1945; Moorhead Memo, November 1945, FBNA/ACC170–74-5/Box120/File1230–1 [UNO] #2 (1945).

66 Moorhead to Anslinger, 22 November 1945; General Federation of Womens' Clubs Resolution, 1 December 1945; Anslinger to Moorhead, 28 November 1945, FBNA/ACC170–74-5/Box120/File1230–1 [UNO] #2 (1945).

67 Moorhead memo, 29 November 1945; State Department to American Embassy, London, 30 November 1945; Moorhead memo, December 1945, FBNA/ACC170–74-5/Box120/File1230–1 [UNO] #2 (1945).

68 Memo of meeting: International Organization for Narcotics Control, 30 November 1945, FBNA/ACC170–74-5/Box120/File1230–1 [UNO] #2 (1945).

69 Steinig to Anslinger, Demember 1945; Moorhead memo, 8 December 1945; 'Narcotic Control Plan Praised', *New York City Journal*, by Ray Richards, 14 December 1945; Anslinger to Hoo, 17 December 1945, FBNA/ACC170–74-5/Box120/File1230–1 [UNO] #2 (1945).

70 Moorhead memo, December 1945, FBNA/ACC170–74-5/Box120/File1230–1 [UNO] #2 (1945).

71 Statement by UK Rep., 17th Plenary of UNGA, 29 January 1946, in FBNA/ACC170–74-5/Box120/File1230–1, UN 1st Session (1946).

72 Anslinger to Hoo, 24 January 1946, FBNA/ACC170–74-5/Box120/File1230–1 [UNO] #3 (1946)

73 Anslinger to Hoo, 3 December 1945, FBNA/ACC170–74-5/Box120/File1230–1 [UNO] #2 (1945).

74 US Delegation to Secretary of State, 23 January 1946; Record of Phone Conversation, 30 January 1946; Morlock to Mulliken, 1 February 1946, FBNA/ACC170–74-5/Box120/File1230–1 [UNO] #3 (1946).

75 US Delegation to Secretary of State, 5th, 12 & 19 February 1946; Moorhead to May and Chamberlain, February 1946, FBNA/ACC170–74-5/Box120/File1230–1 [UNO] #3 (1946).

76 Anslinger note attached to US Embassy memo, 29 January 1946; Moorhead to Malcolm, 14 February, 1946; Moorhead to Henderson, 14 February 1946, FBNA/ACC170–74-5/Box120/File1230–1 [UNO] #3 (1946).

77 League of Nation: Transfer to UN of League Activities, 26 August 1946, in FBNA/ACC170–74-5/Box120/File1230–1, UN 1st Session (1946).

78 Sharman to Anslinger, 20 August 1946, FBNA/ACC170–74-5/Box120/File1230–1, [UNO] #4.

Chapter 4

1 Section drawn from: Report of the Work of the Board, October 1946, FBNA/ACC170–74-5/Box120/File1230–1, UN 1st Session (1946).

2 Felkin to Anslinger, 8 November 1945, FBNA/ACC170–74-5/Box20/File0660, Japan Postwar 1945.

3 Anslinger to Turner, 28 December 1945, FBNA/ACC170–74-5/Box17/File0660, Post War Germany (1945).

4 Report of the Work of the Board, October 1946, FBNA/ACC170–74-5/Box120/File1230–1, UN 1st Session (1946).

5 DSB, Estimated World Requirements of Dangerous Drugs in 1945 ([LON], 1944) in BNA-FO371/50649.

6 CND Statement by Harry Anslinger, regarding the narcotic situation in the US Zone in Germany, December 1946, FBNA/ACC170–74-5/Box120/File1230–1 United Nations First Session #1 (1946).
7 Renborg: Note on the Organization of Drug Control in Germany During Occupation; Anslinger to Breidenbach, 21 November 1945, FBNA/ACC170–74-5/Box17/File0660, Post War Germany (1945).
8 Jonathan Lewy, 'The Drug Policy of the Third Reich', *Social History of Alcohol and Drugs* 22, no. 2 (2008): 144–67.
9 Breidenbach memo: Narcotics Control in Germany, September 1945, FBNA/ACC170–74-5/Box17/File0660, Post War Germany (1945).
10 Anslinger to Director, Civil Affairs Division, War Department, 13 June 1945; Hilldring to Anslinger, 18 June 1945; Hilldring to Anslinger, 3 July 1945; Memo: Location of Personnel and Records of Reichsopiumstelle, 29 July 1945, FBNA/ACC170–74-5/Box17/File0660, Post War Germany (1945).
11 Felkin memo on Paris Meeting, 6 September 1945; Weatherwax to Anslinger, 23 August 1945; 'Berlin Black Market Booming'; 'Sky Is Limit on Watches, Dope', Press Clipping, 5 July 1945, FBNA/ACC170–74-5/Box17/File0660, Post War Germany (1945).
12 Weatherwax to Anslinger, 26 July 1945; Felkin memo on Paris Meeting, 6 September 1945, Weatherwax to Anslinger, 23 August 1945; Memo: Narcotic Control - Germany, 13 September 1945, FBNA/ACC170–74-5/Box17/File0660, Post War Germany (1945).
13 Anslinger note attached to Felkin memo on Paris Meeting, 6 September 1945, FBNA/ACC170–74-5/Box17/File0660, Post War Germany (1945).
14 Anslinger to Breidenbach, 3 October 1945; Breidenbach to Anslinger, 20 September 1945; Breidenbach memo: Narcotics Control in Germany, September 1945, FBNA/ACC170–74-5/Box17/File0660, Post War Germany (1945).
15 Anslinger to Breidenbach, 3 October 1945, FBNA/ACC170–74-5/Box17/File0660, Post War Germany (1945).
16 Col. Howard Hansen to Public Health Branch, USFET, 27 September 1945; Breidenbach to Anslinger, 21 October 1945; 'De Gaulle Set Against Plans for Central Rule in Germany', *The Stars and Stripes*, 14 October 1945, FBNA/ACC170–74-5/Box17/File0660, Post War Germany (1945).
17 Memo: Brief for the British Representative on Item 11 of the Agenda, 1 October 1945, BNA-FO 1032/696.
18 Memo: Control of Narcotics in Germany, 12 October 1945, BNA-FO 1049/266.
19 Harris to Lambert, 25 September 1945, BNA-FO 1032/696.
20 Fryer to Strang, 6 November 1945, BNA-FO 1049/266.
21 Memo: Control of Narcotics in German, 20 November 1945, BNA-FO 1032/696.
22 Memo, re. 'Narcotic Situation in Germany', August 1946, FBNA/ACC170–74-5/Box17/File0660 Germany Postwar #2 (1946).
23 Breidenbach to Anslinger, 10 December 1945, FBNA/ACC170–74-5/Box17/File0660, Post War Germany (1945).
24 Memo: Enquiries from the PCOB, 11 January 1946, BNA-FO 1032/696.
25 Memo: Reply to the PCOB, 24 January 1946, BNA-FO 1032/696.
26 Breidenbach to Anslinger, 2 January 1946, FBNA/ACC170–74-5/Box17/File0660 Germany Postwar #2 (1946).

27 Giuliani to Anslinger, 11 April 1946, FBNA/ACC170-74-5/File0660 Germany Postwar #2 (1946).
28 Ibid.
29 Memo: Status of [PCOB], 24 May 1946, BNA-FO 1032/696; Breidenbach to Anslinger, 10 September 1946; Anslinger to Giuliani, 23 April 1946, Giuliani to Anslinger, 11 April 1946, FBNA/ACC71-A-3554/Box17/File0660, Germany Postwar #2 (1946).
30 Giuliani to Anslinger, May 1946, FBNA/ACC71-A-3554/Box17/File0660, Germany Postwar #2 (1946).
31 Giuliani to Anslinger, 18 June 1946; Giuliani memo, 26 June 1946, FBNA/ACC71-A-3554/Box17/File0660, Germany Postwar #2 (1946).
32 Statement by Harry Anslinger, US Rep to CND, regarding the narcotic situation in the US Zone in Germany, December 1946, FBNA/ACC170-74-5/Box120/File1230-1 [UN] 1 Session #1 (1946).
33 Giuliani to Anslinger, 18 June; 9 July; 13 July 1946, FBNA/ACC71-A-3554/Box17/File0660, Germany Postwar #2 (1946).
34 Giuliani Memo re. 'Narcotic Control in British Zone of Occupation', 27 June 1946, FBNA/ACC71-A-3554/Box17/File0660, Germany Postwar #2 (1946).
35 Giuliani to Williams, 12 August 1946; Giuliani to Anslinger, 28 August 1946, FBNA/ACC71-A-3554/Box17/File0660, Germany Postwar #2 (1946).
36 Giuliani to Anslinger, 11 September 1946, FBNA/ACC71-A-3554/Box17/File0660, Germany Postwar #2 (1946).
37 Ibid.
38 CND Statement by Harry Anslinger, December 1946, FBNA/ACC170-74-5/Box120/File1230-1 [UN] First Session #1 (1946).
39 Giuliani to Anslinger, 11 September 1946, FBNA/ACC71-A-3554/Box17/File0660, Germany Postwar #2 (1946).
40 Ibid.
41 Felkin to US Secretary of State, 28 September 1946, FBNA/ACC71-A-3554/Box17/File0660, Germany Postwar #2 (1946).
42 Giuliani to Anslinger, 13 October 1946; Giuliani to Anslinger, 7 November 1946, FBNA/ACC71-A-3554/Box17/File0660, Germany Postwar #2 (1946).
43 Ibid.
44 Ibid.
45 UN Resolution, December 1946, FBNA/ACC71-A-3554/Box17/File0660, Germany Postwar #2 (1946).
46 Giuliani to Anslinger, 24 December 1946; Draft Report to Health Committee, January 1946, FBNA/ACC71-A-3554/Box17/File0660, Germany Postwar #2 (1946).
47 Giuliani to Anslinger, 15 January 1947, FBNA/ACC71-A-3554/Box17/File0660, Germany Postwar #2 (1946).
48 [LON] Report: 'The Drug Situation and the Control of Narcotic Drugs in Japan', 1 December 1944, FBNA/ACC170-74-5/Box20/File0660, Japan (1946).
49 Ibid.
50 'Jap-Fostered Drug Traffic to be Quashed', *El Paso Times Herald*, 19 August 1945, FBNA/ACC170-74-5/Box20/File0660, Japan (1946).
51 Memorandum of Conversation between Morlock and Dr. Sze, 29 August 1946, FBNA/ACC170-74-5/Box120/File1230-1, [UNO] #4.

52 I am indebted to Peter Reuter for suggesting this as a possible reason in private discussions.
53 'Horizon', Indianapolis Star, Isadore Kirk, 20 August 1946, FBNA/ACC170–74-5/Box120/File1230–1, [UNO] #4.
54 Memo of Conversation: 'War Crimes Office desire to obtain evidence …', 11 October 1945; Speer to Anslinger, 29 November 1945; Anslinger to Bransky, 28 December 1945; Mulliken to Col. Hornaday, 26 December 1945, FBNA/ACC170–74-5/Box20/File0660, Japan Postwar 1945.
55 Sharman to Anslinger, 20 August, 1946, FBNA/ACC170–74-5/Box120/File1230–1, [UNO] #4.
56 Memorandum for the Imperial Japanese Government, 12 October 1945; See numerous press clippings, e.g. 'Jap Opium Trade Frozen', *The Washington Daily News*, 18 October 1945, FBNA/ACC170–74-5/Box20/File0660, Japan Postwar 1945.
57 General MacArthur Memorandum to Commanding General, XXIB Corps, 14 October 1945; '$50,000,000 in Opium Seized by MacArthur in Narcotics Drive', Associated Press, 30 October 1945; Anslinger to Oyler, 26 November 1945, FBNA/ACC170–74-5/Box20/File0660, Japan Postwar 1945.
58 Speer to Anslinger, 20 November 1945, FBNA/ACC170–74-5/Box20/File0660, Japan Postwar 1945.
59 Ibid.
60 Memorandum: 'Statements of Drug and Pharmacy Section Official … ', 26 November 1945; Oyler to Anslinger, 21 December 1945; Anslinger to Speer, 30 November 1945, FBNA/ACC170–74-5/Box20/File0660, Japan Postwar 1945.
61 Anslinger to Col. Sans, October 1946, FBNA/ACC170–74-5/Box120/File1230–1 United Nations First Session #1 (1946).
62 Minutes of Meeting held at Colonial Office, 6 April 1945, BNA-CO 852/666/3.
63 Ibid.
64 Ibid.
65 Ibid.
66 Ibid.
67 Walsh to James, 18 June 1945, BNA-CO 852/666/3.
68 Walkingshaw to Campbell, 31 May 1945, BNA-CO 852/666/3.
69 Goodwin to Walsh Atkins, 13 June 1946, FO371/59608.
70 Gage Minute, File: 'British Opium Policy for Burma', 1 July 1946, BNA-FO371/59608.
71 Goodwin to Walsh Atkins, 15 August 1946, FO371/59608.
72 Goodwin Minute, UN 2446, 18 October 1946, BNA-FO371/59609.
73 Draft Reply to State Department's Note of 8 August 1945, October 1946, BNA-FO371/59609.
74 Morley to Government of Burma, 8 November 1946, BNA-FO371/59611.
75 Draft Reply to State Department's Note of 8 August 1945, October 1946, BNA-FO371/59609.
76 Department of State to British Embassy, 27 December 1946, BNA-FO371/67641.
77 Morley to Coles, 17 October 1946, BNA-FO371/59611.
78 Ibid.
79 Goodwin to Morley, 8 November 1946, BNA-FO371/59611.
80 Coles to Morley, 4 November 1946, BNA-FO371/59611.
81 Lord Pethick Lawrence to Noel-Baker, 25 January 1946, BNA-FO371/57108.

82 Quoted in Lord Pethick Lawrence to Noel-Baker, 25 January 1946, FO371/57108.
83 Memo of Coversation: Minor and Morlock, 11 October 1945; Anslinger to Morlock, 25 October 1945, FBNA/ACC170–74-5/Box120/File1230–1 [UNO] #2 (August–October 1945).
84 Acting Secretary of State to American Embassy, Tehran, 26 July 1945; American Embassy Tehran to Secretary of State, 31 July 1945, FBNA/ACC170–74-5/Box171/File1230–14, Control in Various Countries (1944-5).
85 M. Mahmoud Fateh, 'Prohibition of the Cultivation of the Poppy and the Advantages of this Measure for Iran', *Journal of Tehran*, 1–8 October 1945, FBNA/ACC71-A-3554/Box19/File0660, Iran (Persia) #3 (1946).
86 Murray to Secretary of State, 3 January, 1946; Translation of Prime Minister's Radio Address, 21 March, 1946; Memo: 'Iran', April 1946; Tehran Embassy to Secretary of State, 7 May 1946, FBNA/ACC71-A-3554/Box19/File0660, Iran (Persia) #3 (1946).
87 Paraphrase of Telegram from Tehran, 7 May 1946; various news clippings in file; Copy of Remarks by Hon. Walter H. Judd, 29 May 1946, FBNA/ACC71-A-3554/Box19/File0660, Iran (Persia) #3 (1946).
88 Qavam orders prohibition of opium', 24 June 1946; Decree of the Council of Ministers, 14 July, 1946; Memo: 'Opium prices in Iran – Quarter ended March 31, 1946', 31 May 1946; Foley to Morlock, 15 July, 1946, FBNA/ACC71-A-3554/Box19/File0660, Iran (Persia) #3 (1946).
89 Memo by J Forrest Crawford, 1 August 1946; Memo: 'Opium prices in Iran – Quarter ended September 19th, 1946', 31 October 1946, FBNA/ACC71-A-3554/Box19/File0660, Iran (Persia) #3 (1946).
90 Wright to Anslinger, 22 October 1946; Wright Memo: the opium Situation in Iran, October 1946, FBNA/ACC71-A-3554/Box19/File0660, Iran (Persia) #3 (1946).
91 Anslinger to Wright, 6 November 1946; Henderson to Wright, 6 November 1946, FBNA/ACC71-A-3554/Box19/File0660, Iran (Persia) #3 (1946).
92 Markovic to Anslinger, 15 May, 1939, FBNA/ACC71-A-3554/Box25/File0660, Turkish-Yugoslavia Agreement (1932–46).
93 Anslinger to Fuller, 14 November 1940; Anslinger to Sarhan, 13 December, 1940, FBNA/ACC71-A-3554/Box25/File0660, Turkish-Yugoslavia Agreement (1932–46).
94 Morlock to Anslinger, November 1945, FBNA/ACC71-A-3554/Box25/File0660, Turkish-Yugoslavia Agreement (1932–46).
95 See William McAllister, *Drug Diplomacy in the Twentieth Century*, 144–9.
96 Meeting minutes: 'Axis Europe and Morphine Supplies', 24h December 1943, BNA-FO371/44095.
97 Memo: Economic Warfare Division, American Embassy, 15 April 1944, BNA-FO371/44095.
98 Peterson to Foreign Office, 7 December 1945, BNA-FO371/48731.
99 'Turkey Notifies U.S. of Accord on Opium Sales', Washington Post, 16 July 1945, FBNA/ACC170–74-5/Box171/File1230–14, Control in Various Countries (1944–5).
100 Dawson-Hutchinson to Gedes, 5 January 1945, BNA-FO371/48731.
101 British Embassy, Washington, to Foreign Office, 10 April 1945, BNA-FO371/48731.
102 Warburton to Lomax, 23 May, 1945, BNA-FO371/48731.

103 Howard to Lord Halifax, 31 May 1945, BNA-FO371/48731.
104 Halifax to Foreign Office, 6 July 1945, BNA-FO371/48731.
105 Angora to Foreign Office, 15 October 1945, BNA-FO371/48731.
106 Lomax to Warburton, 18 April 1945, BNA-FO371/48731.

Chapter 5

1 UK Del to FO, 24 September 1946, BNA-FO371/59609.
2 Minutes, UN 2828, 5 October 1946, BNA-FO371/59609.
3 Winant to Secretary of State, 19 September 1946, FBNA/ACC170–74-5/Box120/File1230–1 United Nations Protocol First Session #14 (1946–9).
4 Minute, UN 2633, 2 October 1946, BNA-FO371/59610.
5 Greenwood, *Britain and the Cold War, 1945–1991*, 8.
6 Memo, December 1946, FBNA/ACC170–74-5/Box120/File1230–1, UN 1st Session (1946).
7 Reid to Anslinger, 13 December 1946, FBNA/ACC170–74-5/Box120/File1230–1, UN 1st Session (1946).
8 Report: 'Opium Prices in Iran', 3 July 1947, FBNA/ACC170–74-5/Box121/File1230–1, UN CND 2nd Session (1947).
9 Johnson to Secretary of State, 30 November 1946, FBNA/ACC71-A-3554/Box19/File0660, Iran (Persia) #3 (1946).
10 Report: 'Opium Prices in Iran', 3 July 1947; Bolster, 'Notes on Current Agricultural Situation – Iran', 28 May 1947; Anslinger note attached to memo, 'Government Collection of Illegal Opium Crop', 4 June 1947, FBNA/ACC170–74-5/Box121/File1230–1, UN CND 2nd Session (1947).
11 White to Anslinger, 9 May 1948, FBNA/ACC170–74-5/Box121/File1230–1, UN 3rd Session #1 (1947–8).
12 Anslinger to Wright, 29 April 1948, FBNA/ACC170–74-5/Box121/File1230–1, UN 3rd Session #1 (1947–8).
13 Ibid.
14 Draft: Treaty of Peace with Japan, Control of Narcotic Drugs, February 1948; Memo of Conversation, 19 January 1948; Sharman to Anslinger, 21 November 1947; Sharman to Anslinger, 18 November 1947, FBNA/ACC170–74-5/Box121/File1230–1, UN CND 2nd Session (1947).
15 Sharman to Anslinger, 7 November 1947; Memo of Conversation, 19 January 1948, FBNA/ACC170–74-5/Box121/File1230–1, UN CND 2nd Session (1947).
16 US Delegation ECOSOC Position Paper, 17 February 1947, FBNA/ACC170–74-5/Box120/File1230–1, ECOSOC Position Papers (1947).
17 US Delegation to Secretary of States, 12 March 1947, NA, ACC170–74-5, Box 120, File 1230–1, UN 1 Session #2 (1947-50).
18 Sharman to Anslinger, 3 January 1947, FBNA/ACC170–74-5/Box120/File1230–1, UN 1st Session #2 (Jan 1947–June 1950).
19 US Delegation Position Paper CND, 20 June 1947, FBNA/ACC170–74-5/Box121/File1230–1, UN CND 2nd Session (1947).
20 UN CND, 2nd Session, 'Summary Record of the Fifteenth Meeting', 4 August 1947; Sharman to Anslinger, 21 May 1947, FBNA/ACC170–74-5/Box121/File1230–1, UN CND 2nd Session (1947).

21 US Delegation ECOSOC Position Paper, 17 February 1947, FBNA/ACC170-74-5/Box120/File1230-1, ECOSOC Position Papers (1947).

22 Stanton to Secretary of State, 31 January 1947; UN CND, 2nd Session, 'Summary Record of the Fourteenth Meeting', 1 August 1947, FBNA/ACC170-74-5/Box121/File1230-1, UN CND 2nd Session (1947).

23 UN CND, 2nd Session, 'Summary Record of the Fourteenth Meeting', 1 August 1947, FBNA/ACC170-74-5/Box121/File1230-1, UN CND 2nd Session (1947).

24 Anslinger to Wright, 29 April 1948, FBNA/ACC170-74-5/Box121/File1230-1, UN 3rd Session #1 (1947–8).

25 UN CND, 2nd Session, 'Summary Record of the Fourteenth Meeting', 1 August 1947, FBNA/ACC170-74-5/Box121/File1230-1, UN CND 2nd Session (1947).

26 Richard Harvey Brown, 'The Opium Trade and Opium Policies in India, China, Britain, and the United States: Historical Comparisons and Theoretical Interpretations', *Asian Journal of Social Science* 30, no. 3 (2002): 623–56, https://doi.org/10.1163/156853102320945420.

27 US Delegation Position Paper CND, 20 June 1947; UN CND, 2nd Session, 'Summary Record of the Fourteenth Meeting', 1 August 1947, FBNA/ACC170-74-5/Box121/File1230-1, UN CND 2nd Session (1947). The reasons for the shift are not yet clear and require further research.

28 US Delegation ECOSOC Position Paper, 17 February 1947, FBNA/ACC170-74-5/Box120/File1230-1, ECOSOC Position Papers (1947).

29 UN CND, 2nd Session, 'Summary Record of the Fourteenth Meeting', 1 August 1947, FBNA/ACC170-74-5/Box121/File1230-1, UN CND 2nd Session (1947).

30 US Delegation Position Paper CND, 20 June 1947, FBNA/ACC170-74-5/Box121/File1230-1, UN CND 2nd Session (1947).

31 Secretary General to US Secretary of State, 23 April 1947, BNA-ACC170-74-5, Box 120, File 1230-1, UN 1st Session #2 (1947–50).

32 UN CND 2nd Session, 'Record of the Seventeenth Meeting', 5 August 1947, FBNA/ACC170-74-5/Box121/File1230-1, UN CND 2nd Session (1947).

33 Ibid.

34 Ibid.

35 UN CND 2nd Session, 'Record of the Fifth Meeting', 26 July 1947; Morlock to Anslinger, 15 January 1947, FBNA/ACC170-74-5/Box121/File1230-1, UN CND 2nd Session (1947).

36 Sharman to Anslinger, 29 January 1947, FBNA/ACC170-74-5/Box120/File1230-1, UN 1st Session #2 (1947–50).

37 Anslinger to Sharman, 3 February 1947; 'Examination of the Report … of [ECOSOC]', 15 January 1947, FBNA/ACC170-74-5/Box121/File1230-1, UN CND 2nd Session (1947).

38 Sharman to Anslinger, 29 January 1947, FBNA/ACC170-74-5/Box120/File1230-1, UN 1st Session #2 (1947–50).

39 Anslinger to Sharman, 24 January 1947, FBNA/ACC170-74-5/Box121/File1230-1, UN CND 2nd Session (1947).

40 UN CND 2nd Session, 'Record of the Seventeenth Meeting', 5 August 1947, FBNA/ACC170-74-5/Box121/File1230-1, UN CND 2nd Session (1947).

41 CND: Third Session – Report of the UK Delegate, 2 June 1948, BNA-FO371/72915.

42 'Statement by the United States Representative', 30 July 1947; UN CND 2nd Session, 'Record of the Seventeenth Meeting', 5 August 1947, FBNA/ACC170-74-5/Box121/File1230-1, UN CND 2nd Session (1947).
43 Memo of Conversation, 'Report of the [CND] – Resolution Regarding Mexican Production of Opium Poppy', 4 February 1948, FBNA/ACC170-74-5/Box121/File1230-1, UN 3rd Session #1 (1947–8).
44 Ibid.
45 Ibid.
46 CND, Provisional Agenda of the Third Session, 10 March 1948, FBNA/ACC170-74-5/Box121/File1230-1, UN 3rd Session #1 (1947–8).
47 Memo: Statement by Anslinger re. Production in Mexico, 10 March 1948; Secretary of State to US Ambassador Mexico, 25 March 1948, FBNA/ACC170-74-5/Box121/File1230-1, UN 3rd Session #1 (1947–8).
48 Reveley to Morlock, 20 April 1946, FBNA/ACC170-74-5/Box121/File1230-1, UN 3rd Session #1 (1947–8).
49 Report on the Third Session of CND May 3–22, 1948, FBNA/ACC170-74-5/Box121/File1230-1, UN 3rd Session #1 (1947–8).
50 Coles to Anslinger, 27 October 1947; Anslinger to Coles, 17 November 1947, FBNA/ACC170-74-5/Box121/File1230-1, UN 3rd Session #1 (1947–8).
51 Anslinger to Delevingne, 25 November 1947, FBNA/ACC170-74-5/Box120/File1230-1, UN 1st Session #2 (1947–50).
52 Amidone was later to become more widely known as Methadone.
53 Draft Brief for UK Delegation, ECOSOC VII, 1948, BNA-CAB134/390.
54 US Delegation ECOSOC Position Paper, 17 February 1947, FBNA/ACC170-74-5/Box120/File1230-1, ECOSOC Position Papers (1947).
55 CND, 2nd Session, 'Summary Record of Second Meeting', 24 July 1947, FBNA/ACC170-74-5/Box121/File1230-1, UN CND 2nd Session (1947).
56 Anslinger to Delevingne, 25 November 1947, FBNA/ACC170-74-5/Box120/File1230-1, UN 1st Session #2 (1947–50).
57 'Draft Protocol to Bring under International Control Drugs Not Covered by the 1931 Convention', 16 December 1947; Foley to Secretary of State, 17 February 1948; Anslinger to Tennyson, 7 May 1948, FBNA/ACC170-74-5/Box120/File1230-1, UN 1st Session #2 (1947–50).
58 Memo: Agenda for the Third Session of the CND, 23 March 1948; Memo: 'CND: Chairmanship', 15 April 1948, FBNA/ACC170-74-5/Box121/File1230-1, UN 3rd Session #1 (1947–8).
59 Proposed Statement of US Rep re. Opium Smoking in French Indochina, Undated, FBNA/ACC170-74-5/Box121/File1230-1, UN 3rd Session #1 (1947–8).
60 Landon to Butterworth, 23 April 1948, FBNA/ACC170-74-5/Box121/File1230-1, UN 3rd Session #1 (1947–8).
61 Benninghoff to Morlock, 27 April, 1948, FBNA/ACC170-74-5/Box121/File1230-1, UN 3rd Session #1 (1947–8).
62 Steinig to Anslinger, 9 April 1948; Anslinger to Steinig, 20 April 1948; Memo re. Article 23 of the 1931 Convention, undated, FBNA/ACC170-74-5/Box121/File1230-1, UN 3rd Session #1 (1947–8).
63 Ibid.
64 CND: Third Session – Report of the UK Delegate, 2 June 1948, BNA-FO371/72915.
65 Ibid.

66 Ibid.
67 Ibid.
68 Ibid.
69 Ibid.
70 Statement by US Rep. regarding the Opium Situation in Siam, Third Session CND, 1948, FBNA/ACC170-74-5/Box121/File1230-1, UN 3rd Session #1 (1947–8).
71 I am indebted to Nigel Ashton for highlighting the broader context of Anglo-Iranian relations underpinning narcotics controls discussions.
72 CND: Third Session – Report of the UK Delegate, 2 June 1948, BNA-FO371/72915.
73 Moorhead to Anslinger, 6 August 1948, FBNA/ACC170-74-5/Box121/File1230-1, UN 3rd Session #1 (1947–8).
74 CND: Third Session – Report of the UK Delegate, 2 June 1948, BNA-FO371/72915.
75 Ibid.
76 Draft Brief for the General Assembly: Item 4(D): Narcotic Drugs, 20 September 1948, BNA-FO371/72915.
77 CND: Third Session – Report of the UK Delegate, 2 June 1948, BNA-FO371/72915.
78 Ibid.
79 Draft Brief for the General Assembly: Item 4(D): Narcotic Drugs, 20 September 1948, BNA-FO371/72915.
80 Ibid.
81 Ibid.
82 US Position Paper: Third Session CND, 29 April 1948; Report on the Third Session of CND May 3–22, 1948, FBNA/ACC170-74-5/Box121/File1230-1, UN 3rd Session #1 (1947–8).
83 Steinig to Anslinger, 19 August 1948; Steinig to Anslinger, 25 November 1948, FBNA/ACC170-74-5/Box121/File1230-1, UN 3rd Session #1 (1947–8).

Chapter 6

1 Quote: 'Report of the Commission on Narcotic Drugs', 21 February 1947, BNA-IOC (47)52, BNA-CAB134/381.
2 Anslinger to Vaille, 4 January 1951, FBNA/ACC170-74-5/Box121/File1230-1, UN 5th Session #4 (1950–1); The importance of Vaille to the Franco–US alliance would be demonstrated later when his removal from CND in 1958 saw France quickly shake off its leadership role and work to deprecate the importance of international drug control efforts.
3 For example: 'Hoover Group Asks Shift of Narcotics Unit', *Drug Trade News*, 18 April 1949; 'Now What? From Washington', *American Druggist*, April 1949; Foley (Under Secretary of Treasury) to Dickerson, 9 June 1949, FBNA/ACC 170-74-4/Box49/File0280-3, The Commission on Organization of the Executive Branch of the Government #1 (1949).
4 Giuliani to Anslinger, 20 May 1947; Statement by Anslinger to UN CND, July 1947, FBNA/ACC170-74-5/Box121/File1230-1, UN CND 2nd Session (1947).
5 German Political Department to Cadogan, 19 May 1950, BNA-FO371/88824.
6 Draft Brief for UK Rep, 4 Session CND, May 1949, IOC (49)84, BNA-CAB134/397.
7 Priss Minute, US 1811/36, 25 April 1950, BNA-FO371/88824.
8 Boomstra memo, 'Coca Production and Trade – Peru', 10 June 1947, FBNA/ACC170-74-5/Box121/File1230-1, UN CND 2nd Session (1947).

9 ECOSOC 12th Session Position Paper, 1949, FBNA/ACC170-74-5/Box121/File1230-1, UN 5th Session #1 (1949–50).
10 Ibid.
11 Sharman to Anslinger, 21 July 1950, FBNA/ACC170-74-5/Box121/File1230-1, UN 5th Session #2 (1950).
12 Draft Brief for UK Rep, 7th Session CND, 29 March 1952, IOC (52)12, BNA-CAB134/944.
13 Draft Brief for UK Rep, ECOSOC XII, 6 February 1951, IOC (51)14, BNA-CAB134/410.
14 See Fonda correspondence, FBNA/ACC170-74-5/Box121/File1230-1, UN 5th Session #2 (1950).
15 Draft Brief for UK Rep, 4th Session CND, May 1949, IOC (49)84, BNA-CAB134/397.
16 Murray to Thornton, 18 September 1950, BNA-FO371/88825.
17 Thornton to Murray, 23 September 1950, BNA-FO371/88825.
18 Collins, 'War, Decolonisation and The Birth of the Illicit Opium Trade in Burma'.
19 See BNA-FO371/106691.
20 Collins, 'Imperial Drug Economies, Development, and the Search for Alternatives in Asia, from Colonialism to Decolonisation'.
21 Memo, British Legation, Saigon, 10 June 1953, BNA-FO371/106801.
22 British Legation, Saigon, 3 July 1953, FO371/106801.
23 Draft Brief for UK Rep, ECOSOC XII, 6 February 1951, IOC (51)14, BNA-CAB134/410.
24 See press clippings in FBNA/ACC170-74-5/Box121/File1230-1, UN 5th Session #1 (1949–50).
25 Thornton to Seopes 19 December 1950, BNA-FO371/88826.
26 Foreign Office to UK Delegation, 9 November 1950, BNA-FO371/88826.
27 Minute, US 1811/92, 21 November 1950, BNA-FO371/88826.
28 Seopes to Thorton, 11 December 1950, BNA-FO371/88826.
29 Thornton to Seopes 19 December 1950, BNA-FO371/88826.
30 Report: 'Informational on Opium Production and Traffic by the Chinese Communists', 18 November 1950, FBNA/ACC170-74-5/Box121/File1230-1, UN 5th Session #4 (1950–1).
31 Remarks of Soviet Representative on CND, 5 May 1952, FBNA/ACC170-74-5/Box122/File1230-1, UN 7th Session #1 (1952).
32 See press clippings; Anslinger Remarks, 8th Session CND, April 1953, FBNA/ACC170-74-5/Box122/File1230-1, UN 8th Session (1953).
33 Draft Brief for UK Del, ECOSOC 16th Session, 16 June 1953, IOC (53)90, BNA-CAB134/950.
34 US Delegation Position Paper, CND 4th Session, 9 May 1949, FBNA/ACC170-74-5/Box121/File1230-1, UN 4th Session #4 (1949–50).
35 Report by British Delegate, CND 4th Session, 20 June 1949, IOC (49)123, BNA-CAB134/398.
36 Ibid.
37 Draft US Delegation Position Paper, ECOSOC 8th Session, 1949, FBNA/ACC170-74-5/Box121/File1230-1, UN 4th Session #2 (1949).
38 Draft Brief for UK Rep, 4th Session CND, May 1949, IOC (49)84, BNA-CAB134/397.

39 Report by British Delegate, CND 4th Session, 20 June 1949, IOC (49)123, BNA-CAB134/398.
40 Ibid.
41 Ibid.
42 Draft Brief for UK Rep, 4th Session CND, May 1949, IOC (49)84, BNA-CAB134/397.
43 Ibid.
44 Report by British Delegate, CND 4th Session, 20 June 1949, IOC (49)123, BNA-CAB134/398.
45 Draft Brief for UK Rep to ECOSOC XII, 8 February 1951, IOC (51)12, BNA-CAB134/410.
46 US Delegation Position Paper, CND 4th Session, 9 May 1949, FBNA/ACC170–74-5/Box121/File1230–1, UN 4th Session #4 (1949–50).
47 Draft US Delegation Position Paper, ECOSOC VIII, 1949, FBNA/ACC170–74-5/Box121/File1230–1, UN 4th Session #2 (1949).
48 Anslinger Statement, CND, 19 May 1949, FBNA/ACC170–74-5/Box121/File1230–1, UN 4th Session #2 (1949).
49 Memorandum by the Secretary General on the ad-hoc Committee, 30 September 1949, FBNA/ACC170–74-5/Box121/File1230–1, UN 4th Session #3 (1949).
50 Anslinger Statement, CND, 19 May 1949, FBNA/ACC170–74-5/Box121/File1230–1, UN 4th Session #2 (1949).
51 Memo of Conversation: Steinig and Morlock, 25 Jan 1950, FBNA/ACC170–74-5/Box121/File1230–1, UN 4th Session #4 (1949–50).
52 Merrill to Anslinger, 9 December 1949, FBNA/ACC170–74-5/Box121/File1230–1, UN 4th Session #4 (1949–50).
53 Draft US Position Paper, 5th CND, 15 February 1950, FBNA/ACC170–74-5/Box121/File1230–1, UN 5th Session #2 (1950).
54 Merrill to Anslinger, 9 December 1949, FBNA/ACC170–74-5/Box121/File1230–1, UN 4th Session #4 (1949–50).
55 Merrill to Secretary of State, 8 December 1949, FBNA/ACC170–74-5/Box121/File1230–1, UN 4th Session #4 (1949–50).
56 Merrill to Anslinger, 9 December 1949, FBNA/ACC170–74-5/Box121/File1230–1, UN 4th Session #4 (1949–50).
57 Memo of Conversation: Steinig and Morlock, 25 Jan 1950, FBNA/ACC170–74-5/Box121/File1230–1, UN 4th Session #4 (1949–50).
58 Memo of Conversation: Steinig, Kotschnig, Morlock, 25 Jan 1950; Sharman to Anslinger, 27 December 1949, FBNA/ACC170–74-5/Box121/File1230–1, UN 4th Session #4 (1949–50).
59 Draft Brief for UK Rep, 4th Session CND, May 1949, IOC (49)84, BNA-CAB134/397.
60 Hutson to Steinig, 15 December 1949; Steinig to Hudson, 13 February 1950; Memo: 'Narcotic Drug Control', 1950, FBNA/ACC170–74-5/Box121/File1230–1, UN 5th Session #2 (1950).
61 Murray Minute, 27 July 1950, US 1811/70, BNA-FO371/88825.
62 Draft Brief for UK Rep. for Joint Committee of Producers and Manufacturers, 3 November 1950, IOC (50)206, BNA-CAB134/408.
63 Ibid.
64 Ibid.

65 Dyar to State Department, 25 August 1950; Anslinger to Sharman, 12 September 1950; US Delegation to Secretary of State, 15 August 1950, FBNA/ACC170–74-5/Box121/File1230–1, UN 5th Session #3 (1950–1).
66 Report by UK Rep, Joint Committee of Producers and Manufacturers, 30 January 1951, IOC (51)9, BNA-CAB134/410.
67 US Del Position Paper, 6th Session CND, 12 April 1951, FBNA/ACC170–74-5/Box121/File1230–1, UN 5th Session #3 (1950–1).
68 Draft Brief UK Del, 6th Session CND, 27 March 1951, BNA-IOC (51)39, BNA-CAB134/410.
69 Ibid.
70 Report by UK Rep, 6th Session CND, 29 June 1951, IOC (51)69, BNA-CAB134/411.
71 Ibid.
72 Ibid.
73 Ibid.
74 Report by UK Rep, 6th Session CND, 29 June 1951, IOC (51)69, BNA-CAB134/411.
75 Ibid.
76 Ibid.
77 Ibid.
78 Greenwood, *Britain and the Cold War, 1945-1991*, 117–18.
79 British Embassy Tehran to Foreign Office, 14 March 1952, BNA-FO371/98721.
80 Logan to Pilgrim, 2 April 1952, BNA-FO371/98721.
81 Walker to Logan, 20 May 1952, BNA-FO371/98721.
82 Ibid.
83 Confidential Report by the US Rep to 8th Session CND, Undated, FBNA/ACC170–74-5/Box125/File0355, Loose Files 1953 Opium Conference (1953); Report by UK Rep, 8th Session CND, 29 May 1953, IOC (53)67, BNA-CAB134/950.
84 Confidential Report by the US Rep to 8th Session CND, Undated, FBNA/ACC170–74-5/Box125/File0355, Loose Files 1953 Opium Conference (1953).
85 Anslinger to Sharman, 2 March 1953, FBNA/ACC170–74-5/Box122/File1230–1, UN 8th Session #3 (1953).
86 Report by UK Rep, 8th Session CND, 29 May 1953, IOC (53)67, BNA-CAB134/950.
87 Anslinger Remarks, 8th Session CND, April 1953, FBNA/ACC170–74-5/Box122/File1230–1, UN 8th Session (1953).
88 Report by UK Rep, 8th Session CND, 29 May 1953, IOC (53)67, BNA-CAB134/950.
89 Kotschnig to Anslinger, 27 October 1952; Anslinger to Vaille, 19 February 1953; US Position Paper, UN Opium Conference, 4 May 1953, FBNA/ACC170–74-5/Box125/File0355, Loose Files 1953 Opium Conference (1953).
90 Memo: Observations on the Protocol, 31 October 1952; Hoare to Anslinger, 19 January 1953; US Suggested Textual Amendments to Draft Protocol, 15 January 1953, FBNA/ACC170–74-5/Box125/File0355, Loose Files 1953 Opium Conference (1953).
91 Draft Brief for UK Del, Conference on the Draft Protocol, 21 April 1953, BNA-CAB134/950.
92 Hoare to Anslinger, 15 December 1952; Anslinger to Hoare, 30 December 1952; Hoare to Anslinger, 19 January 1953; Memo: Observations on the Protocol, 31 October 1952, FBNA/ACC170–74-5/Box125/File0355, Loose Files 1953 Opium Conference (1953).

93 Draft Brief for UK Del, Conference on the Draft Protocol, 21 April 1953, BNA-CAB134/950.

94 FBN: Memorandum of Comments, 18 November 1952, FBNA/ACC170–74-5/Box125/File0355, Loose Files 1953 Opium Conference (1953).

95 Morlock to Anslinger, 24 December 1953; Anslinger to Vaille, 9 February 1953; Vaille to Anslinger, 6 March 1953, FBNA/ACC170–74-5/Box125/File0355, Loose Files 1953 Opium Conference (1953).

96 For a discussion of Franco–US tactics at this conference see: McAllister, *Drug Diplomacy in the Twentieth Century: An International History*, 179.

97 UN Opium Conference, Protocol and Final Act, 23 June 1953; *New York Times*, 'UN Pact Limits Opium Production', 28 June 1953, FBNA/ACC170–74-5/Box122/File1230–1, UN 8th Session (1953).

98 US Study of Provision of 1953 Protocol requiring amendment to domestic legislation, undated, FBNA/ACC170–74-5/Box125/File0355, Loose Files 1953 Opium Conference (1953).

99 UN Opium Conference, Protocol and Final Act, 23 June 1953; Statement by Conference President, 18 June 1953; Anslinger Statement to US Senate Foreign Relations Committee, 17 July 1954; US Study of Provision of 1953 Protocol requiring amendment to domestic legislation, undated, FBNA/ACC170–74-5/Box125/File0355, Loose Files 1953 Opium Conference (1953).

100 See press clippings; Anslinger to Morlock, 29 October 1953, FBNA/ACC170–74-5/Box122/File1230–1, UN 9th Session #1 (1953–4).

Chapter 7

1 Quote: Giordano to Anslinger, 13 May 1959, FBNA/ACC170–74-5/Box123/File1230–1, UN 14th Session (1959).

2 US Del Position Paper, 9th Session CND, undated; Secretary of State to American Embassy, Tehran, 12 November 1953, FBNA/ACC170–74-5/Box122/File1230–1, UN 9th Session #1 (1953).

3 IOC (54)84, 19 June, BNA-CAB134/958.

4 Sharman to Anslinger, 19 February 1954, FBNA/ACC170–74-5/Box122/File1230–1, UN 10th Session #1 (1955).

5 Memo by the Secretariat, 'Unified Convention on Narcotic Drugs', 2 March 1949, FBNA/ACC170–74-5/Box121/File1230–1, UN 4th Session #2 (1949).

6 Report by UK Rep, 7th Session CND, 28 June 1952, IOC (52)88, BNA-CAB134/945.

7 'The Single Convention on Narcotic Drugs; Comments and Possibilities', Herbert May, *UN Bulletin on Narcotics*, January–April 1955, FBNA/ACC170–74-5/Box122/File1230–1, UN 10th Session #1 (1955).

8 Report by UK Rep, 5th Session of CND, 6 February 1951, IOC (51)13, BNA-CAB134/410.

9 US Del Position Paper, 9th Session CND, undated, FBNA/ACC170–74-5/Box122/File1230–1, UN 9th Session #1 (1953).

10 Report by UK Rep, 8th Session CND, 29 May 1953, IOC (53)67, BNA-CAB134/950.

11 Draft Brief for UK Del, ECOSOC 16th Session, 16 June 1953, IOC (53)90, BNA-CAB134/950.

12 Yates to Fonda, 24 September 1953, FBNA/ACC170–74-5/Box122/File1230–1, UN 9th Session #1 (1953).
13 US Del Position Paper, 10th Session CND, 15 April 1955, FBNA/ACC170–74-5/Box122/File1230–1, UN 10th Session #2 (1955).
14 Memo for US Delegate, undated, FBNA/ACC170–74-5/Box122/File1230–1, UN 9th Session Agenda (1954).
15 IOC (54)84, 19 June 1954, BNA-CAB134/958.
16 US Del Position Paper, 10th Session CND, 15 April 1955, FBNA/ACC170–74-5/Box122/File1230–1, UN 10th Session #2 (1955).
17 Walker to Anslinger, 2 March 1955, FBNA/ACC170–74-5/Box122/File1230–1, UN 10th Session #2 (1955).
18 Ibid.
19 Walker to Anslinger, 2 March 1955, Anslinger to Walker, 21 March 1955; Note Attached to Anslinger to Walker, 21 March 1955, FBNA/ACC170–74-5/Box122/File1230–1, UN 10th Session #2 (1955).
20 IOC (59)47, 2 June 1959, BNA-CAB134/2073.
21 Anslinger to Tennyson, 13 May 1958, FBNA/ACC170–74-5/Box123/File1230–1, UN 13th Session #2 (1958–9); McAllister, *Drug Diplomacy in the Twentieth Century*, 178.
22 IOC (54)84, 19 June, BNA-CAB134/958.
23 Anslinger to Sharman, Dec 14th, NA, RG 170-74-12, Box 170, File 1230, Folder: Transfer of Narcotic Commission to Geneva, 1954.
24 McAllister, 'A Limited Enterprise: The History of International Efforts to Control Drugs in the Twentieth Century', 364.
25 Vaille to Anslinger, 5 April 1955, FBNA/ACC170–74-5/Box122/File1230–1, UN 10th Session #2 (1955).
26 IOC (54)84, 19 June, BNA-CAB134/958.
27 Statement by US Rep, 9th Session CND, 19 April to 14 May 1954; Extension of Remarks by Rep. Zandt, 8 June 1954; Hoover to Anslinger, 18 February 1954; Speer to Anslinger, 15 March 1954; Speer to Nagahama, 6 April 1954; Nagahama to Speer, 12 June 1953, FBNA/ACC170–74-5/Box122/File1230–1, UN 9th Session Wayland Speer's Reports Relating to Communist Narcotic Traffic in Far East; Session General Correspondence Relating to Communist Narcotic Traffic in the Far East.
28 Memo of Conversation, 'Illicit Narcotics Traffic', 13 April 1954; Statement by US Rep, 9th Session CND, 19 April to 14 May 1954, FBNA/ACC170–74-5/Box122/File1230–1, UN 9th Session General Correspondence Relating to Communist Narcotic Traffic in the Far East.
29 IOC (54)84, 19 June, BNA-CAB134/958.
30 Ibid.
31 IOC (56)29, 13 April, BNA-CAB134/1268.
32 IOC (55)26, 30 March, BNA-CAB134/964.
33 Statement by PRC Foreign Ministry, 2 July 1954; Martin comments on Anslinger's Proposed Statement, 4 April 1955; Statement by US Rep Anslinger, 10th Session CND, 18 April to 13 May 1955, FBNA/ACC170–74-5/Box122/File1230–1, UN 10th Session #1 (1955); Gamson to Speer, 8 March 1955; State Department memo, 'Proposed Statement . . . by H. J. Anslinger', 26 April 1955, FBNA/ACC170–74-5/Box122/File1230–1, UN 10th Session #2 (1955).

34 US Del Position Paper, 11th Session CND, 13 April 1956; Confidential Report of the Acting US Rep, 11th Session CND, 5 July 1956, FBNA/ACC170-74-5/Box122/File1230-1, UN 11th Session (1955–6).
35 Reports on Illicit traffic 1957, UNS1815/5, 16 March; UNS1815/11, 1 April; UNS1815/12, 30 March; UNS1815/13, 10 April, BNA-FO371/129981.
36 Green to Errock, 15 April, UNS1815/14, BNA-FO371/129981; British Embassy Rangoon to UN department FO, 1 April 1957, UNS1815/11, BNA FO371/129981.
37 Ibid.
38 IOC(60) 53, 31 May 1960, BNA-CAB134/2078.
39 UN Department to UK Embassy Rangoon, 3 July 1957, UNS1815/13, BNA-FO371/129981.
40 IOC (60)53, 31 May, BNA-CAB134/2978.
41 IOC (58)32, 11 April, BNA-CAB134/2067.
42 US Del Position Paper, 11th Session CND, 13 April 1956, FBNA/ACC170-74-5/Box122/File1230-1, UN 11th Session (1955–6).
43 Ibid.
44 Confidential Report of the Acting US Rep, 11th Session CND, 5 July 1956, FBNA/ACC170-74-5/Box122/File1230-1, UN 11th Session (1955–6).
45 US Del Position Paper, 11th Session CND, 13 April 1956; US Del Report, 11th Session CND, 5 July 1956, FBNA/ACC170-74-5/Box122/File1230-1, UN 11th Session (1955–6).
46 IOC (59)47, 2 June, BNA-CAB134/2073.
47 Memo: 'Increase in Opium Production', 21 August 1954, FBNA/ACC170-74-5/Box122/File1230-1, UN 10th Session #1 (1955).
48 Tabibi Statement, 10th Session CND, undated; Anslinger to Morlock, 28 April 1955, FBNA/ACC170-74-5/Box122/File1230-1, UN 10th Session #2 (1955).
49 IOC (56)29, 13 April, BNA-CAB134/1268.
50 XII Session: Minutes, 16 April 1957, UNS1815/16, BNA-FO371/129981.
51 Draft Letter to Parliamentary Under Secretary, 23 April 1957, UNS1815/23, BNA-FO371/129981.
52 IOC (56)47, 16 June, BNA-CAB134/1269.
53 US Del Report, 11th Session CND, 5 July 1956, FBNA/ACC170-74-5/Box122/File1230-1, UN 11th Session (1955–6).
54 Draft Letter to Parliamentary Under Secretary, 23 April 1957, UNS1815/23, BNA-FO371/129981.
55 Ibid.
56 Summary of the Points at issue, 25 April 1957, UNS1815/23, BNA-FO371/129981.
57 Private correspondence with Nigel Ashton.
58 Commander Noble to PUS Mr. Simon, 29 April 1957, UNS1815/23, BNA-FO371/129981.
59 Mr. Simon (PUS) to Mr. Noble, 1 May 1957, UNS1815/24, BNA-FO371/129981.
60 Green to Errock, 15 April 1957, UNS1815/16, BNA-FO371/129981.
61 US Del Position Paper, 11th Session CND, 13 April 1956, FBNA/ACC170-74-5/Box122/File1230-1, UN 11th Session (1955–6).
62 Draft US Del Position Paper, 12th General Assembly, August 1956, FBNA/ACC170-74-5/Box123/File1230-1, UN 12th Session (1957).
63 Anslinger to Vaille, 28 May 1956; Vaille to Anslinger, 17 May 1956, FBNA/ACC170-74-5/Box122/File1230-1, UN 11th Session (1955–6).

64 Siragusa to Anslinger, 10 May 1956; Merrill to Anslinger, 12 May 1956; Confidential Report of the Acting US Rep, 11th Session CND, 5 July 1956, FBNA/ACC170–74-5/Box122/File1230–1, UN 11th Session (1955–6).
65 Gauntlett to Sam Hoare, 6 May 1957, UNS1815/17, BNA-FO371/129981.
66 Draft letter to PUS, April 23 1957, UNS1815/23, BNA-FO371/129981.
67 IOC (57)55, 21 June, BNA-CAB134/2063.
68 Draft US Del Position Paper, 12th General Assembly, August 1956, FBNA/ACC170–74-5/Box123/File1230–1, UN 12th Session (1957).
69 US Del Position Paper, 28 April 1958; Memorandum for Commissioner, 1 May 1958, FBNA/ACC170–74-5/Box123/File1230–1, UN 13th Session #1 (1958).
70 Memorandum of conversation between Anslinger and Secretary General Hammarskjold, 30 March, NA, RG 170-74-12, Box 170, File 1230, Folder: Transfer of Narcotic Commission to Geneva, 1955.
71 McAllister, *Drug Diplomacy in the Twentieth Century*, 189.
72 State Department Memorandum, Jan 25th, NA, RG 170-74-12, Box 170, File 1230, Folder: Transfer of Narcotic Commission to Geneva, 1955.
73 IOC (55)26, 30 March, BNA-CAB134/964.
74 IOC (55)88, 30 June, BNA-CAB134/965.
75 Interim report on happenings of Commission, May 16th, UNS1815/32, BNA-FO371/129981.
76 Memorandum of conversation between Anslinger and Secretary General Hammarskjold; Victor Riesel, 'Shift Opium Control to Europe? No!', *The Cincinnati Enquirer*, Dec 6 1954; Anslinger to Page, Jan 25 1955; Anslinger to Sharman, 14 Dec 1954, FBNA/ACC170–74-12/Box170/File1230, Transfer of Narcotic Commission to Geneva, 1955.
77 UN Narcotics Division to Secretary of State, March 10, 1955; Memorandum of conversation between Anslinger and Secretary General Hammarskjold, FBNA/ACC170–74-12/Box170/File1230, Transfer of Narcotic Commission to Geneva (1955).
78 IOC (56)47, 16 June; IOC (56)39, 4 june, BNA-CAB134/1269.
79 IOC (57)55, 21 June, BNA-CAB134/2063.
80 IOC (58)46, 12 June, BNA-CAB134/2069; Foreign Office to Green, 7 May 1958, UNS1815/28, BNA-FO371/137059.
81 IOC (59)47, 2 June, BNA-CAB134/2073.
82 William McAllister cites 'dismal results' and a high relapse rate at the US institutions in Lexington and Fort Worth, *Drug Diplomacy in the Twentieth Century*, 191.
83 Musto, *The American Disease*, 235. Edwin M. Schur, *Narcotic Addiction in Britain and America The Impact of Public Policy* (Oxfordshire: Taylor & Francis, 1962).
84 For historiographical discussion of the 'British System' see: John Strang and Michael Gossop, eds., *Heroin Addiction and the British System: Origins and Evolution* (Oxfordshire: Routledge, 2005).
85 Anslinger to Green, 8 May 1958, FBNA/ACC170–74-5/Box123/File1230–1, UN 13th Session #1 (1958).
86 Remarks of M. L. Harney, Symposium on the History of Narcotic Drug Addiction Problems, 27 March 1958, FBNA/ACC170–74-5/Box123/File1230–1, UN 13th Session #1 (1958).

87 Anslinger to Lande, 11 June 1958, FBNA/ACC170-74-5/Box123/File1230-1, UN 13th Session #2 (1958-9).
88 IOC (54)84, 18 June; IOC (54)104, 29 June, BNA-CAB134/958.
89 Green to Hoare, 16 May 1957, UNS1815/32, BNA-FO371/129981.
90 IOC (59)47, 2 June, BNA-CAB134/2073.
91 US Del Position Paper, 11th Session CND, 13 April 1956; Confidential Report of the Acting US Rep, 11th Session CND, 5 July 1956; Anslinger to Huang, 28 May 1956; Anslinger to Vaille, 28 May 1956; Anslinger to Boening, 9 July 1956, FBNA/ACC170-74-5/Box122/File1230-1, UN 10th Session #2 (1955).
92 Draft Instruction - American Consulate General at Hong Kong, undated, FBNA/ACC170-74-5/Box122/File1230-1, UN 11th Session (1955-6).
93 Hossick to Anslinger, 1 April 1957; Anslinger to Hossick, 10 April 1957, FBNA/ACC170-74-5/Box123/File1230-1, UN 13th Session (1958).
94 US Del Position Paper, 28 April 1958, FBNA/ACC170-74-5/Box123/File1230-1, UN 13th Session (1958).
95 Anslinger to Vaille, 8 April 1959, FBNA/ACC170-74-5/Box123/File1230-1, UN 14th Session (1959).
96 See discussion between Sir S Hoare and Mr. Greenfield, 14 May 1958, UNS1815/34, BNA-FO371/137060.
97 IOC (58)46: 12 June, BNA-CAB134/2068.
98 State Department telegram to US embassy in Ottawa, 13 June 1958, NA RG 59 File 340.19 #4; Conversation of ECOSOC XXVI Agenda w/ Mrs. Bell of State Department of Narcotics, 28 May 1958, UNS1815/38, FO371/137060.
99 Anslinger to Penteado, 4 June 1958, FBNA/ACC170-74-5/Box123/File1230-1, UN 13th Session #2 (1958-9).
100 Report by UK delegation, 25 July 1958, UNS1815/54, BNA-FO371/137060.
101 Anslinger to Penteado, 7 July 1958, FBNA/ACC170-74-5/Box123/File1230-1, UN 13th Session #2 (1958-9).
102 Anslinger to Vaille, 8 April 1959, FBNA/ACC170-74-5/Box123/File1230-1, UN 14th Session (1959).
103 McAllister, *Drug Diplomacy in the Twentieth Century*, 204.
104 Siragusa to Anslinger, 29 April 1960, FBNA/ACC170-74-5/Box123/File1230-1, UN 15th Session #1 (1960).
105 IOC (54)84, 19 June, BNA-CAB134/958.
106 IOC (55)88, 30 June, BNA-CAB134/965.
107 IOC (56)47, 16 June, BNA-CAB134/1269.
108 Confidential Report of the Acting US Rep, 11th Session CND, 5 July 1956, FBNA/ACC170-74-5/Box122/File1230-1, UN 11th Session (1955-6).
109 Hayes to Anslinger, 28 January 1957; Confidential Report of the Acting US Rep, 11th Session CND, 5 July 1956, FBNA/ACC170-74-5/Box122/File1230-1, UN 11th Session (1955-6).
110 Hoare to Gauntlett, 6 March, UNS1816/5; Hoare to Anslinger, 11 March, UNS1816/5, BNA-FO371/129982.
111 Gauntlett to Hoare, 6 May, UNS1815/17, BNA-FO371/129981.
112 IOC (57)55, 21 June, BNA-CAB134/2063.
113 Vaille to Anslinger, 12 May 1958, FBNA/ACC170-74-5/Box123/File1230-1, UN 13th Session #2 (1958-9).

114 Anslinger to Yates, 11 April 1958, FBNA/ACC170–74-5/Box123/File1230–1, UN 13th Session #1 (1958).
115 IOC (58)46, 12 June, BNA-CAB134/2068; Green to Hoare, 2 May, UNS1815/31, BNA-FO371/137060.
116 Report on the first week of the Commission: Minutes, 14 May, UNS1815/31, BNA-FO371/137060.
117 Anslinger to Hayes, 28 May 1958; Anslinger to Flues, 27 May 1958, FBNA/ACC170–74-5/Box123/File1230–1, UN 13th Session #2 (1958–9).
118 Delegate to Anslinger, 22 May 1958, FBNA/ACC170–74-5/Box123/File1230–1, UN 13th Session #2 (1958–9).
119 Ibid.
120 UD Del Report, 13th Session CND, April 28–May 30 1958, FBNA/ACC170–74-5/Box123/File1230–1, UN 13th Session #1 (1958).
121 Merrill to Herter, July 1959, FBNA/ACC170–74-5/Box123/File1230–1, UN 14th Session (1959).
122 IOC (59)47, 2 June, BNA-CAB134/2073.
123 Tennyson to Anslinger, 14 April 1959, FBNA/ACC170–74-5/Box123/File1230–1, UN 14th Session (1959).
124 Vaille to Anslinger, 16 April 1959; Anslinger to Vaille, 8 April 1959; Tennyson to Anslinger, 14 April 1959; Quoted in Anslinger to Yates, 4 June 1959, FBNA/ACC170–74-5/Box123/File1230–1, UN 14th Session (1959).
125 IOC (61)3, 11 Jan, BNA-CAB134/2082.
126 Siragusa to Anslinger, 21 April 1960, FBNA/ACC170–74-5/Box123/File1230–1, UN 15th Session #1 (1960).
127 Siragusa to Anslinger, 29 April 1960, FBNA/ACC170–74-5/Box123/File1230–1, UN 15th Session #1 (1960).
128 Siragusa to Anslinger, 7 May 1960, FBNA/ACC170–74-5/Box123/File1230–1, UN 15th Session #2 (1960).
129 Comments on Illicit Traffic – Report of the Committee on Illicit Traffic, undated, FBNA/ACC170–74-5/Box123/File1230–1, UN 16th Session (1961).
130 See correspondence: Siragusa to Anslinger, April 1960; Draft Statement of United State Delegate, Illicit Traffic Committee, 29 April 1960, FBNA/ACC170–74-5/Box123/File1230–1, UN 15th Session #1 (1960).
131 IOC (61)61, 9 May, BNA-CAB134/2084.
132 Anslinger to Vaille, 16 March 1961, FBNA/ACC170–74-12/Box170/File1230, Single Convention #3 (1961).
133 IOC (61)61, 9 May, BNA-CAB134/2084.
134 Vaille to Anslinger, 15 March 1961, FBNA/ACC170–74-12/Box170/File1230, Single Convention #3 (1961).
135 McAllister, *Drug Diplomacy in the Twentieth Century*, 206.
136 Press Release: 'Conference Debates Prohibition on Cultivation of Cannabis Plant', 8 February 1961; Statement by delegation of Hungary, 20 March 1961, FBNA/ACC170–74-12/Box170/File1230, Single Convention #3 (1961).
137 McAllister, *Drug Diplomacy in the Twentieth Century*, 206.
138 Anslinger to Vaille, 16 March 1961, FBNA/ACC170–74-12/Box170/File1230, Single Convention #3 (1961).
139 Report of US Delegation to the UN Conference for the Adoption of a Single Convention on Narcotic Drugs, 19 April 1961, FBNA/ACC170–74-12/Box170/File1230, Single Convention #4 (1961).

140 Ibid.
141 Ibid.
142 Ibid.
143 Ibid.
144 Ibid.
145 Anslinger to Francis, 5 April 1961; Anslinger to Hayes, 4 April 1961, FBNA/ACC170–74-12/Box170/File1230, Single Convention #4 (1961).
146 Anslinger to Vaille, 8 March 1961; Vaille to Anslinger, 15 March 1961, FBNA/ACC170–74-12/Box170/File1230, Single Convention #3 (1961).
147 Anslinger to Flue, 26 May 1961, FBNA/ACC170–74-12/Box170/File1230, Single Convention #4 (1961).
148 Memo, 18 March 1961, FBNA/ACC170–74-12/Box170/File1230, Single Convention #3 (1961).
149 Anslinger to Kennedy, 29 March 1961, FBNA/ACC170–74-12/Box170/File1230, Single Convention #3 (1961).
150 McAllister, *Drug Diplomacy in the Twentieth Century.*
151 The United States Views of the Single Convention on Narcotic Drugs, undated, FBNA/ACC170–74-12/Box170/File1230, UN Single Convention.
152 US Del Report, 17th Session CND, 15 August 1962, FBNA/ACC170–74-12/Box170/File1230, Single Convention #6 (1962).
153 Copehart to Anslinger, 31 July 1961, FBNA/ACC170–74-12/Box170/File1230, Single Convention #4 (1961).
154 Beesley to Anslinger, 26 July 1961; Anslinger to Vaille, 10 July 1961, FBNA/ACC170–74-12/Box170/File1230, Single Convention #4 (1961).
155 Carroll to Anslinger, undated, FBNA/ACC170–74-12/Box170/File1230, Single Convention #5 (1961–2).
156 Memo of Conversation, 21 September, 1962, FBNA/ACC170–74-12/Box170/File1230, Single Convention #6 (1962).
157 British Embassy Washington to Horn, 19 September 1962, UNS18112/68, BNA-FO371/161050.
158 Green to Key, 6 September 1962, UNS18112/66, BNA-FO371/161050.
159 See clippings FBNA/ACC170–74-12/Box170/File1230, Single Convention #4 (1961).
160 Green to Anslinger, 26 February 1962, FBNA/ACC170–74-12/Box170/File1230, Single Convention #5 (1961–2).
161 Mission to Greece and Turkey on Narcotic Treaties, 3 May 1962, NA, RG 170-74-12, Box 170, File 1230, Folder: Single Convention.
162 For use in discussion with Curran, 1962, NA, RG 170-74-12, Box 170, File 1230, Folder: Single Convention.
163 Flues to Secretary of the Treasury, 3 May 1962, FBNA/ACC170–74-12/Box170/File1230, UN Single Convention.
164 Ibid.
165 Ibid.
166 Postscript, Flues to Treasury, 3 May 1962, FBNA/ACC170–74-12/Box170/File1230, UN Single Convention.
167 Cusack to Giordano, 17 September 1962, FBNA/ACC170–74-12/Box170/File1230, Single Convention #6 (1962).
168 See FBNA/ACC170–74-12/Box170/File1230, Single Convention #7 (1962–3); US Embassy New Delhi to Secretary of State, 1 May 1962, FBNA/ACC170–74-12/Box170/File1230, Single Convention #6 (1962).

169 Anslinger to Vaille, 20 June 1962, FBNA/ACC170–74-5/Box123/File1230–1, UN 17th Session (1962).
170 Bernes to Reed, 13 May 1963; US Delegation Geneva to Secretary of State, 23 April 1963, FBNA/ACC170–74-12/Box170/File1230, Single Convention #8 (1963–5).
171 Ratification by Turkey, 9 August, UNS18110/24, BNA-FO371/172756.
172 US Del Report, 17th Session CND, 15 August 1962, FBNA/ACC170–74-12/Box170/File1230, Single Convention #6 (1962); For examples of UK's ratification efforts see: BNA-FO371/172756.
173 UN Bulletin on Narcotics – 1965 Issue 1: 'Coming into force of the Single Convention on Narcotic Drugs, 1961'. www.unodc.org/unodc/en/data-and-analysis/bulletin/bulletin_1965-01-01_1_page002.html (accessed 18 September 2014).

Chapter 8

1 For a discussion of the politicisation of INCB's work see: Joanne Csete, 'Overhauling Oversight: Human Rights at the INCB', ed. John Collins, *Governing the Global Drug Wars*, LSE IDEAS Special Reports, October 2012. https://eprints.lse.ac.uk/47122/1/Governing%20the%20global%20drug%20wars%28published%29.pdf.
2 United Nations, 'Commentary on the Single Convention on Narcotic Drugs, 1961' (New York: United Nations Secretariat, 1973), 263. www.unodc.org/documents/treaties/organized_crime/Drug%20Convention/Commentary_on_the_single_convention_1961.pdf.
3 Joseph Spillane and William B. Mcallister, 'Keeping the Lid On: A Century of Drug Regulation and Control', *Drug and Alcohol Dependence* 70, no. 3 (2003): S5–12. https://pubmed.ncbi.nlm.nih.gov/12759194/.
4 William B. McAllister, 'The Global Political Economy of Scheduling: The International–Historical Context of the Controlled Substances Act', *Drug and Alcohol Dependence* 76, no. 1 (5 October 2004): 3–8. https://doi.org/10.1016/j.drugalcdep.2004.02.012.
5 United Nations, 'Commentary on the Single Convention on Narcotic Drugs, 1961', 1973, 53.
6 Ibid., 53.
7 Ibid., 51–2.
8 Ibid., 52.
9 Ibid., 51–2.
10 Ibid., 68.
11 Ibid., 53.
12 Ibid.
13 Ibid.
14 Ibid., 54.
15 Ibid., 54.
16 Ibid., 55.
17 Ibid., 57.
18 Ibid., 58.
19 Ibid., 59.
20 Ibid., 60.
21 Ibid., 64.

22 Ibid., 92.
23 Ibid., 92.
24 Article 2, United Nations, *Single Convention on Narcotic Drugs of 1961 as Amended by the 1972 Protocol* (New York: United Nations, 1961).
25 United Nations, 'Commentary on the Single Convention on Narcotic Drugs, 1961', 1973, 65.
26 Ibid., 67.
27 Ibid., 66.
28 Ibid., 66.
29 Ibid., 74.
30 Ibid., 90.
31 Ibid.
32 Ibid., 77.
33 Ibid., 77, footnote 23.
34 Ibid., 77.
35 Ibid., 78.
36 Ibid.
37 Ibid., 88.
38 Art. 1, para. (e), *Convention on Psychotropic Substances of 1971* (New York: United Nations, 1971). www.unodc.org/unodc/en/treaties/psychotropics.html.
39 United Nations, 'Commentary on the Convention on Psychotropic Substances, 1971' (New York: United Nations, 1976), 15.
40 Ibid., 30.
41 Ibid.
42 Ibid.
43 Ibid., 31.
44 Ibid., 30.
45 Ibid., 32.
46 Ibid., 33.
47 Ibid.
48 United Nations, 61.
49 WHO Expert Committee on Drug Dependence, 'Seventeenth Report', WHO Technical Report Series, n.d.
50 United Nations, 'Commentary on the United Nations Convention Against Illicit Traffic in Narcotic Drugs and Psychotropic Substances 1988' (New York: United Nations, 1998).
51 United Nations.
52 United Nations.
53 United Nations, 7.
54 Preamble, United Nations, *United Nations Convention against Illicit Traffic in Narcotic Drugs and Psychotropic Substances, 1988* (Vienna: United Nations, 1988). www.unodc.org/pdf/convention_1988_en.pdf.
55 UNODC, 'A Century of International Drug Control', 8.
56 Article 3, United Nations, *United Nations Convention against Illicit Traffic in Narcotic Drugs and Psychotropic Substances, 1988.*
57 United Nations, 'Commentary on the United Nations Convention Against Illicit Traffic in Narcotic Drugs and Psychotropic Substances 1988', 81–82.

58 John Collins, 'Losing UNGASS? Lessons from Civil Society, Past and Present', *Drugs and Alcohol Today* 17, no. 2 (2017): 88–97.
59 Latin American Commission on Drugs and Democracy, 'Drugs and Democracy: Toward a Paradigm Shift', February 2009. www.globalcommissionondrugs.org/the-latin-american-commission-on-drugs-and-democracy.
60 The Global Commission on Drug Policy, 'War on Drugs' (New York: GCDP, 2011), www.globalcommissionondrugs.org/reports/war-on-drugs/.
61 Juan Manuel Santos, 'Re-Examining the Drug Problem Through a Fresh Lens', ed. John Collins, *Governing the Global Drug Wars*, LSE IDEAS Special Reports, October 2012, 2.
62 Adam Williams and Nacha Cattan, 'Biden Says Drug Legalization Debate Is Totally Legitimate', *Bloomberg News*, 3 June 2012. www.bloomberg.com/news/articles/2012-03-05/biden-visits-mexico-honduras-amid-calls-to-debate-drug-strategy.
63 Organization of American States, 'Scenarios for the Drug Problem in the Americas, 2013–2025' (Cartagena de Indias: OAS, 2012). www.oas.org/documents/eng/press/scenarios_report.pdf.
64 William R. Brownfield, 'Trends in Global Drug Policy' (New York City, 9 October 2014). http://fpc.state.gov/232813.htm.
65 John Collins, 'The State Department's Move to a More Flexible Diplomatic Policy on Drugs Is a Rational Approach to a Difficult Question', *USAPP* (blog), 1 December 2014. http://blogs.lse.ac.uk/usappblog/2014/12/01/the-u-s-new-more-flexible-diplomatic-doctrine-on-drugs-is-a-rational-approach-to-a-difficult-question/.
66 United Nations General Assembly, 'Our Joint Commitment to Effectively Addressing and Countering the World Drug Problem' (New York: United Nations, 19 April 2016).
67 Martin Jelsma and David Bewley-Taylor, 'UNGASS 2016: A Broken or B-r-o-a-d Consensus?', *Transnational Institute* (blog), 5 July 2016. www.tni.org/en/publication/ungass-2016-a-broken-or-b-r-o-a-d-consensus.
68 Rick Lines and Damon Barrett, 'The Human Rights Win at UNGASS on Drugs That No One Is Talking About and How We Can Use It', 9 May 2016, https://hrcessex.wordpress.com/2016/05/09/the-human-rights-win-at-the-ungass-on-drugs-that-no-one-is-talking-about-and-how-we-can-use-it/.
69 Jelsma and Bewley-Taylor, 'UNGASS 2016: A Broken or B-r-o-a-d Consensus?'; Martin Jelsma, 'UN Common Position on Drug Policy – Consolidating System-Wide Coherence', Transnational Institute, December 2019, www.tni.org/en/publication/un-common-position-on-drug-policy-consolidating-system-wide-coherence.
70 Collins, 'Losing UNGASS? Lessons from Civil Society, Past and Present'.

Chapter 9

1 'Ethical' description comes from: McAllister, 'Reflections on a Century of International Drug Control', 13.
2 John Strang and Michael Gossop, 'Misreported and Minunderstood – the "British System" of Drug Policy', in *Heroin Addiction and the British System: Origins and Evolution*, ed. John Strang and Michael Gossop (Oxfordshire: Routledge, 2005), 1.
3 Bewley-Taylor, *International Drug Control*.

4 Nadelmann, 'Global Prohibition Regimes: The Evolution of Norms in International Society'.
5 John Collins, 'A Brief History of Cannabis and the Drug Conventions', *AJIL Unbound* (October 2020), 280.
6 Bewley-Taylor, *International Drug Control.*
7 Collins, 'Evaluating Trends and Stakeholders in the International Drug Control Regime Complex', 1 April 2021.
8 Ibid., 2.
9 Ibid.
10 Martin Jelsma and David R. Bewley-Taylor, 'The UN Drug Control Conventions: The Limits of Latitude', Series on Legislative Reform of Drug Policies (Transnational Institute and International Drug Policy Consortium, March 2012). www.tni.org/sites/www.tni.org/files/download/dlr18.pdf.
11 Collins, 'Evaluating Trends and Stakeholders in the International Drug Control Regime Complex', 2.
12 Collins, 'A Brief History of Cannabis and the Drug Conventions', 279.
13 Frank Biermann et al., 'The Fragmentation of Global Governance Architectures: A Framework for Analysis', *Global Environmental Politics* 9, no. 4 (2009): 15. https://doi.org/10.1162/glep.2009.9.4.14.
14 Damon Barrett, David Bewley-Taylor, and Martin Jelsma, 'Fatal Attraction: Brownfield's Flexibility Doctrine and Global Drug Policy Reform', *Huffington Post* Politics UK (blog), 18 November 2014. www.huffingtonpost.co.uk/damon-barett/drug-policy-reform_b_6158144.html.
15 Collins, 'A Brief History of Cannabis and the Drug Conventions'.
16 Biermann et al., 'The Fragmentation of Global Governance Architectures', 16.
17 Ibid., 16.
18 C. Wilfred Jenks, 'The Conflict of Law-Making Treaties', *BYBIL* 3 (1953):, 403; Martti Koskenniemi, 'Fragmentation of International Law: Difficulties Arising from the Diversification and Expansion of International Law', in *Report of the Study Group of the International Law Commission*, United Nations, 2006, 10. http://legal.un.org/ilc/documentation/english/a_cn4_l682.pdf.
19 Koskenniemi, 'Fragmentation of International Law', 10.
20 Ibid., 11.
21 Damon Barrett, 'Reflections on Human Rights and International Drug Control', in *Governing the Global Drug Wars*, ed. John Collins (London: LSE, 2012). https://eprints.lse.ac.uk/47122/1/Governing%20the%20global%20drug%20wars%28published%29.pdf; Richard Lines, *Drug Control and Human Rights in International Law* (Cambridge, Cambridge University Press, 2017). https://books.google.co.uk/books?id=zNqiDgAAQBAJ.
22 Jacob Cogan et al., 'Fragmentation of International Legal Orders and International Law: Ways Forward?', in *American Society of International Law. Proceedings of the Annual Meeting* (Washington: Cambridge University Press, 2011), 123–32; Martti Koskenniemi and Pivi Leino, 'Fragmentation of International Law? Postmodern Anxieties', *Leiden Journal of International Law* 15, no. 3 (2002): 553–79. https://doi.org/10.1017/S0922156502000262.
23 Cogan et al., 'Fragmentation of International Legal Orders and International Law', 24.
24 Ibid., 124.

25 Ibid.', 124.
26 Koskenniemi, 'Fragmentation of International Law'.
27 Sally Engle Merry, 'Legal Pluralism', *Law and Society Review* 22, no. 5 (1 January 1 1988): 870.
28 UK All Party Parliamentary Group on Drug Policy Reform, 'Guidance on Drug Policy: Interpreting the UN Drug Conventions', 2015.
29 Nico Krisch, *Beyond Constitutionalism: The Pluralist Structure of Postnational Law*, 1st ed., Oxford Constitutional Theory (Oxford, New York: Oxford University Press, 2010), 27.
30 Ibid.
31 Ibid., 27.
32 Ibid.
33 Ibid., 27.
34 Eileen Denza, 'The Relationship between International and National Law', in *International Law*, ed. Malcolm D. Evans, 4th ed. (Oxford, New York: Oxford University Press, 2014), 437.
35 Koskenniemi, 'Fragmentation of International Law', 13.
36 Anne Peters, 'The Refinement of International Law: From Fragmentation to Regime Interaction and Politicization', *International Journal of Constitutional Law* 15, no. 3 (2017): 671. https://doi.org/10.1093/icon/mox056.
37 Ibid., 672.
38 Ibid., 673.
39 Stephen D. Krasner, 'Structural Causes and Regime Consequences: Regimes as Intervening Variables', *International Organization* 36, no. 2 (1982):186.
40 Ibid., 186.
41 Kuyper, 'Global Democratization'.
42 Krasner, 'Structural Causes and Regime Consequences', 186.
43 Kuyper, 'Global Democratization'.
44 Ibid.
45 Collins, 'Rethinking Flexibilities',
46 Jeff Colgan, Robert Keohane, and Thijs Van de Graaf, 'Punctuated Equilibrium in the Energy Regime Complex', *The Review of International Organizations* 7, no. 2 (2012): 117.
47 Bewley-Taylor, *International Drug Control.*
48 Mills, 'Cocaine and the British Empire'.
49 James Windle, 'How the East Influenced Drug Prohibition', *The International History Review* 35, no. 5 (October 2013): 1185–99.
50 John Collins, 'War, Decolonisation and The Birth of the Illicit Opium Trade in Burma', in *Historical Perspectives on Organised Crime and Terrorism*, ed. James Windle et al. (London: Routledge, 2017).
51 Collins, 'Regulations and Prohibitions'; Douglas Clark Kinder, 'Bureaucratic Cold Warrior: Harry J. Anslinger and Illicit Narcotics Traffic', *Pacific Historical Review* 50, no. 2 (1 May 1981): 169–91.
52 Raustiala and Victor, 'The Regime Complex for Plant Genetic Resources', 279.
53 McAllister, 'Reflections on a Century of International Drug Control'.
54 Collins, 'Regulations and Prohibitions'; McAllister, *Drug Diplomacy in the Twentieth Century*; Taylor, *American Diplomacy and the Narcotics Traffic.*

55 Raustiala and Victor, 'The Regime Complex for Plant Genetic Resources'; Oran Young et al., *Institutional Interplay: Biosafety and Trade* (Tokyo, Japan: UNU, 2008). http://search.proquest.com/docview/903905443/.

56 Valbona Muzaka, 'Linkages, Contests and Overlaps in the Global Intellectual Property Rights Regime', *European Journal of International Relations* 17, no. 4 (2011): 755.

57 Ibid., 756.

58 Colgan, Keohane, and Van de Graaf, 'Punctuated Equilibrium in the Energy Regime Complex'; Raustiala and Victor, 'The Regime Complex for Plant Genetic Resources'.

59 UNDP, 'Addressing the Development Dimensions of Drug Policy'.

60 *Buenos Aires Herald*, 'Mujica Blasts UN Official Raymond Yans over Marijuana Law', 15 December 2013. www.buenosairesherald.com/article/147539/mujica-blasts-un-official-raymond-yans-over-marijuana-law (accessed 8/10/2015)

61 Private discussions, Commission on Narcotic Drugs, 2015.

62 Kuyper, 'Global Democratization'.

63 Ibid., 620.

64 Ibid.

65 Collins, 'Losing UNGASS?'.

66 Muzaka, 'Linkages, Contests and Overlaps'.

67 Laurence R. Helfer, 'Regime Shifting in the International Intellectual Property System', *Perspectives on Politics* 7, no. 1 (2009): 39–44.

68 Kuyper, 'Global Democratization'.

69 Keohane and Victor, 'The Regime Complex for Climate Change'.

70 Colgan, Keohane, and Van de Graaf, 'Punctuated Equilibrium in the Energy Regime Complex'; Raustiala and Victor, 'The Regime Complex for Plant Genetic Resources'.

BIBLIOGRAPHY

Official Documents

Great Britain

- British National Archives, Kew:
  - Cabinet Records
    - CAB 134: Steering Committee on International Organisation
  - Foreign Office
    - FO 371: General Correspondence, Political
    - FO 938
    - FO 1014
    - FO 1032
    - FO 1049
    - FO 1050
  - Home Office
    - HO 45: Dangerous Drugs
  - Colonial Office
    - CO 323
    - CO 554
    - CO 852
    - CO 859

United States

- NARA II, College Park Maryland
  - Washington National Records Centre
    - Record Group 170: Records of the Federal Bureau of Narcotics
    - Record Group 59: General Records, Department of State

Published Official Documents

United Nations

- *Bulletin on Narcotics*, New York, United Nations.

Private Collections

Butler Library, Columbia University, Oral History Research Office, *The Reminiscences of Herbert L. May.*

Books and Journal Articles

Barrett, Damon. 'Reflections on Human Rights and International Drug Control'. In *Governing the Global Drug Wars*, edited by John Collins. London: LSE, 2012. https://eprints.lse.ac.uk/47122/1/Governing%20the%20global%20drug%20wars%28published%29.pdf.

Barrett, Damon, David Bewley-Taylor, and Martin Jelsma. 'Fatal Attraction: Brownfield's Flexibility Doctrine and Global Drug Policy Reform'. *Huffington Post Politics UK* (blog), 18 November 2014. www.huffingtonpost.co.uk/damon-barett/drug-policy-reform_b_6158144.html.

Becker, Howard Saul. *Outsiders: Studies in the Sociology of Deviance.* Free Press, 1997.

Bello, David. 'The Venomous Course of Southwestern Opium: Qing Prohibition in Yunnan, Sichuan, and Guizhou in the Early Nineteenth Century'. *The Journal of Asian Studies* 62, no. 4 (2003): 1109–42. https://doi.org/10.2307/3591761.

Bentham, Mandy. *The Politics of Drug Control.* New York: Macmillan, 1998.

Berridge, Virginia. 'Illicit Drugs and Internationalism: The Forgotten Dimension'. *Medical History* 2, no. 45 (2001): 282–8.

Opium and the People: Opiate Use and Drug Control Policy in Nineteenth and Early Twentieth Century England. London: Free Association Books, 1999.

Bewley-Taylor, David R. *International Drug Control: Consensus Fractured.* Cambridge: Cambridge University Press, 2012.

Bewley-Taylor, *The United States and International Drug Control, 1909–1997.* London: Continuum, 1999.

Biermann, Frank, Philipp Pattberg, Harro Van Asselt, and Fariborz Zelli. 'The Fragmentation of Global Governance Architectures: A Framework for Analysis'. *Global Environmental Politics* 9, no. 4 (2009): 14–40. https://doi.org/10.1162/glep.2009.9.4.14.

Block, Alan A. 'European Drug Traffic and Traffickers between the Wars: The Policy of Suppression and Its Consequences'. *Journal of Social History* 23, no. 2 (1 December 1989): 315–37.

Bradford, J.T. *Poppies, Politics, and Power: Afghanistan and the Global History of Drugs and Diplomacy.* Ithaca: Cornell University Press, 2019. https://books.google.co.uk/books?id=iapzDwAAQBAJ.

Brook, Timothy. 'Opium and Collaboration in Central China 1938–1940'. In *Opium Regimes: China, Britain, and Japan, 1839–1952*, edited by Timothy Brook and Bob Tadashi Wakabayashi. Berkeley: University of California Press, 2000.

Brown, Richard Harvey. 'The Opium Trade and Opium Policies in India, China, Britain, and the United States: Historical Comparisons and Theoretical Interpretations'. *Asian Journal of Social Science* 30, no. 3 (2002): 623–56. https://doi.org/10.1163/156853102320945420.

Brownfield, William R. 'Trends in Global Drug Policy'. US Department of State press office. New York City, 9 October 2014. http://fpc.state.gov/232813.htm.

Bruun, Kettil, Lynn Pan, and Ingemar Rexed. *The Gentlemen's Club: International Control of Drugs and Alcohol*. Chicago, IL: University of Chicago Press, 1975.

Buenos Aires Herald. 'Mujica Blasts UN Official Raymond Yans over Marijuana Law', 15 December 2013. www.buenosairesherald.com/article/147539/mujica-blasts-un-official-raymond-yans-over-marijuana-law (accessed 8/10/2015)

Campos, Isaac. *Home Grown: Marijuana and the Origins of Mexico's War on Drugs*. University of North Carolina Press, 2012.

Chouvy, Pierre-Arnaud. 'Drug Trafficking in and out of the Golden Triangle'. In *An Atlas of Trafficking in Southeast Asia. The Illegal Trade in Arms, Drugs, People, Counterfeit Goods and Natural Resources in Mainland*, 1–32. I.B. Tauris, 2013. https://hal.archives-ouvertes.fr/hal-01050968.

Cogan, Jacob, Nele Matz-Lück, Mario Prost, and Sahib Singh. 'Fragmentation of International Legal Orders and International Law: Ways Forward?' In *American Society of International Law. Proceedings of the Annual Meeting*, 123–32. Washington: Cambridge University Press, 2011.

Colgan, Jeff, Robert Keohane, and Thijs Van de Graaf. 'Punctuated Equilibrium in the Energy Regime Complex'. *The Review of International Organizations* 7, no. 2 (2012): 117–43.

Collins, John. 'A Brief History of Cannabis and the Drug Conventions'. *AJIL Unbound* (October 2020).

'Breaking the Monopoly System: American Influence on the British Decision to Prohibit Opium Smoking and End Its Asian Monopolies, 1939–1945'. *International History Review* 39, no. 5 (February 2017): 770–90.

'Evaluating Trends and Stakeholders in the International Drug Control Regime Complex'. *International Journal of Drug Policy* 90 (1 April 2021): 103060, https://doi.org/10.1016/j.drugpo.2020.103060.

'Imperial Drug Economies, Development, and the Search for Alternatives in Asia, from Colonialism to Decolonisation'. *Drug Policies and Development* (27 August 2020): 43–63. https://doi.org/10.1163/9789004440494_004.

'Losing UNGASS? Lessons from Civil Society, Past and Present'. *Drugs and Alcohol Today* 17, no. 2 (2017): 88–97.

'Regulations and Prohibitions: Anglo-American Relations and International Drug Control, 1939–1964'. London School of Economics and Political Science (LSE), 2015. http://etheses.lse.ac.uk/3107/.

'Rethinking "Flexibilities" in the International Drug Control System – Potential, Precedents and Models for Reforms'. *International Journal of Drug Policy* 60 (2018): 107–14.

'The State Department's Move to a More Flexible Diplomatic Policy on Drugs Is a Rational Approach to a Difficult Question'. *USAPP* (blog), 1 December 2014. http://blogs.lse.ac.uk/usappblog/2014/12/01/the-u-s-new-more-flexible-diplomatic-doctrine-on-drugs-is-a-rational-approach-to-a-difficult-question/.

'War, Decolonisation and the Birth of the Illicit Opium Trade in Burma'. In *Historical Perspectives on Organised Crime and Terrorism*, edited by James Windle, John Mirrison, Aaron Winter, and Andrew Silke. Oxfordshire: Routledge, 2017.

Convention on Psychotropic Substances of 1971. New York: United Nations, 1971. www.unodc.org/unodc/en/treaties/psychotropics.html.

Courtwright, David. 'A Short History of Drug Policy or Why We Make War on Some Drugs but Not on Others'. In *Governing the Global Drug Wars*, edited by John Collins. London: LSE IDEAS, 2012. https://eprints.lse.ac.uk/47122/1/Governing%20the%20global%20drug%20wars%28published%29.pdf.

Csete, Joanne. 'Overhauling Oversight: Human Rights at the INCB'. Edited by John Collins. *Governing the Global Drug Wars*, LSE IDEAS Special Reports, October 2012. https://eprints.lse.ac.uk/47122/1/Governing%20the%20global%20drug%20wars%28published%29.pdf.

Denza, Eileen. 'The Relationship Between International and National Law'. In *International Law*, edited by Malcolm D. Evans, Fourth Edition. Oxford, New York: Oxford University Press, 2014.

Edwards, Lee. *Missionary for Freedom: The Life and Times of Walter Judd*. Paragon House, 1990.

Engle Merry, Sally. 'Legal Pluralism'. *Law and Society Review* 22, no. 5 (1 January 1988): 869–96.

Friman, H. Richard. *NarcoDiplomacy: Exporting the U.S. War on Drugs*. Ithaca: Cornell University Press, 1996.

Ghiabi, Maziyar. *Drugs Politics: Managing Disorder in the Islamic Republic of Iran*. Cambridge University Press, 2019. https://books.google.be/books?id=HoOWDwAAQBAJ.

Gootenberg, Paul. *Andean Cocaine: The Making of a Global Drug*. University of North Carolina Press, 2009.

Greenwood, Sean. *Britain and the Cold War, 1945–1991*. St. Martin's Press, 2000.

Hansen, Bradley. 'Learning to Tax: The Political Economy of the Opium Trade in Iran, 1921–1941'. *The Journal of Economic History* 61, no. 1 (1 March 2001): 95–113.

Helfer, Laurence R. 'Regime Shifting in the International Intellectual Property System'. *Perspectives on Politics* 7, no. 1 (2009): 39–44.

Hoopes, Townsend, and Douglas Brinkley. *Franklin Delano Roosevelt and the Creation of the U.N.* Yale University Press, 1997.

Jelsma, Martin. 'UN Common Position on Drug Policy – Consolidating System-Wide Coherence'. Transnational Institute, December 2019. www.tni.org/en/publication/un-common-position-on-drug-policy-consolidating-system-wide-coherence.

Jelsma, Martin, and David Bewley-Taylor. 'UNGASS 2016: A Broken or B-r-o-a-d Consensus?' *Transnational Institute* (blog), 5 July 2016. www.tni.org/en/publication/ungass-2016-a-broken-or-b-r-o-a-d-consensus.

'The UN Drug Control Conventions: The Limits of Latitude'. Series on Legislative Reform of Drug Policies. Transnational Institute and International Drug Policy Consortium, March 2012. www.tni.org/sites/www.tni.org/files/download/dlr18.pdf.

Jenks, C. Wilfred. 'The Conflict of Law-Making Treaties'. *BYBIL* 3 (1953).

Keohane, Robert O, and David G Victor. 'The Regime Complex for Climate Change'. *Perspectives on Politics* 9, no. 1 (2011): 7–23.

Kinder, Douglas Clark. 'Bureaucratic Cold Warrior: Harry J. Anslinger and Illicit Narcotics Traffic'. *Pacific Historical Review* 50, no. 2 (1 May 1981): 169–91.

'Shutting Out the Evil: Nativism and Narcotics Control in the United States'. In *Drug Control Policy: Essays in Historical Comparative Perspective*, edited by William O. Walker III. Pennsylvania State University Press, 1992.

Koskenniemi, Martti. 'Fragmentation of International Law: Difficulties Arising from the Diversification and Expansion of International Law'. *In* Report of the Study Group of the International Law Commission. United Nations, 2006. http://legal.un.org/ilc/documentation/english/a_cn4_l682.pdf.

Koskenniemi, Martti, and Pivi Leino. 'Fragmentation of International Law? Postmodern Anxieties'. *Leiden Journal of International Law* 15, no. 3 (2002): 553–79. https://doi.org/10.1017/S0922156502000262.

Kranton, Rachel, and Anand V. Swamy. 'Contracts, Hold-Up, and Exports: Textiles and Opium in Colonial India'. *American Economic Review* 98, no. 3 (1 June 2008): 967–90. https://doi.org/10.1257/aer.98.3.967.

Krasner, Stephen D. 'Structural Causes and Regime Consequences: Regimes as Intervening Variables'. *International Organization* 36, no. 2 (1982): 185–205.

Krisch, Nico. *Beyond Constitutionalism: The Pluralist Structure of Postnational Law*. 1st ed. Oxford Constitutional Theory. Oxford, New York: Oxford University Press, 2010.

Kuyper, Jonathan W. 'Global Democratization and International Regime Complexity'. *European Journal of International Relations* 20, no. 3 (2014): 620–46. https://doi.org/10.1177/1354066113497492.

Latin American Commission on Drugs and Democracy. 'Drugs and Democracy: Toward a Paradigm Shift', February 2009. www.globalcommissionondrugs.org/the-latin-american-commission-on-drugs-and-democracy.

Lewy, Jonathan. 'The Drug Policy of the Third Reich'. *Social History of Alcohol and Drugs* 22, no. 2 (2008): 144–67.

Lines, Richard. *Drug Control and Human Rights in International Law*. Cambridge: Cambridge University Press, 2017. https://books.google.co.uk/books?id=zNqiDgAAQBAJ.

Lines, Rick, and Damon Barrett. 'The Human Rights Win at UNGASS on Drugs That No One Is Talking About and How We Can Use It', 9 May 2016. https://hrcessex.wordpress.com/2016/05/09/the-human-rights-win-at-the-ungass-on-drugs-that-no-one-is-talking-about-and-how-we-can-use-it/.

Maule, Robert. 'British Policy Discussions on the Opium Question in the Federated Shan States, 1937–1948'. *Journal of Southeast Asian Studies* 33, no. 2 (June 2002): 203–24.

'The Opium Question in the Federated Shan States, 1931-36: British Policy Discussions and Scandal'. *Journal of Southeast Asian Studies* 23, no. 1 (March 1992): 14–36.

McAllister, William B. 'A Limited Enterprise: The History of International Efforts to Control Drugs in the Twentieth Century'. PhD Dissertation, University of Virginia, 1996.

Drug Diplomacy in the Twentieth Century: An International History. New York: Routledge, 2000.

In *Governing the Global Drug Wars*, edited by John Collins. London: LSE, 2012. https://eprints.lse.ac.uk/47122/1/Governing%20the%20global%20drug%20wars%28published%29.pdf.

'The Global Political Economy of Scheduling: The International–Historical Context of the Controlled Substances Act'. *Drug and Alcohol Dependence* 76, no. 1 (5 October 2004): 3–8. https://doi.org/10.1016/j.drugalcdep.2004.02.012.

McCoy, Alfred W. *The Politics of Heroin: CIA Complicity in the Global Drug Trade, Afghanistan, Southeast Asia, Central America, Colombia*. 3rd ed. Brooklyn, NY: Lawrence Hill Books, 2003.

McWilliams, John C. *The Protectors: Harry J. Anslinger and the Federal Bureau of Narcotics, 1930–1962*. Newark: University of Delaware Press, 1990.

Meyer, Kathryn, and Terry M. Parssinen. *Webs of Smoke: Smugglers, Warlords, Spies, and the History of the International Drug Trade*. Oxford: Rowman & Littlefield, 2002.

Mills, James H. *Cannabis Britannica : Empire, Trade, and Prohibition 1800–1928: Empire, Trade, and Prohibition 1800–1928*. Oxford: Oxford University Press, 2003.

Cannabis Nation: Control and Consumption in Britain, 1928–2008. Oxford: Oxford University Press, 2012.

'Cocaine and the British Empire: The Drug and the Diplomats at the Hague Opium Conference, 1911–12'. *The Journal of Imperial and Commonwealth History* 42, no. 3 (2014): 400–419.

Morgan, H. Wayne. *Drugs in America: A Social History, 1800–1980*. Syracuse University Press, 1981.

Musto, David F. *The American Disease: Origins of Narcotic Control*. 3rd ed. London: Oxford University Press, 1999.

Muzaka, Valbona. 'Linkages, Contests and Overlaps in the Global Intellectual Property Rights Regime'. *European Journal of International Relations* 17, no. 4 (2011): 755–76.

Nadelmann, Ethan A. 'Global Prohibition Regimes: The Evolution of Norms in International Society'. *International Organization* 44, no. 4 (1 October 1990): 479–526.

Organization of American States. 'Scenarios for the Drug Problem in the Americas, 2013–2025'. Cartagena de Indias: OAS, 2012. www.oas.org/documents/eng/press/scenarios_report.pdf.

Paoli, Letizia, Victoria A. Greenfield, and Peter Reuter. *The World Heroin Market: Can Supply Be Cut?* Oxford University Press, 2009.

Peters, Anne. 'The Refinement of International Law: From Fragmentation to Regime Interaction and Politicization'. *International Journal of Constitutional Law* 15, no. 3 (2017): 671–704. https://doi.org/10.1093/icon/mox056.

Raustiala, Kal, and David G. Victor. 'The Regime Complex for Plant Genetic Resources'. *International Organization* 58, no. 2 (2004): 277–309. https://doi.org/10.1017/S0020818304582036.

Richards, John F. 'Opium and the British Indian Empire: The Royal Commission of 1895'. *Modern Asian Studies* 36, no. 2 (2002): 375–420. https://doi.org/10.1017/S0026749X02002044.

Russell, Thomas. *Egyptian Service: 1902–1946*. Murray, 1949.

Santos, Juan Manuel. 'Re-Examining the Drug Problem Through a Fresh Lens'. Edited by John Collins. *Governing the Global Drug Wars*, LSE IDEAS Special Reports, October 2012, 2–3. https://eprints.lse.ac.uk/47122/1/Governing%20the%20global%20drug%20wars%28published%29.pdf.

Schur, Edwin M. *Narcotic Addiction in Britain and America: The Impact of Public Policy*. Oxfordshire: Taylor & Francis, 1962.

Spillane, Joseph, and William B. Mcallister. 'Keeping the Lid On: A Century of Drug Regulation and Control'. *Drug and Alcohol Dependence* 70, no. 3 (2003): S5–12. https://pubmed.ncbi.nlm.nih.gov/12759194/.

Stein, S. D. *International Diplomacy, State Administrators, and Narcotics Control: The Origins of a Social Problem*. Aldershot: Gower, 1985.

Strang, John, and Michael Gossop, eds. *Heroin Addiction and the British System: Origins and Evolution*. Oxfordshire: Routledge, 2005.

eds. 'Misreported and Minunderstood – the "British System" of Drug Policy'. In *Heroin Addiction and the British System: Origins and Evolution*, edited by John Strang and Michael Gossop. Oxfordshire: Routledge, 2005.

Taylor, Arnold H. *American Diplomacy and the Narcotics Traffic, 1900–1939: A Study in International Humanitarian Reform*. Durham, NC: Duke University Press, 1969.

The Global Commission on Drug Policy. 'War on Drugs'. New York: GCDP, 2011. www.globalcommissionondrugs.org/reports/war-on-drugs/.

'The Hague International Opium Convention'. The Hague, 1912.

Traver, Harold H. 'Colonial Relations and Opium Control Policy in Hong Kong, 1841–1945'. In *Drugs, Law, and the State*, edited by Harold H. Traver and Mark S. Gaylord. New Brunswick: Transaction Publishers, 1992.

Trocki, Carl A. 'Opium and the Beginnings of Chinese Capitalism in Southeast Asia'. *Journal of Southeast Asian Studies* 33, no. 2 (2002): 297–314. https://doi.org/10.1017/S0022463402000152.

Opium, Empire and the Global Political Economy: A Study of the Asian Opium Trade, 1750–1950. Oxfordshire: Routledge, 1999.

UK All Party Parliamentary Group on Drug Policy Reform. 'Guidance on Drug Policy: Interpreting the UN Drug Conventions', 2015.

UNDP. 'Addressing the Development Dimensions of Drug Policy'. New York: United Nations Development Programme, June 2015. www.undp.org/content/undp/en/home/librarypage/hiv-aids/addressing-the-development-dimensions-of-drug-policy.html.

United Nations. 'Commentary on the Convention on Psychotropic Substances, 1971'. New York: United Nations, 1976.

'Commentary on the Single Convention on Narcotic Drugs, 1961'. New York: United Nations Secretariat, 1973. www.unodc.org/documents/treaties/organized_crime/Drug%20Convention/Commentary_on_the_single_convention_1961.pdf.

'Commentary on the Single Convention on Narcotic Drugs, 1961'. New York: United Nations, 1973.

'Commentary on the United Nations Convention Against Illicit Traffic in Narcotic Drugs and Psychotropic Substances 1988'. New York: United Nations, 1998.

United Nations. *Single Convention on Narcotic Drugs of 1961 as Amended by the 1972 Protocol*. New York: United Nations, 1961.

United Nations Convention against Illicit Traffic in Narcotic Drugs and Psychotropic Substances, 1988. Vienna: United Nations, 1988. www.unodc.org/pdf/convention_1988_en.pdf.

United Nations General Assembly. 'Our Joint Commitment to Effectively Addressing and Countering the World Drug Problem'. New York: United Nations, 19 April 2016.

UNODC. 'A Century of International Drug Control'. Vienna: United Nations, 2008. www.unodc.org/documents/data-and-analysis/Studies/100_Years_of_Drug_Control.pdf.

Walker III, William O. 'Bibliographic Essay'. In *Drug Control Policy: Essays in Historical and Comparative Perspective*, edited by William O. Walker III. Pennsylvania State University Press, 1992.

ed. *Drug Control Policy: Essays in Historical and Comparative Perspective.* Pennsylvania State University Press, 1992.

Opium and Foreign Policy: The Anglo-American Search for Order in Asia, 1912–1954. Chapel Hill: University of North Carolina Press, 1991.

WHO Expert Committee on Drug Dependence. 'Seventeenth Report'. WHO Technical Report Series, n.d.

Williams, Adam, and Nacha Cattan. 'Biden Says Drug Legalization Debate Is "Totally Legitimate"'. *Bloomberg News,* 3 June 2012. www.bloomberg.com/news/articles/2012-03-05/biden-visits-mexico-honduras-amid-calls-to-debate-drug-strategy.

Windle, James. 'How the East Influenced Drug Prohibition'. *The International History Review* 35, no. 5 (October 2013): 1185–99.

Yanli, Gao. 'Judd's China: A Missionary Congressman and US-China Policy'. *Journal of Modern Chinese History* 2, no. 2 (December 2008): 197–219.

Young, Oran, W. Bradnee Chambers, Joy Kim, and Claudia Ten Have. *Institutional Interplay: Biosafety and Trade.* Tokyo, Japan: UNU, 2008. http://search.proquest.com/docview/903905443/.

Yung-Ning Hoo, Mona. *Painting the Shadows: The Extraordinary Life of Victor Hoo.* London: Eldridge and Co., 1998.

Zhou, Yongming. *Anti-Drug Crusades in Twentieth-Century China: Nationalism, History, and State Building.* Oxford: Rowman & Littlefield, 1999.

INDEX

For EU product safety concerns, contact us at Calle de José Abascal, 56–1°,
28003 Madrid, Spain or eugpsr@cambridge.org.

www.ingramcontent.com/pod-product-compliance
Lightning Source LLC
LaVergne TN
LVHW011809200926
848484LV00005B/1114
* 9 7 8 1 3 1 6 5 1 2 3 2 6 *